D1206833

All Our Years

The Autobiography of

ROBERT MORSS LOVETT

All Our Years

New York • THE VIKING PRESS • 1948

FIRST PUBLISHED BY THE VIKING PRESS IN MAY 1948

PUBLISHED ON THE SAME DAY IN THE DOMINION OF CANADA

BY THE MACMILLAN COMPANY OF CANADA LIMITED

PRINTED IN U.S.A.

AMERICAN BOOK–STRATFORD PRESS, INC., NEW YORK

To My Students

Preface

I HAVE been asked many times to write my memoirs. So long as I was employed I could answer that I had no time. Now in retirement I have to quote Milton: "Hence with denial vain, and coy excuse."

Moreover, certain aspects of my career having become matters of public attention, I feel that it is incumbent on me to explain my attitude toward World War I, World War II, the Russian Revolution, efforts for peace through neutrality and collective security, United States colonial administration, socialism and communism. My dismissal from national service together with Dr. Goodwin Watson and Dr. William E. Dodd, Jr., has become a *cause célèbre* in the textbooks. From this point of view the appendix is the most important part of the book.

The best of my life has been given to education in the broader sense, including work with various organizations to promote peace and social welfare. As I look back I realize that my students have been the chief justification of my existence.

I owe so many obligations to so many people in connection with this book that I could fill this page with their names. I owe my gratitude especially for reading the manuscript in preparation to my long-time colleague Dr. Ferdinand Schevill, and to former students Miss Elizabeth Greenebaum (Mrs. George Herzog), Miss Martha Dodd (Mrs. Alfred K. Stern), and Miss Bessie Zaban (Mrs. Howard Mumford Jones). To Robert O. Ballou of the Viking Press my thanks are inexpressibly great.

ROBERT MORSS LOVETT

Table of Contents

Part I

Part II

Appendix

Part I

"Behold the life at ease. It drifts."

I. *Roxbury*, 1871–1888

I

SIR THOMAS BROWNE once described his life as a miracle of forty years. My life began with what I fear was regarded as a miracle, or an intimation of a miraculous future. In the year 1870 Christmas Day came on Sunday, and I came with it, about half-past ten in the morning, as the church bells were ringing and pious folk were heeding their call. I early learned to regard this distinction as a misfortune. In childhood the celebration of my birthday with appropriate ceremony and gifts tended to be forgotten in the major significance of Christmas; and in old age when I should be glad to forget my birthday the coincidence is an inevitable reminder. Even my grandchildren mock the event by singing:

> God rest you merry, grandchildren,
> Let nothing you dismay,
> For Jesus C. and Grandpipi
> Were born on Christmas Day.

A more serious cause of embarrassment was the expectation which was aroused in the family of which I was the firstborn—a child of promise. My mother read with special unction the Bible stories of Sarah, of Manoah's wife, of Hannah, and cast me in her mind for a part suggested by Isaac, or Samson, or Samuel. My effort to live up to these hopes led to precociousness, and this in time caused an optimism in regard to my achievements of which possibly the last sign is the fact that some twenty-three publishers have expressed a blind but generous faith in this book. Very early I became accustomed to disappointment—of others.

The city of my birth was a minor source of distinction, felt by me as a child, and respected even to this day. Boston in 1870 was a city of some three hundred thousand people, holding fifth place in population, and, more than this, richest of all American cities in colonial, revolutionary, and anti-slavery memories. It was a shrine of patriotism with the Old South Church, the Old North Church, Bunker Hill, the Old State House, Faneuil Hall, the Old Granary Graveyard. It was the gateway to Cambridge, where Longfellow, Lowell, and Norton wrote in the shadow of Harvard, and the approach to Concord, where Emerson shone in cloudy mysticism. Whittier at Amesbury was not far away. All this glory was part of the inheritance of a boy born in 1870, of which he became slowly conscious, and it cast a mild reflection on the South End where the middle class, sharply differentiated from the Brahmins of Beacon Hill and the Back Bay, was making a stand against the slum.

A group of young men who had grown up in that neighborhood had joined the Boston Cadets, gone to war with the Cadet regiment (the 45th Massachusetts), and returned to enter business, gathered about William Poland of the contracting firm of William C. Poland and Son. William the son married Sarah Ellen Everett Lovett, and his house on East Concord Street became the home of his parents-in-law and his brothers-in-law, who also married and produced offspring. My Aunt Nellie was the most beautiful and goodhearted woman I have ever known, and I do not believe that the complicated household irked her in the least; but the overcharged domestic magazine finally exploded and scattered the three young families. Mine was blown to Roxbury, which about that time was annexed to Boston.

My first recollections are of a block of three brick houses on Dudley Street at Mount Pleasant, occupied by three friendly families who were connected by business and church relations. I fancy that my life there was much like that described by Ruskin in *Praeterita*, in its deprivations. Like him, I was never allowed to experience any danger or hardship. Like him, I saw no society except the immediate neighbors and had no training in manners. My sister, born when I was three and a half, gave me a limited companionship. Later, visits to my Poland cousins among the hills of Milton or at the shore of Squantum, and association with their group of young people at West Roxbury, taught me to be ashamed of my ineptitude out-of-doors and my shyness with my contemporaries. These visits, and others to my aunt at New Bedford, were a corrective to the limitations of my suburban existence. And as I came to know my parents and appreciate their anxious care of me, I came to love them. When my brother was born I was nineteen and fully awakened to affection. I used to impress on his young mind the formula: "If Sidney wants anything, Bobbo will go get it for him." He never took advantage of my offer.

My paternal grandparents were always dear to me. My grandfather was the first of a line dating from 1636 to change the inherited name John to Augustus, and to leave Beverly in Essex County for Boston. There he became secretary of the Hope Insurance Company and succeeded to the presidency in the year in which five ships were lost by storm, fire, or mutiny between the coast of Malabar and the Strait of Sunda, reducing the capital by half. After the liquidation of the company he became an agent, but was not very successful. He and my grandmother lived with their daughter, and after Grandma's death he came to live with us. His misfortunes never quenched his sprightly spirit. It was he who took me to see all the sights of Boston, and to Beverly to recall the fame of that port in the era of the clipper ships. He was short, rotund, with a gray beard cut square and humorous brown eyes. I recall him most characteristically on Fourth of July, putting cannon crackers under pots and pans confiscated from the kitchen, lighting the fuses from his cigar, and skipping nimbly away as the tinware soared skyward.

My grandmother, Mary Ann Bishop of Newburyport, was suited to him in every way, an adorable old lady. With her, cheerfulness became at times exuberant, and she feared to go to funerals lest her sense of humor should betray her into inextinguishable laughter. I inherited this failing. When she came "to spend the day" with us her pockets were full of filberts, and today that sweet, modest little nut brings her back more vividly through taste than through sight. She used to take me for walks on which her chief preoccupation was to avoid dogs, which she discerned from any distance. Dogs in those days were chiefly Newfoundland, whose friendly advances seemed to her a prelude to hostilities, necessitating a scuttle around the corner or into an alley. Fear of Newfoundland dogs was a condition of my childhood until I went to school and found from the reading-books that they were chiefly occupied in saving children from drowning.

Undoubtedly the dominant factor in our family was my mother. Elizabeth Russell was born in New Bedford, left an orphan as a child, and brought up by her older sister Emily. She early developed a strong character and a sense of self-dependence. She became a schoolteacher, and after her marriage in 1868 she remained essentially a teacher and a disciplinarian. She was intensely religious. God, immortality, duty, were her chief concerns. She did not echo the adjectives with which George Eliot qualified the first two as inconceivable, unbelievable, but she accepted fully the verdict: "How absolute and peremptory the third!" I was the first object of such consideration. She was a ladylike figure, stately rather than beautiful, her natural seriousness intensified by long periods of illness which kept her in bed. During such times Aunt Emily came to take care of the family. I was always good at such times, but my sister was a little devil. I remember sitting priggishly at the bedside while Emmy ran about, pursued ineffectually by my aunt, while my mother exhorted, "Whip her, Emily. Whip her." Poor Aunt Emily, thin and wisplike, could not catch the child, much less punish her.

My mother's illness contributed to my father's acceptance of matriarchy. He was a handsome man of thirty when I was first acquainted with him, nearly six feet tall, with bright blue eyes in sharply angled sockets, and red whiskers and mustache. He was, like Ruskin's father, an entirely honest merchant, selling insurance in State Street in partnership with the popular Lispenard Stuart Jordon in the firm Jordon, Lovett and Company, founded by their respective fathers in 1849. He, like my mother, was deeply religious, a youthful pillar and deacon of Shawmut Congregational Church, a favorite of the distinguished pastor Dr. E. B. Webb. He conducted prayers regularly after our seven o'clock breakfast, relying much, of course, on the pious clichés of the Epistles, such as his invariable "Be diligent in business, fervent in spirit, serving the Lord." Immediately on rising from his knees he sat down to read carefully all the insurance policies written in his office the day before.

A true history of life, as Sherwood Anderson remarked, is a history of moments, for it is only in rare moments that we live. I can recall very few such moments in this early period of my life, but one recurs to me as having perhaps a certain symbolism. A block from our house was a small provision store to which I was sometimes sent to bring home a yeast cake or a quart of milk. This made me feel very important and trustworthy. I usually lingered in the shop, hoping to be invited to ride on the high seat of the delivery wagon beside the driver, but my orders were always small enough to be delivered by hand. One day as I was waiting to proclaim "I want a yeast cake," I heard a lady say, "I want a green squash." The words fascinated me, and I went about the shop repeating, "I want a green squash." For a time no one paid any attention to me, but finally when all the orders had been made up the delivery man caught up a great green squash by the stem and, after threatening me with it playfully, tossed it into the wagon and hoisted me to the seat. It all took place so quickly that I could not halt the march of events even if I had known how. I hoped the ride would be a long one, but our house was nearest, and in less than a minute I was swung off my perch and swept into the kitchen and the squash was beside me on the table. The Irish maid burst into protest. "What'll I be doin' with that?" "Master Bobby ordered it," explained the man. Renewed expostulation and reply brought my mother downstairs. It was clear that I had told a lie in order to enjoy a ride. I was held over for my father's return to be properly punished, but that was nothing to the humiliation of losing face with the storekeeper and his driver, who strode off indignantly, dangling the squash by its stem.

2

Why we left the dignified brick house in Mount Pleasant for the comparative squalor of Quincy Street I never knew. I conjecture that my father's younger brother Henry, who was in business with my grandfather, was careless in accounting to his companies in regard to premiums and that my father had to bail them out, probably at the expense of his entire savings. At any rate, we moved to a double house which we shared with my uncle's family. My mother bore this with Christian fortitude, but when after two years Uncle Henry moved to a large house with spacious grounds in Newton, and made not the slightest effort to pay his debt to my father, she could not always remember that charity suffereth long and is kind. For five years more we stuck in the lower middle-class slum, an acre of houses of the same hideous pattern, painted gray, set close to the street and to each other. Ours had a narrow strip of turf at one side and a small back yard. One of the reasons that Quincy Street was considered degraded was that it led directly to an Irish settlement known as Cherry Valley. It fed my inferiority complex to answer truthfully the question "Where do you live?" I used to reply defensively, "I live at Sixteen Quincy Street, but I'm not a Mick." It did not help matters when our neighbor, Dr. D. W. Waldron, the jovial city missionary, pretended to discover that the former name of Quincy Street was Piggery Lane.

Two notes of gentility our family maintained. We kept a servant at three dollars a week—and I remember with gratitude two or three pleasant Irish girls who took care of us during my mother's illnesses—and we always went to the country for a month in the summer. I recall Dunbarton, Lebanon, and Mont Vernon in New Hampshire, Hubbardston and Grafton in Massachusetts, pleasant villages where we stayed at small boarding houses or with families who took in paying guests. The best of these excursions was to North Woodstock, at the gateway to the White Mountains. This visit was, however, the scene of a humiliation which I have never forgotten. At the hotel, proudly known as the Parker House, were two boys a little older than I—Philip Littell and his cousin John, quite on their own. Phil was a charming lad in knickerbockers, with smooth stockings over finely turned shanks. My mother was charmed with his cultivated voice and manners, and if she had known Meredith would have quoted Lady Mountstuart Jenkinson: "He has a leg." I met John on our common ground of baseball, but Phil was remote and indifferent. He was reading *The Decline and Fall.* Since I prided myself on my historical knowledge, I one day contrived to mention casually "Lord Catham." He looked up from his book. "I believe it is usually pronounced Chatham," he said dryly. The wound was cauterized fifty years later when I reminded him of the incident. "Was I such a son-of-a-bitch?" he murmured.

As I contrast my childhood with that of other autobiographers I recognize that it was a misfortune to grow up in a suburb lacking the intimate associations of a small town or a city block. Roxbury was particularly unfortunate since it had lost its corporate character by annexation to Boston. We were too distant to take advantage of urban opportunities. But there were compensations. Transportation was by horse-car, the Metropolitan green and the Highland plaid competing for our patronage on Warren Street. To hop on or off the car without stopping it was a point of honor, and to stand on the platform and chat with the conductor a privilege. Once a conductor shared his misogyny with me as a lady crossed the platform, leaving an odor of musk behind her. "I always think a woman's real smell must be something nasty if she has to cover it up with that stuff."

Conductors were an intimate factor in suburban life and so was the crew of fire engine Number 24 at the corner of Warren and Quincy. I sat for hours in conversation with the latter, hoping for an alarm, to see Jerry and Babe dash from their stalls, stand under their self-adjusting harness, and in two minutes leap out the doors, their top-heavy engine swaying behind them. A real fire was an event. We raced the engine and stood beside it in its steaming agony, shouting, "Play away, twenty-four!"

Fires were, however, more than fun in our family. My father's insurance business had been nearly wiped out in the Boston fire of '72. It was thrilling to hear him tell of the fight to keep the fire from crossing Washington Street, and of saving Hovey's store by hanging wet blankets from the windows. I used to retell these tales to my friends at the engine-house, who, however, would not concede much credit to a civilian.

Another public character was the lamplighter who made his rounds evening and morning with his torch, which had a wrench for turning the gas on and off. Finally there was the policeman. An arrest was, next to a fire, the biggest event in our juvenile world. Patrolman Parker was a pleasant man with a full beard like those of many Civil War generals. I have forgotten how I happened to get into his bad books—something about dissecting a dead cat, I believe. He talked to me seriously one day about how sorry he would be to run me in, and then suddenly changed the conversation to the United Woodmen of America of which he would be pleased to have my father a member. I saw at once the advantage of this connection and wearied my father with importunity on the subject, but to no avail.

Houses were heated by coal furnaces (ours conservatively managed later by me), lighted by gas, furnished with ice from the ice cart which lumbered along with a tail of children catching rides on the back step and snatching slivers of ice, and well supplied with water from Lake Cochituate. Occasionally an itinerant dealer advertised his wares, "Buy a lob; buy a lob. Two for a quarter," or a junk man passed by with the cry, "Old bottles, old boots, old rags, old shoes," as melancholy as that of the death cart in Defoe's *Plague Year*, "Bring out your dead."

Our household kept the New England maxims: "Eat it up. Wear it out. Make it do." If I didn't like the food I was told, "You must learn to like it." Even now I hate to give up my clothes until I am sure they are beyond repair. We had a lot of black walnut furniture, now prized as antiques, and an assortment of miscellaneous articles, a penholder and a pencil, two pairs of scissors, a big and a little, a watchman's rattle, a boot jack, a checker and backgammon board, two packs of cards (one for whist and a smaller one for euchre), a bed pan often lent throughout the neighborhood (I being the Mercury), a student lamp, an ax, a hatchet, and a hammer. I recall these things with affection. Food was very plentiful—steak, potatoes, and hot biscuits or muffins for breakfast at seven, tapering down through a moderate meal of fish or cold meat with vegetables and pudding at noon, to a light supper at night when my father came back from his office. On Saturday night and Sunday morning baked beans with brown bread and "Indian pudding" doubtless accounted for some dereliction from church on my part.

The world of my childhood was almost that of a hundred years earlier, certainly nearer to it than to the world of today. The first inkling of the wonders to be came when my father was at the Centennial Exposition in 1876. My mother received a letter printed in type instead of written with a pen. It was a miracle; the neighbors flocked in to see it. About the same time Uncle William was reported to have held a conversation by means of a tube and a wire with Professor Dolbear a mile away, but Uncle William was a romantiker. Then my grandfather took me to see a great sputtering incandescent lamp at the corner of Washington and Dover Streets; it made the street gaslights shrink palely into the surrounding darkness as if they knew their time had come. Next the streetcar lines were electrified.

Coming back to Chicago in 1898 from a trip abroad, I saw twenty horseless buggies and carryalls lined up for a race around the city along the boulevards. Only two went the route. Early in the next century my friend Charles Manly, assistant to Dr. Langley of the Smithsonian Institution, invented an engine so light and so powerful that it would fly a heavier-than-air machine. What a pity, it was said, that an eminent scientist like Dr. Langley should lend his name and that of the Smithsonian to such foolishness! Charles took off twice on the bank of the Potomac with a push from a catapult, but couldn't develop speed enough, and the crown went to the Wrights. Wireless came next, and moving pictures, and radio, and votes for women, and birth control, and now the atomic bomb—but I am getting ahead of my story, except for my thesis that the acceleration of the pace of the world has changed from arithmetical to geometrical progression.

3

When I was six I was sent to school after my mother's preliminary visit to the teacher. There was a fine new brick schoolhouse on Quincy Street, but it drew its clientele from the Irish settlement, and accordingly I went to the Monroe Street school, an old shabby wooden building, where in one room Miss Burrill taught the first two grades reading, writing, spelling, arithmetic, and geography. School hours were from nine to twelve and two to four. On rainy days work was halted while we listened for the fire alarm at a quarter to twelve to announce that school would continue until one with no afternoon session.

The school yard was divided by a high fence, half for boys and half for girls. At the foot of the yard stood the "backhouse," similarly divided. Our half was adorned with caricatures and verses reflecting the grosser functions of the body. When later Professor William I. Thomas told me of the implications of such rhymes, which a sociologist in Vienna had collected in six volumes, I regretted that I had not memorized a few to add scientific interest to these pages. The "backhouse" was a frequent resource in the long hours of thralldom. The teachers tried to mitigate the harsh request "May I go out?" to "May I retire?" with the result that "Teacher, please may I go out and retire?" gave a specific meaning to the ladylike word.

My cousin Harry, who then lived next to us, entered school with me and was the occasion of an episode in my life which I can scarcely believe ever happened, yet which is as clear in my mind as my unconscious lie about the green squash. It happened that a room was opened in the upper story for the second grade. I was kept at home by a sore throat the day of the transfer, and my cousin informed the teacher that I had left school for good. When on my return I found that I had lost my promotion I was grieved, and the extreme disappointment of my mother turned sorrow into indignation. I felt that I was the victim of a plot. I detested the lower room full of retarded children. Miss Burrill tried to compensate by making me her pet, and as I had nothing more to learn in that class I became a monitor, and soon an informer, and as such earned the undying hatred of that little band of six-year-olds. No one knew who next would be denounced. When the teacher left the room I took charge and let my eyes rove balefully over the group of trembling infants to whom I would indicate by a glance or a gesture the next victim. They were thoroughly terror-stricken, and as crime diminished it became necessary to invent it in order to assert my authority. One day I ventured beyond the usual accusations of whispering, getting out of seats, making bad smells. When the teacher returned I reported the conduct as excellent, and while a sigh of relief was going up I reluctantly added "except." The sigh died to silence. "Except," I rushed on, "Wessie Rock called me a darn old shitass." Horror! Wessie was summoned to the front and stood there, a fat, red-faced little boy, unable to control the train of events. I trembled. Of course he would deny it and twenty voices would affirm the denial. My throne tottered. "Where did you learn such words?" asked the teacher reproachfully, and Wessie answered, "Boys." Saved! But as I returned to my seat while Wessie Rock expiated an uncommitted sin by standing in the corner, I felt remorse and shame. The next day I was sent upstairs to the higher grade—to my mother's delight.

I should explain that what turned me into a Nero or Caligula for a few weeks was somewhat the result of the enormous importance of education in my home. My mother, as a former schoolteacher, took an unwholesome interest in my school life, rather resented by my teachers, who had never imagined a parent-teacher association. My failure of promotion, though clearly attributable to my cousin's careless falsehood, remained a cloud in the family. As I advanced through the regular grades of Boston's excellent school system it was my mother's ambition always to have me at the head of the class. Except for once, I never was better than number two or three, but the emphasis on high marks and good behavior was always a limiting influence on my life.

When I came to school one September morning we were assembled and marched to an imposing brick building on Dale Street, the Lewis Grammar School. I was eight and a half years old, and spent five years there under teachers whom I recall pleasantly except for the free use of the rattan. The practice of corporal punishment had a curious psychological effect. Every boy feared it and wanted it at least once. Whipping on the open hand with a thin rattan was the approved form. Teachers were discussed and appraised according to might of arm and persistence in swinging it. Some punishments were inflicted lightly, immediately on the offense, but on a serious occasion the guilty one was held over until after school. Then the news spread through the building, and the atmosphere was that of Reading Gaol on the night before an execution. Little groups stood about to congratulate or condole with the victim. "How many times did he hit you?" "Did you cry?" The girls looked at his hands marked by heavy red welts. If the equal-rights-for-women movement had been prominent in those days I am sure that ardent feminists would have protested against their exclusion from the pleasures and pains celebrated by the Marquis de Sade.

My parents' trust in education was not limited to public school. I was sent to Sunday school, dancing school, riding school, and the New England Conservatory of Music to train my ear. To dancing school I went most unwillingly and positively refused to go to the ball with which it closed, thereby embarrassing my family and the girl whom I had asked to be my partner. I cannot imagine how I got away with this contumacy except that my mother regarded dancing as on the whole a frivolous pastime unnecessary, if not unfit, for a Christian, and sent my sister and me only from a sense of the importance of manners. For the same reason I was sent to Draper and Hall's riding school, duly equipped and provided with a card for ten lessons. The riding master kept me circling the tanbark ring at a closed trot for nine of them. On the tenth day he was absent and his place was taken by an assistant, who encouraged me to post, canter, and gallop. In spite of this initiation I did not return for another card, and it was not until twenty years later that I found in riding my chief recreation.

My parents were musical and delighted to have my childish voice blend with theirs in the hymns that we sang on Sunday evenings, but I could not guide voice by ear. I was given lessons, and my mother drilled me beside the piano, but in vain. Part of the trouble was that I despised music as much as I did dancing, and this scorn I lay to the silly words which we sang in school. My approach to music was through meaning, not sound. I did not know that words were unimportant except to represent notes. I hated to be made to sing about the joys of spring—"Come May thou lovely ling'rer"; the suffering of the planted seed—"Little seed now must thou go"; the lesson of the bees—"Listen to the bee's brisk hum, Let us hear what says she"; and especially the pleasures of life—"Come and see how happily we spend the day, Always joining cheerfully in school or play." I hated myself for uttering such nonsense. I was glad to be excused from singing and sat patiently among the "non-singers," who were called on only when volume rather than quality was demanded. I remember a musical festival on a long, hot afternoon in Mechanics Hall when we had only one line, which we gave with real feeling: "O hold–me–up–*my God!*" Years later I used to chant the ballad of Abdul the Bulbul Ameer as my contribution to an intimate evening entertainment. Once my hostess sportively asked the distinguished pianist Rudolph Reuter to play my accompaniment. I apologized in advance for any inadequacy in my performance on the ground that I had been a non-singer at school. As he struck the last chord he turned to me. "Did you say a non-singer? I should have said an anti-singer."

4

I have written of education as if it were the chief end of my being in these early years. It was not so regarded in the home, where first place was held by religion. Sunday school afforded a link between the two. Although we lived in Roxbury we attended Shawmut Church in Boston, which my grandfather and father had helped to found, but as the journey was too long to be taken twice a day I was entered for Sunday school in the afternoon at the Walnut Avenue Congregational Church.

We kept up the distinction between members of the church and members of the congregation. Only the former were entitled to consider themselves "saved." My grandfather was not "saved" and used to walk out before communion, while my mother and father remained to partake of the bread and wine. A hundred years earlier the members of the congregation, outnumbering the "saved," would have declared themselves Unitarians and taken possession of the church property on the secession of the elect; but theological passions had cooled, and while to deny the divinity of Christ was properly regarded as a reason for permanent exclusion from His presence, to accept it, even if one did not join his church by profession of this faith, put one into the class of nominal Christians for whom there might be a chance. The case of Grandpa intrigued me greatly, and I often argued it with my mother. I was assured that we cannot win heaven by our good deeds. The evil of Grandpa's example in making respectable a certain lukewarmness in religion was pointed out. The necessity of a public profession was insisted on. "For whosoever shall be ashamed of me, of him shall the Son of Man be ashamed when He shall come in His own glory." That was logical enough—but nevertheless I remained ashamed of Jesus.

My theological discussions with my mother took place on the parlor sofa. These conversations always moved into the field of personal religion, and the state of my soul was probed and found to be unsatisfactory. Signs of grace were lacking. All this was painful to me, but how much more so to my mother! The mother of a son who stands before a judge to be sentenced to be hanged unless proof of innocence is forthcoming suffers in extremity. The mother of a son already condemned to eternal agony would suffer more were it not for the reprieve during which he might clear himself by accepting pardon through a process which seems easy and yet is so difficult to grasp. The explanation of this difficulty to my mother's mind was original sin, for which the blood of Christ was the atonement. Although she did not quote Pascal, she had the same thought that it was incredible that anyone of intelligence should not devote himself to mastering the theological intricacies of the way of salvation, the alternative being so dreadful.

We went to church on Sunday mornings to listen to the eloquence of the Reverend Edward Bonaparte Webb in the brick church on the corner of West Brookline and Tremont Streets. In the days of the prosperity of the church, before the South End lost all its best families to the Back Bay, my father leased his pew on the floor and we sat in the gallery, whence I could look down on the charms of the beautiful Fanny Smith. Dr. Webb was a handsome man, with the white whiskers made popular by General Burnside. He enjoyed great distinction as the friend and former pastor of James G. Blaine—"My Blaine," he said with reverence. Only two things I remember from his sermons—two names. I learned that Charles Darwin confessed that science had killed his love of poetry, and that the death of Karl Marx had revealed a vast network of revolutionary organizations throughout Europe.

On days when stomach-ache, sore throat, or some chore like clearing the sidewalks of snow released me from church-going, I was allowed to substitute the learning of a chapter of the Bible. I exhausted the Psalms of moderate length and then was put into the Gospel According to Saint John. I could make time for myself on the Psalms but lost out on the Gospel.

Making me learn the Bible was one of the best things my mother did for me, far better than reading it with her, a chapter a day until we got bogged down in the genealogical tables in Chronicles. I took my chapter every morning just after my cod liver oil; when the medicine was discontinued the reading fell off. Later I read The Acts of the Apostles with my father, whose Christianity was less theological and more for action than my mother's. He was the superintendent of a mission supported by the church in the slums of Harrison Avenue, and used to spend Sunday afternoon in conducting Sunday school, with occasional sorties against those whom he described as "lewd fellows of the baser sort" who had inherited the spirit of Paul's persecutors. He was a deacon in the church and passed the contribution box and the bread and wine on Communion Sundays, while my grandfather concerned himself with the choir, fairs, and other non-essential side lines.

The "end of the world" was a subject of much preoccupation. I thought about it a good deal with a divided mind. We had a song book left from Father Kemp's Old Folks' Concerts, which contained a description of the Last Day:

> On Cherubim, on Seraphim
> Full royally He rode
> And on the wings of mighty winds
> Went flying all abroad—

which Professor Barrett Wendell pronounced one of the grandest things in Elizabethan poetry. Of course I wanted to see it—if I was sure of salvation. But I wasn't sure and on the whole preferred to be among those rising quietly and inconspicuously from their graves. The prophecy of Mother Shipton was much quoted:

> The world unto an end will come
> In eighteen-hundred-and-eighty-one.

This was much too imminent. I made it part of my nightly prayer to direct God's attention to the manifest appropriateness of dealing in round numbers. "Please, God, don't come before the year two thousand." People then were more afraid of destruction by the wrath of God than today of destruction by the wrath of man.

I was definitely ashamed of Jesus, and I was embarrassed by the too ostentatious piety of our family. One of the neighbor boys once asked me with a puzzled expression, "Why do you have the prayers?"

It was in my period of shameless falsehood. "What do you mean?"

I replied. "We don't." But the next morning, as I lifted my face from the red plush chair where I buried it during my father's supplications, I was disconcerted to see three boys balancing on our high back fence on a level with our sitting-room window.

The only time I was proud of our religion was when Moody and Sankey came to Boston. A great tabernacle was built for the services, a choir was enlisted in which my parents sang, and tickets of different colors were issued for seats in different parts of the house. They were in great demand. My family had the distribution of them in our section of Roxbury; neighbors came to the house to ask for them, and I, a boy of ten, went about as messenger, handing out choice seats in order of merit. I remember being allowed to attend the service only once, when I sat with my parents in the choir. I was greatly impressed by the sight of hundreds of people weeping when Mr. Sankey sang of "the Ninety and Nine." "What are they crying for?" I asked. "They are sorry for the lost sheep," said my father. "They are weeping for you," said my mother pointedly. Years later I was sent to Northfield in the hope that Moody would bring to fruition the seed that Dr. Webb had planted and my mother watered. I was introduced to him. "A chip off the old block," he announced. He was wrong.

Gibbon palliates his conversion by remarking that at least he fell by a noble hand. My surrender was mainly due to the Reverend A. J. Gordon of the Clarendon Street Baptist Church, whose hymn, together with "Just as I am without one plea," melted my hard heart. It is strange that I should have yielded to music what I refused to logic. The setting was a series of revival meetings held in Roxbury by the Reverend B. Fay Mills. These were not grandiose affairs such as Moody's, but more intimate gatherings in the different churches. The second stanza of Mr. Gordon's hymn won me:

> I love thee, my Saviour, who first lovéd me
> And purchased my pardon on Calvary's tree.
> I love thee for wearing the thorns on thy brow;
> If ever I loved thee, my Jesus, 'tis now—

that and the last line of "Just As I Am":

> O Lamb of God, I come, I come.

I came.

For a time everything was joy and gladness at home. All the pious friends of the family offered congratulations. I was the lost sheep, the prodigal son. King's Daughters offered me shy hands or passed me notes at school. Then came the reaction. I was prepared to join the church, but which? I was strong for Shawmut, where the Reverend William Elliot Griffis had succeeded Dr. Webb—Griffis, who had written *The Mikado's Empire*, whose sermons were magnificent in their appreciation of the Bible as literature (especially The Song of Solomon, in which he cut out the nonsense in the margin about Christ and the church paying compliments to each other), and who wrote me a fine manly letter about my conversion. My mother, who had long resented the dichotomy in our religious life between church and Sunday school, thought that I should join the Walnut Avenue Church by whose ministrations I had been saved. In the interval I began to read the Bible for myself and was struck by the fact that the Gospels were themselves uncertain as to the vital point of our faith, the divinity of Christ. What was the sense of the long genealogy tracing his earthly ancestry? If he was the Son of God, why "extol the stem of Jesse's rod?" When it came to the words "conceived by the Holy Ghost, born of the Virgin Mary," I could not take it. I told my mother. If she had known the Church Fathers she would have quoted Tertullian, "*Certum quia impossibile est.*" Instead she fell back on the text, "They that do His will shall know of the doctrine," and on prayer. I tried both. My real prayer would doubtless have been that of many Christians and Bible students: "Dear God, please cut out the genealogies." Of course it was too late to ask God to revise the Bible, but why, in a work every word of which was dictated by the contact man of the Trinity, should this awkward dilemma appear? My mother suggested that it was there as a trial of faith. What really troubled me was the horror of backsliding in the face of my world. I had professed loyalty to Jesus, and love. Now I was denying him like Peter, betraying him like Judas, condemning him like Pilate. I was both Barabbas and the impenitent thief. I was crucifying my Lord afresh and putting him to an open shame. My father and mother were very tender with me. Later, when Phillips Brooks was preacher at Harvard, I went to see him at my mother's urgency. He was magnificent, but on the great and vital question of the divinity of Christ he was uncommunicative. I fear that he thought me a pious prig or an atheist seeking an argument. At any rate, he dismissed me with the flattering but to me meaningless text, "Ye are all Gods."

I felt among other pangs the disgrace from which my family suffered in the eyes of their world, and their far keener disappointment in my heavenly hopes. I tried to make it up to them by the only means at all comparable to their sense of loss. I went out for school and college honors and became more than ever the victim of the obsession with high marks. Dr. Mills later became a Unitarian, and this helped to reconcile my mother, who saw in the heresy of the physician of souls the reason why the inoculation did not take.

5

Next to religion and education the leading interest in our family was war. My father had served in the War between the States, not, I grieved to realize, with high distinction. He had been a corporal in the 45th Massachusetts, a nine-month regiment which saw some action in North Carolina. Once, at a regimental reunion, Colonel Charles R. Codman told how the regiment, on its way home, was held in reserve for the army at Gettysburg. As he gloated over the probable losses I felt that I would have risked my father's life for his participation in that glorious fray.

I was born six years after the end of the war, and when I was a child it was still a leading topic of conversation and dominated the political scene. The visitors at our house were nearly all veterans, and we visited them in turn. The prevailing opinion seemed to be that the war had ended too soon, and that the South was merely waiting its chance to "try it again." I was fascinated by war. I spoke war pieces at school, beginning one afternoon when I was nine with "The Battle of Ivry," to the amazement alike of teacher and pupils, and I followed with poems of the Civil War by Frank Gassaway. I read Greeley's *American Conflict* and acted out the whole war with paper soldiers in an attic assigned to me as a playroom. This was a manly sport, far above childish play, and I deeply resented the family's description of it as playing with paper dolls. The entire action, beginning with Bull Run, culminating at Gettysburg, and ending at Appomattox, took months to rehearse. Some of the bitterest moments of my childhood were those in which, on coming home from school, I found the armies swept away by the broom of the servant (for the room had to be cleaned), or thrown out of strategic positions by an incursion of my little sister, who early manifested pacifist prejudices.

The outdoor sport I enjoyed most was "playing soldier," organizing a company and marching at the head, resplendent in epaulets and sash cut out of red flannel, reminiscent of winter underclothes. I had no competition for this leadership, for the recruits were of the type later known as cannon fodder, innocent of any notion of why they were drafted into service. The Irish boys mocked at this parade when we skirted their territory. Sometimes stones put us to rout, but occasionally we abandoned decorations and wooden weapons and, armed with coal shovels to protect our faces, made a display of force in the vacant lots which constituted a kind of no-man's land between our respective settlements, calling on the traditional enemy to come out. They came in a swarm, and then my military science was useful in defending our flanks. Ammunition was plentiful. My father often remarked on the pockmarked surface of our coal shovel.

My knowledge of war was increased when one summer my father took me to a reunion of veterans at Gettysburg, where I refought the battle: on the first day, in the village, where General Reynolds was killed; on the second day, scouting along the Union lines on Cemetery Ridge; on the third day, charging with Pickett across the valley from Seminary Ridge; and on the fourth day, with a map, I captured Lee's army, which Meade so carelessly allowed to escape. The veterans of our party were very decent to me, taking turns in guiding me over the battlefield and identifying various features, but I could not find anyone to check the strategy by which I stopped Lee's retreat. By the fourth day everybody was tired and bored, as I suspect was the case in the battle itself.

There was a rally of the survivors of the Second Corps in the auditorium, and its commander, General Daniel Sickles, was on hand to defend his course in precipitating action on the second day, by which he claimed to have won the battle. Perhaps he did, in that the mauling his corps took in the peach orchard and wheat field may have given Lee the idea that the Union line could be broken by Pickett's charge. Backstage, before Sickles' appearance, several comrades struggled with his wooden leg while the hero groaned and cursed. At length it came off, and General Sickles, on crutches, swung out on the platform, his dangling pantaloon suggesting the leg he had left on the battlefield. It was a great speech. "Sickles held diamonds—and diamonds were trumps." The symbol of the corps was the diamond.

Military ambition caused a serious lapse in my education. There was in our suburb a famous school, the Roxbury Latin, to which my mother wished to send me, with an eye to college and the pulpit as my future career. I was determined to go to the English High School in Boston because that institution contributed two battalions to the Boston School Regiment and elected the colonel in alternate years with the Boston Latin School. It offered the best preparation for West Point. I may say at once that my military career was a disastrous failure. The basis of promotion was skill in handling a musket. Prize drills were held by various organizations in the city, and the school year was closed by a final exhibition in which competitors were lined up to go through the manual of arms under the eyes of judges who disqualified them for errors, as in a spelling match. In my mind I saw myself winning medals and finally becoming colonel, or at least a major. I did not realize how utterly inept I was at anything requiring co-ordination of eye and hand. On the first day of drill under the instruction of a second-year boy I showed my awkwardness and was liberally cursed, until with weariness, anger, and disappointment I passed out and fell with my heavy musket in a loud clatter to the floor. Arms and the man did not cohere. That day was a forecast of three years of humiliation. I was always placed in the rear rank, and when there was a redivision of privates I was among those transferred to another company. My first year of high school was one of low marks and only "passable" behavior. After that I braced up, because in appointing officers in the third year the teachers took account of scholarship. I achieved a first lieutenancy in a company under another high-stand boy as captain. At the annual prize drill our company was the worst.

6

If my boyhood was not unhappy it was drab. On Quincy Street I was a leader until an unfortunate episode caused my downfall. I had organized a baseball team, and as I possessed a bat and a league ball I became captain and pitcher. At bat I was a total loss, and on the occasion of a game with the Irish team my recruits persuaded me to take the important post of umpire. Cut to the heart, I consented to be kicked upstairs. The Irish boys, however, did not know what an umpire was for, and at every decision against them gathered about menacingly. When I tried to even matters by a sop to the

Celtic Cerberus, my own comrades surged up in an angry wave, and in the end I was chased by both teams. I was not sorry when we moved up the hill to Gaston Street, where we had a garden with pear and cherry trees. Unfortunately I never got into the gang in our new neighborhood.

The most normal part of my childhood was spent with my cousins the Polands. My kind Aunt Nellie used to invite me every summer for a week, usually extended to three or four. There were five children, a real family. Joe, a year older than I, became my guide and inspiration. Together we threaded the woods of Blue Hill, as Chingachgook and Uncas in *The Last of the Mohicans*. For a while the Polands lived in Cambridge, where Uncle William, a contractor, was building Memorial Hall. Then they moved to Milton, and later to Squantum, where we had swimming, sailing, and clams steamed on the beach. From there they went to West Roxbury, where they became the nucleus of a group of young people who made me conscious of the deficiencies in my home life. Helen, the beautiful eldest, and Joe and Charlie were gracious in sharing their friends with me. The Polands wove a streak of bright plaid in the gray fabric of my life. It was a sad day when my uncle took the family to Livermore, Colorado, and I saw them no more for a season. Helen and Joe came back to the East and have happily renewed themselves in their children. For human qualities—gaiety, affection, generosity, humor—they remain the best family I have ever known.

Their departure when I was fourteen left a depression in my life which was filled about this time by New Bedford.

I have said that the Lovetts came from Beverly, and my visits there with my grandfather were reminiscent of the great aristocratic tradition of clipper ships to China and Java. My other grandfather, whom I never saw, was Henry Russell, a painter by trade, who went from Nantucket to New Bedford sometime after the War of 1812. There his older daughter Emily married Captain Dan'l Wood, of a famous whaling family, and brought up her little orphan sister, who was my mother. My aunt was not an exciting person though she had made the voyage with her husband around Cape Horn to Honolulu, where she had had her picture taken, riding horseback with wide skirts flying. She was strong for good manners, read me lessons on tipping my hat to ladies, and gave me ten dollars for refraining from picking my nose for a year. Since I received only one dollar for repeating the Ten Commandments, I was left for a time in doubt of the relative values of worldly and other-worldly etiquette, which later led me to appreciate Richardson's novels where the two are in such perfect balance. In fact, now that I think of it, our family belonged somewhere in the background of *Clarissa.*

My uncle was a horse of a different color. He had gone to sea at fourteen in one of his father's whalers, had risen to be a captain, and had been wrecked in the Okhotsk Sea and burned by the *Shenandoah.* That event, he used to say, was the best day's work in his life, and he delighted to tell how under the expert guidance of government accountants he had submitted to the Alabama Claims Commission a bill, including the oil he had taken and the oil he expected to take, calculated at the price determined by their loss.

After the pay-off he retired and watched the decline of the whaling industry through the rise of petroleum. Every afternoon he put on his tall hat and frock coat and went "down-street" to sit with other retired captains in the rear of Charley Haskell's hat store. As a little boy I was taken along for the walk, and I used to wait patiently to hear something of the great life these men had lived in the Arctic. I was constantly disappointed at the conversation, which was entirely local gossip. There was one among them at whom I gazed with special interest. That was Captain Craig, a crooked, shriveled little man who had been mouthed by a whale. I wanted terribly to hear about that, but I was warned never to refer to it. To have your boat knocked from under you by a bump of a whale's head was not good whalesmanship, and Captain Craig probably got what was coming to him, but his feelings should be spared.

I could not connect these mild old gentlemen with the dangers and horrors of whaling. I realized that they were a cut under the clipper-ship aristocracy of Salem and Beverly, but I was indignant years later when I read in Professor Samuel Eliot Morison's *Maritime History of Massachusetts* his description of the black-leg crews and brutal captains of whaling ships. My uncle had gone to sea at fourteen in his father's ship, following his older brothers, Charles and James. They had graduated to become ship owners and gentlemen, not to be distinguished by me from the aristocrats of Essex County. I thought of whaling as a family tradition of progress from cabin-boy to captain and owner. I wrote in my mind a letter of protest to Professor Morison. But just then, through the death of my father, my uncle's papers came to me, and among them a number of notes signed by the crew at the end of each voyage acknowledging the receipt of five or ten dollars from the captain in compensation for being beaten up. One was for fifty dollars on the allegation that the complainant had been knocked unconscious and held head down in a barrel of oil for twenty minutes.

My Uncle Dan had a horse for driving to Padan Aram; my Uncle Rowland, on my mother's side, taught me to sail; but my chief resource was the Baylor boys, who lived opposite my uncle's house on Seventh Street. Courtenaye Baylor was about my age and introduced me to a crowd of boys and girls like those at West Roxbury. We boys went swimming naked at Crow Island and more respectably at Fair Haven, took the girls sailing and afterwards for ice cream at Bates's, played tennis on the Swaine School courts, and went on picnics to Horse Neck.

Those were the years of the revival of races for the America's Cup. The New York Yacht Club used to put in at New Bedford on its annual cruise northward, and I have never seen a more beautiful sight than that fleet of graceful sloops and schooners rounding the buoy and breaking out spinnakers for the run home. One of the boys, a summer visitor like myself, was Joseph Delano Hitch. He was a relative of Mr. Malcolm Forbes who allowed us on board the *Puritan* the year she beat the *Genesta*. Delano was a great name in New Bedford. I have often smiled at the decorative effect of the pronunciation of the name by political orators and radio announcers, with the accent on a long "a"—De-lā′-no. We called it just "Dulno."

At the grass-grown docks four or five old whaling vessels were tied up, the riggings and tops of which offered admirable practice for the seafaring career to which my uncle destined me when the price of whale oil should make it profitable again to put to sea. In spite of the cotton mills, which were making a new reputation for New Bedford, everybody was hoping for a turn in the market. There were hundreds of barrels of oil covered with seaweed on the docks, awaiting a chance to move. It never came.

The New Bedford I like to remember is that of the seventies—the old waterfront exactly as described in the opening pages of *Moby Dick*, the pleasant middle-class houses climbing up the hill, the magnificence of County Street with the courthouse and Judge Grinnell's pillared mansion. I often wished that my mother had chosen to live in New Bedford instead of Roxbury.

7

Undoubtedly, apart from excursions to the Polands and New Bedford, the happiest time of my childhood was spent in reading and acting out what I read. The first serious book I owned was Higginson's *Young Folks' History of the United States.* I knew it by heart and was insulted when the only poor teacher at the Lewis School consumed time in class by making us copy it, page after page. Then came Dickens' *Child's History of England*, which annoyingly stopped at 1688. I remember now the vivid phrasing of Dickens' prejudices, against Dunstan, for example, and Henry VIII, who left a "blot of blood and grease" on the fair page of his country's story. I delighted in a lively account of the Revolutionary War, *The Boys of Seventy-Six*, by Charles C. Coffin, who sat in the opposite gallery from us in church. *The Boys of Sixty-One* was disappointing; Greeley's *American Conflict* had carried me beyond Coffin. I devoured Charlotte M. Yonge's histories of France, Germany, Greece, and Rome, acquiring from her, as from Dickens, certain monstrous misconceptions. Dickens was a violent Protestant, Miss Yonge an Anglo-Catholic, and both were vigorous propagandists. I always resented the "Young Folks" in a title and felt that the author was putting something over on us. Even *The Youth's Companion* was under suspicion because of its title.

For lighter reading there were the annual appearances of the *Bodley Books* by Horace E. Scudder and the *Zigzag Journeys* by Hezekiah Butterworth, two faint luminaries of the deepening twilight of New England's Indian Summer. These came regularly as Christmas gifts. Far more exciting was Oliver Optic, whom I procured from Drake's circulating library. Then there was *The Chatterbox,* also a regular Christmas gift, that remarkable miscellany of sketches, poems, stories, and once a serial, *Honor Bright and the Four-Leaved Shamrock*. Hōnor ("o" as in omega) was a lovely girl, but my first literary love affair was utterly unworthy of a serious reader of history and travel. I fell for a dashing little girl named Dotty Dimple, in an interminable series of books by a lady who called herself Sophie May. I resented it bitterly when the author abandoned Dotty Dimple for a new heroine, Flaxie Frizzle. I remained faithful and reread Dotty. Of course I felt the disgrace of reading girls' books, and used to send my sister to ask our neighbor who had the whole lot to lend her *Little Prudy's Captain Horace* or some such humiliating title. Thank God the Elsie Dinsmore books never came my way!

I must say a word in defense of a class of books much depreciated by critics—the Sunday school library books. At the Walnut Avenue Sunday school we were allowed two a week. I didn't like to carry them home in their gray cambric covers, identifying me as a Sunday school boy—I was ashamed of Jesus—but the delight of reading them on Sunday evening was compensation. Some of them I remember today after sixty years: *Froggy's Little Brother*, a pathetic tale of two abandoned waifs in London; *The Little Brown Girl*, the heroine being a juvenile replica of Fanny Price in *Mansfield Park; An Island Home*, about an attractive Southern family. I have always maintained that the way to a child's heart in fiction is to give him children with whom he would like to be associated, as is so truly the case with such classics among children's books as *Hans Brinker*, *Castle Blair*, and some of Louisa M. Alcott's books. The *Bodley Books* were about natural children with whom one could be intimate, while the *Zigzag Journeys* had to be made with an unconscionable group of prigs.

At home we had Longfellow's poems and Tennyson's, Whittier's *Snow-Bound* and *The Tent on the Beach*, Jean Ingelow's verses and Bryant's *Iliad*. The crown of the library was the Excelsior edition of Dickens, which I was forbidden to touch. I got a cheap paper edition of *Pickwick Papers*, which I concealed in the bathroom and read on Saturday nights until the bath water grew cold. At New Bedford there was not much to read, though my aunt borrowed *Tom Sawyer* for me; but the Polands had everything heart could wish. There were Marryat's novels and Cooper's *Leather-Stocking Tales*. Above all, they had Elijah Kellogg's stories of the Indian wars. These had the irresistible charm of bringing the reader into the frontier settlement of Wolf Run, and making him a companion of Sammy Summerford and Tony Stewart, to the extent of adopting their very imperfect English. My mother noticed this decline in culture after a visit to the Polands and was quick to infer the cause.

When my mother took me to "spend the day" with some family friends, my first, and sometimes my only, interest was in the bookcase. I always found something to suit my catholic taste and could pass the time happily until it was time to go home, which I often accepted with real reluctance. Once my mother rebuked me for telling my hostess that I had had a splendid time, when on the contrary

I had "had my nose in a book all day." I protested. "I thought it was good manners, Mama." "It is never good manners to tell a falsehood." "But it was true. I was reading the *Last of the Huggermuggers*." "It couldn't possibly *sound* true," replied my mother, and this set a new standard of veracity, a pragmatic one. What's the use of telling the truth if nobody believes you?

We had no plays in the family library, except Shakespeare, and never went to the theater. I got into trouble in the lowest class of grammar school by remarking, when the teacher was telling us about Lincoln's death, "He shouldn't have gone to the theater." But when Booth and Salvini came to Boston to play *Othello* the tabu was lifted. A clerk in my father's office was deputized to take me. William Hazeltine had been colonel of the Boston School Regiment, and so the occasion had a double significance for me. He got the last seat available in a corner of the second gallery of the Boston theater and squatted beside me, calling my attention to the "business," which I should otherwise have missed, as well as to certain liberties which Booth took with the text. He commended the pudicity which omitted "between the sheets" from the line:

'Tis rumored that between the sheets
He hath performed my office.

The performance that afternoon is fixed in my memory—the furious rage of Othello, more impressive because Salvini spoke in Italian, and the gentle insinuating guile of Iago. The antagonists were perfectly matched. Since then I have seen Coquelin in *Cyrano*, Duse in *Francesca da Rimini*, Bernhardt in *Phèdre*, Nazimova in *Ghosts*, but *Othello*, double starred, seen when I was fourteen, remains for me the acme of the theater.

8

The first reference to politics that I remember was the question, "Who're *you* for?" And a boy's reply, "Hayes and Wheeler." The long contest over the election was settled for us in favor of Hayes by the pronouncement of Grandpa. "He has a bullet in him," a war record being the first requirement of a successful candidate for office. I still have an impression, drawn from the heated talk of my father's cronies, that if the Electoral Commission had decided in Tilden's favor the Loyal Legion would have marched on Washington to prevent his inauguration. When President Hayes visited Boston my grandfather took me to see him, standing in a white hat in front of the Hotel Brunswick. Hayes became unpopular with Loyal Legionnaires and Grand Army men. His pledge not to accept a second term was interpreted as reflecting doubt on his election, which I have no doubt he felt, and his policy of appeasement of the South was regarded as a sign of weakness and stimulated the demand for Grant's return to the White House in 1880. I stood with Conkling and his three hundred and eight delegates for the third term, though my grandfather was a fanatic for Blaine, a "Blainiac" as the *Boston Advertiser* called him. In 1884 he came home one afternoon waving a newspaper and proclaiming, "The fourth ballot brought him."

Grandpa took me to the big Republican rallies in the campaign of 1884. I remember a seductive song by a male quartet:

Blaine is a statesman brave and true,
  Put him through! Put him through!
Stand by the old red, white and blue,
  Put him through!
Peace to the nations east and west;
Peace to the land we love the best,
Blaine is the man of all the rest,
  Put him through!

Put him through! Put him through!
Rally to your leader boys,
  Put him through!
Peace and prosperity he'll renew.
  Put him through!

It was a shock to descend from such spiritual heights in Tremont Temple to the streets full of marching men with torches, chanting:

Blaine! Blaine! James G. Blaine!
God save the liar from the State of Maine!

Or the conclusion of one of his letters to a certain Mr. Fletcher:

Burn this letter. Burn this letter.
Kind regards to Mrs. Fletcher.

One reason for Blaine's appeal to our middle-class public was that he represented distrust and hatred of England. Memories of the

Revolution and the War of 1812 were revived by the support given to the Confederacy during the Civil War and not appeased by the Alabama Claims decision. England was our hereditary enemy. Like the South, she was "waiting to do it again." Both were cherished political assets of the Republican party. In Massachusetts we had the scholar in politics, Henry Cabot Lodge, "waving the bloody shirt" at the South, and Blaine was the plumed knight, especially of the Irish. It was an irony of politics that he was defeated by the Reverend Mr. Burchard's speech characterizing the Democratic party as the party of "Rum, Romanism, and Rebellion." Grandpa always believed that Burchard was planted by enemies at the reception to Blaine at the Astor House, and that his habitual epigram was printed beforehand for distribution at Catholic churches in New York the following day.

Foreign affairs came into my life by way of a picture in *Harper's Weekly* of the Austrian Army entering Bosnia after the Treaties of Berlin. Somehow that scene has remained in my memory, connected by organic filaments, to use Carlyle's expression, with the tragedy that befell my family, and others, exactly forty years later. At school I was always ahead in current events, especially those of a military nature. There were Indian wars, and Custer's last fight and massacre, which Uncle William attributed to the jealousy of President Grant, who "planned it that way." There was the Afghan war and the Zulu war with the death of the Prince Imperial. The British bombardment of Alexandria and smashing of Arabi Pasha stirred Uncle William's wrath. We had the jingo song, and another:

> John Bull is not afraid of a fight to keep his trade,
> For his commerce he will always highly prize.
> But he'd make a better show if when e'er he struck a blow
> He'd take a *fellah* of his size.

The revolt of the Mahdi in the Sudan with the siege of the garrisons at Sinkat and Tokar was still more exciting, and we followed breathlessly the expedition of Sir Garnet Wolseley to rescue Gordon at Khartoum. I wrote an essay on the war between Serbia and Bulgaria.

When I was in high school Edwin D. Mead was leading a movement to interest young people in history. Under his inspiration Mrs. Mary Heminway offered prizes of a hundred dollars to pupils graduating from high school for historical essays. Mine was on "The

Political Thought of Sir Harry Vane," which opened the way to later interests in the English Civil War and Milton, and perhaps in civil liberties. I read my essay one evening in Mrs. Heminway's parlor to a group of distinguished old Bostonians whose names greatly impressed my mother. This success led to an invitation to deliver a lecture in the summer course at the Old South Church on "Thomas Jefferson and the Louisiana Purchase," which Mr. Mead kindly published in the *New England Magazine*.

I graduated from the regular course of the English High School with a Franklin Medal, a bunch of Lawrence prizes, and a platform part in the school exhibition, which the English teacher called "Imagination in Fiction" and the headmaster altered to "Some Novels." In my family, worldly success for the moment submerged otherworldliness. I had no difficulty in exchanging West Point for Harvard.

II. *Harvard*, 1888–1893

I

HARVARD COLLEGE in 1888 was still the dominating element in the institution that was becoming Harvard University. President Charles W. Eliot, after nearly twenty years of persuasion, had converted the faculty to the elective system in the curriculum, which had the effect of adapting the college course to preparation for the professional schools. This relaxation of prescription was reflected in the requirements for admission. Dr. Eliot had the English High School in Boston especially in mind as one of the schools from which students might be drawn for the new and liberalized Harvard, and the headmaster, Francis A. Waterhouse, was eager to co-operate. The college preparatory course in the Advanced Class, after the formal graduation, attracted five members of the class of 1887 to become candidates for Harvard. Latin, Greek, Chemistry or Physics, History, English, French, German, Algebra, Geometry, and Astronomy, were the subjects which we had to continue or review in one crowded year. We had to take all the examinations at one time. There were four days of concentrated and differentiated mental activity in June, when with a motley crowd of sub-freshmen we were shepherded from building to building by proctors under the direction of W. W. Nolan, later a famous tutor known as "the Widow."

The day he enters college is one of the time-marks in the life of the American boy. I had been fortunate in drawing a room in Thayer Hall. It was the least gracious of the college buildings, something between a barn and a factory, but it looked out upon the Yard, then shadowed by the elms beneath which so many saints and sages and soldiers had walked and talked. Opposite were venerable Hollis and Stoughton where these worthies had lived, and to the right my view caught the broad, kindly face of Holworthy. In between was the pump, whose rattle and gurgle day and night kept alive the memory of the days when Harvard was merely another New England country college. Now that Harvard was entering the modern world as a university, we cherished such memories though they were fading. The freshman-sophomore rush on "Bloody Monday" was bloody only in the newspapers. Bonfires in the Yard no longer summoned the proctors from their dignified leisure but were suppressed by a mercenary gestapo known as the Yard committee.

The ordeal of entrance examinations passed, we entered the intellectual cloud-cuckoo land under the elective system. I proposed to take all knowledge for my province, and spent the first fortnight of the term in sampling courses in medieval history, literature, philosophy, science, and art. In the end an upper classman wrote out my registration card—Latin A, Greek A, English A, History 1, Natural History 4.

In both Greek and Latin I had the incomparable advantage of the teaching of James Rigdon Wheeler. The experience of reading the classics with that superb exponent of the Greek spirit is one to be cherished always. For the rest, my courses were too easy. I found myself at the close of the year a high-stand man, committed more deeply than ever to the superstition of high marks. It was, however, a grand moment in my life when, early in the next year, I stood next to Allen Benner, always number one, to receive a "detur" from the hand of Charles Eliot Norton—Carlyle's *French Revolution*, bound in crimson leather stamped with the college arms.

I had intended to make history my major subject, but I found the courses in European history by Silas Macvane and Edward Channing a repetition of textbooks. Professor Albert Bushnell Hart was developing a new method in American history, but that field did not attract me. Accordingly I accepted George P. Baker's suggestion to switch to English. At that time the chief distinction of the English Department was the emphasis on writing. Dr. Eliot proposed to maintain the traditional culture of Harvard, threatened by the loss of social exclusiveness and of the protection of the classics, by required courses in English writing. He called a classmate, Adams Sherman Hill, from the *Chicago Tribune* to develop this field. LeBaron R. Briggs left the Greek Department to conduct the freshman English course. Sophomore were obliged to write themes every fortnight, which all members of the department shared in correcting. Juniors and seniors wrote forensics which Baker made his special concern. Far from discouraging

Election the required courses stimulated it, and Professor Barrett Wendell's English XII, with its novelty of daily themes, reached an enrollment of over two hundred. English V was Professor Hill's special course, limited to twenty-five. His method is aptly described by Charles M. Flandrau in his clever book *Sophomores Abroad.* On one occasion a student who had been savagely scored rose to protest that he was too discouraged to write again. Professor Hill laid down his glasses and replied that his function was fulfilled, not to encourage bad writing but to discourage it, to protect literature from incompetent writers.

I took English V once with Professor Briggs and again with Professor Hill. With gratitude to them I can quote Matthew Arnold:

> For rigorous teachers seized my youth
> And purged its faith and trimm'd its fire.

I have spent a good part of my life as teacher, editor, and consulting critic in passing forward their instruction, but I know that it was a mistake for me to abandon history, which has always been my chief intellectual concern, for English literature, in which I had a keen literary and sociological, but a meager scholarly, interest.

2

I believe that those of us who were at Harvard in the late eighties and early nineties would echo Norman Hapgood's appraisal in his autobiography, *Changing Years:* "If there could be a place intellectually more attractive than Harvard University toward the end of the nineteenth century, my imagination does not give it form." This period was a golden age in the history of Harvard. The setting sun of the classics cast a mellow glow from the horizon, like Christianity in an age of science. We had, for the most part, ceased to live in them, but we held them in affection. Meanwhile the intellectual excitement arising from the new freedom in choice of studies was contagious. Although the elective system, unguided, was properly criticized as tending to a scattering of interest and energy, its immediate effect was stimulating and broadening, especially in breaking down regimentation within the narrow frames of class solidarity. Instead of following the same prescribed routine, men of the same college age pursued different lines and brought various material into discussion. Again, a freshman or sophomore might sit next to a junior or senior in lecture room or laboratory and belong to the same departmental club. Perhaps as a result of being treated as adults undergraduates developed a certain sense of superiority, what was called "Harvard indifference." Although Harvard had a rigid hierarchy of clubs rising from the Institute of 1770 through the Dickie and the Fly to the Porcellian or Med. Fac., most undergraduates were unconcerned with it. The tragedies of Yale men who failed to make Bones or Keys were incomprehensible to us. The case was best put by my classmate Hutchins Hapgood. "We're too much interested in life," he said, "to care to succeed in it."

I suffered from the juxtaposition of upper classmen in my freshman year when in History I found myself by alphabetical selection seated next to a big bald man named Longworth. I knew he was a crew man and a sport, and therefore was not surprised when he usually laid his head on his arms and slept steadily throughout Dr. Gross's lectures, though I resented the fact that he took up so much space on the narrow table. I was flattered, however, when just before the mid-year examinations, with no apology, he appropriated my notebook.

On the other hand, I gained from several upper classmen more than I can thank them for. The chief of these was Norman Hapgood, who was editor-in-chief of *The Harvard Monthly*. Looking about for new material, he heard of me, probably through Professor Baker. He called at my room one day in the spring of my sophomore year, a racquet and set of tennis balls in hand. As he carelessly proposed that I should submit an article, he knocked the balls about and, missing one occasionally, he would dive under desk or couch to retrieve it. Charmed by this informal approach, I hastened to comply. In the end I was elected an editor of the magazine, the most important event of my college years.

The Harvard Monthly had been founded by a group of remarkable men of the class of 1886, headed by Alanson Bigelow Houghton, whose promise as a poet was defeated by the Corning Glass Works. It enjoyed the unique distinction among college publications of being admitted to Poole's index of magazine literature. The most distinguished of all the farmer members of the *Monthly* was George Santayana. He returned to Harvard from Germany in my sophomore year and became an elder statesman to the editorial board. His spiritual autobiography, in the form of a sequence of sonnets, appeared in the magazine while I was editor, by far the most important contribution I published.

Once I suggested to Santayana that he give a party in his rooms to which we would invite our not-yet-successful aspirants, as a mark of appreciation and encouragement. He used to make a pleasant drink of light wine and Apollinaris water, but it was called a punch and our party was so described in the invitation. On the afternoon before the party Dean Briggs came to my door in some excitement to say that the invitations must be recalled. President Eliot would not approve of a member of the faculty serving punch to undergraduates. Santayana's academic future was at stake! I explained the harmless nature of the drink, but, after all, punch was punch. I hurried over to see Santayana, who took the matter quite coolly. "Let's call it a beer," he said.

In explanation of the scandal it should be said that punch was the traditional drink of Harvard in those days—a base of claret strongly impregnated with rum and flavored with maraschino. On Commencement Day each returning class held open house in a room on the college Yard and vied in the potency of the liquid entertainment. The procession of alumni to Memorial Hall might have been described by an unfriendly commentator as "drunk and disorderly." Among undergraduates punch was also the usual drink at clubs and informal gatherings. The Signet, a quiet literary circle, had rooms immediately below the riotous D.K.E., or Dickie, and we watched with interest a large purple stain on our ceiling which seemed to expand from week to week. Naturally punch became anathema to the authorities. Finally the Corporation assigned rooms for alumni gatherings at Commencement only with a prohibition against it. I have gathered that after undergraduates were furnished with individual bathrooms in the modern "Houses" the brewing of beer replaced the mixing of the bowl.

3

Our existence could hardly be called Spartan, and yet there were lapses from what we now think of as civilization. The preferred dormitories were in the Yard. None had central heating or running water, and we bought wood and coal for our small grates and carried water from the basement up two, three, or four flights of stairs.

Except in a few privately owned dormitories, like Beck Hall, there were no baths except in Hemenway Gymnasium. I remember at an election to the Signet it was solemnly urged in favor of a nominee that he took his cold bath every morning "like an Englishman." The only toilets were in the basements—in Hollis and Stoughton none at all. A scandalous daily theme described with mordant humor the plight of a student in Hollis with diarrhea on a winter night, sitting in his overcoat, ready for a dash to the Holworthy "mine." Once President Eliot, in a rarely expansive mood, dated the use of this term from the time when the single comfort station behind University Hall bore that appellation. The *Boston Herald* once cited as an example of the feebleness of Harvard wit a conversation reported in *The Lampoon.* "First Student: 'I'm going to my room.' Second Student: 'I'm going to mine.' "

The administration was equally primitive. Letters to Secretary Frank Bolles, asking questions of importance to an anxious candidate for admission, were answered at length in his own handwriting, and notes from President Eliot were also handwritten, though they were laconic. The entire body of records seemed to be kept by a lady known as Carrie Harris, who had inherited the office from her father. It was a notable innovation when the university bought a typewriter and appointed George Washington Cram as Recorder.

Through Norman Hapgood I met his brother, Hutchins, who joined our class in the sophomore year; he proved to have an original mind and a taste for intellectual adventure which were my delight for fifty years. Through Norman I also came to know members of the faculty. His parents had moved from Alton, Illinois, to Cambridge, where they were appreciated in academic circles much as visitors from Mars. They spent the summers at Seal Harbor, Maine, to which resort came Professors Charles C. Everett, Crawford H. Toy, and others, along with Norman's undergraduate friends. The walks to Somes Sound or Prettymarsh, or up Green Mountain, were a peripatetic school of philosophy. Mrs. Toy was a hospitable hostess at Seal Harbor and in Cambridge where her home was a civilizing influence for me as for other raw youths.

4

The English and Philosophy Departments were the two which exerted the most widespread influence upon undergraduates. George

Lyman Kittredge returned to Harvard from Exeter in my freshman year, and at once laid the basis for his dominating career as colleague and successor of Francis J. Child. For the famous two-year course in Shakespeare I came under the latter. Both masters used the same method—a minute study of the text of seven plays each year, with much thumbing of Schmidt's *Shakespeare Lexicon* for parallel references, useful on examination papers. There was no mention of the fact that Shakespeare had a personal history or that he wrote for the Elizabethan stage. Professor Child was contemptuous when a committee of students requested the substitution of the sonnets for one of the plays. His method of conducting the class was to summon to the front row eight students to read and comment on the text, while the rest of the class listened or slept. If by chance this panel was exhausted, however, and the professor began to range at large through the class, there was consternation. One day when he had given way to a pardonable display of temper at the repeated lack of response, the next reader took up the line from *King Lear* in a mild voice of expostulation: "What! Art thou mad?" Again, after a number of drafted students had responded with "Not prepared," the rebuke came pat from the text: "Then shall you go no further. It is the cowish terror of his spirit that dares not undertake."

Professor Child was one of the survivals of the old Harvard. I liked to remember that James Russell Lowell had rehearsed the "Commemoration Ode" with him under the trees of the yard. Lowell himself could be seen walking about Cambridge in ambassadorial dignity of frock coat and tall hat.

Another professor blessed by time was Francis Bowen, who formerly had occupied a settee rather than a chair of philosophy, political economy, and what there was of political and social science. In this field a new star was rising. Frank W. Taussig became czar of Pol. Econ. 1 and 2, to rival Kittredge in his long reign. He practiced the Socratic method based on John Stuart Mill's *Principles of Political Economy* and earned among generations of discomfited students the designation Stinker Taussig.

A further link between past and present was Charles Eliot Norton —a link also between England and America, for he had gone into the battle of the Carlyle family against Froude and he was a friend of Ruskin. It was a sacred occasion when one of us discovered the charming passage in Ruskin's *Praeterita* which describes their meeting as young men on Lake Geneva. Norton's courses, like Shaler's in geology, were discursive, and therefore popular. Some years later, on a visit to Harvard, I saw a continuous line of students during a class hour descending the fire escape from the second story of Massachusetts Hall. "That's Norton's course," was the explanation. It would not have happened in my day. The fiery denunciations of the vulgarity and corruption of modern society, in Ruskin's best vein, held even Porcellian men. Like Ruskin's, Professor Norton's mind was extremely gregarious. One morning he opened his lecture with a few reminiscently thoughtful remarks on the place of the water closet in civilization. Like many of his colleagues, he was hospitable. A party at Shady Hill was a feature of the Christmas season for students who could not go home. At a gathering about his fireplace, when he was expounding his religious views, a student inquired innocently if Ruskin shared the same "pagan consciousness." "You think I am a pagan?" asked the author of *Church Building in the Middle Ages.* The student apologized, explaining the eulogistic sense of the term in a generation that was brought up on Omar Khayyám.

In philosophy there were three professors—George Herbert Palmer, William James, Josiah Royce—and Santayana. In my junior year they combined to give a general course, Introduction to Philosophy, in which each took a special field—ethics, psychology, logic, and metaphysics. James, for some reason, chose logic, and constantly delighted the class by putting syllogisms on the blackboard which sometimes did not work out. Then he would throw down the chalk and call out to the bright lad who was marking attendance, "Mr. Gifford, Mr. Gifford, please take this over."

Ralph Waldo Gifford was one of the ablest students in our class. He was tutor to the James family. His appearance on the platform gave him authority. I was flattered when he suggested to me that we should jointly offer a "seminar" in preparation for the final examination. The seminar system had become an institution under the management of "Widow" Nolan. His assistants attended large courses and took full notes, from which a synthesis was prepared which in three or four hours gave a review of the course covering the questions expected on the final examination. As the course in philosophy was new, the Widow had not got around to digesting it, so that our seminar had no competition. On a hot June night my rooms in Thayer were filled with a crowd that extended into the corridor. The pitchers went on frequent journeys to the pump. We charged the usual fee of three dollars, but accepted IOU's. We bore lightly on logic, on the ground that James would necessarily be easy, and on psychology, of which Santayana had admitted to the class that he knew little, but Gifford on metaphysics was exhaustive. In his exposition of Leibnitz's doctrine of monads he defined God as the Monad Monadorum. The acolyte of the department who read the examination books remarked that semester on the frequent recurrence of that term.

Palmer was the professor whom I knew best. He was a Hegelian. Accordingly, in his ethics course I wrote an enthusiastic thesis on Thomas Hill Green's *Prolegomena to Ethics*, and a disparaging criticism of Mill's *Utilitarianism*. Both Professor and Mrs. Palmer were extremely kind to me in college and afterwards. He was a Worldly Wiseman among idealists. One bit of his wisdom I seem to have followed consistently: "Attach yourself to institutions," along with another from William James, the iconoclast: "Be open to all appeals."

5

I came to Harvard as one of five freshmen from the English High School and thus lacked the easy initiation into college life enjoyed by those who came from the usual preparatory schools. In my second year I joined Delta Upsilon, the only society at Harvard which kept up its connection with a national fraternity. Such connection was not popular. The D.K.E. had become a local sophomore society whose members might graduate the next year into Alpha Delta Phi, thus committing the crime of dual unionism. When Delta Upsilon achieved distinction in later years through Heywood Broun and Robert Benchley, it too suffered a split, most of its members forming a local D.U. club.

In Delta Upsilon I found a group of men from Phillips Academy in Andover. There were Allen R. Benner, the first scholar in our class, later the famous Zeus of Andover, William T. Brewster, and Carlos C. Closson. The two last came from Lawrence, Massachusetts, as did Fred N. Robinson, of '91. I had a leaning toward Phillips Andover because my grandfather had been a pupil there, and I found companionship among its graduates. For Benner I had immense respect and something of awe. His character, like that of Professor Wheeler, seemed to reflect the nobility of the classics which he studied and taught throughout his life. I was more intimate with Billy Brewster and Carlos Closson. With them and Robinson I took summer trips, walking and camping in the White Mountains.

It was in my second year Latin course that I heard Professor C. L. Smith call "Mr. Moody," and listened to a voice that I can hear today, full, clear, rich in overtones, reading with animation some lines from *Phormio*. I did not know its owner for some time afterwards, but a sonnet in the *Monthly* on "A Chorus of Wagner" assured me that it was the voice of a poet. I met William Vaughn Moody at the meeting of the *Monthly* board when we both became members. A well-knit figure, of medium height, a ruddy face under wavy flaxen locks, eyes of cold blue except for frequent gleams of humor, lips sensitive and sensuous, such was the youth who became my closest companion in college and who was always the object of my deep admiration. We were thrown together necessarily by a common interest in the *Monthly*, but I remember chiefly our walks, when, as Norman Hapgood said of Moody's conversation, we chased a metaphor all around Sky Pond or across the Harvard Bridge to Boston. It is in the light of Moody's companionship that I see again the pine woods of Arlington Heights in the sunlit snow of a winter afternoon, or feel the soft velvet darkness of Mount Auburn, where once we were benighted and had to scale the dangerously tall iron gates to escape.

In those days Moody was learning his business from Tennyson, Browning, Keats, Shelley, Wordsworth. He imitated them all with skill, but there emerged also the authentic note of his own genius. He had years of struggle before him to subdue the tendency to lushness of line and luxuriance of color that made Santayana say that his poetry reminded him of stained-glass windows. It was Moody's tragedy that when he had achieved a more austere and controlled style in "The Death of Eve," a new school of poets was taking possession of the stage. That he was the most powerful exponent in America of the older poetry was recognized by Amy Lowell, chief of the Imagists, who remarked speculatively in conversation about him, "I wonder if he could have held us back."

One of my pleasantest experiences in connection with the *Monthly* was the recruiting of lower classmen for the staff. Since the class of '90 the editorial board had never had more than two or three active members. I found several promising students who in their later careers in college and afterwards revived the former distinction of the paper—Edward Kennard Rand and John Rathbone Oliver of

'94, Joseph Trumbull Stickney, '95, and Philip Henry Savage, "Special." Rand and Stickney became my very close and much loved friends. Rand was a shy and deprecating youth in his patient citadel on the top floor of Matthews Hall. He protested that he was not a writer, only a "grind," a root out of dry ground without form or comeliness of style. As an undergraduate he became known to Latinists throughout the country when at short notice he replaced Stickney, who was taken ill, in the title part of *Phormio* as given by the Latin Department. He became the perfect college don, with immense learning carried lightly at all times and never more happily than when drawn upon to feed a fine sense of humor. Once I heard this humor break into exquisite drollery. As toastmaster at an alumni banquet of the Signet, he raised the flowing bowl and made as if to send it around the table; then, looking down at the diminutive figure beside him of Professor John Livingston Lowes, he remarked sadly, "No, something must be left for the rest," and he turned to the other side. I last saw Rand at the Harvard Tercentenary, as Pope Professor, gorgeous in the robes of world-wide academic distinction, distributing compliments to the guests with noble Latin eloquence. Of all the speakers on that occasion only he spoke without manuscript.

Joseph Trumbull Stickney was an immediate contrast to Rand. Rand had come to Harvard from a Watertown high school, from a suburban environment like my own. Stickney's family had lived for many years in Europe. His father had been a teacher of the classics, and from him and from tutors Stickney had acquired a European culture. In college dramatics he took with equal ease parts in Latin, French, or German. At our first meeting, as he stood in his doorway to admit me, I saw a tall, very handsome youth with a charming dignity touched by a shade of deference. He read me several poems, and I engaged him at once for the *Monthly*.

My relation with Stickney during the following year illustrated the breaking down of barriers and easing of class restrictions which marked the Harvard of that epoch. I was a graduate student and assistant in English. Stickney was a sophomore, but during this year when Moody was in Europe I found in the former my chief companionship. Officially I read his themes; unofficially, his poetry. An attack of measles confined him to his room, where I tended him, without a thought of spreading the disease. Having been brought up in Europe, Stickney threw himself passionately into American life, but he was not enthusiastically received. Santayana in his autobiography records Stickney's rejection by a group of his contemporaries who had formed a circle for reading poetry with, "The others didn't like him." It was later in Paris that I recognized Stickney's true background, where, like Santayana's, "my memory prefers to place him."

An innovation of great personal importance to me occurred during my years at Harvard. Before that time the Institution for the Collegiate Instruction of Women, popularly known as the Harvard Annex, had been completely ignored by Harvard students. There arrived on the scene, however, a group of girls who made such indifference impossible and who could not be ignored. The Comedy Club brought men and girls together. *The Harvard Advocate* set up a committee of associate editors from the Annex, and perforce the *Monthly* followed. The Browning Club used to meet alternately at Cambridge homes and in college rooms. It startles me today to remember that young women used to gather in the evening in my rooms in Thayer with no protest from the college authorities. A Poetry Club was formed, and the Peripatetic Club for walking and canoeing. It seemed that we were becoming civilized.

6

With all these temptations to frivolity I was ambitious to become a leader in the campaign against what was held to be Harvard's besetting sin of "indifference." I made this the theme of editorials in the *Monthly*. Since the old society of Christian Brethren had become a branch of the Y.M.C.A. and was open only to members of orthodox churches, we organized a new society known as the Religious Union. It was the period when social settlements were being founded, following the example of Toynbee Hall in London and Hull House in Chicago. Robert Erskine Ely, then a clergyman in Cambridgeport, enlisted a few students in imitating them. We hired rooms in the old Prospect Hotel in Central Square and announced classes to be taught by Harvard students and instructors. As the Prospect Progressive Union was only fifteen minutes' walk from the Yard, actual settlement seemed unnecessary, though Carlos Closson joined Ely in residence for a time. The idea made an immediate appeal. If slogans had been in vogue we might have advertised, "Purge yourself of indifference at the Prospect Union." Professors were cordially willing to lecture to a courteous audience consisting mostly of middle-class tradesmen and clerks eager for self-improvement. Two occasions I especially remember. William James spoke on hypnotism, giving himself an alibi at the outset by stating that nearly everyone could hypnotize but comparatively few could be hypnotized. No one in that hardheaded audience proved susceptible. Santayana gave a lecture on St. Francis and the beauty of poverty, which left his hearers, whose interest in the Union was largely of a practical nature, somewhat aghast.

During my last year as an undergraduate I had the supreme satisfaction of being important. I stood at the head of the class, Benner having temporarily succumbed to the required course in forensics. I was president and chief marshal of Phi Beta Kappa, editor-in-chief of the *Monthly*, president of Delta Upsilon and the Senior Literary Society, the O.K. Tom Lamont, who was the most generally popular member of the class, put me into the "Hasty Pudding." But my most prized distinction was my election as class poet. I had greatly desired to be orator, but the caucus which was apportioning class offices decided that Hugh Landon had a superior claim to that office, and with much hesitation I undertook the poem. Six years before Alanson Bigelow Houghton had delivered a very notable poem impregnated with the pessimism of a time when every Harvard intellectual had his Omar Khayyám at hand or in mind. The haunting weariness of Houghton's strophes obsessed me.

> More fleet than love, light living for a day,
> More vain than barren husks of ruined corn
> The years with weary eyes have fled away
> Through hidden ways, and paths no feet have worn.
> And gone are those who sought for higher things,
> And those who heard the singing echoing strings
> Of some diviner song that would not stay;
> The age is feeble as a Samson shorn.

I determined that my poem should be a complete answer to Houghton—a challenge to doubt and hesitation, a call to arms. I was greatly flattered when Santayana congratulated me, but a little disappointed when he added, "It was so simple."

7

The summer after Class Day I went to Europe with Norman Hapgood and his classmate Louis H. Dow, who ever after was my close friend. Moody was leading a boy about the continent while preparing him for college and joined us in Switzerland. An American youth's first view of Paris is an unforgettable experience, a favorite theme of Henry James, but nowhere touched on so happily as by Carl Van Vechten in *Peter Whiffle*. Next to this I recall a chance meeting with William James, who joined our party when we were all befogged at Gletsch. My passion for mountains awoke at Zermatt, where I persuaded the rather indifferent party to an ascent of the Cima di Jazzi. Great were the preparations therefor. Two guides and a porter carried great packs of provisions and drink for one night at a mountain hut. At two in the morning we set forth in thick mist and drizzling rain. About eight o'clock the guides halted and declared that we were at the crest. There was no way of checking this assertion, and we meekly took the trail they indicated as leading to Italy. As we descended the sky cleared, the mist rolled away as swiftly as a stage curtain is raised, and from our background of bleak mountain range we saw Italy, bright in sunlight, the long spurs of green foothills and valleys dotted with villages and farms, and the trail leading down to Domodossola. No more perfect approach could have been imagined to that lovely land.

A factor in my happiness that summer was the release from a great anxiety as to my future. I had feared that my career in college marked a climax beyond which there was nothing higher. I had felt keenly the responsibility of success and the importance of capitalizing on it. I had hesitated between the Divinity School, drawn by the personal attraction of Professors Everett and Toy, and the Law School, where my upper-class friends, Norman Hapgood and Philip S. Abbot, were stars. In the end it seemed to me that nothing more glorious could be imagined than a place on the Harvard faculty, and under the encouragement, and I think the affectionate interest, of Professor Hill, I accepted an assistantship in English and simultaneously entered the Graduate School.

That autumn of 1892 saw new blood infused into the Harvard faculty. President Eliot had already sought to correct the ingrowing tendency of departmental self-sufficiency by bringing from Manchester University Professor W. J. Ashley, an economist of the inductive school, to offset Taussig's rigid deductive teaching. Professor Ashley regularly brought to his class a refreshing glass of milk and egg (and what else?), which he placed on his desk beneath his tall hat and drank on the half hour amid cheers. Professor James brought Münsterberg, and his students promptly proclaimed, "*Ein Münsterberg ist unser Gott.*" Eliot had also planted several promising graduates on traveling fellowships in Europe. Three of these returned to Harvard in 1892—Arthur Richmond Marsh and Edward Cummings to introduce into the curriculum the novelties of comparative literature and sociology, and Lewis Edwards Gates in modern English literature and composition.

As a graduate student I was immensely attracted by all these representatives of the new learning. I might have chosen sociology if I had had the necessary preliminary training in political economy. I was fascinated by the personality and scholarly outlook of Professor Marsh. He was supposed to be Eliot's choice as a counterweight to Kittredge's philological influence in the English Department, which was even then becoming dictatorial. Those of us who had somewhat resented Kittredge's textual method rallied to Marsh, but we soon realized that the latter was no match for the great scholar and that we had hitched our wagons to a falling star. With Gates I was brought into contact as his assistant. English 22 was a new sophomore course, and since it carried exemption from the required sophomore themes its enrollment passed one hundred and fifty. A long theme was required every fortnight and, for part of the year, a short theme every day. I staggered under the load of two-thirds of the long themes and all the "dailies." There were compensations. The class included a number of men whose ability as writers won later recognition—Charles M. Flandrau, Joseph Trumbull Stickney, Pierre La Rose, Henry Milner Rideout, and Arthur S. Pier, to mention only those whose names recur to me.

Gates had the qualities of a first-rate critic of literature—scholarship, sensibility, a sure sense of values, and a brilliant style. Except for reviews of poetry in the *Nation* and a small volume of essays, he expended his gifts on lectures to undergraduates and comments on their efforts. His talents were not wasted, however, as the names of his pupils who attained distinction in American letters show. He lived a solitary in his rooms in Matthews Hall. I persuaded him to take his meals at our table of graduate students in Memorial Hall, but he was not an easy companion. Although we met at least twice a day at table he communicated with me chiefly by letters. A click of my letter drop, and when I reached the door there would be only the sound of retreating footsteps two floors below. His letters were incisive. It was said that when annoyed at night by the pounding of his radiators he would write a note to President Eliot and scurry with it across the campus to the President's door. He also taught at the Harvard Annex, where his relations with his girl pupils, who were enormously intrigued by him, showed a fearful fascination. To his morbidly sensitive nature his later mental illness brought acute suffering.

The year was one of many other happy relations and pleasures, but I felt more and more anxiously that it was a mistake. I thought of it as a year of lost momentum. I did not realize that it conditioned my life for all the years to follow. It was in discouragement, weariness, and reaction from the strenuous year previous that I went in for a very conscious reversal of form. The Laodicean Club was partly a joke, designed to *épater* the Cambridge bourgeoisie, partly a reassertion of the traditional Harvard indifference. It was amusing to hear Professor Toy read out with denunciatory emphasis the judgment upon the church of Laodicea. "Because thou art neither hot nor cold, therefore will I spew thee out of my mouth." It was gratifying to be told that Professor Baker commented scornfully, "I did not think Lovett was so *young*." But the club was also a genuine expression of a mood common to young men pausing on the border between college and the world and taking refuge from reality and responsibility in a mood of quietism and cynicism.

The meetings of the club were in my rooms; the refreshments, lukewarm tea and Tokay instead of punch. The members were George Santayana, elected pope, Norman and Hutchins Hapgood, W. F. Harris, Arthur S. Hayes, and possibly one or two others. The second meeting was devoted to canonizing the saints of Laodicea, each member proposing a candidate. Harris sponsored Horace. One of the Hapgoods offered Goethe, probably on the ground that he

> Neither made man too much a god,
> Nor God too much a man.

Omar Khayyám was elected without difficulty. Since we needed a virgin my own choice was Lucrezia Borgia, who exercised a wise indifference in difficult circumstances. Santayana's candidate was God.

Since the Laodiceans could not be enthusiastic even about their church, it was the rule that if at any meeting a quorum should be present the club should *ipso facto* cease to exist. As a result, the second meeting was the last.

8

Among the recent editors of the *Monthly* the most promising aspirant to literary success was Robert Herrick of the class of '90. He was teaching at the Massachusetts Institute of Technology when called to the University of Chicago, then just established. I was greatly flattered when toward the end of my post-graduate year Herrick asked me to go with him. At first I had no idea of accepting. I had a romantic attachment to Harvard. I liked to think of it as somehow the New England equivalent of an English university in academic dignity and richness of culture and association. In my junior year I wrote a Bowdoin Prize essay on "A Study of Cardinal Newman," and was possessed by the idea of an Oxford Movement at Harvard, though not directed to the same ends. I used to read the passage in Newman's *Apologia* in which he wrote of taking the snapdragon growing on the wall of Trinity College as a symbol of his lifelong residence in the university, with a longing that so it might be with me. My attachment extended even to my homely rooms at Thayer 57, which I retained though I might have had free quarters as proctor in another entry. Newman's influence brought a resurgence of the religious emotion to which I had been conditioned in my childhood—oddly enough, contemporary with my lapse into Laodiceanism. Contrary to both tendencies, I had a leader whom I admired and venerated in President Eliot. He was the very spirit of the Harvard I knew, one utterly remote alike from the Oxford of the early nineteenth century and the church of Laodicea. When Eliot advised me to stay at Harvard I considered the matter settled.

Nevertheless Herrick and his friends were urgent. President Harper invited me to visit the University of Chicago, and as the Columbian Exposition of 1893 had just opened I accepted the opportunity to see the university and the fair. I was a good deal impressed by both, and by the city which had already begun its cultural progress with the establishment of the Art Institute, the Symphony Orchestra, and Hull House. Nevertheless, I was not convinced and returned to Cambridge, so far as I knew to stay. I told Professor Marsh of my decision and boyishly revealed my romantic attachment to Harvard and my feeling that all my future was bound up in remaining in and of it. He listened with an expression of extreme distaste. "For God's sake," he exclaimed, "get away. Go anywhere." It was revealing. In a flash I knew that he was right. I was growing soft, a parasite, dependent on the teachers who had been my intellectual hosts.

I went to see President Eliot the same day and told him that I thought it would be best for me to leave Harvard. It was near Commencement, and he was very busy, working over those beautifully laconic appraisals of the eminent men on whom he was to confer honorary degrees, but he patiently went over the ground, spoke of the future he designed for Harvard, the uncertain fortunes of the new university, the horrors of life in Chicago. He ended. I sat speechless. A minute passed, perhaps two or three. Then I heard a faint, courteous sigh and quickly rose. "At any rate," he said, "I shall give you the appointment you have earned for next year, in case you should change your mind." This was an ironic thrust. The winter before Dr. Mackenzie of Lawrenceville had asked Eliot to recommend an English master. Dr. Eliot was very anxious to place a Harvard man in that school, and it was virtually at his bidding that I visited Dr. Mackenzie and accepted the position. On returning to Cambridge I withdrew. I expected that Eliot would be disgusted. He was kind. After thinking a few moments, as if weighing his words, he said, "It was permissible." My behavior was a part of the uncertainty and anxiety over my precious career which that year rode me like a night hag.

9

I fancy that Eliot may have been reminded in my case of the problem with which he had been confronted in his younger days when he decided to leave Harvard for the new Massachusetts Institute of Technology. When he threatened to make the new institution a genuine rival, the Corporation elected him president of Harvard, but the Board of Overseers refused to approve the election for a year, after which they were obliged to accept a *fait accompli*. He made his way slowly, leading his faculty step by step in his plan to make Harvard the first of American institutions of higher learning. To develop Harvard into a university he supported the professional schools, as older alumni thought, at the expense of the college. To fit the college curriculum to the demands of professional training he converted the faculty to the elective system. In the well-founded belief that at least one of the four college years was educationally unnecessary, he tried to induce his colleagues to reduce the prescribed course to three years. This proposal was under discussion when I was editor of the *Monthly*. The strongest point against it was made by William James, who argued that residence within academic walls and in the midst of cultural associations was a life value which should not be diminished. The popular protest from alumni and students was based on the sacred hierarchy, freshman, sophomore, junior, senior. Which year could be cut out, it was asked, without destroying the symmetry of the temple of learning? In the end Eliot succeeded only in permitting ambitious students to complete the required eighteen courses for the A.B. degree in three years.

President Eliot lacked popularity among undergraduates because of his dislike of intercollegiate athletics. He had rowed in the Harvard boat in his undergraduate days, but the fanatical emphasis on organized sports coming to the fore in the nineties aroused his disgust. A victory of Harvard in football occurred in 1890, when Yale was defeated twelve to six. The event was so unusual and unexpected that we did not know how to take it. We had read of celebrations in freshwater colleges and noted that one invariable feature was to drag the team, posed on the top of a tally-ho coach, to the president's house. So it was done. Dr. Eliot stood on his porch and offered congratulations, but he added that what most impressed him in his reading of the game was the magnificent rally which Yale made in the last ten minutes. Since we all realized that if those minutes had been prolonged Yale would have tied the score, this peroration was not received with cheers.

The luncheon of the Harvard Chapter of Phi Beta Kappa on the day after Commencement always found Eliot in magnificent form. He usually dissected the oration of the morning, and if the orator was able to come back the occasion was not without excitement. One year the orator was General Francis A. Walker, president of the Massachusetts Institute of Technology. Walker gave the learned society a shock by taking as his subject college athletics, which he appeared to regard as the chief reason for Harvard's existence. There was no love between him and Eliot, and when the latter arose after luncheon we all knew what was coming—and it came. He began by remarking that General Walker knew his subject, for he came to all the games at Harvard while rigidly excluding such frivolities from his own institution. He proceeded to tear up his opponent's arguments one by one, until there was nothing left of the original fabric. General Walker had already asked to be excused from speaking.

Tact was not Eliot's strong point. Sometimes his promptness in rejecting a courteous lead was disconcerting. At another Phi Beta Kappa luncheon Professor W. W. Goodwin, who was presiding, referred felicitously to President Eliot's impeccable and elegant Latin in his conduct of the Commencement exercises the day before. The President followed with a declaration that the use of Latin on that occasion was an anachronism and he intended thereafter to employ English.

President Eliot was disliked by the patricians, partly because of his policy of making Harvard democratic, and he was unpopular with the masses, partly because he was a natural aristocrat. The Boston papers were furious in their attacks on political grounds. He was a liberal of the school of John Stuart Mill, a believer in free trade, a mugwump who set good government above party. A pronounced individualist, he could not see by what right labor unions limited freedom of contract between worker and employer. He always spoke out. The wrath of press and public reached a crescendo when in the Mormon tabernacle at Salt Lake City he spoke of the courage and fortitude by which a civilization and an economy had been built up in the wilderness. His comparison of this exploit with that of the Pilgrim Fathers in Massachusetts was furiously resented. His stern and lofty bearing set him apart from his own faculty and students. He sat alone in Appleton Chapel every morning and alone he strode across the Yard to University Hall. Once on Dean Briggs' advice I joined him to ask his approval of the founding of the Religious Union. We walked to his office, and I was surprised to find him immediately cordial and evidently pleased at being consulted. I seem to remember the first occasion of his approach to the body of undergraduates as that on which Major Henry L. Higginson presented Soldiers' Field to the university in memory of four of his comrades who fell in the Civil War. President Eliot's reply was eloquent of the nobler conception of that struggle. In the end he conquered by sheer force of personality the coldness and indifference with which the collegiate body of my day regarded him. In later times there was both affection and pride in the greeting by alumni gatherings, when his presence was always toasted by singing, "Here's a health to King Charles."

10

Among the girls who were lifting the Harvard Annex to the distinction of Radcliffe College Ida Mott-Smith was the most brilliant and handsome. Her parents were among the New England pioneers of Hawaii. Her father, Dr. John Mott-Smith, had played an important part in the government of the islands under Kalakaua, and was actually their minister to the United States. In the face of the disgraceful participation of the State Department and the Navy in the conspiracy to overthrow the monarchy, he insisted on guarantees of safety and compensation for the Queen, and thus incurred the hostility of many of his old associates, now in the Provisional Government of the islands. A gallant and useful life ended in disappointment.

His wife, Ellen Paty, was the daughter of the Harbor Master of Honolulu in whaling days. My Uncle Dan had known him well. Indeed, Hawaii was part of the romance of our family and of New England. Missionaries and whalers gave it the glamour both of heavenly and earthly success. When Queen Kapiolani and Princess Liliuokalani came to Boston and rode in royal state with the mayor, it was a popular triumph; and although the Republican papers snarled at spending twenty-four thousand dollars to entertain two Kanakas, the Mott-Smiths shared the radiance spread by royalty.

The Mott-Smiths' home on Newbury Street was one of exuberant gaiety and charm. There were seven children and they reminded me of my cousins the Polands in their closely knit diversity. The children brought home guests as they liked for meals. On my first invitation I fear that I passed as a pagan, by continuing conversation at one end of the long table while the youngest girl invoked divine blessing at the other.

I knew Ida Mott-Smith in the Browning Club started by Algernon Tassin in my senior year at Harvard. I was on easy terms with the other girls, even the austerely beautiful Mary White Ovington, but with Ida I was shy. I resented Will Moody's remark that he went to the club only to look at Miss Mott-Smith's neck, and was hotly jealous when gossip reported that Miss Mott-Smith was seen sitting on the grass in the Boston Public Garden with Norman Hapgood. When my paper on Cardinal Newman attracted some attention I was invited to read it to a group of Annex girls at the Mott-Smith home, and when I was elected class poet the Idler Club, of which

Miss Mott-Smith was a leading spirit, invited me to tea to meet Oliver Wendell Holmes, who had been class poet in 1845. My own class poem was read in Sanders Theatre to two people, President Eliot and Ida Mott-Smith.

The summer after my graduation Will Moody returned from abroad, and I was very keen on his society. We spent some time in Cambridge, revising Bulfinch's *Age of Fable* for a hundred dollars, and then went for a cruise out of New Bedford. I had in mind, however, that a party had been planned for Waterville, New Hampshire, of which I was fairly sure Ida Mott-Smith would be a member, and when Moody left I made for that sequestered spot. The usual professorial colony was there, all most sympathetic. One gentleman congratulated me on the speed and persistence of my courtship, qualities which I seldom exhibited. At any rate I was too happy to be embarrassed when a telegram from Mrs. Mott-Smith was read out on the telephone, "Yes. Mother's love to both."

III. *Chicago*, 1893–1896

I

THE PLUNGE from the tepid atmosphere of Cambridge to the chilly winds of Chicago was both unpleasant and invigorating. The city was emerging from its triumph of the Columbian Exposition into the financial panic of 1893. The collapse was the more severely felt in Chicago because of the strain of carrying the fair. At the University Convocation in October President Harper found it necessary to assure his new faculty that the payroll would be met. This assurance was based on the fact that the Board of Trustees included the men who were responsible for the forward movement of the city in all directions. Martin A. Ryerson, who became chairman of the Board, and Charles L. Hutchinson, its treasurer, were in Paris when the Demidoff collection of Dutch masters came on the market and bought it at once to make the first notable contribution to the Art Institute, knowing that their colleagues would support them. This was an instance of the enterprise which carried the ambitious cultural projects of the city, including the university and the fair, through the depression.

The Columbian Exposition was the triumph of the feudal barons under whom Chicago had grown great. Its challenge to the world denounced the reputation which the city bore of materialism, cruelty, and clownishness. The noble group of buildings, white against the blue of the lake, were in their unity of design a symbol of the co-operation which was the secret of Chicago's success. The great collection of works of art, an exhibition unequaled in the world, the assembly of men and women of world-wide distinction, lent a cosmopolitan splendor to a city which had hitherto cherished its provincialism. But the sunshine of a brilliant afternoon was paling, shadows were falling. The financial strength of the country, which had made the enterprise possible, was failing. Nothing in the history of the city is more characteristic than the way in which the magnates stood up to their responsibilities in the face of danger and depression and carried on to the end.

2

I arrived in Chicago on a chilly, cloudy night in late September and found Robert Herrick glooming in a cheap boarding house. The next morning, still under a gray sky, we took the cable car to the university, where even President Harper's cordial greeting did not soothe our melancholy. The first view of the university was depressing. The gray stone buildings marked the corners of a square of four city blocks. They were vaguely of English Gothic, but four stories gave them a high-shouldered effect suggesting industry. The campus was a rough sand-lot with a swamp marked by a few scrub oak trees, where frogs croaked us to sleep at night. It was all bleak and grim, with little academic grace or charm. We took rooms on the first floor of a dormitory called Graduates Hall and dug in for the winter.

For a month we enjoyed the fair, but the contrast between its artificial glory and the squalor of the real city was appalling. Chicago had not yet accomplished its original task of lifting itself out of the mud. Wooden sidewalks often were on different levels, connected by short flights of steps. The long avenues leading to the west were mostly unpaved. Trucks and wagons drawn by horses or mules swayed along wide expanses of highway, now sinking to the axles, now rising on islands where the wooden paving had not yet been swallowed by the mud. They were like caravels on a turbulent sea. The effects of the fire of 1871 were still visible in the lines of dwellings in the ugly architectural style of the seventies, interrupted by shanties with entrances below the level of the street. The aftermath of the fair showed in whole blocks standing vacant and hotels boarded up. We foraged for food among restaurants which afforded studies in deterioration and frequently closed before our meal tickets were used up. Worst of all was the spectacle of poverty —men, women, and children marching to the garbage dumps and, in spite of unoccupied buildings galore, sleeping in jails or the City Hall. From our windows in Graduates Hall we saw Coxey's army of unemployed straggle north to seek shelter and food in the city. It was in keeping with this contrast that the summer of the fair—

the most splendid triumph achieved by an American city in the sight of the world—was followed in the winter by the most terrific arraignment of any city since the Hebrew prophets denounced Babylon, in W. T. Stead's *If Christ Came to Chicago.*

Moreover, there was acute fear in the community. The shadow of the events of seven years earlier still rested on the city. Anarchism, interpreted in terms of violence and terrorism by Johann Most, had made progress among the great mass of foreign-born workers in Chicago. The strike at the McCormick Reaper Works in 1886 had resulted in riots and shooting by the police; taking advantage of the exasperation, some unknown person had thrown a bomb into a squad of police marching to break up a peaceful public meeting in Haymarket Square. Seven writers for anarchist papers, some of whom had spoken at the university, had been arrested and tried, and four of them executed. It was a shocking travesty on justice in which Judge Elbert Gary, sitting on the bench with prominent ladies beside him as guests, boasted of making the law as he went along. In 1893 Judge Gary could still pose as the savior of society.

Among the ladies invited to see, as another judge later expressed it, what Gary "did to those anarchist bastards," was the future Mrs. Herrick. Her account of the feeling in Chicago at the time, the paroxysm of hate and fear that seized the city, is recalled in Herrick's novel *One Woman's Life.*

Much of the horror of the winter we escaped by reason of the remoteness of the university from the city. Although as a result of the fair the Illinois Central had elevated its tracks and provided a suburban service, the open flat cars sometimes drenched by spray from the lake, our usual transportation was by streetcar operated by cable. The route followed an incredibly mean thoroughfare misnamed Cottage Grove Avenue, described by Herrick in *The Web of Life:*

> Block after block, mile after mile, it was the same thing. No other city on the globe could present quite this combination of tawdriness, slackness, dirt, vulgarity, which was Cottage Grove Avenue. India, the Spanish-American countries, might show something fouler as far as mere filth, but nothing so incomparably mean and long.

3

I had not known Robert Herrick at all well at Harvard. He had been graduated just before I joined the staff of the *Monthly*, but he had honored us with his presence at the first meeting which I attended. My impression was of a youth of truly classical figure and beauty, and of an icy manner which he obviously tried to thaw. He had brought with him the manuscript of a story, a characteristic study of New England life, "From Shirtsleeves to Shirtsleeves," and in inviting our comment he was careful to say condescendingly that he "wished Lovett would give his opinion because he was writing fiction." From that moment Herrick's literary career became a constant interest in my life. And not in mine alone. No man I have known was more fortunate in his friends. The earlier editors of the *Monthly*, George Rice Carpenter, George P. Baker, Bernard Berenson, Philip S. Abbot, and Jefferson B. Fletcher, who married Herrick's beautiful sister Agnes, were devoted to him. Professor Palmer, a cousin of his mother's, was eager to be a guide and counselor. Later, William Dean Howells was an affectionate critic of his novels and Clyde Fitch of his efforts in the drama. Recently, in going over his papers, I found in the packages of letters, carefully preserved, a monument to friendship.

Robert Herrick was not a personal influence in my decision to go to Chicago—I was not even sure that I liked him—but he was a factor in keeping me there. During our first year he was endlessly concerned lest I should quit. I remembered a Swiss story of an old man and his grandson who lingered too late in their chalet in the high Alps and were snowed in for the winter. The grandfather exhausted ingenuity in providing alleviation for the boy's loneliness, the final *coup* being the finding of a copy of Thomas à Kempis. I used to joke with Herrick over his grandfatherly solicitude for my comfort, entertainment, and success. He was extremely fastidious in person and economy, and my carelessness in our menage probably pained him. When President Harper asked me to become his assistant at an increase in salary, Herrick, with extremely apologetic good will, advised me to get a good suit of clothes.

Next to Herrick's companionship in that first Chicago year I found my chief resource in two colleagues who lived in Graduates Hall, Oliver J. Thatcher and Ferdinand Schevill. They were in the Department of History. Thatcher was a picturesque academic figure. From Wilmington, Ohio, he had gone abroad, studied church history with Harnack at Berlin, traveled in the East, written a book on the Apostolic Church, and become a professor at Alleghany Seminary. He "lost his faith," as the saying was, and, a theological outcast, took refuge in Harper's Cave of Adullam. He was a passionate devotee of football, on the field every afternoon in the season as a volunteer coach, and tutoring the members of the team in the evening to keep them eligible to play. A painful event of his career was the allegation that when acting as linesman in an important game he danced about so enthusiastically after a small gain that he forgot to advance the line.

I suppose that the lambs of every college faculty are subject to the temptation of finance. Possibly the prominence of the financial background in the psychology of the University of Chicago rendered us rather less resistant than others. At any rate, I remember several waves of speculation that swept the faculty—gold mines recommended by a professor of geology, New York real estate introduced by a professor of sociology, apple orcharding in Montana promoted by a popular football star. Thatcher, on deciding to live for this world rather than the next, became a speculator, the chief supporter of an inventor, one Joe Symons, who turned up from Boise, Idaho, with a scheme for raising water from a stream by an endless chain of buckets which were filled and hoisted by the force of the current. "Buckets," as it was nicknamed, achieved the dignity of incorporation, and when several members of the Department of Political Economy were known to be purchasers of stock the rest of us followed their lead. Prices soared on the university bourse. One enthusiastic economist expressed the opinion that it was unimportant whether the Symons Water Elevator ever lifted a pail of water. It could sustain itself in the atmosphere of confidence of the investing public, who were already making money by selling stock to each other. He telegraphed to Mr. Rockefeller to come to Chicago at once in order to swim in the golden flood. Mr. Rockefeller replied to President Harper that he thought the faculty should stick to education and abjure finance. An investigation followed, and all intrafaculty deals were canceled. The up-to-the-minute economist went to a home for the mentally ill.

Thatcher never lost faith in Symons, who appeared year after year with something new—a loader, a ditcher, finally a flying machine, built, he explained, "to fly like the gulls." We certainly flew like them.

Of Ferdinand I need say little here. As my closest companion for more than fifty years, as an essential part of my memories, a sharer in the joys and sorrows of my life, he will appear often in my reminiscences. As Sterne of Uncle Toby, I may write later on:

> You perceive that the drawing of my Uncle Toby's character went on gently all the time—not the great contours of it—that was impossible—but some familiar strokes and paint designations of it were here and there touched on as we went along, so that you are much better acquainted with my Uncle Toby now than you was before.

4

The founder of the university, as of the Standard Oil Company, was John D. Rockefeller, a Baptist. According to the legend, his spiritual adviser, the Reverend F. T. Gates, held that good works were a passport to heaven, and so gave Mr. Rockefeller to understand. At any rate, Rockefeller promised six hundred thousand dollars to re-establish the University of Chicago, which had closed its doors in 1887, on condition that the Baptist Social Union would raise four hundred thousand more. He selected for president the most prominent Biblical scholar of the denomination, William Rainey Harper, Professor of Hebrew at Yale. If Mr. Rockefeller thought that a million dollars was sufficient to establish a modern university, President Harper soon enlightened him. In the course of time the Rockefeller fortune was drawn upon to upwards of a hundred million.

A few months after I joined the faculty President Harper asked me to be his special assistant in addition to my teaching. Thus from almost the beginning of my residence in the university and within a year of its opening I was drawn into close connection with its structure and development, a witness of its trials and errors and its triumph, in all of which the president was the major factor.

Dr. Harper was the greatest possible contrast to my former chief. Physically, where Eliot was tall, lean, with a look of race, Harper was short, fat, and undistinguished of features. Where Eliot was by nature aristocratic, Harper was characteristically of the people and superficially commonplace. Where Eliot offered to the world an appearance of coldness and inaccessibility, Harper was warm, genial, enthusiastic, approachable. Undoubtedly he was the man for the occasion which Mr. Rockefeller had created. His vision of a great institution of learning persisted in spite of meager resources. His faith in himself and his work, his power of communicating his enthusiasm and making friends, his tolerance in dealing with co-workers and students, all were indispensable to the founding of the University of Chicago.

As President Eliot represented the temper of New England raised to a higher power, so did Dr. Harper that of the Middle West. He was generous to a fault in his judgments of people and in his eagerness to aid them. When it was a question between the university and an individual member of the faculty or student in a matter of discipline, he used to say, "I won't dismiss him under fire," or "I'll give him another chance. The institution can afford it; the man can't." Once while discussing a peculiarly difficult case he peered around the edge of his desk to see if the Dean of the Faculties was sitting at the desk opposite, and said in explanation: "Mr. Judson is a merciless man." (He was not.) With all his humanity and optimism Dr. Harper was not the dupe of his temperament. I remember one occasion when he put his hand on my knee and said, "Lovett, I sometimes think we're all rotten," characteristically including himself.

Dr. Harper's generosity in money matters, personal and official, was embarrassing in both categories. He was constantly taking responsibility by guaranteeing assistance to young men and women. It was difficult for officials to dismiss a student whom the president had invited to come to the university at his expense. As editor and co-author of a series of language textbooks, written on the "inductive" method, he had a considerable income, which he sacrificed by selling his copyrights on accepting an appointment to the Chicago Board of Education, an important step toward integrating the school system with the university.

Dr. Harper was not an ascetic. He loved good food, good wine, good music. He enjoyed leisure and sleep. At the same time he was a terrifically hard worker. He believed that every member of the faculty should be a student in other departments than his own, a teacher, a research scholar, and bear a share in the administration, as well as contribute to the social life of the campus and of the city. He continued to teach classes in Hebrew, to attend lectures by his colleagues, to carry on research, and to maintain an elaborate web of social relations. Of men in the faculty who followed his example a number broke under the strain, especially of administration, which in view of the novel and complicated structure of the university was exacting. In my first years, in addition to teaching and secretarial duties, I took courses in Dante and Old English, and was head of the dormitory for undergraduate men and of the Board for the Recommendation of Teachers. Anything in the nature of research was crowded out of my program. Dr. Harper was anxious on this point and frequently asked me why I did not take a doctor's degree. I truthfully pleaded lack of time.

His habitual greeting at our daily interview was, "What ideas have you this morning?" I was fairly prolific in them at first, but soon found that each one he accepted (and he was hospitable) added to my burden, and I became more sparing of suggestions.

His doctor advised bicycling for exercise, and as he pedaled slowly I could walk alongside, notebook in hand. I think there was something of exhibitionism in his industry, and certainly in mine. It was in the Chicago spirit to combine recreation and work, to make every minute count. Sometimes late in the afternoon he would drop off for ten minutes' sleep, but invariably his question on waking was, "What have you been thinking up?" He liked to make appointments at obscene hours. When he invited Professor Manly, another tremendous worker, to a conference at six in the morning he enjoyed Manly's protest: "I hardly ever sit up so late, Mr. President."

Dr. Harper was by every instinct a liberal, but he had not surveyed the whole field. He gave the university a charter of freedom of teaching, research, opinion, and speech, but he was thinking in terms of what was known as the higher criticism of the Bible. Economic heresies were new to him, but he dealt with them in his usual spirit of consideration for the individual. One case was plausibly represented as a departure from academic freedom at the behest of the Founder. I remember seeing a letter from Mr. Rockefeller to President Harper, inquiring, "Who is this man whom I am accused of dismissing from your university?" Obviously the founding of the university by the greatest capitalist in America made it sensitive to charges of capitalistic influence and inclined to lean backward to avoid them. No one can testify with better right than I to the fact that no other institution in the United States ever exhibited such tolerance of unorthodox opinion and behavior as the University of Chicago.

Mr. Rockefeller's early gifts were wisely made contingent on the contribution of equal sums by others. President Harper was therefore committed to a campaign for raising money for objects which at best were imperfectly understood by the community. The success of the Hebrew scholar in dealing with the world of business and finance was amazing. A businessman stopped at the Newberry Library one day to inquire from the librarian the name of a ruined city of the Orient which he had heard but forgotten. After several guesses Baalbec was suggested. Right. The inquirer explained that in the smoking room of a Pullman the man from the university had pictured the desolation of Baalbec in such moving terms that he had made a subscription to equip an expedition to excavate its ruins.

One of the most important gifts to the university was quite fortuitous. President Harper received a letter from Charles T. Yerkes offering a million more or less for an observatory, which was, in fact, erected at William Bay, Wisconsin, and which made the university at once a center of exploration and research in astronomy. It was said that this was a gesture to restore faith in the donor's resources and credit which had been somewhat shaken. It was apparently successful, since Mr. Yerkes celebrated the acceptance of his gift by a dinner to the faculty at which champagne flowed freely.

President Harper was no less successful in his fishing for men, and with the same lack of initial orientation. He had decided at the outset that the University of Chicago should pay larger salaries to its heads of departments than any similar institution. He was thus able to raid successfully his older rivals. For the first year he had on temporary appointment Professor Francis H. Mall of Johns Hopkins, who selected the staff in various departments of science. Five distinguished scientists were taken at one swoop from Clark University—Michelson, Donaldson, Whitman, Nef, and Loeb. From Cornell he drew William Gardner Hale in Latin, James Laurence Laughlin and Adolph C. Miller in Political Economy. From Yale he brought his brother, Robert F. Harper, in Semitics, as well as Frank F. Abbott in Latin, Edward Capps in Greek, and William B. Knapp in Romance Languages. Professor Paul Shorey came from Bryn Mawr, and a miscellaneous lot from Denison University, where President Harper had once taught. Even college presidents were glad to accept positions at the new university. President T. C. Chamberlain came from the University of Wisconsin, to be head of the Department of Geology, bringing with him Rollin D. Salisbury. President Albion W. Small came to the Department of Sociology from Colby University, and two years later President John W. Coulter, the botanist, came from Indiana University. The greatest catch of all, in public appeal, was Professor Hermann E. von Holst from Freiburg in History. President Harper saw the necessity of bidding high for such men, and the salary of seven thousand dollars for head professors was for the time the highest reward for what Veblen irreverently called the "hire learning."

One advantage of residence in the University of Chicago in its first years was association with these eminent men. The small faculty, remote from the city, was drawn together by a common feeling of exile. The older men who had set up homes were very hospitable to us youngsters. Though the financial chasm between a head professor and an instructor seemed immeasurable, the social gap was easily bridged. Academic distinctions, it is true, were cherished even to absurdity. Going out of chapel one day I heard an inquiry: "Who was the fellow who fainted?" And the answer: "It wasn't a fellow. Only a student."

Another relief in the thinness of the social atmosphere in which we lived was afforded by the hospitality of a section of the merchant aristocracy of the city, some of whom became trustees of the university. Families of Spragues, Bartletts, Glessners, McCormicks, exercised a kindly patronage. Another alleviation was afforded by the women's houses on the campus. In these early days the female students came, on the whole, from a higher social level than the male. This could be accounted for by the fact that boys of richer families continued to follow family traditions and go to the Eastern colleges, while the girls came to the local institutions. Thus we had a group of girls from the city who exercised a refining influence on their co-educated classmates. Mrs. Alice Freeman Palmer was the first Dean of Women, and under her administration the three women's halls were oases of civilization. Beecher, Kelly, Foster, had as heads three remarkable women—Elizabeth Wallace, who was a citizen of the world in every sense, Marion Talbot, who succeeded Mrs. Palmer as dean, and Myra Reynolds, a humane scholar. Miss Wallace, in her autobiography, has described the very first year of the university with a sense of comedy which is my envy and despair.

5

In educational policy Herrick and I did not see eye to eye with the president. As a teacher at Chautauqua Dr. Harper had found that by holding classes twice a day he could increase fourfold the amount of Hebrew instilled into his students. Accordingly he made the units of instruction courses meeting twice a day for a "term" of six weeks, or for the quarter, entitled respectively a major or double major. A minor was a course meeting once a day for six weeks; a double minor, for twelve weeks. President Harper was a great teacher. Few could equal the energy that he threw into class work or the enthusiasm with which he inspired his students. But while the study of language in the elementary stage undoubtedly profited by this intensification of effort and extension of time spent with the instructor, other subjects required a different ratio of time between class work or lectures and private study or reading. Obviously, in English literature or composition less time in the lecture room and more in reading or writing over a longer period are desirable. In fact, the six weeks major soon disappeared and the conventional unit came to be designated by the awkward term "double minor."

The division of the academic year into quarters instead of semesters was an essential part of the plan. As one advantage the summer quarter was raised from its irregular contribution as a "summer school" to full equality with the other periods. For another, the four working quarters a year for three years enabled a student to take his degree in that time, and an instructor to earn a year of leave of absence—a device which I promptly adopted. Theoretically a student could enter college at four dates in the year, and could be absent in any quarter, or two, or three, according to convenience or necessity. As the several curricula leading to the degrees A.B., Ph.B., S.B., were rigidly prescribed, this arrangement theoretically implied that all essential courses should be given every quarter. This proved impossible, and the student's program might fall into serious dislocation.

President Harper realized further that many students could not profit by more than two years of college work. He therefore divided the four-year course into Junior College and Senior College—an innovation that has been adopted throughout the country—and proposed to induce the unprofiting to leave at the end of six quarters with the Junior College Certificate. The bribe was not sufficient. The authority of the four-year course could not be shaken. Only fifty years later was this convention broken by President Hutchins, in granting the A.B. on a two-year basis.

Coming from Yale, with a faculty largely recruited from Eastern colleges, President Harper brought high academic standards, including admission strictly by examination. It soon became necessary, however, to adopt the method in vogue throughout the Middle West of admission by certificate from secondary schools. Originally Eastern men on the faculty put a ban on fraternities, but again the influence of the environment was too strong. An underground movement set in, student clubs were formed, often with the connivance of members of the faculty, looking toward affiliation with Delta Kappa Epsilon, Alpha Delta Phi, and so on, and the ban was lifted.

President Harper originally took a high view of athletics. A regular department of physical culture and athletics was headed by Amos Alonzo Stagg of Yale, who initiated his academic career with a series of lectures on the history of athletics from the Greeks and Persians onward. Stagg's heart was not with the Greeks but with his football team. So were the hearts of many of his colleagues. Business interests soon identified athletic success of the university with the dignity of the metropolis. Alumni, when there were any, became as fanatical as those of Princeton or Yale. In the end, football at the University of Chicago became subject to the same evils as in other institutions—the recruiting of players, relaxation of academic standards to make players available, boastful excitement throughout the student body before, and bitter recrimination after, the big games. The University of Chicago has atoned for the errors of its youth by being the first of the larger American universities to sweep out the whole mess of intercollegiate athletics.

All these compromises were accepted after opposition by the small group of Harvard men on the faculty, among whom Herrick was outstanding for bitter speech. It was finely characteristic of Dr. Harper that he never resented open criticism. It never occurred to me, as his assistant, that the official connection implied support of his policies. I see now that his accommodation to the temper of the Middle West was necessary. The university had got off to a flying start, but the essential condition of its continuation was acceleration. Mr. Rockefeller conditioned his gifts on local support, and the local mind was unduly impressed by success, which it evaluated in terms of size and speed. The president, with full faith in his mission, committed his greatest patron, his trustees, and his supporters in the city to financial obligations far beyond their original intentions, and the only justification he could offer was progress in terms easily recognized.

The fact that an institution of imperial ambitions was founded on what might be described as one of Mr. John D. Rockefeller's shoestrings made money a dominant factor in its early psychology. Though President Harper airily rejected the conservatism of the trustees, remarking one day that he could not conduct a university hampered by a budget, he suffered the keenest anxiety about ways and means until his death, of which this anxiety was perhaps a contributory cause. The faculty and even the student body were infected. A gift of three million dollars under the usual conditions from Mr. Rockefeller was hailed as if it were a football victory with a campus celebration as Professor von Holst delivered an oration in defense of Mr. Rockefeller's business methods. A crowd of girls from Kelly Hall bore a banner which greedily announced: "Kelly wants three million more." When Mr. Rockefeller visited the university four years after its opening he was greeted by the students with the chorus:

> John D. Rockefeller, wonderful man is he.
> Gives all his spare change to the U. of C.
> He keeps the ball a-rolling in this great varsity;
> He pays Doctor Harper to make us grow sharper
> For the glory of the U. of C.

6

During my second year at the University of Chicago I had an opportunity to reconsider my decision, so painfully arrived at, to leave Cambridge. In the course of the year the Secretary of Harvard University, Frank Bolles, died and President Eliot offered me the position in a letter, very characteristic of him.

Harvard University,
Cambridge, November 5th, 1894.

Private.

Dear Mr. Lovett,—

I should like to have you return to the service of Harvard University as Secretary, in the place of Mr. Bolles. You might do this at any time, before September 1st, 1895, which would be convenient to you and proper in view of your obligations to Chicago University. I suppose you have a general notion of the duties of the place. They are multifarious and incessant, including a general correspondence, the keeping of the records of the University Council and the Faculty of Arts and Sciences, the getting employment for under-graduates and graduates, the maintaining relations with graduates who are teachers, and the writing of articles for the Graduates' Magazine and the daily press. You are well qualified for the place; and the work which Mr. Bolles laid down ought to be taken up. The salary of the office is rather higher than the salary of a teacher of the same academic standing; because the vacation is much shorter, and because the Secretary can hardly become a man of science, although, as in Mr. Bolles's case, he can become a man of letters. I should propose as a first salary $1500. a year. You would have the assistance of a stenographer and typewriter all the year round.

Although you will of course be free to consult confidentially the friends whose advice you will value, I request that this proposal remain completely private.

Very truly yours,
(Signed) Charles W. Eliot

Needless to say, the letter touched me deeply. I went to Cambridge and had my last conversation with the man whom I so intensely admired. But the reasons that impelled my original decision still existed. I felt more strongly than ever that closely attached personally as I should be to President Eliot, I should be more and more an inferior copy. Moreover, my experience had raised doubts as to the entire wisdom of his educational policy, especially of the elective system. Above all, I saw myself absorbed, as Frank Bolles had been, in the university. I was not ready to resign myself to administration. I was beginning to think of myself as primarily a teacher. Mr. Eliot conceded that I might continue as a member of the English Department, but I knew that teaching would be a remote issue. At Chicago I had a feeling of freedom, both as to the present and the future. Two more years at the university would set me free for two years of Europe. With great regret I told Mr. Eliot once more that I could not accept his offer.

7

The first group of students who came to the University of Chicago, drawn by the novelty and fame of Dr. Harper's experiment, was as remarkable as the faculty. Indeed, the latter soon was reinforced from the ranks of its students. In the English Department we enlisted as colleagues James Weber Linn, Nott William Flint, and Edith Burnham Foster, afterwards Mrs. Flint. These recruits from the student body mediated between the "highbrow" Harvard teachers and the Middlewestern scene, and were responsible in large part for the happy relations which existed in our section of the Department. Herrick and I took a great interest in these youngsters, and the letters which passed when either of us was away were full of approving comment on their work. We both admired Nott Flint, who was our first tragedy. He died of a brain tumor in 1905.

Among the undergraduates of this early and distinguished group was Harold L. Ickes, who, as a convinced son of the Middle West, resented the importation of the Harvard influence. He didn't like our accent. I was conducting an examination for Ferdinand Schevill, and as we were too poor in those early days to have the questions printed or mimeographed I took the easy device of reading them to the students. When I reached a crucial subject in the Schmalcaldic League and War, Master Ickes arose in his place and pointed out courteously but firmly that the regulations of the university explicitly provided that students should have copies of examination papers. I replied that Dr. Schevill as a historian respected documents, and if such a Magna Charta existed he would have taken account of it instead of directing me to give out the questions orally, but Master Ickes stood his ground. Suppose, he said, a student misunderstood a word like Schmalcaldic, in an unfamiliar dialect, and wrote an irrelevant answer—and how many students could spell Schmalcaldic anyway? I yielded to this reasoning and covered the blackboards with the text. Since that time I have often met Mr. Ickes in connection with his support of one good cause or another in Chicago or Washington. He never let me get away without reminding me of this incident. I think he enjoyed his triumph over me in 1896 as much as that over Pauley fifty years later.

During my second year at the university I was head of Snell House, a dormitory for undergraduate men, largely occupied by the football team and several local societies which were being cultivated by national fraternities. My predecessor was Stagg, who escaped by marriage. On one occasion when he entertained his charges on a sleigh ride his ungrateful guests threw him out and trolled him several miles back to the campus. I looked for the worst. On the contrary, it was a pleasant year. The height of disorder was an occasional water fight between hostile forces of the second and third floors, which converted the staircase into a cascade. One evening there was a bonfire in front of the hall to celebrate a football victory. The fire department turned out; the students cut the hose;

the police were summoned, and the sergeant with a squad of four men threatened to search the house for the malefactors. As I stood at the entrance confronting the sergeant and his squad and demanding a search warrant, I heard a warning cry from above and jumped back to avoid a pailful of water which inundated the officer to the delight of all.

A pleasant episode of my residence was a call from Mrs. Snell, the donor of the building. She was not clear as to the relation of the university to the fair, and having read in the paper a statement that the buildings of the latter were to be destroyed, she hastened from her West Side home to inquire. When she was assured of the permanence of her gift she was responsive to a hint that our common room lacked furniture. A few days later there arrived, items: portrait in oil of Mr. Snell, ditto of Mrs. Snell, a sofa and two overstuffed chairs, a rug, a table, a family Bible, and a spittoon.

8

Difficulties in regard to daily bread were solved for Herrick and me by his marrying, and setting up a joint menage with Professor Laughlin, which I was permitted to join for meals. Professor James Laurence Laughlin was head of the Department of Political Economy and a fierce conservative. He brought William Hurrell Mallock to the university to give a series of lectures attacking socialism. I had read Mallock's *New Republic* and expected to hear table talk as well as lectures in the brilliant, incisive vein of his famous satire. On the contrary, Mallock was bored and dull both at the table and on the platform.

The chief excitement of the summer of 1894 was the strike which, beginning with the workers at Pullman, came to involve all the railroads having connections at Chicago. Night after night we saw the western sky red with the light of burning cars. Grant Park was white with the tents of soldiers sent by President Cleveland on the pretext that the strikers were interfering with the mails, a charge hotly denied by Governor Altgeld. The strike was broken by injunction. Eugene Debs, president of the American Railway Union and director of the strike, spent a year in prison. One of our visitors was John Graham Brooks, who came to investigate the strike and report to President Cleveland. He assured us that the burning cars were fired by the railroad companies for propaganda purposes. Our table talk included the action of Governor Altgeld in pardoning the two survivors of the anarchist delusion and condemning the judicial murder of the victims of judge-made law. The "free silver" issue was looming up as the campaign of 1896 approached, and Professor Laughlin used to read us his replies to a popular exponent of the heresy known as Coin Harvey. In spite of much personal kindness from my host I had an instinctive hostility to his economic thinking.

An enterprise in which Professor Laughlin took the lead was the "settlement," which it had become incumbent for every full-geared university to nourish. In this I was his lieutenant. The settlement opened in rooms above a feed store, on Gross Avenue in the Stockyards district. Later a building was contributed by Charles L. Hutchinson. Mary E. MacDowell was the first head resident and became an important figure in the civic life of Chicago. In our need of funds we planned a course of lectures to be given by professors in the houses of prominent citizens on the North Side. To ask for such hospitality was my task. I had the help of one of the notable women of Chicago, Mrs. Otto Matz, who led me by the hand from one hostess to another. Of course the first house to be obtained was Mrs. Potter Palmer's—the others followed easily. My trump card was von Holst, to be played at Mrs. Palmer's. Unfortunately he was ill, and Mr. Laughlin substituted with his favorite lecture on Political Economy and Christianity, of which I remember chiefly his characterization of Jesus as an exponent of thrift rather than poverty. Mr. Potter Palmer looked in on the assembly of ladies in the art gallery and, evidently pleased with the talk, handed me a five-dollar bill.

Professor Laughlin had as his first assistant Adolph C. Miller, afterwards a distinguished member of the first Federal Reserve Board, created under the law which his chief helped to write. A holder of a departmental fellowship who was also the working editor of *The Journal of Political Economy* and teacher of a course in socialism was Thorstein Veblen. As I used to meet him on his way to his chief's sanctum, a long, lean, cadaverous figure, with smoldering eyes in a pallid, usually unshaven face, I thought of the description of William Langland, the "Long Will" reputed author of *The Vision of Piers Plowman.* A few years later, in the series of books beginning with *The Theory of the Leisure Class,* Veblen unveiled a vision of society in the twentieth century as devastating as was Langland's in the fourteenth.

9

In June 1895 I married Ida Mott-Smith. Our wedding was a joyous affair. I was saved from the embarrassment of choosing between Norman and Hutchins Hapgood for best man by the fact that Hutchins had gone to Japan with Leo Stein. My men-at-arms were Allen Benner, Billie Brewster, Will Moody, and Ernest Mott-Smith. Ida's father and mother were in Honolulu, so her brother Harold led her down the stairs, to the strains of a march from *Tannhäuser* (irrelevant but imposing), to where I stood in front of Dr. A. V. G. Allen, wondering if twenty dollars would be enough. It was what my father had paid in 1868.

Professor Laughlin had lent us his house for the summer, but we had hardly arrived in Chicago before Ida was summoned to Honolulu by the death of her father, and the illness, soon fatal, of her mother. On her return to Chicago we took a large apartment at 5488 East End Avenue. Will Moody had been persuaded to join the English Department, and he and Ferd Schevill shared one of the big rooms. We took on for dinners Ken Rand, also an addition to our faculty, and Billy Hapgood, the third of that distinguished family. What I recall chiefly about the year is the extraordinary cheapness of living. Sharing all expenses—rent, food, service—the four of us paid about eight dollars each a week. My second memory is of the general hilarity, punctuated by dinners in a private room at the Bismarck Restaurant, where steaks of continental size and Pschorrbräu beer contributed to an occasional gaudy night. I see after fifty years Ferdinand Schevill perched precariously on a radiator to sing, but protesting instead, "*Je ne me sens pas bien ici*," and Will Moody dancing in tails an interpretation of the ditty, "Twinkle, twinkle, little star." Rand refused to drink, but he loyally shared in the general hangover the next morning. We were sufficient unto ourselves and left the rest of the faculty and the city to go their several ways.

I took advantage of the quarter system to work for three full years, and I had a year of accrued leave to which I stipulated the addition of another year of absence. So in the summer of 1896 we left Chicago for Boston, where was born, in the pleasant Mott-Smith house on Newbury Street, the son who bore my name without fear or reproach until his gallant death in the Belleau Wood twenty-two years later.

IV. *Abroad*, 1896–1898, 1902–1903

I

We sailed from New York on the North German Lloyd steamer *Ems*. With us were the baby, three months old, a nursemaid, and my sister-in-law May, who was beginning her career of adventure and conquest. We landed in Genoa and promptly took the train for Florence, where we found quarters in the admirable pension of Signora Traverso, in the Palazzo Alberti opposite the Ponte alle Grazie.

One object of residence in Florence was to renew acquaintance with Bernard Berenson, whom I had met four years before. Berenson had been an editor of the *Monthly* in 1887, and in the intervening decade had become one of the leading art critics of the world. Almost on arrival he took us over, and when the cold became severe he found for us the Villino Illingworth on the hillside above the piazza of Fiesole. It was heated by a great porcelain stove for which we bought coal from the tram company. From its courtyard we looked out over the valley of the Arno, the city with Brunelleschi's dome in the center. When we took possession in December the hills above us were white with snow, but by February it was warm enough in the full southern exposure of the courtyard to breakfast out of doors.

That winter in Florence was of the happiest. One element was the low cost of living, for the exchange was heavily in favor of the dollar. As a result of the Abyssinian fiasco, Italy was suffering a national humiliation which seemed to be reflected in a chastened spirit and behavior. A recovery was faintly in view when the Principe di Napoli was cheered as he rode through Florence to the Pitti Palace with his Montenegrin bride, but the triumph was modest, as befitted an alliance with the smallest of the Balkan states. Latin peoples are more attractive in defeat than in victory. It is hard to realize that within a generation the kindly, courteous, reasonable people we knew could become enthusiastic participants in the arrogant, vulgar, brutal regime of fascism. It is still harder to understand how English and Americans could repudiate the Italy which reflected the spirit of the Risorgimento in Croce and Matteotti in favor of the Italy of Balbo, Farinacci, and Mussolini.

Through Berenson we obtained cards of admission to the public galleries. Mornings we spent in the Uffizi, Pitti, Accademia, Bargello, in the churches, Santa Maria Novella and Santa Croce, or the monastery of San Marco. Afternoons we drove to San Miniato or in the Cascine. The winter twilight found us at Doni's or Giacosa's for chocolate, before returning to the villino on the hill for dinner.

We had a wonderful cook. Louisa Guazzini had worked for Professor and Mrs. Palmer, to whom she referred affectionately as "I Palmeri," and for the Herricks. Signor Errico was the hero of her life. Louisa was a grand purveyor. She quickly formed an alliance with the clergy through a person described as *la sorella del canonico*, from whom came delicious *vino santo* and sometimes a *bel capone*. More important, we shared with the monastery the good bread from the city instead of the hard unsalted local bake. Louisa was infatuated with the baby and led an admiring populace on his progress in an iron perambulator down the lane to the piazza. The native *bimbi* became "Bimbles" on his American tongue, by which name he was always known in the family.

Berenson was a superb teacher. He had just published his book on the Florentine painters of the Renaissance and undertook to initiate me into the principles and methods of scientific art criticism practiced by Morelli and himself. This criticism, having as its purpose the correct attribution of works of art, was similar to objective literary scholarship in distinguishing the authorship of early works. It had a commercial use, however, in determining values for art dealers and purchasers, and thus gave a financial basis to the art critic, previously rewarded only through writings and lectures. It distinguished the professionals from mere appreciators like Ruskin, Pater, and Vernon Lee. With two years of freedom before me I was tempted by the prospect, but I soon realized that I did not have any genuine interest in this world of tactile values of which Berenson and his associates talked so learnedly. I went back to books.

Here too Berenson was omnivorous and omniscient. He liked company on a walk, and I profited by the fact that most of his guests were not pedestrians. He used at the outset to stand me up for the delivery of some idea or theme, recalling the Cambridge habit of serious conversation. He had a prodigious memory, of which I have a recent example. I wrote a review of Rosa Luxembourg's letters about the time of her death. Twenty years later Berenson wrote me recalling the review and asking me to obtain a copy of the book for him. It was disappointing to find it out of print.

2

Toward spring Ferdinand Schevill turned up in Florence. He and I rode our bicycles to Pisa by way of Pistoia and Lucca, staying a day at the latter, where we saw *Tosca* violently performed by the local opera troupe. If I revisit Italy, presumably as a ghost, Lucca will be my favorite haunt. We made another expedition, by way of San Gimignano, to Siena, of which he was later to write one of the best examples of the art of the historian, a character sketch of that marvelous city. From Siena we went to the monastery of Monte Oliveto, where we inspected the magnificent paintings by Sodoma. Our guide was a lecherous old monk who identified *il suo moglie* with a sly mixture of genders. After luncheon we started for Pienza. The map showed the road as making two sides of an oblong. It naturally occurred to us to take the diagonal across country. It rained. The clay soil was so slippery that we could keep our feet only with difficulty. The countryside was infested with the ferocious long-horned cattle against which we were warned by Baedeker, and in running to avoid them we frequently fell and rose well plastered with yellow clay. Childe Roland's country was no worse.

Emerging on the hard highway we were utterly at a loss as to direction. We guessed. After an hour's march through the gathering darkness we came upon a dwelling, unlighted and defended by several dogs. Their furious barking brought a response from an upper window which informed us that we had guessed wrong. After a drink from a green-encrusted water trough we wearily took the road back that promised no end. But, without warning, we brought up against the closed gates of Pienza. On being admitted, we found the town in darkness, and stumbled our way to the inn, where we made a sparse supper on Bologna sausage and dry bread.

The next day we visited the dismantled palace of the Piccolomini, which servants were trying to render habitable for the return of their young lord. The whole city with its palaces and public buildings bears the mark of the genius of Aeneo Sylvio, whose birthplace was reconstructed in the mood of the Renaissance of which he was so eminent a patron, and named Pienza in honor of his brief papacy as Pius II. We could have spent a profitable week in that forgotten mausoleum of the great humanist, but hunger forbade. We left before noon to walk, happily down hill, to Montepulciano, where, also happily, the food and wine were delicious.

3

I joined my family at Siena, and we set out on a zigzag journey by carriage from one town to another through Tuscany and Umbria. Perugia and Assisi were places of longer stay, but the short visits to Todi, Montefalco, Orvieto, Foligno, are not to be forgotten—the Benozzo Gozzoli paintings at Montefalco, the Signorelli's and the wine at Orvieto, the Madonna of Foligno.

At Rome I picked up a germ which made travel extremely trying. However, we made the journey to Venice and settled at the Casa Frollo on the Giudecca, where Will Moody arrived later.

We spent long afternoons on the Lido and evenings on the Grand Canal. I remember Will's tenor joining the voices of the singing gondoliers.

Mornings we gave dutifully to galleries and churches, the Doges' Palace and San Marco, basking in the richness of Carpaccio and Veronese, Titian and Tintoretto, after the austerity of the Florentines. It was at the annual exhibition of modern painters that Will saw a picture of the Day of Judgment with an angry God passing between windrows of naked, tortured bodies—a bad painting which was the origin of his great poem, *The Masque of Judgment.*

One of our projects was a bicycle trip to Asolo, which was still reminiscent of Robert Browning. As I was more comfortable at rest than in motion, I spent much of my time at the café where various notables dropped in during the day. The postmaster repeated daily his tale of the posting of *Asolando* to London and the notice of its safe arrival at the publisher's, which the poet had showed him with praise for his efficiency. The *syndaco* took us to call on Miss Sarianna Browning, to ask her to persuade her nephew to lease us one of the six or seven villas which he owned. Robert Barrett Browning was a stout little man, bald and red-faced, a sort of caricature of his father. He told with humor of a little girl who on being presented to him stood at gaze for a moment and then inquired, "Can it be that you are the child of those two glorious poets?"

Barrett Browning cordially invited us to inspect his villas, one after another, but each inspection developed a reason why he could not part with it even for a summer. The weather became hotter, and we took to sleeping on the hillside beneath the *rocca*, the ruined castle where Katharine Cornaro, "Kate the Queen," listened to the page who sang his love while fitting her hawks their jesses. We talked of going north. The *syndaco* argued that it would be dangerous for the baby to go *subito subito* from the heat of Venice to the cold of the mountains. My sedentary habits exposed me to his arguments. Will, meanwhile, spent the days pursuing his explorations and his loves with the freedom of his bicycle.

On the evening fixed for our departure he did not appear, and I took the road alone in the twilight for Feltre. In the early morning I mounted the omnibus, saw my wheel hoisted to the top, and took a last backward look. Far down the road there was a cloud of dust no bigger than a man's hand, from which slowly emerged my companion, pedaling furiously. The driver delayed his start until Will drew alongside and out of breath climbed to the seat beside me. After a time he drew out excusingly a little square of paper, on which in a girlish hand was written the equivalent of "*Non suerdate di me*," signed Annunziata.

4

We joined Ida at Belluno and drove to Cortina, where we settled for the summer amid the terrific mountain forms of the Dolomites—Cristallo, Tofana, Sorapis. Outlined against the clear sky, they looked like a stage setting of papier maché through which a fist could be thrust, but on contact they proved resistant. They gave Moody the setting of *The Masque of Judgment*, on which he worked mornings, complaining bitterly of the loquacity of Raphael, "the affable archangel." He was reading Milton, in preparation for his edition of the poems, and my familiarity with the Bible was called on to supplement his sketchy Sunday schooling.

Will and I made one memorable trip afoot to the north to gaze at the terrors of the Drei Zinnen, the Rosengarten, and a mountain, unnamed for us, which bore upon its face great red splashes, as if it had been hacked with a gigantic ax. On a lovely morning we made the circuit of the Marmolada, the only snow-covered peak among the Dolomites. The sight of its gently sloping snowfields was an inexpressible relief to eyes weary with looking at the sullen brown faces of its neighbors. A snow-clad mountain is more human and civilized than a huge rock, savage in its nudity. On the Marmolada where a long slope of snow met in a sharp edge a flower-sprent green field we stripped and rolled shivering down the snow to feel on the warm grass the sudden release from tension, which sent us both to sleep.

Later that morning we passed through a village to which our mail had been forwarded. In mine was the *Boston Weekly Transcript* with William James' address at the unveiling of Saint-Gaudens' monument to Colonel Robert Gould Shaw on Boston Common. We were both moved. I remembered the story of Shaw's march down Beacon Hill at the head of the Black Regiment, the 54th Massachusetts, greeted by hisses and jeers from the Somerset Club, whose members were the sons of the men who had tried to lynch William Lloyd Garrison, the grandfathers of those who did lynch Sacco and Vanzetti. That morning saw the genesis of "An Ode in Time of Hesitation." When Moody returned to Boston he saw the magnificent bas-relief and wrote a tribute, no less distinguished than Saint-Gaudens', to a hero who broke the bonds of class and color to fall leading the men whom he fought to make free, and to lie among them. "Bury him with his niggers."

From the Dolomites we went on to the Hohe Tauern and made the easy ascent of the Grosse Venediger, where we parted, I to return to Cortina, Will to make for Italy. He injured his leg on the descent and at Innsbruck suffered the first of the serious illnesses which preceded his early death. He recovered, went back over the Brenner Pass to Italy, rode by night to Genoa, where he lay desperately ill and partly unconscious, until one morning he awoke with the sense that this was the date set for his sailing, and by an effort of will got up, packed, made his way to the steamer, climbed into his berth, and stayed there until the landing in New York.

5

To learn to know a city in the shortest time possible the search for a family dwelling is recommended. We covered London from

Chelsea to St. John's Wood, and finally found through an agent the house we wanted on Hampstead Heath. It stood just high enough to escape the fog, which from the foot of the lawn rolled away over London like a sea, while the house and garden stood in the palely smiling sun—at least this was our first impression. The occupying family, composed of a matriarch, daughters, and sons-in-law, turned cold on learning that we were Americans, lacking references, with two babies, *uno fuore* and *uno in corpo*, as Louisa put it. Then began a long negotiation, conducted through the agent. One closet or room, one article of furniture after another, was withdrawn from the lease; one restriction after another was imposed on the tenants. We agreed to everything provided we could keep the roof. At long last the English were forced to admit, much to their agent's confusion, that they did not wish to let the house anyway. We had won a Pyrrhic victory, and were so exhausted that we went into winter quarters with the Misses Rowlands at 13 Queen Square, where my older daughter was born in January.

We knew almost no one in London except the doctor and the dentist. Ida's family had an old friend in Bishop Staley, formerly Bishop of Honolulu, whose sister-in-law, known to the young Staleys and to us as Aunt Selina, lived at Sydenham. She duly bade us to luncheon. We duly went. I found myself, encased in a new Prince Albert, the sole male amid a bevy of elderly suburban ladies agreeably reminiscent of *Cranford*. After an excellent luncheon Aunt Selina invited me to smoke. I accepted with alacrity, and we all adjourned to the conservatory, which was fitted to conserve nothing except frozen meat. The ladies looked at me, expectation shining in their eyes, as if about to witness an eruption of Vesuvius. A sense of impotence grew upon me as I realized that Aunt Selina was relying on the Englishman's habit of carrying a pipe, for which my best clothes afforded no accommodation. I had not even a cigarette. At last Aunt Selina apologized for having no tobacco and led the shivering flock back to the fire.

6

It was with great joy that we moved to Paris in the spring. As one of my brothers-in-law, Harold Mott-Smith, was living on the Boulevard Montparnasse, we took an apartment near by on the rue Léopold-Robert. Harold was president of the American Art Students' League, and naturally we saw a good deal of his friends. We particularly liked Henry Ossawa Tanner, the half-Negro painter. His picture "The Raising of Lazarus," to be exhibited at the Salon, had been bought for the Luxembourg. The exhibits of the two Salons were united that year at the Palais de l'Industrie, and the battle line between old and new was sharply drawn. Bouguereau and Carolus-Duran were out. The Impressionists were going. Cézanne and Gauguin were rising. Caillebotte had presented a gallery of moderns to the Luxembourg, referred to by American students as "the chamber of horrors." Rodin's heroic statue of Balzac was shown that year at the new Salon, representing the master in his dressing gown, his face alight with inspiration. An angry crowd surged about the statue, cursing the sculptor who had so vilified the novelist. Ultimately a guard was set to prevent the desecration of a monument by a great realist to the master of all realism. It was exciting to be among people who took art so seriously. The supreme moment of the Salon that year, however, was the triumphal passage of Cléo de Mérode through the hall, negligently swinging an immense white fur boa between the swaying lines of the admirers, not of a second-rate dancer in the Opéra ballet, but of the mistress of the King of the Belgians.

I planned that spring to join my classmate Billy Brewster and his friend Ben Borland in Spain, but the threat of war kept me in Paris. At last there came a telegram informing me that the American Ambassador had assured my friends that Spain had yielded to the demands of the United States. I engaged passage to Madrid, but I didn't get there. A day or two later Congress declared war. I was therefore in advance of the confessions of history, aware that my country had committed that greatest of crimes, a war without a cause.

The war with Spain was the first international event to have a strong impact on my thought and feeling. I heard from home of the frantic efforts of the Hearst and Pulitzer papers to excite public opinion to war, the obvious motive being that war news is the most salable of all news; of the clamor of Theodore Roosevelt, whose motive was equally obvious; and of the weakness of McKinley, under the pressure of party leaders to whom a successful war meant a political victory. I also saw the horror and disgust of continental Europe, which seemed to realize that the cynical negation of diplomacy in favor of battle, the ranging of the United States among the imperialistic powers, was a sinister prelude to the century which was to see the breaking down of such barriers as civilization had been able to place in the path of its own destruction. The defeat of the effort of the European powers to mediate, by the adroitness of Sir Julian Pauncefote, revealed Great Britain as the Mephistopheles leading the United States Faust to sell its soul for worldly power and glory. I was glad to see the senseless prejudice against Great Britain, with which I was familiar from boyhood, vanish, but I suspected wily Albion of using us for its own purposes, especially luring us into complicity in bearing the White Man's Burden. The record of events, the destruction of the feeble Spanish fleets, the vainglorious victory of San Juan Hill, the conquest of Puerto Rico, and the atrocities in the Philippines left me with a disgust as well as a horror of war and made me a pacifist.

7

Brewster and Borland left Spain and I joined them at Orléans. We spent ten days in the Loire country, seeing the chateaux, Blois, Chinon, Amboise, and the exquisite Chenonceaux, visited by Henry James and charmingly described in his *Little Tour in France*. Most rewarding, in Baedeker's phrase, was Bourges, with its magnificent cathedral and its Burgundy wines, especially Moulin-à-Vent. Ben Borland was a fat boy but agile. No flight of steps daunted him, and the narrowest apertures were wide enough for him to wriggle through. His sophistication was immense. Throughout our journey he used to remind us that Rostand's play *Cyrano de Bergerac* was about to open at the Porte Saint-Martin with Coquelin *aîné* as Cyrano. The evening of our arrival in Paris we had an experience that none of us will forget. At the rise of the curtain we were overwhelmed by the spectacle on the stage, crowded with an amazing multitude of types, in the midst of which Cyrano emerged, mounting a chair to forbid Montfleury to act. From that magnificent entrance the hero never faltered. Whatever may be thought of Rostand as poet and playwright, he incontestably created a perfect character part for the supreme actor of his day.

Brewster and I made a bicycle tour of Normandy and Brittany later that spring, of which the cathedrals of Rouen and Amiens, the perfect Gothic church at Coutances, the monastic rock of Saint-Michel, are memories. So are the cheeses, which we discussed critically as we had the wines of Burgundy—Pont-l'Evêque, Port Salut, and especially Camembert, a luscious example of which we ate in twilight with great praise, only to find with a light that it had already been predigested by cheesy worms which had to be drowned in our stomachs by drafts of Norman cider. Nor can I forget the *escargots* which the waiter fed us in our beds at Rennes, while our clothes, sodden with the rain which had caught us on the way, steamed by the fire.

I saw a good deal of Joe Stickney in Paris. He was writing his thesis on gnomic sentences in Greek literature for his Docteur ès Lettres degree. My memories of the city are brightest through him. The background suited him perfectly; whether it was in his little apartment in the rue d'Assas, or, as I like to remember him, striding like a young god across the Champs Elysées to join us at Laurent's. His enthusiasm was magnificent and charmed older men, like Henry Adams.

Stickney was in certain respects a more modern poet than Moody. He inherited and was educated in a classical tradition, which gave an austerity and simplicity to his poetry such as Moody acquired slowly and with effort. I have always thought that Stickney's *Prometheus Pyrphuros* in its severe restraint was a finer treatment of the subject than Moody's richly romantic *The Fire Bringer*. Moody suffered in reputation from the change in the whole spirit and direction of poetry which set in after the first decade of the century, and Stickney never caught the ear of critics or public. Lately Conrad Aiken and Edmund Wilson have begun to make him known.

8

In the summer we returned to England. A visit which we were bound to make was to Bishop Staley, retired to the country curacy of Croxall near Lichfield. The English Midlands were at their best, and the Croxall rectory, across the lawn from the Norman church, was reminiscent of all that I had read and dreamed in college of the external beauty of the Anglican confession. The bishop, a wizened little figure in gaiters and shovel hat, seemed to walk out of Trollope when he told us of his reception by "the King of the Sandwich Islands, who instructed me to impress on his people the beauty of holiness by the splendor of ecclesiastical services and the adornment of my person."

We called the baby "the pibroch" because of her wailing, but on examination by the bishopess it came out that as yet she had not been named. Thereupon the bishop inveighed against the sin of submitting an unchristened child to the dangers of the ocean and of Hell, and declared that the omission must be made good the next day. That night we resumed the six-months-old discussion of the name. I wanted something dashing and French—Georgette, Yvette, Yvonne. Ida wanted to distinguish one of her girl friends—Gertrude, Sophie, Blanche, Edith, Margaret, or Beatrice. We came to no agreement. The next morning we continued the argument even as we set forth across the green to the church, the bishop bearing a ewer of water from the Jordan, his lady carrying other ecclesiastical accessories, and the servants trailing behind. We stood at the font, Mrs. Staley as godmother holding the baby, the bishop raising a wet hand and asking what name. A pause. Mrs. Staley forced a decision. "Quick. I shall drop her," she whispered. It sounded like a threat, and no one could tell how far the baby would fall, perhaps clear through to Hell to delight God and his saints with the spectacle of her sufferings. Although of a deeply religious nature, I refused to give them that satisfaction. The name before all others to conjure up Hell is Beatrice. So I answered, and Beatrice it was and is.

9

During the next few years we were back and forth between Europe and America. Ida took the children to Spain in the spring of 1901, and leaving them at Gibraltar with the excellent English nurse we had acquired in London, enjoyed the trip which I had missed because of the war. I crossed later with my father and joined the family at Liverpool. In London John and Alice Corbin told us about the Marienhalden, on the Wallensee, east of Zurich, and after a few weeks at Pourville we settled in the Alps for the rest of the summer. It was at Samaden in the Engadine that we heard of the assassination of President McKinley. The English people at the hotel were extremely sympathetic, but with memories of the Spanish War and the murderous campaign against the Filipinos then proceeding, we were rather cold. The English, by a sort of national instinct that seemed to affect all classes, were then promoting an *entente cordiale* with the United States. I felt this a short time later at Munich when at a memorial service for McKinley in the Frauenkirche young men in top hats and frock coats stood at the doors proclaiming, "*Nur Engländer und Amerikaner.*"

I left my family in Munich and returned to Boston, where Moody and I finished the *History of English Literature* that bears our names. I had been urged by my classmate, Pitts Duffield, then with Scribner's, to undertake this work, and was fortunate to find in Moody a collaborator. We worked closely together, and the book owes much to the model of his impeccable style and his refusal to accept any merely conventional treatment. In a letter returning my draft he phrased the ideal to which the book owes its long-continued popularity: "Be as brief as a love spasm, and as pleasant."

I returned to Europe by the Mediterranean route, and as it happened sat at table beside Martin A. Ryerson, president of the Board of Trustees of the University of Chicago. I admired him as one of the most generously cultivated men I ever knew. He was a wise collector, especially of pictures, and his critical sense was acute in other fields. I meant to take advantage of the excellent cellar of the North German Lloyd, and at our first luncheon I ordered a bottle of wine. Mr. Ryerson consulted the wine card and advised me that the wine I had chosen had no special merit and directed my attention to the Berncastler Doctor of a certain year. Thereafter he supervised my choice. He permitted himself, apparently against doctor's orders, a small sip of each new bottle to validate the selection. His knowledge of vintages gave me an idea, which I discussed with him, of an institution to introduce discrimination in taste as an element in culture by means of a curriculum in wines. A select class might visit, in a succession of summers, the wine cellars of Europe, taking advantage of the hospitality of growers, who would naturally be sympathetic with the noble experiment. The first summer would be spent in France, beginning with the Bordeaux, taking next the wines of the Rhône and Burgundy, then the champagnes. The course would culminate with brandies and liqueurs. The second summer would be devoted to Italy, the third to Germany and Hungary, and the fourth to the Iberian peninsula. Mr. Ryerson was quite interested in working out the details on paper, but when it came to practical measures of introducing the course into the elective list of the university he became doubtful. In vain I urged the duty of a university, which aspires to the teaching of universal knowledge, to include so important a field, and to make the despised sense of taste contribute to American culture by becoming a vehicle of discrimination and higher criticism. Mr. Ryerson felt that a university of which, by its charter, two-thirds of the trustees were professing Baptists was not in a position to initiate so desirable an extension of the educative and cultural process. I thought that the miracle in Cana of Galilee should convince the Baptists that there was no innate conflict between water and wine—and then and there, as more than once in my life, a perfectly sound and serious idea lapsed into farce through a misapplied sense of humor. Mr. Ryerson suspected satire and closed up. The institution would have been of immense service to American culture in the Volstead age, when the sense of taste for finer values nearly perished through disuse and corruption.

10

The ship docked at Naples, and I made my way through Italy to rejoin the family in Munich. We soon left for Paris, which, when we arrived, was enjoying the mild gaiety of mi-carême and the brightness of early spring, all the more effulgent after the gloom of the German winter. Harold Mott-Smith had moved to Auteuil, and we settled near by in the Villa Montmorency, the house said to have been the home of the Goncourts. It was a lovely old mansion with a garden and trees of its own within the grounds of the villa. Auteuil in those days of horse transportation was a long way from the center of the city. *Fiacre* drivers hated to go there, and we found it best to settle firmly in the vehicle before giving the address. Sometimes the driver would pretend ignorance and along the way would stop to ask colleagues for direction—and sympathy. "*J' vais à la compagne. C'est dommage, n'est-ce pas? Au revoir, mes amis,*" in a voice that suggested, "It may be for years, and it may be forever."

It was in this house that my younger daughter was born, it might be said over the telephone. We had engaged a distinguished *accoucheur*, Dr. Lepage, who lived in Montmartre. Telephones were not usual in Paris then, but Lamar Middleton, correspondent of the *Chicago Daily News*, who lived near us, had one, and by this means I undertook to keep Dr. Lepage informed hour by hour of the progress of events. I remember that more than one connection had to be made to get through to Montmartre, but the operators became interested and cleared the line for me with, "*C'est le monsieur qui va avoir un enfant à Auteuil,*" "*Les peines sont très fortes,*" and "*Venez, Monsieur, avec grande vitesse.*" When the baby was born there was an informal reception and much favorable comment and congratulation from which emerged the realistic note when Marie, the *bonne à tout faire* remarked, "*Vous êtes bien débarrasée de ça, Madame!*" A day or two later a young gentleman called "*pour visiter l'enfant.*" I told him that Mademoiselle was not old enough to receive callers, but he explained that his visit was not social, merely to corroborate the sex so that there should be no question later of military service. It was indicated that I should have to report the child's birth and name at the *mairie*. More friends than I expected appeared as sponsors at luncheon, and when we adjourned to the *mairie*, somewhat flown with wine, I felt encompassed by a great cloud of witnesses, who described themselves as of fantastic names, ages, and occupations. Harold Mott-Smith claimed to be a *marchand de bois*. When the *régisseur* asked his prescribed questions there was a confusion of answers until he threw down his pen and demanded, "*Qui est le père?*" To which I replied firmly in the formula of Louis XIV, "*Le père, c'est moi.*" When it came to the name of the child he burst out in irritation, "Rut'?" It wasn't in the classical dictionary or in the calendar of saints. The Bible? What is that for an authority! Only after it was explained that the name Ruth was only for American use and would not offend French nomenclature did he inscribe it, growling, "*Nom d'un nom! Quel nom est celui-là!*"

Among those visiting the newly born was her little cousin, who a day or two later came down with whooping cough. We feared the worst. Whooping cough is far more severe in France than in the United States. It is a dangerous disease even for adults. I have seen strong men clasping trees in the Champs Elysées during a *crise*, and if a suspicious cough is heard on an omnibus the cry "*la coqueluche*" goes up from the passengers and the dangerous carrier is promptly evicted. There was no record of so young a child having recovered, but a skillful physician and a devoted English nurse won, with the help of the baby. She knew by instinct that the *crises* must be avoided, and lay quietly for hours without an unnecessary movement or a cry. Her recovery was a miracle.

II

Later that spring I went to London for a few weeks to exchange the delay and confusion of the Bibliothèque Nationale for the comparatively efficient service of the British Museum.

I was invited one evening to a dinner at the Authors Club, which turned out to be amusing. At the outset the chairman announced acidly that the guest of the evening, the Lord Chief Justice, had preferred to dine with the Australian cricketers, but then remarked that in times of similar embarrassment he always followed the rule "play the Americans," and after peering at the list of guests he called on me.

I tried the conventional opening with a story, probably ancient even then, of a London bus driver who beckoned to the guard and, pointing over his shoulder at a passenger, muffled up and reading the *Times*, identified him as the Archbishop of Canterbury. The guard was skeptical but agreed to inquire. Touching his cap he asked, "Beg parding, Sir, but to decide a bet between my mate and me, *are* you the Harchbishop of Canterbury?" The passenger replied uncordially, "What the bloody hell is it to you whether or not I'm the Archbishop of Canterbury?"

There was a riot. Members rocked on their chairs and cried "Oh! Oh!" and "Hear! Hear!" and made other sounds by which the English are accustomed to express dissent or approval. Apparently it was the first time they had heard "bloody" as a spoken word in polite society. I thought naïvely that if the audience went off at half-cock with such an explosion the conclusion would be a triumph. It was not. At the return of the guard to his driver with the sorrowful admission, "You was right, Bill. It *is* His Grice after all," there was only an embarrassed titter.

As we left the table a gentleman took my arm kindly and introduced himself as Mr. Bruce-Joy, the sculptor, who had done more outdoor work than any man in England. "I've been in America," he said. "I like your humor. These chaps didn't get it, but you and I know that it really wasn't the Archbishop?" I admitted that I had suspected it. "Of course," he went on, "Dr. Temple is addicted to the use of intemperate language. He used to be a schoolmaster. But he wouldn't have been riding on top of an omnibus in London." I agreed that it was not probable. Several other gentlemen in the course of the evening took occasion to make sure that I was not under a misapprehension. At last, feeling that an apology was somehow due, I said to the chairman that I feared I had spoken irreverently of an exalted and sacred personage. I might have spared myself the trouble. "I enjoyed it," he declared bluntly. "I like to hear those Anglican fellows shown up. I'm a Scotch Presbyterian myself."

12

I have never known a city so tingling with excitement, so stimulating and yet so agreeable, so *sympatico*, as Paris in the early years of the century. The naturalistic movement was at its height, with the Théâtre Antoine, and it had reached the operatic stage. I remember Joe Stickney exclaiming as I met him one day after an absence, "Do you know what's sending us all to sleep with girls? It's *Louise*." Mary Garden had replaced Sybil Sanderson in the title part at the Opéra Comique, and the city was in an uproar over the girl from Hyde Park, Chicago. We went and went again, never satiated with the theme, so mournfully tender in Mary Garden's voice:

La grande ville a besoin de nos filles.

But already symbolism was emerging from its secret places and becoming a public issue. In the year which saw the success of Charpentier's *Louise*, Debussy was putting the story of Pelléas and Mélisande into opera. It was only a year or two later that I heard Mme. Yvette Guilbert, in a charming *conférence*, deplore the passing of literature from the clear if harsh light of realism into the shadows of mysticism. Along with the serious drama the French farce kept its old-time power of sheer pleasure-giving. At the Palais-Royale and the boulevard theaters, Les Variétés and Les Nouveautés, one could see worthy successors of Labiche–Capus' *Les Deux Ecoles*, or *Miquette et Sa Mère* by Flers and Caillavet.

Among our less serious occupations Harold and I undertook to make a study of the *cafés chantants* of Montmartre, the objective being a book or series of articles of which he would furnish the illustrations and I the text. This interest led us to the Boîte à Fursy, which had replaced, in name at least, the Chat Noir on the rue Pigalle. That was an enticing cabaret, and we became regular patrons. The small auditorium accommodated perhaps a hundred people. The curtain went up on a meeting of the Chamber of Deputies, with "Mephisto *aîné*" in the high seat. If a late guest chanced to enter, the chairman rang the bell and the audience greeted the newcomer with song:

Une seconde. Voici du monde.
Chantons en ronde
Jusqu'on soit placé.
Tra la, tra la, tra la la la la–etc.

Then the performance went on with one song after another in mordant criticism of the government. During the intermission everyone adjourned to the lobby. Fursy, stocky, black-browed, genial, went about among his guests, discussing the new plays at the Antoine or theatrical politics—he afterwards became director of the Odéon. Later there was a *revue* with more satire on public events. The entertainment was always essentially the same, but we never grew tired of it, anticipating the moment when a flamboyant female would arise in the audience and proclaim, "*Je suis la mère de la belle Otéro. Je suis très féministe*," and follow with a tirade on woman's place in society. Above all, we awaited the appearance of Odette Dulac, far more beautiful than Cléo de Mérode, who sang a heartbreaking song with the refrain:

Il y a toujours une moitié du monde
Qui se fiche de l'autre moitié.

We visited other cafés—the stunt cafés like Le Néant, where the tables were coffins, the lights were mortuary candles, and the waiters, brothers of the misericordia in black robes, masked, solemnly handed out the drink as ordered, "*Voici votre poison.*" The best were the simple little establishments, each serving a special quarter, with its own poet *chantant*, who commented on affairs of the day. M. Millerand, the Socialist deputy, had entered the ministry of the aristocratic Waldeck-Rousseau, and his efforts to keep up with the Joneses among his colleagues were satirized in a ballad "*Un bal masqué chez M. Millerand.*" The famous Humbert *escroquerie* was a recent scandal. Mme. Humbert for years had borrowed large sums from conservative financial institutions on the basis of a safe deposit box in which two rich Americans, the Crawford brothers, were supposed to have deposited a fortune for her ultimate benefit. When the Crawfords ceased an existence which was always fictitious, and the box was opened, the catalogue of its squalid contents in lugubrious recitative made a refrain on the theme of the vanity of human wishes.

The Dreyfus case was in its last stage, only awaiting the formal vindication of the victim and his restoration to the Army. The bitterness, disillusionment, and indignation at the revelation of the perfidy of high Army officers found expression in the press, especially in Ernest Vaughan's *L'Aurore*, which had published Zola's famous letter "*J'accuse.*" The anger against the Army blew into flame the latent anti-clericalism of France, since the Church was on the whole anti-Dreyfusard. It was thought necessary for the preservation of the republic to take education out of clerical hands, and Waldeck-Rousseau initiated this policy, pursued with violence by his successor, Emile Combes. Ecclesiastical schools were closed and teaching orders of priests and nuns driven into exile. On the whole, however, the period was one of recovery of the Third Republic from another of the crises which marked its history. The national repentance for the cruel injustice meted out to one man is almost unexampled in history. In spite of wounds self-inflicted and scars which remained, *l'affaire Dreyfus* was a sign of the restoration of health in the body politic. Like Italy, France profited by defeat; the civilized epoch after the Franco-Prussian War, commemorated by Henri Lavedan in *Le Bon Temps*, reached a culmination in the Dreyfus purge. Thereafter came the descent from Zola, Anatole France, Picquart, Waldeck-Rousseau, to Déroulède, Maurras, Léon Daudet, and Poincaré.

13

For the summer we took a villa at L'Etang-la-Ville on the longer route by rail to Saint-Germain. It was an adventure to depart from or arrive at the Gare Saint-Lazare, where the personnel seemed to regard each train as a new phenomenon, and the long delay in the tunnel gave one to think that we had been forgotten entirely; but once the train emerged from the darkness and the squalor of the faubourg, the journey home became a thing of delight. It was a painter's country, already subdued to landscape art by men's hands through long generations of toil. It brought out clearly the difference between the civilized schools of French painting and the masters of the raw scenery of America.

L'Etang-la-Ville comprised a row of villas on the edge of a plateau, from which the ground fell off sharply to the village, on the site of the swamp which gave it its name. The villas were on the border of the Forest of Marly, one of the loveliest forests in France. It must have escaped destruction in the Franco-Prussian War, for thirty years of growth could scarcely have accounted for the magnificent trees which shaded the grass-grown avenues and alleys. Our favorite walk on Sundays was to St. Nome-la Bretèche, at the farther extremity of the forest, where there were a railroad station and a pleasant café.

Ferd Schevill and Will Moody were both in Paris that summer, the latter reading the whole body of Greek tragedy with Joe Stickney in preparation for his *Fire Bringer*. Meanwhile Ferd and I, impelled by a sense of duty, took off on our bicycles for Reims and then turned south, with Carcassone, Nîmes, and Arles in view. At Bourges I fell a victim to Moulin-à-Vent, and spent a day in the hotel while Ferd devoted it to the cathedral. After that, bicycling lost its charm for me. The country was hot, dusty, dull. One late afternoon we rode into Clermont-Ferrand, thinking only of a drink and a bath. At the hotel the former was at once forthcoming, but the bath called for consultation, preparation, mobilization of pails of hot water, sheets, and towels. At last the signal was given, and the entire personnel of the establishment escorted us to the cellar of Roman architecture, wherein stood a marble vessel so large that as we submerged, one at each rounded end, our feet met in the middle. Attendants stood about, but we were in no hurry to leave that caressing water in velvet marble. Tolstoy says in *Childhood* that his earliest memory is of the smooth surface of a bathtub. It will be my latest. We emerged from the delicious warmth of the water into the delicious coolness of the cellar and the ministrations of the attendants, for whom also the occasion was doubtless memorable. Relaxed in body and morale we returned by train to Paris and L'Etang-la-Ville.

V. *Chicago*, 1898–1909

I

My doubts as to my future course in academic work persisted during my first years abroad. In my letters to Herrick I find myself constantly reverting to my interest in history, with a vague hope that I might transfer to that field. I wrote in September 1897: "I confess that I haven't the least scrap of enthusiasm left for the teaching of literature. I have a firm conviction that literature is already taught too much, not too little. For handling literature as literature few men have any distinct vocation; I doubt if I have. Ida thinks I had better peg away at history, and advises me to burn my ships by resigning from Chicago."

My decision to return to the university in 1898 was determined in part by the news which reached me of the appointment of John M. Manly as head professor in the Department of English. I had known Manly at Harvard, where as a member of the English Club I noticed that almost every topic that came up was concluded with, "What does Dr. Manly say?" As the first student in the Graduate School of Modern Language he blazed the way for a brilliant following, which included Fred N. Robinson, W. H. Schofield, and W. T. Brewster. Brewster and I took his course in Old English one summer. Years later, when at an examination for a doctorate at Chicago I was sharing a text of *Beowulf* with Manly, he reminded me of the time we had read it in the summer of 1891. Manly's own examination for his Ph.D. degree at Harvard became a legend. Not since the young Jesus confronted the doctors in the temple had established intellectual authorities been so surprised and astonished. As this was then a novel occasion we were curious to know what questions were propounded and how they were answered. "What did Kittredge ask, and Child, and Hill?" When the question came to Wendell, Manly replied, "Oh, he didn't ask anything. He just gave me a cigar." After Manly had taken his degree he returned to Harvard. Why? What more had the institution to give him? Professor Hill had answered dryly, "He is reading the Harvard Library."

In addition to a marvelous memory, Manly had a happy faculty of improvisation. His objection to the theory that one William Langland was the author of all three versions of *Piers Plowman* took its rise from the discovery that a leaf from the original manuscript had dropped out and been lost. As soon as De Vries' theory of mutations modified the Darwinian idea of evolution by the slow accretion of variations, Manly saw its application to the development of literary forms the history of which, according to the Darwinian principle, was chiefly composed of missing links.

I thought that Manly would hardly remember me from our brief intercourse at Harvard, but as I crossed the campus for the first time after my return, a taxicab passed me, stopped, and from it sprang the slight, lithe figure of the man whom I always thought of as "the master of those who know." The meeting began a friendship of the most intimate kind, which lasted without interruption for forty years. Manly's first exploit after coming to Chicago was a devastating criticism of an edition of pre-Shakespearean plays by Professor Alois Brandl of the University of Berlin. I saw in his work on this review the fascination and romance of scholarship. He forgot his classes, his food, his sleep. He lost the distinction between night and day. He showed keen delight in catching the Berliner in a multitude of errors; and in the courteous acrimony of his style he recalled the malevolence, though not the manners, of Renaissance controversialists. In the persistence with which he carried forward his work through the years, despite increasing ill health, he recalled the character in Browning's "Grammarian's Funeral."

Manly's work was an effect of his intense avidity for life, which also showed itself in other ways. He enjoyed good fellowship, and his keen, dry wit contributed to any gathering. He never missed a cue. At the celebration of Milton's tercentenary in London he scored a hit with his English hosts by remarking, "Milton, if living at this hour, would be a leader in every liberal cause except that of the advancement of women." He naturally had a discriminating appreciation of literature, and he adored Ben King and "Ironquill" among our poets. His "daily strength for daily needs" he found in Omar Khayyám, but I think he did not honestly subscribe to Omar's contempt for scholarship. He wrote a series of epigrams in skeptical comment on life, full of a homely wisdom like Ben Franklin's. He was a stoic in work and an epicure in pleasure, fond of good food, good drink, good talk. Unfortunately his intense application led him to by-pass his meals and to rely on whisky for nourishment. Against this addiction he fought a heroic battle. It was a mark of the humane liberalism of the University of Chicago to accept his failing as sickness. Manly well repaid the university for its generous understanding.

2

Manly's coming increased the tempo of our section of the university in many ways. As head professor he gave to the English Department a distinction equal to those of other schools. Promising young men and women came for graduate work, and the staff was recruited from their number—Charles R. Baskervill, George Sherburn, David H. Stevens, Thomas A. Knott, James R. Hulbert, Edith Rickert. They were all devoted to Manly, and Miss Rickert and James Hulbert were closely associated with him in such projects as the variorum *Canterbury Tales* and the *Dictionary of the American Language*. Oddly enough, Manly, one of whose epigrams on scholarship was "Milton's name was John, not George," always said Hurlbert for Hulbert. I used to be reminded of Cardinal Gibbons' reply when asked about the Pope's infallibility: "He always calls me Jibbons."

Manly's reorganization of the English Department involved a change from the aesthetic to the historical approach in the study of literature. Hitherto our discussions had turned on such questions as: What is literature? Is Macaulay literature? Manly defined the basic discipline in six period courses each occupying a quarter, running from the sixteenth century through the nineteenth. The Harvard group in the department was enthusiastically in favor of the plan, and we boldly divided the field. Moody did a fine piece of work in the seventeenth century, although he resented the conjunction of teaching and literature. "At every lecture I slay a poet," he remarked when he handed in his resignation. The department was undermanned for carrying out Manly's plan. Eventually I believe that I taught all six basic courses with the satisfaction at least of beginning the training of better scholars than I. Before the advance of my own pupils I retreated from the sixteenth century to the nineteenth. I also gave courses on the history of the novel and several seminars in that field.

My interest in Milton began with a call to speak of his political thought on the occasion of the tercentenary of his birth. Then, as there was a demand for a Milton course, I rashly took it on, perpetrating some monstrous howlers the first time. George Sherburn and David H. Stevens were among the students who were subjected to my initiation. My approach to Milton was by way of the English revolution and Puritan theology. George Sherburn once said to me, "You don't teach literature; you teach history and sociology with literature as a side line." It was true, but I defended the method. I felt that my generation was essentially historically and socially minded, and that literature approached from that point of view had a wider and more immediate appeal to our age. Once attention and interest directed to any aspect of literature was secured, literary values would make themselves felt to the extent of a person's sensibility to them.

My own experience in discovering an appreciation of music is in point. My mind was awakened to the construction of the symphony, to the use of the *leitmotif* in operas, and enjoyment of music in itself followed. Similarly with painting and sculpture: the concentrated attention which Berenson taught me to give to determine the attribution of a picture meant in the end a far more genuine appreciation than I gained from Ruskin's or Pater's dithyrambs. I have always distrusted the efforts of teachers to inspire pupils with their own ecstasies. I have felt that the approach through elaborate aesthetic theory or technical analysis would reach comparatively few. The highest use of literature is to make it a part of experience, and to forward this process it is advisable to take it up where it is most nearly in contact with the life of the age in which we are living. The teaching of literature *as such* therefore seems to me far less profitable or necessary than promoting the comprehension of the life from which that literature sprang. The example of the makers of literature should prove decisive on this point. How few men have written greatly in illustration of a theory or to solve a problem in metrics or aesthetics! How many have written nobly because they were burning with a sense of the importance of what they had to say!

Many years later I had a debate with Gertrude Stein on her visit to the university, in which I fared badly, as to whether propaganda can be literature. Our positions were diametrically opposed. I held to the literal meaning of propaganda as those things which ought to be propagated or published, and maintained that most great literature fell into this category—the Bible, Greek tragedy, Dante, Milton. Even the Earl of Essex and the Earl of Southampton found *Richard II* propaganda for their mad attempt to take control of the kingdom in the last days of Elizabeth. Miss Stein held that while propaganda is found in the writers mentioned, their claim to literature exists in spite of, not because of, this element. The case of Shelley is in point. Though Shelley wrote with an earnest revolutionary purpose in *The Revolt of Islam*, and even in *Prometheus Unbound* was an advocate of vegetarianism, it is obvious that enjoyment of his poetry may be independent of such considerations. For me, however, the introduction to that poetry through a view of Shelley's experience of life enhances its interest. I should never have read *The Revolt of Islam* except from a sense of professional duty if it had not been for the introduction marking it as an allegory of the French Revolution. Milton and Dante come alive through some understanding of their politics and theology. I like to read *King Lear* as having a reference to King James' proclivity for giving away the royal demesne to his favorites.

I am sorry that I did not remain primarily a student during these years when learning was easy for me. Because of the scarcity of college teachers in the early nineties I advanced too rapidly. In my enforced association with eminent scholars I had to assume a virtue though I had it not, and from a kind of false shame concealed my ignorance. I have never made any contribution to knowledge. The chief value of my teaching has been in the organization of fields which I have seen my students enter with success and for which they have sometimes been generous enough to thank me. I take more than pleasure in a letter I received later from a scholar of distinction:

Department of English
Cornell University
Ithaca, N. Y.

187 Goldwin Smith Hall
August 8, 1918

My dear Professor Lovett,

You do not, of course, remember that I was once your student; yet the first course in graduate work that I ever had was at Chicago under your direction. The splendid training that you gave me in Elizabethan literature helped to determine all my subsequent work, and the inspiration I derived from you has enabled me to give the same course here for many years. I have always been grateful.

Sincerely yours,
Joseph Q. Adams

I went to the University of Chicago to teach writing and never entirely gave up courses in this field. There, as in literature, I had the satisfaction of seeing my pupils do better work than I ever could. Here, again, my approach was through matter rather than form. I tried to interest the students in recognizing the value of their own material. Instead of giving out formal assignments—a description, a personal essay, an argument, a story—I tried to make them aware of what experience they controlled which might provide subject matter to exercise their pens or typewriters.

That change in the mechanics of the production of literature is significant. In my early years of teaching everything was written in longhand. It has seemed to me that a change in the instrument of composition has resulted in a general change in style, somewhat like that produced by the substitution of oral dictation for writing. I noticed this in the work of Robert Herrick, many of whose novels I read in manuscript. The meticulous accuracy of expression of his early books gave way to a looseness which I attribute to his Oliver typewriter. I believe that a corresponding laxness in correction on the part of teachers has occurred. The very difficulty of reading handwriting keeps the critical mind at strain. Gone are the days when we reduced a student's theme to a palimpsest overlaid by exceptions in red ink based on Hill's *Principles of Rhetoric*. In fact, I recognize that our first dereliction at Chicago was allowing a red pencil and then any pencil in place of red ink as the critic's weapon.

Another weakness was laxness in enforcing rewriting. In one of my first classes I had as a pupil Samuel Rawson Harper, the president's oldest son. I knew that Dr. Harper in his keen oversight of everything that went on in the university would not fail to go over his son's themes; and to let him know that the Harvard critics were doing their duty I gave that young man's pages a special overhauling. The president was impressed and asked one day if I would designate a member of my department to go over some work of his own. I was told by his secretary later than on receiving the manuscript back he looked it over ruefully for a few minutes. "Flint says rewrite," he murmured. "We won't do it." Accordingly we did not reform President Harper's style, but I hope we were of some use to Samuel in his later writing on Russian literature and politics.

3

During these years my association with Robert Herrick grew into strong friendship. We had in common our job—to develop writing at the university. In Herrick's view this implied writing ourselves and stimulating our young colleagues and students to write for professional publication. This was in marked contrast to the tendency at Harvard, where the *Monthly* and the *Advocate* were the goals. Our joint management of our division was a constant preoccupation, attested by hundreds of letters which passed between us in his absence or mine—letters filled with estimates of the work of our young colleagues and details of administration respecting the size of classes and fixing of standards. In this routine Moody loyally took his part, though with a heavy heart. We gained another colleague from Harvard in Lindsay Todd Damon, who joined Herrick in the production of a standard textbook, *Composition and Rhetoric*, the well-known "Herrick and Damon."

Like Moody, Herrick was building a literary career. He first emerged in *Scribner's Magazine* in 1894 with a story, "The Man Who Wins," which became the title of a small volume of stories published a year later. His first novel, *The Gospel of Freedom*, was the product of his year in Italy, 1895–96, for which association with art critics provided the somewhat satirically handled background. After his return to Chicago he wrote a series of American novels, *The Web of Life*, *The Real World*, *The Common Lot*, *Together*, each showing a stronger grasp of his material and closer construction. The university, through its flexible quarter system, allowed Herrick great freedom in his teaching arrangements and the apportionment of his time, but as he gave less time to academic engagements his conscientious scruples became more troubling, until in 1922 he resigned.

Herrick's novels belong strictly to the school of realism and social criticism which flourished during the quarter century before the First World War. For each he cultivated a specific background through which the personal problem emerged in the old terms of individual *versus* society, with the animus against egoism. He was an academic writer in view of his concern with technique, his careful planning of structure. I wrote him in regard to his first novel that what appealed to me most was the way in which everything drew steadily in a definite direction, though I felt that the pull was not always strong enough. I early recognized that Herrick was forced to rely on situations that he had seen and characters that he had known, and many were the arguments we had when I felt that he had trenched upon private interests and violated personalities. He always denied this, but I refused to accept his denials. Rather, I believe that he considered his art important enough to justify the sacrifice of these interests and persons.

A case which proved my point arose when Henry Goddard Leach, editor of the *Forum*, was looking out for an academic novel as a serial. I recommended Herrick, who had often spoken of a generalized view of college life to be known as "The Pleasant Walks of Academe." Both Manly and I urged Herrick to maintain this conception and avoid a picture of the University of Chicago. Herrick could not work that way. He fell back on his accustomed method and even chose a title, *Chimes*, which had a specific and esoteric reference in the history of that institution. We resented especially his treatment of the first two presidents of the university, who had been generous in granting him freedom and support for his career and defending him when some of the trustees were scandalized at his realism.

I remain proud and happy in my friendship for Robert Herrick. I take satisfaction in the renewal of his reputation and the recognition of his place in serious American fiction, in witness of which I take leave to quote so good a critic as Newton Arvin, who cites *The Common Lot*, *The Memoirs of an American Citizen*, and *Together* as "three of the most impressive works in our literature," and Herrick as "the most human, the most capacious, and the most truly critical mind at work in American fiction since Howells and Norris."

4

Herrick's sense of the sterility of our social soil led to the founding of a dining club which became known as the Windbag. The members were Adolph Miller, Ferdinand Schevill, Manly, Herrick, Moody, and I. We met about once a fortnight at one another's houses, and I have never heard better talk. Manly was always in great form, but no better than in another gathering known as the Thompson Street Poker Club, of which the leading spirit was Philip S. Allen. I am grateful to Allen for breaking down my New England habit of parsimony. I came to Chicago as what was known in our expressive metaphor as a "tightwad." Allen had an unerring instinct for money in someone else's pocket, and an invincible charm for abstracting it in the interest of the company's thirst for another bottle of champagne.

Allen was an academic type of a species occasional elsewhere but never in such perfection. He was a sport of the first water. He had been a famous center rush on the Williams College eleven, and after a year or two in Germany he was recruited by Stagg to fill the same position at Chicago while pursuing his studies for a Ph.D. in German. Allen admired Manly and caught his enthusiasm for learning. He devoted himself to the late Latin and medieval romantic lyric, on which he wrote two excellent books. He and Manly established a quarterly, *Modern Philology*. As a teacher he had a great following among the students, recruited year after year, and held enthusiastically attended salons in his office, prolonging class hours. He was a picturesque figure on our campus, maintaining the tradition of the personality-plus professor.

Another intimate friend of Manly's and of mine was William Isaac Thomas. He came to the university in a small administrative position, created for him by President Harper, to take his degree in sociology in a department of which he became the most distinguished member. Sociology in the last century seemed to be divided between the theorists, interested in a philosophy of society, and the philanthropists, interested in practical amelioration. Thomas turned the attention of his pupils to the actual phenomena of social life by case studies and statistics. He made sociology a science.

I came to know Thomas well on one long day in a summer quarter when he received news that one of his boys had been drowned at the resort in Michigan where his family was staying. There was no train until evening, and all day we sat together, talking of this and that, but always his mind returned to the question—which? It was not Bill, the oldest, because Bill could always take care of himself. It was not Ed, because Ed was too cautious to be caught in a situation he couldn't handle. It could not be the youngest boy because the others would never have given him up. It was the last, caught in a current so swift that the older boys had been helpless.

Among the first people I had met at Chicago was a man a few years older than I, Joseph Edward Raycroft. He was then an undergraduate, studying medicine, and assisting Stagg in the Department of Physical Culture; later he became university physician. He was another example of President Harper's faculty for attracting valuable personalities who would fit into the very flexible structure of the institution. Raycroft was called to Princeton in 1911 as director of athletics by President Wilson. During the First World War he was in charge of athletics in the Army and later was the director of the American team in successive Olympic games. His last position was as president of the Board of Managers of the New Jersey Hospital for the Insane. He has maintained a scholarly interest in physical culture, thus illustrating Dr. Harper's belief in its place in intellectual life.

University life at Chicago was much enriched in the early years by George and Louise Vincent. George Vincent was another of the early comers who blurred the distinction between faculty and students. The son of Bishop John H. Vincent, founder of Chautauqua, he had grown up in that institution. From Yale he had come to Chicago in President Harper's personal following to study sociology, and he took his doctor's degree *summa cum laude*. He joined the faculty, and became a popular teacher and administrative officer. He had cultivated public speaking, not as the fine art of Cicero, but as a rapid, clear, forcible means of communication, much enhanced by anecdotes, of which he prudently kept a store, and by genuine wit which caught unfailingly the note of the moment. Vincent's intelligence, fairness, and good humor made him an admirable Dean of the Junior Colleges and later Dean of the Faculties. His sense of play was a refreshing element in an institution inclined to take itself too seriously. Among his promotions were two comic operas, *The Deceitful Dean* and *The Academic Alchemist*, which were joint faculty and student productions for the benefit of the University Settlement. Vincent would invite a number of us to dinner, posit the theme, and we would set to work with Weber Linn's facility in light verse as our main resource. Louise Vincent was the scenic artist and stage manager. *The Deceitful Dean* was really good satire. *The Academic Alchemist* was a bit overelaborate and heavy. It furnished an excellent device, however, to give the rather self-conscious university a chance to laugh at itself.

Among other projects Vincent brought saddle horses from the West and established a faculty riding club. I had never recovered from my early educational experience at Draper and Hall's Academy in Boston, but under Vincent's stimulus I found riding my best means of exercise and outdoor enjoyment, and soon bought a horse of my own. Louise Vincent organized basketball and other games for the sedentary faculty. She was strong for out-of-doors, for camping, hunting, and mountain-climbing, in which I envied her daring and skill.

5

All these people I have mentioned were close associates of President Harper. Indeed, nearly everyone on the faculty at this time was his personal choice and a subject of his special interest. As the university halted in its progress after the turn of the century, and promises could not be fulfilled nor ambitions gratified, there was opposition and recrimination, but the recognition of the fact that the president was perhaps fatally ill shed gloom over the entire university.

The relation between the Founder and Dr. Harper was close. Mr. Rockefeller's original interest in re-establishing the University of Chicago was due to its connection with the Baptist denomination. It was a stipulation in the charter that the president must be a Baptist minister, but Mr. Rockefeller had already elected Dr. Harper, as the outstanding scholar in the Baptist Church, and accordingly the stipulation was waived. Thenceforward President Harper held the confidence of the Founder in spite of his addiction to what was called the higher criticism, which excited the fury of the "hardshell" wing of his denomination. The break between them came not as had been prophesied on religion, but on financial grounds. Mr. Rockefeller was increasingly restive over Dr. Harper's policy of operating on a deficit which by 1903 had reached upwards of two hundred and sixty thousand dollars. He hesitated to accept further calls and suspended his annual contributions to the endowment. This action was particularly embarrassing to President Harper, who at that time proposed to add a Medical Department to the university, based on the leading local institution, the Rush Medical School. Mr. Rockefeller was counted on to match the sum of a million dollars raised locally, but Dr. Harper's million included old books, old bones, old surgical instruments contributed by the profession, which Mr. Rockefeller refused to accept, leaving the university in a highly compromising situation. There were rumors of President Harper's resignation, which he scornfully denied. Undoubtedly anxiety over the future added to a physical condition resulting from overwork and bad hygiene.

Early in 1905 President Harper informed his closest friends that he was threatened. On February 22 members of the faculty gathered at the Quadrangle Club to hear the result of an operation which confirmed the threat. Nevertheless, he continued his various activities, completing his commentary on the book of Hosea, his final contribution to the scholarship that he loved. In September he went through the exhausting ceremonies of Convocation in which he had always taken great pleasure and pride. In spite of periods of intense pain his resolution to live and work was never stronger. Slowly he yielded. One by one, at his home, he saw members of the faculty, at least all those who had been with him from the beginning, and spoke of his interest in the future of each one and of his hopes for the university. We remembered the kindness of our leader, his praise of whatever we had done to deserve it, his forgetfulness of opposition and forgiveness of injuries. There had been much that was pretentious and sordid in the early history of the University of Chicago, but the great achievement remained, consecrated by ferocious labor in life and courage in death. His death on January 10, 1906, brought out a great tribute from the city. It realized that another of the titans who had made its history, and the most unselfish of them all, was gone. In the dignity with which he met the end he deserved Milton's lines from *Samson Agonistes:*

> Nothing is here for tears, nothing to wail
> Or knock the breast, no weakness, no contempt,
> Dispraise, or blame, nothing but well and fair,
> And what may quiet us in a death so noble.

6

The natural successor of President Harper was the Dean of the Faculties, Harry Pratt Judson, in whose hands the administration had largely rested during the president's illness. He became acting president on Dr. Harper's death. In the next year he was elected president. George Vincent succeeded him as Dean of the Faculties,

James R. Angell became Dean of the Senior Colleges, and I became Dean of the Junior Colleges. In addition I acted as secretary of the English Department. I always enjoyed administration, largely because of the character of the men I worked with or under. President Harper was an inspiration. Vincent made the meeting of routine bodies, even the curriculum committee, lively and interesting. When Dean Angell and I had adjoining rooms, I looked forward to office hours enlivened by his intelligence and humor. He would have been an admirable president of the University of Chicago, and it is the chief weakness of Dr. Judson's administration that he failed to provide for such a successor. As both Manly and Herrick were absorbed in their special activities, I found the English Department, with a group of brilliant young people, chiefly in my hands. Their scholarly allegiance was to Manly, but I was responsible as a sort of top sergeant for their academic discipline.

I count it as one of my chief services to the university to have influenced President Judson and Dean Vincent, in spite of their economy program, to call Dr. William A. Nitze to the headship of the Romance Language Department, which he raised to the first rank in the country. Another addition which I successfully urged was that of Dr. Tom Pete Cross to the English Department, to give courses in Celtic and medieval literature. The name Tom Pete was not then a household word in American scholarship, and Dr. Judson queried whether these presumable nicknames might not be extended in the university *Register* to Thomas Peter.

7

A great factor in our life in Chicago has always been the Lake Zurich Golf Club. This institution is so unique and at the same time so characteristic of Chicago that it deserves a page or two. Lake Zurich is thirty-seven miles from Chicago, one of the small lakes that dot northern Illinois, Wisconsin, and Minnesota. A Chicago lawyer, Charles B. Wood, had defended in court the title to the land on the northern shore of the lake, and in the settlement conceived the idea of finding a buyer for some seventy acres by founding a golf club, the second such club to be formed near Chicago. Its members were city men, but one of my colleagues, Frederick I. Carpenter, was a Chicagoan and knew Wood's partner, Horace Oakley. Carpenter approached me, and as I have always joined everything when invited (except the Socialist party), I accepted. Soon all my intimate friends at the university were members.

The clubhouse faced the lake. It was a simple structure, built for an incredibly small sum in 1896, with two big rooms on the ground floor, ten bedrooms above, and a dormitory under the roof. We used to go by train on Saturdays to Barrington and thence by Peters' livery to the club—six miles, which in snow or mud was an hour's ride. The fare was two bits, known as "Peters' pence." The driver was Henry Pingle, whence the drive was known as "pingling." His substitute, a lame boy named Max, had a habit of sleeping behind his horses, and nearly extinguished the club when the crowded four-seated bus swung across the E. J. and E. tracks barely ahead of a train.

The stations we passed on the Northwestern railway were pathetically suggestive of wishful thinking—Park View, Park Ridge, Mount Prospect, Arlington Heights—the rolling country did not actually begin until we reached Barrington. The nine-hole course at Lake Zurich was not exciting, but it was a pleasant relief from the monotonous prairie landscape through which we had come. When I first saw the links there were many trees, hickories and oaks, but the former suffered from a blight and disappeared after furnishing (for a generation) fuel for the big fireplaces. My wife and I were so keen on the country and golf that we built a cottage next to the clubhouse in the same simple style—no heat but fireplace and stoves, no hot water, no inside toilets. Our week-ends in winter were austere; the occasional summers we spent there were hot and dry, but we always arrived with the sixteenth-century poet Surrey's exclamation: "How glad I was that I had gotten out!"

8

One of the ambitions of Chicago was to become a literary center. It had already to its credit a novelist, scornfully characterized by Matthew Arnold as "a man by the name of Roe," whose *The Opening of a Chestnut Burr* and *Barriers Burned Away* were best-sellers in the seventies. A more strenuous school of fiction was represented by Hamlin Garland, whose stories drawn from his early life in Wisconsin (collected in 1890 in *Main-Traveled Roads*) were hailed by William Dean Howells in the eighties as the promise of truthful fiction in the Middle West. Garland was the leader of a group of which Lorado Taft, the sculptor, and Henry Blake Fuller were members. Fuller began his career with romance, *The Chevalier of Pensieri-Vani* and *La Chatelaine de La Trinité*, but turned to the realism of Chicago in *The Cliff Dwellers* and *With the Procession.*

Garland, encouraged by the generous approval of Howells, passed on the patronage to his younger contemporaries. Herrick rather resented it, but I appreciated the kindly spirit with which Garland greeted the two novels which I published in 1904 and 1907.

Both novels began with children whose characters inevitably lost the appeal of childhood as they emerged into the light of common day. For the opening of the first, *Richard Gresham*, I invented the episode of the flight of the boy's father from arrest, but for the second, *A Winged Victory*, I had the scene caught from the porch of my cottage at Lake Zurich—two little girls with a smaller boy between them fleeing down the country road from an angry farmer with a horsewhip. One girl broke away and escaped; the other stood fast and confronted the pursuer with the child in her arms. *The Dial*, then the chief literary organ of the Middle West, objected that my characters were feebly drawn and that it was not clear what I wanted my readers to think of them. The *Nation*, however, remarked that "of the latter part nothing is to be said but that the childhood story is a matter for wonder and gratitude." To the same effect George Carpenter wrote to Herrick: "His story all falls to pieces and yet, My! how he does get children."

Robert Herrick and I used to have long discussion on the art of fiction. He always worked with existing persons as characters (except in *The Memoirs of an American Citizen*), while my characters were always imagined. This difference accounted for the firmer texture of his work and, of course, for its social significance. One remark of his I cherish. "Your books," he said one day, "have what I never get—emotion."

The literary ambition of Chicago was also breaking out in unexpected places. Shortly after my return from Paris Dr. Harper called me to his office and handed me a pretentious large paper volume entitled "The Merchant Prince of Cornville." He explained that the author, a leading real-estate dealer named S. E. Gross, had reason to think that his work had been plagiarized by Rostand in *Cyrano de Bergerac* and hence had submitted it to the university for a report. The fee was a hundred dollars. I was amused at being chosen as an expert. The external evidence was the allegation that the author of

"The Merchant Prince" had sent the manuscript to Coquelin in 1894. It had not been accepted. The internal evidence was the fact that the hero had a large nose and the situation in which an accomplice replaces the lover under his lady's window. It was impossible to check the external evidence of plagiarism in view of its inherent improbability, but for the similarities in material I submitted a list of plays in which the same phenomena appeared, as common property of the romantic stage. Mr. Gross welched on the payment of the fee, and I was not summoned to the witness stand when he sought and obtained an injunction to prevent Richard Mansfield from playing *Cyrano* in Chicago. The injunction held when Coquelin and Bernhardt came to the city. I was in Paris then and wrote Herrick of the stupefaction with which the news was received, before the *cafés chantants* converted it into inextinguishable laughter. The episode properly receives a page in *Chicago: The History of Its Reputation,* by Lewis and Smith. Mr. Gross could not be restrained from being a clown, but the judge might have prevented this contribution to the reputation of his city.

VI. *Germany*, 1909–1911

I

I look back on no part of my life with more pleasure than the years from 1909 to 1911, most of which I spent in Germany with my family. The children, aged thirteen, eleven, and seven, had been going to the progressive school of the university and, we thought, needed some stiffer training in general and in foreign speech in particular. Accordingly we sailed on the *Argentina*, of the Austro-American Line, for Trieste in July 1909 with Ferdinand Schevill as attaché.

Since we had read *The Amazing Marriage* we had had a desire to see Carinthia. It had not occurred to us that we should find hordes of visitors in what we had gathered from Meredith was a primitive region. On arriving in Villach in the evening we were met at the station by a dozen porters wearing that look of triumph with which they inform you that they are not there to solicit but to refuse. An obliging cabman drove us about to test their statements, and finally took us to a roadside inn two or three miles out of town.

From Villach we drifted on to the Millstätter See, which we circumnavigated by small steamer. At each stopping place most of the passengers would disembark and rush through the village crying for rooms—*Zimmer*, *Zimmer*. On our return to the starting point I was first ashore and led the pursuit back to a modest lodging house which we had disdained a few hours before and engaged one small room with three beds. The girls struggled nightly to defend a strategic frontier in one, while Robert slept under a table on a pile of rucksacks and accumulating laundry.

Meanwhile Ferd Schevill had been scouting around and found a place at Sand in Taufers-Tal, the Pension Schrottwinkel, where we spent the rest of the summer and the next. The pension was in the steward's lodge of the *Schloss*, which stood above it in ruins. There was a *Weinstube* on the ground floor where the local drinkers gathered for refreshment in the evening. Occasionally a traveling troupe of Tyrolese musicians turned up and entertained the company with old favorites and with topical songs and improvised verses directed at one or another of the audience. It was astonishing how quickly the musicians could catch a hint from the responsive attitude of the listeners and pick out a victim at whom to point their satire, which was usually received good-naturedly, with laughter and backslapping. Once a row was provoked by a song, popular that year, which recounted a series of accidents or misfortunes with the refrain, "*Es war ein Böhm dabei*," to whose presence the various casualties were referred. As it happened there was a Bohemian in the room that evening who resented violently these aspersions. I believe that Ruth frequented the *Weinstube* surreptitiously, for she acquired a repertory of the most vulgar sort which she was easily induced to sing to any company.

The Schrottwinkel contained a number of old porcelain stoves with tiles dating from the Renaissance. The Archduke Franz Ferdinand was an expert, and accordingly sent word that he would visit the pension on a certain day to see the treasures. He arrived with his Archduchess Sophie Chotek, and both were simple and informal, chatting affably with the guests, or so Ida reported. I have always regretted that I was away on a mountaineering trip, and thus missed seeing the man who four years later innocently brought upon the world the greatest burden of horror and woe it had suffered by reason of the death of any man except Jesus.

2

Education was the business that had taken us to Europe, and as we knew Munich from previous visits we went there after our summer in Sand. Karl Marr, born in the United States, was then the head of the American colony by virtue of his position as director of the Academy of Fine Arts. Taking his advice for Robert, we sought out the head of the Institut Röhmer, who had the reputation of putting more knowledge into a boy's head in a short time than any other schoolmaster in Munich. Herr Röhmer was a Prussian who proposed to correct the easygoing way of life of the Bavarians. The institute was largely attended by boys who had to make up lost time in order to pass examinations which would entitle them to a reduction in military service to one year. The instruction was individual or in groups of two or three. Every hour of the day was accounted for, including visits to the Marienbad—fifteen minutes to go, thirty to bathe, fifteen to return. Each week-end there was an *Ausflug*, a trip to the Bavarian Alps. Every other Sunday the boys were given leave under family direction, from ten in the morning to nine at night—a small fund of freedom against which were charged fines for any infraction of rules. The discipline was of the strictest. A few weeks after Robert was immured Herr Marr came to us in some consternation to say that he feared he had been too hasty in recommending the school on its general reputation because friends had told him it was too strict, *zu streng*, for an American boy. By that time, however, Robert had shown that he could take it.

From the beginning no allowance was made for his unfamiliarity with the language. He had to understand, and, with some help from a boy whose mother was English, he did. Intercourse in English, however, was forbidden, and also the reading of English books. He resorted to Shakespeare as most likely to be excused if discovered, and his first letters were full of naïve appreciation of the plays which relieved his homesickness. Of course, pocket money was forbidden, but he had a small gold mine in his mouth from a teeth-straightening operation which had not been completed on leaving home. Somehow on the way to the Marienbad he discovered a pawn shop where a fragment of gold could be exchanged for a mark. Similar evasions of rules were common on the part of Herr Röhmer's young gentlemen, and probably worse things went on in the dormitory, of which all the windows were open at night, as if to freeze the boys into virtue. Soon after Robert's entrance he wrote me to say that I had been misled about the character of the school and to recount the misdeeds of his companions. He added, "I am good because I am so sad."

When we moved to Weimar Ferd Schevill stayed in Munich, and he was duly authorized to lead Robert forth on his free Sunday. His accounts of these experiences were pathetic. He would find his charge full of joyful anticipation. They would set forth happily up the Isarthal to the Starnberger See, and eat a dinner of the best, returning to the city for a café and supper, still cheerful but with shadows gathering as evening drew on. The last hour would find them on a bench in the Englischer Garten, both weeping. Then at nine Robert would race for the institute, Ferd following to boost him over the gate if he was late. A minute would cost an hour on the next fortnightly leave.

As I was called back to Chicago for the winter a consolidation of the family was indicated, and we returned to Munich. I informed Herr Röhmer that I wished Robert to live with his family as the temporary man of the house. The Prussian at first refused. His whole system depended on having his pupils completely under his control. Robert's future career would be frustrated, and as an out-pupil he would demoralize the school. We stood firm, however, and Herr Röhmer yielded. He had received inquiries from other American families and saw the advantage of the connection. He made the arrangement as difficult as possible. Robert had to report at six in the morning to his German master. During the Munich winter six o'clock is as black as midnight. One night when we returned late from the opera Robert was roused by the light and without a word turned out of bed and began to pull on his trousers. When I told him that he had still half the night for sleep, without a word he reversed his movements and fell back into bed. Ida used to rise every morning at five to give him breakfast and make sure that he was on time.

The American connection proved valuable to Herr Röhmer. Three other boys from American families entered the next year. The Herr Direktor was a believer in athletic sports, particularly in a debased form of baseball known as "Deutschball," in which the batted ball was picked up and thrown at the base runner. The appearance on his team of three or four American boys who were used to catching the ball and throwing it with some precision put the Institut Röhmer ahead of the various *Turnverein* teams and other participants in the local league and won prestige for the institute. The star players were not pleased, inasmuch as games were scheduled for Sunday afternoons, interfering with the fortnight leave. The boys bore this with grumbling, but when a petition for freedom on the Fourth of July was denied there was mutiny. Herr Röhmer wrote me indignantly that a "stinkbomb" had been set off in the building, causing an appalling loss of time to the business of education. I was amused to see the Prussian drill-sergeant caught in the same dilemma as the principal of a high school in the United States, unable to expel his star players for serious misdemeanors however the morale of the school might suffer. Herr Röhmer was decorated about this time for services to education in Bavaria, among which doubtless the development of athletics and the prowess of his Deutschball team were remembered.

On our return to Munich we investigated schools for the girls, finally deciding upon the Institut Savaete. I followed with interest the course of their education, especially in the history of Bavaria. The textbook began with the modest statement "*Bayern ist ein binnen Land,*" which naturally led to an admission of naval inferiority. The fact that in the European wars from the sixteenth century onward Bavaria had been on the side of France against Germany, and with Austria against Prussia, was tactfully attenuated. The treatment of Andreas Hofer was especially delicate. This year was the hundredth since Hofer's execution at Mantua, whither he had been escorted by the Bavarian allies of Napoleon. Now Hofer had become a national hero of Bavaria, and Munich vied with Innsbruck in doing him honor. Italians, Austrians, Bavarians in their rifle corps, marched in parades together in the solidarity of the Tyrol.

3

The situation of Bavaria was not happy. In the country districts the Slavic invasion had begun and farms were passing into the hands of Poles. I have always felt that the Western nations did not give enough consideration to the genuine fear of Slavic pressure as a deep-seated cause of World War I. In the cities, Prussians were competing in business, and with their energy and ambition were putting out old Bavarian firms. There was the old rivalry between the first state of Germany and the second, which could always dream of leading a coalition of the South Germans. But the time for that had passed. Bavaria had backed the wrong horse in the Austro-Prussian War of 1866, and the smaller states distrusted her leadership. Bismarck had brought Ludwig II to the point of ceremonially offering the crown of Imperial Germany to the King of Prussia with the threat that the King of Württemberg might be called in to do the honors. Bavarians were an easygoing people, but some of them showed impatience at the recollection of their kings' selling the national birthright—Ludwig I for Lola Montez and Ludwig II for Wagner.

In general, Bavarians were happy in the consciousness of their culture and art, of which Wagner in music, Lenbach in painting, and Thomas Mann in literature were evidence of supremacy. An active literary group gathered about the weekly *Simplicissimus* and Café Käthi Kobus. The Kaiser was not much thought or spoken of, except for an occasional spate of funny stories. When Count Schack died, leaving to the Kaiser his gallery of works of art which had long figured in Baedeker, the city was scandalized. The Kaiser, however, had the good sense to hand the gift over to the municipality. He came to

Munich to make the presentation, but his visit attracted little attention. Ida and the little girls saw him driving from the Bahnhof with no signs of popular enthusiasm. Ruth was disappointed because he did not wear his crown.

There was much good music to be heard in Munich. Herr Mottl conducted the opera, which boasted two great artists, Mme. Matzenhauer and Mlle. Fassbender. The Prinzregententheater had recently been built, following the plan of the theater at Bayreuth, for the production of Wagner's operas. At the charmingly rococo Residenztheater the lighter operas of Mozart were given during the winter. The Kaimsaal had been built for concerts at popular prices, and Weingartner came from Vienna each week to conduct the orchestra, which was not of the first class. On one occasion when the violinist Eugène Ysaye was playing Lalo's *Symphonie Espagnole*, Weingartner suddenly rapped for silence and, linking arms with Ysaye, marched off the stage while the players hung their heads.

The most exciting week in music of my experience was that of the return of Richard Strauss to Munich, from where he had been banished, musically, many years before. His first opera, *Feuersnot*, with text by Hugo von Hofmannsthal, was, like *Die Meistersinger*, a protest against the Beckmessers. Munich rose en masse to greet the return of its former son. In five days the whole repertory of Strauss's work was presented: in the mornings, the chamber music, for which was gathered a superb choir of woodwinds; in the afternoons the symphonic poems; and in the evenings the operas, beginning with the early *Feuersnot* and closing with *Der Rosenkavalier*, which was new in 1911. In the late afternoon or late evening Strauss was to be seen at the Café Luitpold or the Odéon, an engaging figure with his long slender body, bright-crowned head, and delicate hands.

The cafés, baths, and gardens of Munich were part of everyday life. Our favorite café for late afternoons was the Luitpold, where we read the newspapers, and drank coffee at moments when the *Fräuleins* rushed about with their steaming pots crying *frisch gemacht*. The Hofgarten was the place for a sunny Sunday afternoon; when it rained, the Hofbräuhaus was to be preferred. Every room in the great building was crowded, and the singing was tumultuous. In the courtyard endless lines of drivers in rubber coats with steins in hand passed by the faucets. The effect of beer on the Münchener was undoubtedly both soothing and stimulating. One of the men who stood about ready for any commission, a *Dienstmann*, estimated that he drank eighteen half liters a day. "You see," he explained, "what makes me glad to get a job is that I drink a stein as soon as I get it. And what makes me hurry to get it over is that I drink another when I get done." The number and variety of brews gave an opportunity for the exercise of discrimination and criticism in taste, as in the case of wine and tea. Löwenbräu was easily recognized by its sweetness, and Hofbräu, Franciskanerbräu, and Pschorrbräu had distinguishing qualities, but some of the lesser brews were baffling. One annual experience was the bock beer of the Salvatorbräu, served in the Franciskanerkeller a few miles out of town, to which in the early days of April all Munich made a pilgrimage, by horse or foot.

We kept house for two years, first in an apartment on Von der Tannstrasse, where the landlord was unpleasant and constantly involving us in legal difficulties, and then on Prinz Regentenstrasse. Among our friends the Hanfstaengl family was most helpful. Frau Hanfstaengl, of the American Sedgwick clan, was generous always to her fellow countrymen. Her daughter Erna, and the youngest boy, Erwin, or Wini as we called him, were especially appointed to look out for us. Later Wini was in Chicago for a time as secretary to Mr. Harold McCormick. He was in Paris, ill with typhoid fever and nursed by his mother in the first days of August 1914. As an enemy alien, unable to leave and unable to obtain proper treatment, he died—the first tragedy of the war to come personally near to us.

4

Ferd Schevill and I left my family at Weimar and made a journey eastward, stopping first at Vienna. From there we went to Budapest. Five years before World War I no city was more intriguing in its serious ambition and wild gaiety than this little capital on both banks of the Danube. It had a subway, though it extended, it is true, only the short distance from the river to the hilltop which crowned the city. Its cafés rivaled Maxim's; each had its band of Zigeuner musicians and an assigned quota of handsome, vivacious girls ready to entertain foreign visitors in the city or on a week-end trip to the Tatra. It would appear from the crowds abroad on Sunday evening that no family was permitted to stay at home. And why should anyone wish to when the whole city was a city of joy? The Magyars were a courteous people, with the exception of their refusal to understand Ferd's questions or requests in his Berliner speech. Usually I could draw an answer. "Why not?" growled Ferd. "Every sentence you utter is an insult to the German language."

From Budapest we went to Constantinople, which was in an interesting period of transition. The Young Turks had thrown out Abdul Hamid and were setting up a constitutional government. Shevket, Enver, and Talaat were the big names of the new regime.

We visited the Sultan's deserted haremlik on the Golden Horn and rode up and down the water alleys in boats propelled by foot-work, contrived for concubines who, we were told, were scattering throughout Europe the delights once reserved to a single potentate.

The superb voyage across the Aegean on a bright autumn day, every island and promontory with its temples shining white in the sunlight, culminated in our first sight of Athens with the Parthenon glorified by sunset. Greece has the advantage over other lands in that it bursts upon one in its complete splendor after a perfect approach by sea.

The usual way of the tourist in Greece is to join a Cook's party. We decided to avoid the crowd and to work out our itinerary by ourselves. This plan had its disadvantages in that when we arrived at a destination by steamer, the Cook's tourists got the first carriages and the best rooms at the hotels. We had a certain pride in doing the trip as cheaply on our own as could be done on Cook's schedule, and should have succeeded if Ferd had not brought along some gold twenty-mark pieces which he handed out unconsciously in place of twenty francs. This usually happened at places where we were not pleased and meant to cut the tip to the smallest amount. His disgust when he discovered that we had dropped a dollar by mistake was one of my minor satisfactions.

Delphi was our best find—the excavations in the heat and dust recalling vividly the scene of *La Cittá Morta*. I tried Mount Parnassus, but crumpled on the long, dusty, goat-infested way.

Back in Athens once more, we tried to follow the intricacies of Greek politics. Every hour or two a newspaper appeared at the cafés to set the habitués buzzing like a swarm of bees, "eager to hear or tell some new thing." After a half-hour everything would quiet down until the hive was stirred by the next edition. One morning the hotel porter told us mysteriously that there would be a revolution that afternoon and advised us to be in front of the palace. We were there in the midst of a great concourse which was soon stirred by the arrival of armies with banners, made up of the patriotic societies of

Athens. A committee was admitted to the palace. King George I then appeared with his wife and children on the balcony. How many monarchs since Louis XVI have sought to stem revolution by this pathetic appeal to the principle of dynasty! The King of the Hellenes was a bluff, hearty Dane who made no sentimental plea. Apparently his defense of the monarchy was "Take it or leave it." They took it with cheers. The revolution was over.

We intended to go to Montenegro and even calculated how much we were prepared to lose in playing poker with the King, but at Bocce de Cattaro Ferdinand balked and flatly refused to leave the steamer. Nevertheless we went to Herzegovina and Bosnia. Sarajevo was a Turkish city in appearance, with its bazaar, mosques, and minarets. The Austrian administration, excellent in matters of health, protection, and welfare, was regarded with increased suspicion by the Serbs, who feared the provinces would be lost forever to Greater Serbia. When two years later the provinces were formally annexed to the Hapsburg Empire, it started the train of events which exploded in the assassination of the Archduke, who was largely responsible for the policy of building a Slavic state within the Empire.

The chief result of our journey was Schevill's history of the Balkans, published some years later. I left him there to pursue his researches or collect his impressions and made my way by slow trains to Weimar. I stayed a night at Gratz, which was the center of the *Anschluss* movement. In conversation with a citizen at the Kaiser Wilhelm Café I inquired why it was not the Franz Josef Café, and was promptly informed that it would draw no custom under that name. He added, "Franz Josef hasn't showed his face in Gratz for fifty years." The streets were named for enemies of Austria, Prussian heroes, Bismarck and von Moltke, not omitting Frederick the Great. It seemed as if the chief enemies of the Austrian monarchy were German and its best friends the Slavs, but such judgment would have been superficial. The virus of nationalism had worked among all the ingredients of the pot, making Germans, Magyars, Czechs, Serbs, Croats, Poles, Slovaks, and Slovenes alike recalcitrant to melting and fusion.

5

In the three summers spent in Europe, mountain-climbing marked the high spots for Robert and for me. Nothing in my life has been so immediately rewarding. At Sand our first objective was the Schwarzenstein, which dominated the valley. We started early one afternoon, Ferdinand and I, with Robert and Beatrice, and two unnecessary guides. We arrived at the Schwarzensteinhütte above the snow line for supper. Just before bedtime Robert stood in the doorway looking out at the superb panorama of snow-clad peaks under the full moon. "This reminds me of our own Lake Zurich in the winter," he remarked.

The next summer we climbed Mount Ortler, the highest of the Eastern Alps, going up from the Berglhütte with two guides. At the hut, the night before we started, we met a party intending to do a stunt climb of an *Eiswand* that shone in the moonlight across the valley. As our guides were reputed first-rate, the serious mountaineers invited us to join them. Robert's eyes glistened, but a look at the perpendicular wall of ice was enough for me. I was satisfied with the Ortler. We met at the top the parties which had come up by other routes. The sun was just rising on Franz Josef's eightieth birthday, whereat we all sang Haydn's hymn:

Gott erhalte Franz den Kaiser
Unser guten Kaiser Franz—

since prostituted to "Deutschland über Alles." The descent had a troublesome *mauvais pas* at which the guides encouraged us with shouts of "*Keckheit! Nun, ein bischen Keckheit.*" At the worst spot the guides held the rope while we descended; then the head guide held the rope for the second; and we three stood braced on a narrow shelf to catch the leader. As he worked slowly, exploring the possibilities of hand- and foot-holds, we in turn shouted *Keckheit*, whereat he slithered down in a rush that nearly upset us all.

The next day we took the range of mountains that terminated in the Königspitze, the second highest of the Eastern Alps. Starting at midnight from the hut, we easily gained the crest and began to work along the ridge on the snow. The first guide, noting that my hands were bare, told me to put on my gloves. I explained that the gloves had been in my breast pocket, and in squeezing around a sharp corner I must have squeezed them out. The guide gave me some words, which Robert understood better than I did—and enjoyed. Not long after my frozen fingers lost their grip on my pickle, and the heavy ice ax went sliding down the snow field and bounced out of sight. We stood in the dim light of dawn while the head guide told me off in the bitterest speech ever addressed to me. The whole party was endangered by my carelessness.

There was a glorious sunrise on the Königspitze, but we did not linger long. A bad place was ahead, where falling stones were to be expected, and the guides declared that we must pass it before the sun melted the ice which held them fast. We reached it. It was a stony trail, nearly perpendicular, and without my pickle for balance I had to proceed slowly, while the guides stormed and an occasional rockfall from above gave point to their fears. I consoled myself by reflecting on kinds of courage. The guides were apparently fearless in places where they could control the situation. Where it was a matter of chance they were scared. On the other hand, I was frightened when I was responsible for my safety and that of others, but indifferent to a fate out of my control. At that moment I even invited it. Near the bottom we struck a long glissade. Robert shared his pickle with me and we shot down to the Cevedalehütte for breakfast. There we parted from the guides, with congratulations all around. My mishap became a joke, and I wondered whether the indignation had not been a well-played comedy and the compliments on my coolness a nice bit of irony.

6

The Easter of 1911 we joined the general *Ausflug* from Munich to the Italian lakes and went to the Garda See. As usual we took no thought for the morrow, or for the night, and trusted to luck to find rooms for five persons at sight. Every member of the family was a good sport, taking everything that came with gaiety, and this time luck was with us.

From a pleasant pension at Riva, Robert and I set forth to see the Trentino. It was April, too early for ascents, but we counted on getting through the Val Dalgone to Madonna di Campiglio. On the way by train we were accosted by a genial Italian youth sitting opposite who slapped my knee and exclaimed, "American! I saw your gold tooth." I apologized for being the victim of a bad period of dentistry, but he cut me short with, "I've got one. See." It was too far back to be effectively visible, but I changed my tone to one of congratulation. We were united by a national symbol. He explained that he had been a bartender in Trinidad, Colorado, but, learning that his girl was going with another fellow, he had returned to defend his claim. "And this is the chap now," he said as we stopped at a station and a young man entered and sat down in the section with us. The American enjoyed giving in English a character sketch of his rival, who was unconscious of being the subject of discourse. The latter was something of a dandy and wore his clothes well, having just returned from military service at Vienna. As he alighted at a station the man from Trinidad followed with blood in his eye, and an air which threatened the "mussing up" of the Viennese.

We started up the Val Dalgone in high spirits, but as we ascended we encountered snow, as we should have expected. It was heavy going, and we did not reach the height until well on in the afternoon. The going down was worse. It was so slippery that to keep on our feet was impossible, and we continually fell and rolled until stopped by the trees. As it grew dark I realized that we could not make the outlet and decided to try to cross over the mountain wall into the next valley. Fortunately we found a depression between the hills, and after a scramble up the wooded slope we saw the lights of a village in the valley below. On our descent, as we paused above what looked to be an inn courtyard, we heard a voice in English, ill tempered and upbraiding, but I was surely happy to hear it.

In a few minutes we were drying out before a fire and eating, while a company of a dozen men and women who had gathered quickly told of their adventures in the United States. When they heard that we were from Chicago they insisted that we should go on to the next town, Pinzolo, where they assured us we should find many of our neighbors. It was a weary two miles, but escorted by the company we made it after supper and found a numerous party waiting for us.

"Where do you live?" was a first question.

"I live on the Midway Plaisance."

"Is that so? I live at corner of Halsted and Taylor Streets." The original immigrant had followed the knife-and-scissors sharpening trade, and those who had gone after him had learned it before leaving as a sure way to make money. Later they had worked into other professions. The men had voted—by invitation. All expected to return to the States when their savings were exhausted.

The next day we ascended to Madonna di Campiglio, where the snow was hard enough for skiing and there were many to take advantage of it. I had a long talk about Italia Irredenta and, as at Pinzolo, I found no one who wanted to be redeemed. The excellent local administration was contrasted with the graft and misgovernment of the people "down below." Nearly all the people were Italian, and unless they had an upsurge of national feeling during World War I they probably suffered, along with the Austrians at Bozen and Meran, from Wilson's conception of self-determination. After all, the first loyalty of the Tirolese is to the Tirol. Andreas Hofer is the hero of them all, the Bavarians who captured him and the Italians who shot him.

7

The summer of 1911 was marvelous. Every day was a perfect mountain day. We joined Jeff and Agnes Fletcher and their children at Champéry in Switzerland. Two adults plus two are four, and two children plus three are five, a total of nine, a considerable party for which to find places in our happy-go-lucky fashion. After we had climbed the Dent du Midi, Champéry held nothing more to conquer, and Jeff Fletcher, Robert, and I set out on a scouting expedition which took us as far as Chamonix. The intensely hot weather that year had driven people from the cities, and every hotel was full. We advised staying in Champéry, but to our consternation received in reply a telegraph message—"Leaving Champéry. Meet you at Aigle."

I shall not forget the menace of the truck on the railroad platform at Aigle loaded with the luggage of the two families, which towered above me like the mountains over Christian at the beginning of his pilgrimage. It seemed as if the narrow-gauge engine could not draw the load. Fins-Hauts, halfway to Chamonix, had attracted us, and there we stayed "for one night only." Hotelkeepers were rationing their accommodations and exacting pledges of early removal. The next day we moved on to Chamonix. On our earlier visit we had seen rooms at the Hôtel des Alpes and had rejected them as inadequate, but necessity compels. I had learned in Carinthia the importance of being first off a train or boat and keeping ahead of the traffic, and so it was that I beat it through the town and found the same rooms, which now seemed palatial.

The high point of the summer was the Matterhorn, which I had vaguely promised Robert we would do. With strict injunctions from Agnes that Jeff was not to climb we three left Chamonix by the Col du Géant, descended into Italy, and over one of the easy passes to Zermatt. There we found two guides awaiting us. I did not know that when we had passed through Zermatt early in the season Robert had engaged them on his own responsibility. Although the Matterhorn is no longer to be accounted a major ascent, since a cable has been affixed to the steep slope covered by a sheet of black ice just below the summit, still by virtue of its history of long resistance, and the tragedy of its conquest, it occupies a place in the romance of mountain-climbing from which it will not be displaced.

The next morning Robert and I set forth for the hut, leaving Jeff disconsolately behind. It was a surprise to see him turn up in the afternoon with a guide, having broken connubial bonds and defied asthma and a doubtful heart—as always a sport. We made the peak about sunrise.

On our return we found Chamonix as crowded as ever. I spent a night in the jail. We found the two families a difficult combination in traveling and therefore went by different routes to Paris, where we were reunited for a last view of that capital of Europe before the catastrophe. It is probably an *ex post facto* sentiment that in retrospect makes me see that city as tinged with melancholy, though I never enjoyed it more—the theaters, the restaurants, the cafés. We took a long walk through the Forest of Marly, past our one-time home at L'Etang-la-Ville, to the little station of St. Nome-la-Bretèche. The children surrounded us like a covey of birds. It was gay, but it was autumn.

8

The several years I spent in Europe gave me a strong feeling, even a love, for the countries I lived in—Italy, England, France, Germany, Switzerland. I became a romanticist. My affection was drawn by nature, of which my first glimpse was on the journey from Boulogne to Paris past the bright green fields and poplar-bordered roads of Normandy. The lovely upper country of the Seine and the region of the Loire, the Val d'Arno from Fiesole, the English Midlands, the mountains of Bavaria, the Tirol and Switzerland, all remain with me in "the sessions of sweet silent thought." Except in a few instances, I did not know the people individually. Signora Traverso and old Louisa, our Florentine cook, Bishop Staley, Fräulein Dilthey in Weimar, with whom I exchanged English for German, the Hanfstaengls in Munich—I am astonished to think how few. I have no facility in language, and a sustained conversation soon exhausted me. I could hardly ever think of anything worth the trouble of translating. On the other hand, people in the mass attracted me strongly. They were so accessible to observation in the easy informality of churches, cafés, public gardens. I have sat for hours outside the Café de la Paix in Paris, never weary of the vivacity of the boulevards, or at the Café Panthéon, or the Deux Magots on the Left Bank. I remember a Sunday morning at Munich when we went to a *Rodelbahn* on the banks of the Isar, where scores of families sat on their sleds, moving courteously, without pressure, toward the take-off of the long slide through the sun-flecked pine forest to the river.

Compensation for my limited contacts was supplied by Ferd Schevill, who was my frequent companion in Europe and whose culture is completely European. His knowledge of the past constantly kindled my enthusiasm for history, which was another romantic element. Each of the countries I knew appeared to be in its civilization the natural result of forces within itself, and to possess an instinctive disposition for a certain form of organization. This seemed most perfectly worked out in England and Germany. Government in France and Italy was too much affected by imitation. I shared the feeling of Europeans against what was coming to be described as the American invasion. I thought it a crime for one nation to interfere with the government of another either by military force or financial power. I was early an internationalist. It was therefore natural for me to be horror-struck at the attack by my own country upon Spain, and later at our more terrible incursions into Europe and our ignorant efforts to order its life according to the reading of our own history. With a sense of pity and fear I recall in gratitude the privilege of seeing Europe, in its fading sunset it is true, but before it had sunk into irretrievable ruin. Several statesmen, including Napoleon and George Canning, have been reported as claiming to have called upon the New World to redress the balance of the Old. They did not foresee that the effect of that call would be to destroy the balance altogether.

VII. *Chicago*, 1911–1917

I

When we returned to Chicago we found an apartment at 1718 East Fifty-sixth Street, opposite Jackson Park, where we lived until we went to Hull House. It was in 1911 that George Vincent resigned to become president of the University of Minnesota, and as Angell succeeded him as Dean of the Faculties I had as my colleague in the senior colleges Dean Leon C. Marshall. As the latter became more and more absorbed by the College of Business Administration, I found the entire undergraduate body in my charge.

In thinking over these years my most vivid memories are of students. My courses in writing were the basis of more intimate acquaintance than large lecture courses, and the fact that we had a pleasant apartment, conveniently accessible, made hospitality easy, especially in connection with the Poetry Club. One day Harold Van Kirk, a student, called my attention to the fact that there was no course in the English Department specifically in poetry except a learned seminar labeled "English Versification," which dealt with theories chiefly expounded in German. I told him that I should hate to have academic standards applied to anything so personal and spontaneous as poetry and suggested that poetry, like athletics, should be an extracurricular activity, representing appreciative rather than utilitarian values. Why not form a poetry club?

Van Kirk was teaching and conducting boys' clubs at the Abraham Lincoln Center and therefore was limited in time spent on the campus and in association with fellow students. Nevertheless he found four lads of the same mind as himself, and I invited them to dinner, to meet Harriet Monroe, who as editor of the magazine *Poetry* was the recognized head of American poetry in the Middle West. Among the guests I remember especially Donald C. Peattie, now a prolific writer, and Robert Redfield, now Dean of the Social Science Division at the university. After dinner the poets read their verses, which Miss Monroe pronounced deplorable. It has always seemed one of the minor tragedies of college life that Van Kirk was that day taken to the hospital for an infection of the eyes, and as he soon after entered the Army he never attended a meeting of the club.

The next year only two members remained in college, but a new start was made, bringing into the club Glenway Wescott, Yvor Winters, Gladys Campbell, Elizabeth Madox Roberts, Janet Lewis, Vincent Sheean, and later Jessica and Sterling North and George Dillon, all of whom have achieved literary distinction. To stimulate production I offered a prize of twenty-five dollars, for which Vincent Sheean wrote two exquisite short poems. The prize became permanent through the gift of a thousand dollars by Horace Spencer Fiske in memory of his father. The John Billings Fiske prize has amply justified itself, but I have wondered what Mr. Horace Fiske, who was a poet of the older generation, thought of the harvest from his sowing.

Poetry was in the air in Chicago, and the club received much attention. It was entertained by local poets, by Mrs. Arthur Aldis at Lake Forest, by Harriet Monroe and Edgar Lee Masters, and had as guests, often at gatherings at my house, Robert Frost, Wilfrid Wilson Gibson, Carl Sandburg, Alfred Kreymborg, Padraic Colum, James Stephens, and others. The club was, however, fully self-sustaining. At first they read their own verses. I can hear today the light, sweet voice of Elizabeth Roberts reading her children's poems with the perfect touch of childhood shaded with humor. Later Helen Goodspeed, also gifted with a charming voice, was the reader. Helen Goodspeed was more than a poet. She was poetry—a girl with an exquisitely penetrating intelligence and a passion for life which carried her out of and beyond the academic setting. She had strained her heart playing tennis, and her times of intense joy of living were alternated by attacks of terrible pain, which she bore with unflinching gallantry until her death.

I did not encourage the young poets to publish, though Miss Monroe found the club a fund of support for her magazine. I did not wish to be responsible for increasing the flood of immature verse. With prose it was otherwise. Once, in drawing up the objects of a college education, I set down: "To make the student independent intellectually and economically"—not to leave him open to be used by others. Obviously, writing is a business as well as an art—a practical art like architecture. It is the office of a teacher of writing in a university to promote originality by helping a student to find his own best material, advising him as to form, and sometimes putting him in the way of publication. After I became a journalist I found that my usefulness in this last function was much increased.

Once I met a successful young magazine writer who told me with engaging frankness that my class had been of no use to him. He had later gone to Professor Walter B. Pitkin at Columbia. "He psychoanalyzed me," he reported, "and then I got started." I promptly realized my limitations. On the other hand, I had a certain practical sense of the ways of publishers and public. I recall with satisfaction my association with James T. Farrell. He was never in my classes, but he came to me one day with a manuscript of a short story about a boy named Studs Lonigan. I take credit for pointing out that the material suggested a novel rather than a story. I believe I was also responsible for his long and fruitful association with the Vanguard Press, which began with this book. I suggested to its president, James Henle, who raised the question of censorship, that it should be introduced with a foreword by Professor Trotter, the sociologist and authority on boys' gangs. *Studs Lonigan* remains a classic of the life of a boy in the outer courts of the underworld, so different from Aldrich's *Story of a Bad Boy* or Tarkington's *Penrod*. I have always taken great interest in Farrell's progress toward recognition as a writer of honest fiction, as a critic, and as a publicist.

I was not so happy in trying to link Meyer Levin with the Houghton Mifflin Company. His first book, *The Reporter*, is an original presentation of a young newspaperman, whose assignments constantly interfere with his private life, and whose faithful account of episodes and interviews are oddly at variance with the published versions in the Hearst papers. The publishers decided that in Boston they could not print certain words in reporters' vocabulary, which Levin, in the pride of his realistic art, would not change. He came into his own a few years later with *The Old Bunch*, published by the Viking Press.

Among Herrick's pupils was Janet Ayer Fairbank, who was later my good friend, and whose work I was happy to read in manuscript. I believe that *The Smiths* is one of the best novels written of Chicago. She and her sister, Margaret Ayer Barnes, inherited the best traditions of the middle-class aristocracy which made Chicago great. Mrs. Barnes' *Years of Grace*, like *The Smiths*, is a beautiful and pathetic study of parents and children, the tragedy of the generations.

One of the most promising students I ever had was Katharine Keith, who wrote in my class an autobiographical sketch which ran in two numbers of the *Atlantic Monthly* and was afterwards published by Holt as *The Girl.* Katharine was a granddaughter of Edson Keith, one of the group of pioneer merchants who made Chicago. Caught in the panic of 1893, he marched into the lake to his death, in order that his life insurance might be available to save his business and his family. Katharine had something of the same indomitable spirit. Her ambition to write was a flame, but she wrote with infinite attention to detail. For years her work was too precious for the public, but before her death in an automobile accident in France she had one success, *A Crystal Icicle.*

Among others whose early work I had the pleasure of reading is Helen Hull, who is building a growing reputation by fine, clean workmanship; Dorothy Scarborough, who wrote of Texas in *King Cotton* and *The Wind;* Katharine Anthony, whose *Margaret Fuller* was a pioneer in psychological biography; Viola Paradise, whose novels and short stories show flashes of genius. Vardis Fisher came from Idaho to live out his autobiographical epic, *In Tragic Life*, and later to tell the story of the Mormon migration in *Children of God.*

One of the chief policies of the English Department was to resist the demand for a school of journalism. President Harper, though tempted by the vision of a university which should include every feature in vogue elsewhere, stood firmly by us in our view that our work was to teach writing and literature and leave professional journalism to practical experience, which was then easy to obtain in Chicago. Nevertheless, a good many of our students have been highly successful in special journalistic fields, such as literary criticism and foreign affairs. Among critics Howard Mumford Jones, Harry Hansen, and Sterling North are today among the most active and influential; among writers on foreign affairs–Samuel Harper and Anna Louise Strong on Russia, Nathaniel Peffer on China, John Gunther and Vincent Sheean. One of the liveliest journalists today is Milton Mayer, who sat in my classes and took a good-natured revenge by drawing my portrait as "A Dangerous Man." Will Cuppy has made himself the chief critical authority on detective and mystery stories. Janet Flanner found the appropriate medium for her intelligent wit in *The New Yorker.*

At one time the magazine *Asia* was edited by two of our pupils, Gertrude Emerson and Elsie Weil, with Mary Elizabeth Titzel and Ernestine Evans closely connected as free-lancers. Gertrude Emerson later spent a year alone in a village of Northeast Hindustan and wrote a most intimate and revealing book, *Voiceless India.* Ernestine was mistress of too many talents and too interested in everything to devote herself to any specific thing. When she was a journalist in London after the First World War she discovered more good leads than anyone else and characteristically gave them away to her colleagues.

Another pupil whose work interested me greatly was Margaret Wilson, also a writer on India. She was for a long while secretary to a physician who directed a hospital for women in an Indian city of medium size, and she came to know intimately the tragedies of Indian women. She wished to follow the art of Maupassant rather than that of Kipling. After a year in the States without publication she returned to India and resumed her experience, keeping her objective distinctly in mind, with the result that her stories, signed "A Middle-Aged Spinster," were accepted by the *Atlantic Monthly*. She attempted a big novel of three generations about her ancestors in Iowa, which I tried to whip into shape in the conviction that here was the great American novel, but the canvas was too vast. Cut down to a single episode, it won the Pulitzer prize as *The Able McLaughlins.* Later, as wife of the governor of prisons in England, she wrote *The Crime of Punishment* and *One Came Out*, which made me an active supporter of the League to Abolish Capital Punishment.

A number of my students have entered the academic profession after taking the doctor's degree. Helen Sard Hughes wrote her thesis in my field and collaborated with me on the *History of the Novel in England.* She was later head of the English Department and Dean of the Graduate School at Wellesley. Carl Grabo wrote some of the best criticism I ever had from a student. He was appointed one of our instructors, and has written in many fields – philosophy, fiction, social and literary criticism. His recent work on Shelley has thrown new light on the working of the imagination of a poet. Morton Dauwen Zabel took a distinguished doctor's degree and is now a member of the English Department.

My list is already too long, but I recall notably two young men who came from Evansville, Indiana–Odell Shepard, whose *Harvest of a Quiet Eye* is a lovely story of a walking trip in Connecticut, and Paul S. Wood. Odell, who served as lieutenant governor of Connecticut in 1940–41, is now head of the English Department at Trinity College, and Paul holds the same position at Grinnell. Of Howard Mumford Jones, who came as a poet and left as a scholar and critic to follow a peripatetic course which led him finally to an honorary degree at the Harvard Tercentenary and a place on the faculty, I can speak with affection and admiration. He dedicated his life of Tom Moore to me.

I do not claim credit for the success of my students. In the matter of creative writing, so called, I repeat my conviction that literature cannot be taught *directly* in the making any more than in its appreciation. The essence of the matter is an inward vocation which, above all, a teacher is bound to respect. At a dinner given for me by students of the university on my final retirement Meyer Levin said of me:

> He never preached and he never lectured. Yet somehow I got from him a sense of being backed up, approved, as long as I was engaged in finding social truth. If he can be said to have encouraged any single tendency in literature, I believe that in his intangible and yet powerful way he did encourage this tendency. I could never show him anything that I didn't feel was basically good. He's the kind of teacher who continues to look over a writer's shoulder, all through a man's writing life. It is good that he's there.

This is what I hoped to be—"the invisible censor."

2

The early years of the century were marked by a revival of the drama as well as of poetry. Little theaters were springing up all over the country. In Chicago one of the most notable was directed by Maurice Browne. A more ambitious enterprise was undertaken under the lead of Mr. Arthur Aldis and Mr. Arthur Bissel, following the establishment of the New Century Theatre in New York, in order to give a hearing to plays of genuine literary merit, which would be "caviar to the general." For one season the Great Northern Theatre was rented. A play by Robert Herrick and John Harrison Rhodes, *The Maternal Instinct*, and another by Henry Kitchell Webster, achieved a certain *succès d'estime*. Then the guarantors hired Steinway Hall and rebuilt the interior as an intimate little playhouse, like the Residenzetheater in Munich. The director one year was B. Iden Payne, and the company included Walter Hampden and Marie Van Volkenberg. The cosmopolitan repertory extended from Rex Beach's *The Spoilers* to Valdez' *El Gran Galeoto*.

I wrote a play, *Cowards*, based on an experience of Joe Raycroft's, who, as a young medical student, had taken a terrific chance in delivering the baby of a high school girl in her own apartment, while her family was having a party, fortunately a noisy one, in the next room. My play enjoyed a *succès de scandale*. It was seized upon by the birth-controllers as propaganda for their cause. It was damned by Ashton Stevens of Hearst's *Herald-Examiner*, who explained that he reviewed it on the front page along with "murders, divorces and other scandals." Bert Taylor (B. L. T.) carried in his column, "A Line o' Type or Two," a caustic note on what Hearst's men think of their front page. The most devastating comment was Walter Hampden's. As we were having a drink at the Auditorium bar he remarked seriously, "The trouble is with the casting. We all want to play one part." "I suppose that is yours," I replied innocently. "No," said Hampden, "it's the foetus'."

The stir over drama was reflected in the university, where a dramatic club was formed. It had the distinction of producing among the first in this country the Irish plays of Yeats, Synge, and Lady Gregory. It was fortunate in having two girls with lovely voices, Lucine Finch and Vida Sutton, the former a dark, elfin creature, the latter a handsome blonde. Yeats himself, who saw *The Land of Heart's Desire* on his visit to Chicago, complimented the young players on their perfect delivery of his lines.

The effort to make Chicago a literary center was proceeding under the strenuous leadership of Hamlin Garland. He persuaded the recently formed National Institute of Arts and Letters to hold its annual meeting in Chicago in 1911 as a recognition of the city as a home of literature and culture. An essential condition of combating the tendency of Midwestern writers to move to New York was met by Stone and Kimball, who brought their little magazine *The Chap Book* to Chicago, and later expanded into general publication.

Some years before the meeting of the Institute of Arts and Letters Garland had launched a project for promoting cultural interests in Chicago which became of permanent value. Having in mind the Bohemian Club in Boston, the Salmagundi and Players' Club in New York, the Bohemian Club in San Francisco, he proposed to establish a similar institution for local writers, artists, musicians. The trustees of the Chicago Symphony Orchestra allowed a penthouse to be erected on the roof of Orchestra Hall. As space was limited, the best dining-car cook available was engaged. Garland named the club the Cliff Dwellers, from Fuller's novel, with the unhappy result that Fuller repudiated the club altogether.

Fuller became the editor of the literary supplement attached to the *Chicago Evening Post* and made it an important organ of criticism. His assistant was Tiffany Blake, who, like Fuller, was a critic of sensibility and taste. Another assistant, and his successor, was the notable Francis Hackett, who in turn passed the torch on to Floyd Dell, "Jig" Cook, and Llewellyn Jones. These last connected the *Post* with a much more vital literary development in Chicago than that represented by Hamlin Garland, the Cliff Dwellers, and the Institute of Arts and Letters. The credit for what is referred to currently as Chicago's Literary Renaissance belongs to the group which had its headquarters at Schlogl's Restaurant on South Wells Street. The book of autographs kept by Richard, the head waiter, is a collector's item.

The most important contribution to the literary reputation of Chicago was made by Miss Harriet Monroe. In 1913 she obtained contributions to a guarantee fund for the establishment of the magazine *Poetry*. This monthly drew together the emerging poets of the Middle West, Edgar Lee Masters, Vachel Lindsay, Carl Sandburg, and also attracted poets from the entire English-speaking world. Two years earlier Amy Lowell had introduced the Imagists as militant reformers of modern poetry, and they found allies in Harriet Monroe and her magazine.

3

No patronage of university people was so distinguished as that of Mrs. Edith Rockefeller McCormick. As the daughter of the Founder she had a special duty toward us. She organized a club known as "Lovers of Italy," before which Ferd Schevill lectured on Giotto and Mantegna and I read papers on D'Annunzio, Fogazzaro, and Sem Benilli.

Mrs. McCormick had built a superb mansion on Lake Shore Drive, where she proposed to bring together the university and the North Side. As there weren't enough cabs in the livery which served us, the ladies of the faculty monopolized them, and we, their consorts, went by Illinois Central or streetcar and rejoined our spouses in the anteroom. Mrs. McCormick had received as a wedding present from her father a gold dinner service, a source of gratified interest to Chicagoans, as was later the silver coffin of the gangster Dion O'Bannion. Unfortunately Mr. Rockefeller's social ambition ran only to dinner parties of twenty-four, while his daughter's soared to thirty-six. When we sat at her table, eighteen faculty couples to eighteen North Siders, I used to catch the eyes of my colleagues' wives wandering down the line to note whether we were discriminated against in the apportionment of golden vessels. Mrs. McCormick ran her team of servers with military precision. At the too early conclusion of each course the footmen swooped like harpies upon the plates, which they extricated literally between hand and mouth from the unwilling and unready guests.

Another patron of culture in Chicago and a local character somewhat exaggerated in type was Colonel George Fabyan. Colonel Fabyan was a cotton factor. He published a book, entitled *What I Know about the Cotton Trade*, consisting of three hundred blank pages. It had a wide circulation among cotton interests, especially in India, but was not quoted. As a farceur the Colonel was inimitable. When the Department of Agriculture undertook to eliminate the foot-and-mouth disease by compelling farmers to slaughter infected cattle, Colonel Fabyan surrounded his farm on the Fox River by a high barbed-wire fence and enlisted a corps of guards composed of ex-convicts commanded by a West Point graduate. Then, as the cream of the jest, he sued out an injunction forbidding the state to slaughter its own herd at the neighboring state farm at Geneva. He took a great interest in the home for delinquent girls at this village. It was enlivening to hear him call cheerfully at the entrance, "Where are my damned daughters?"

The Colonel was a speculator in junk, and among other purchases he bought the American set-up of the Shakespeare-Bacon controversy. Mrs. Ida Gallup and her niece, experts in reading ciphers, were brought from Boston and pleasantly established in a cottage on his estate with early editions of Elizabethan authors. In italicized passages they found letters peculiar in type which, being put together, conveyed messages to the general effect of Baconian authorship. Apart from the impossibility of a universal conspiracy among typesetters in Bacon's interest, the method proved too much. Within chronological limits most of Elizabethan literature could be and was attributed to Bacon.

One day I received a letter from Ellery Sedgwick, of the *Atlantic Monthly*, saying that he had received a communication in regard to a discovery of great literary importance from Colonel Fabyan with an invitation to visit him which he proposed to accept. He invited me to go along. The meeting of New England and the Middle West, each somewhat exaggerated in its representation, made a comedy which I was happy not to miss.

On our arrival Sedgwick and I were assigned a large room at the top of the house, where we were soon assailed by an incredible burst of sound. The Colonel had installed an orchestrion, which he played for total effect in his drawing-room, with instruments placed in different rooms of the house. The percussion was under our beds.

At dinner there was another terrific racket, this time from the veranda which, we later discovered, was completely enclosed by cages of monkeys and kindred simian types. When they shook their bars in concert the clanking was hellish. I saw the Colonel gently maneuvering Sedgwick toward a cage from which a long hairy arm protruded swiftly, and horned fingers clutched the editor of the *Atlantic* by the collar and shook him like a leaf. He was a good sport. As we were going to bed after other adventures, Ellery asked me if this sort of domestic life was usual in the Middle West.

In the end it appeared that Fabyan wanted to sell a continuation of Bacon's *New Atlantis* which turned out to be the sketch of Utopia in Burton's *The Anatomy of Melancholy*.

If Fabyan's version of the Baconian hypothesis was rejected by scholars it was accepted by higher authority. When another Chicago colonel was producing *Romeo and Juliet* on the screen as Shakespeare's work, Fabyan induced him, for the sake of publicity, to bring suit to enjoin propaganda in favor of Bacon's authorship. A Chicago judge, a friend of both parties, solemnly pronounced the verdict: "Out, Shakespeare! You stole Bacon's plays."

4

Outside the university my chief concern in those years was in getting rich. This ambition led me to look westward—to the fading frontier of America rather than to the culture of Europe. The complex of influences which worked this new disposition is clear in my mind today. First was my horse Jim. I used to ride with Herrick and his younger sister Bessie in the great fields then lying between the university and the industrial city of Pullman. It was Bessie who induced me to buy Jim, who became one of my best friends, full of gaiety and humor. Later I kept him at Lake Geneva at Kellogg Fairbank's and rode week-ends with Janet Fairbank, whose adventurous spirit led us into exploration of the exquisite Wisconsin country. I learned then the fact that man on horseback is a different character from man at the desk.

In the second place there was Fred Nichols. He had been one of my charges in Snell Hall during my second year at Chicago. He was the best athlete we had, halfback on the football eleven, pitcher on the baseball team. I admired his prowess. When he returned to the university years later with a plan of settling a group of professors on an estate in the Bitter Root Valley, Montana, where on each lot of ten acres eight hundred apple trees could be grown, yielding after five years a dollar a tree per annum, the prospect was pleasing. Many of my academic friends were buyers, including a group from the University of Wisconsin.

My first visit to my estate was in 1912 with Henry Gale, who had also been one of my boys in Snell, now professor of physics. The first stage of the journey was to St. Paul, where we bought khaki pants, blue denim shirts, and sombreros. Next came three days on the Northern Pacific, past legendary Butte to Missoula. Thence up the Bitter Root Valley to the Ravalli Hotel at Hamilton, where the walls were decorated with reminiscences of the sport and crime of the pioneers. A drive of thirty miles brought us almost to the apex of the valley where, above the little town of Darby, the orchards already flourishing were spread along a bench among the foothills.

The scenery was magnificent. To the east, the Rockies; to the west, the Bitter Root Mountains, rising eleven thousand feet to the summit of El Capitán. The green valley and hillsides crowned by snow peaks reminded me of the Engadine. The air had a stimulating tang. The clubhouse, with great open fireplaces, was full of cheer. A dashing brook from Tin Cup Lake brought water which was distributed through irrigation ditches. There were trout in the Bitter Root River; trails through the mountains; the promise of a hunting party in the autumn over the divide into the wild Clear Water country of Idaho. I can only describe the whole effect as intoxicating. I was ready to abandon literature for orcharding. Trees seemed more satisfactory than students. Somehow in the course of successive summer visits I became owner of three hundred and forty acres, and twenty-seven thousand trees, apple, cherry, and crab, promising an annual income of that number of dollars, increasing fivefold with the years. When the enterprise was consolidated into a stock company I enjoyed being the whale among the swarm of little fishes.

Every summer I anticipated the journey westward. So eager was I to reach the Bitter Root that I must have passed the Gardiner Gateway to Yellowstone Park a dozen times, untempted. One summer I took Robert to see his inheritance. I was delighted to see him shoot over the head of his bucking horse and leap at once to take the saddle again. One year we went with Fred Nichols and his wife and daughter to Glacier Park, just opened to tourists, and still quite primitive. The deformed mountains were as impressive, though in a very different fashion, as the Dolomites. One afternoon as we were scrambling down a cliff I found a trail promising an easy descent, but Fred Nichols and Robert preferred the hard way. From the bottom I looked up and saw the two figures on a narrow shelf, scouting this way and that for a practicable exit, and as I watched them I had a comfortable feeling that the boy would never be afraid.

When I returned to the Bitter Root in 1916 the bloom was off the fruit. On the bench there were two older orchards which had not suffered from pests, and it was thought that the narrow valley was naturally quarantined. The first year, however, the transcendent crabs showed blight and had to be pulled out. Then came a succession of attacks, that of the Colorado leaf roller being especially ferocious. State inspection and requirements of spraying became a heavy charge. The advantage of the high valley for growing apples with the tang and aroma of northern fruit turned into disappointment. Year after year a late frost caught the blossoms or an early freeze caught the fruit. The orchards specialized in the Mackintosh Red, which was becoming popular, but farmers in Vermont and New York entered the market, and freight rates to the East went up. Each season left a deficit.

Fortunately we had two angels. Among the original small holders were my classmate Alexis I. Du Pont and his younger brother Eugene. While others fell by the wayside they showed the persistence which has been a factor in the career of their distinguished family. Our manager was a University of Wisconsin man, equally persistent. Each spring he and I would proceed to Wilmington, Delaware, where in the great skyscraper, as in a cocoon, nested some sixty-seven Du Ponts. Alexis was always affable, but at the mention of money he took alarm. "I'll have to ask Eugene." Eugene was hard-boiled—"Nothing doing,"—but hospitable. Cocktails—several. An excellent luncheon. Talk of Harvard in the nineties. Jokes about my pacifism threatening the traditional prosperity of E. I. Du Pont de Nemours. I believe that it was sentiment, with something of business pride, that carried the day, and the University Heights Orchard Association lived for another year.

And many others. After our manager took his career elsewhere I lost hope and interest, and though I received notices of annual meetings I did not attend until, in 1938, came a final call for the winding up of the enterprise. I went to New York concerned only with how much of my loss I could charge off against my income.

The meeting took place in the office of the Peyton-Du Pont Company, which I took to be a sort of dog-house where are kept the canine and feline outcasts of the Du Pont family. The only other attendant was the secretary of the company. He told an unvarnished tale of misfortune. The University Heights Orchard Company had become the Mackintosh-Morello Company. It was unable to meet the exactions of the state horticultural inspection. The apple trees were pulled out in favor of cherries. Still under pursuit, the cherry trees were pulled and the estate was put into wheat. Wheat became a drug on the market and was replaced by hogs. These died of cholera. The company tried to sell or give away the property, but it was tied up with a contract to supply water to neighboring farmers. They tried to force the state to take it over for taxes. Finally I suspect they arranged to have someone buy it so that they could charge off the losses against income taxes. That was also my interest.

Part II

"Contention is the vital force."

VIII. *War*, 1917–1918

I

IN 1917 I was forty-six years old. I was enjoying my life in the pleasant walks of academe, very much at ease in Zion. Professor Palmer's advice to me to become a part of an institution had borne fruit. I had grown into the university and was at home in the city of Chicago. Our children were almost perfect. On returning from Germany Robert had gone to Andover, where his great-grandfather had been a pupil, and later to Harvard. At Andover he lived in the house of Master Benner, my college roommate, and at Harvard his adviser was Ken Rand, who was his godfather. Beatrice was at Radcliffe. Ruth was varying the noiseless tenor of our life by becoming a ballet dancer. So we dwelt after the manner of the Sidonians, quiet and secure.

It was almost by accident that I was drawn from academic seclusion and a passive attitude of good will into activities which I had hitherto avoided, preferring the aloofness of cynicism and the seat of the scorner.

The year 1912 had seen the emergence of the Progressive party, which I had not joined. My friends, liberals like Jane Addams, Donald Richberg, Kellogg and Janet Fairbank, had been fanatical supporters of the Bull Moose, but I distrusted Roosevelt from the time of the Spanish War as an imperialist and a self-seeker. When war broke out in Europe two years later I regretted for a time that he was not in the White House, thinking that his energetic diplomacy might have brought Europe to its senses, but in the end I approved Wilson's declaration of neutrality in thought, word, and deed.

The campaign of 1916 was fought on the issue of war or peace. Wilson's appeal was based on the claim of his party: "He kept us out of war." The Republican position was ambiguous. The Progressive party was bound up with Roosevelt's leadership, which demanded intervention on behalf of the Allies. I sat in a box in the

Auditorium looking down on the assembly of earnest men and women who had joined the cause of domestic reform in 1912 and now called on their leader to keep faith. They were betrayed. I saw a famous Harvard professor, Albert Bushnell Hart, gather about him the delegates from Massachusetts and read them Roosevelt's letter advising the nomination of Henry Cabot Lodge in order to facilitate reunion with the Republicans. Professor Hart's face was purple and he trembled with indignation; his associates turned away in disgust. We on the side lines knew that Roosevelt had refused the nomination, but the delegates were entertained by the managers, George W. Perkins, Bainbridge Colby, and Raymond Robins, with plans for the campaign (and reminded profusely of the time of trains leaving Chicago), until the convention was worn down to a frazzle incapable of a demonstration when the word of their leader's desertion became known.

Ruskin had written years before that war existed only by permission and acquiescence of women: Let them go into mourning, wear black, abjure ornament, deny beauty, in unanimous protest against slaughter. His idealism was voiced by the Women's Congress at the Hague in 1915, in their proposal that the neutrals should offer continuous mediation. Later Jane Addams visited the foreign offices of the belligerents and found the plan generally received as statesmanlike. President Wilson promised the support of the greatest of the neutrals in his "peace without victory" speech, until he found that the United States was no longer neutral.

2

In the winter of 1917 the prospects of peace without victory seemed hopeful. The re-election of Mr. Wilson could be regarded only as a mandate of the country, though by a narrow margin, against entering the war. In the preceding December the Reichstag had passed a resolution in favor of accepting arbitration by neutrals. This feeling found expression later in Lord Lansdowne's letter urging a negotiated peace. Kaiser Franz Josef had been succeeded by Karl, at whose instigation Prince Sixtus de Bourbon had approached the French cabinet with proposals to take Austria out of the war. If his letter had been published at the time, it seems probable that the Army and people of France would have demanded peace. On the virtual suppression of the Austrian proposals by Clemenceau and Ribot, Francis Corday remarked bitterly, "Blood is the milk of old men."

Doubtless the election of Wilson led the German High Command to the belief that even a submarine campaign against neutral shipping to cut off supplies to the Allies would not bring the United States into the war. Possibly if von Bernstorff had been allowed to proceed to Germany without delay at Halifax, the immediate cause of war might have been removed by diplomacy. It was reported that in England and France many persons were shocked and disgusted at the action of the United States in declaring war, which nullified all hopes of peace which had been cherished through three winters of discontent.

Immediately after our entrance into the war I was among those who believed that the declaration of war by Congress created an opportunity for a declaration of our will to peace, and its terms. Wilson already had his Fourteen Points in mind. The Allies were dependent on the assistance of the United States. Great Britain had come to the end of her financial resources; France had exhausted her manpower. The first revolution in Russia made doubtful her further participation in the war. Even if the Fourteen Points had not been immediately accepted, the basis of the peace which Wilson desired and died for would have been established and might have replaced the secret treaties among the Allies, of which his official ignorance was to cost many lives including his own. In the spring of 1917, in the game in which the stakes were the lives of millions then alive and yet to be, human decency, civilization, the peace of the world, Wilson held all the high cards. In the intoxication of unwonted popularity he threw them away, and went to Paris two years later with empty hands and only talk to play against fact.

Resentment at the fact that the country had been eased into the situation, so frankly indicated later by Ambassador Page as an alternative between war and panic, and disgust at the folly of the statesmen whom I had trusted, led me to join the movement for closing our commitments before they resulted in spiritual and intellectual bankruptcy. In view of the importance of making known the position of the United States in entering the European war and underwriting the future settlement of Europe, meetings were held in various cities in April 1917 to urge President Wilson to make clear his purpose. A great audience gathered in New York under the chairmanship of Rabbi Judah Magnes. A similar meeting was projected in Chicago. At the outset it was believed that the occasion would command the support of the League to Enforce Peace, which was strong in Chicago under the leadership of Walter L. Fisher, recently Secretary of the Interior in President Taft's cabinet. His son Arthur was secretary of the *ad hoc* committee formed by pacifists and Socialists. There were, so far as I remember, no German-Americans on the committee, but Russia was represented by a schoolteacher by the name of Berg; later he went to China as political adviser to Sun Yatsen, where he was known as Borodin. The Auditorium was engaged for Sunday afternoon, May 27.

The newspapers were not unfriendly at first, but they very quickly developed an attitude that became characteristic of the country during this war. The belligerent spirit inspired noncombatants with a thirst for battle that found expression in a militant home front. Although responsible publishers in general were sensible and fair, city editors and reporters could not be restrained from joining the hue and cry against conscientious objectors, Socialists, German-Americans, and unpopular groups like the I. W. W. Our committee rapidly dissolved. Bill Chenery, now of *Collier's*, said that his paper, the *Chicago Evening Post*, insisted on his withdrawal. In the end the chairmanship went to me by default.

I took every precaution against misrepresentation. The resolutions were carefully scrutinized. I rehearsed my opening address before the remnant of the committee and the other speakers in order to secure general agreement:

> This meeting has been called for the sole and explicit object of representing to the administration the general desire that as soon as possible the war aims of the United States be set forth, together with the terms of peace which represent their fulfillment. . . . This meeting is not held to pass any criticism on the course of our country in entering the war. On the contrary, we fervently hope that Mr. Wilson's belief will be justified that by that course an earlier ending may result. We believe that the power and influence of the United States are capable of imposing on the world the terms of a righteous and lasting peace. It would be a crime unspeakable if for any preventable cause the war lasted one day, one hour, beyond the moment when such terms are attainable. But to know that moment the terms must be known.

I quoted Wilson's defense of peace without victory:

"Only a peace between equals can last; only a peace the very principle of which is equality and a participation in a common benefit." This I believe is a translation into terms of internationalism of Lincoln's "with malice toward none, with charity to all."

It would be worth while to hold such meetings as this if for no other purpose than to repeat these words of Lincoln and of Wilson—so that if possible the warfare that we wage should not add one drop of bitterness to the cup already overflowing of the world's agony. Some may say that the words "Peace without Victory" were spoken before we entered the war—that they were spoken for others, not for the United States. I should reply that if the United States by proposals can secure a righteous peace, that itself will be a victory so far transcending the glory of any achievement of arms that comparison is literally unthinkable. . . .

However that peace comes, it must be a peace with power. This country is rapidly assembling the forces, military and financial, necessary to impose such a peace. We are here to urge that it put behind these mighty engines the moral power to make such a peace as speedily as may be, and for all time. I am not afraid that this country will prove a slacker in war. If I have any fear it is that in the heat of the conflict we shall forget in some measure the ideals of democracy and world peace with which we set out. To guard against this it seems that nothing can be so useful as to have those ideals set forth in a form as explicit as possible as the conditions of the peace for which we are striving.

As I approached the Auditorium on that hot Sunday afternoon I was amazed to see the crowd blocking Congress Street and overflowing into Grant Park. The hall was already packed. It is true that the meeting was hailed as a protest against the war, but the speakers kept within the bounds set by our announced subject. Mary E. MacDowell of the University of Chicago Settlement was one; the Reverend Fred A. Moore, who afterwards lost his pulpit in the war hysteria, was another; Seymour Steadman, the leading Socialist of Illinois, gave a timely warning of possible divergence between our proper objectives in the war and the designs of the Allies. Meanwhile the crowd outside became restless. The police asked me to send our speakers to address an outdoor assembly, but I refused. Within doors we could control the meeting. Outside various soap-box gatherings challenged the clubs of the police. The reporters were naturally more interested in violence than in reason, and the newspapers next morning reduced the whole affair to an anti-war riot.

I shall always believe that if the course we advocated at the Auditorium meeting had been followed the world might have been spared the continuation and disastrous conclusion of World War I, and World War II which that conclusion made inevitable. It may, of course, be argued that if the peace tentatives of 1917 had been successful they would have resulted in a mere truce, during which the armaments race would have been resumed with added zeal. On the other hand, it may be that the Social Democrats in Germany would have gained strength in view of their part in forcing peace, and that a peace without victory would have been an object lesson to all nations of the futility of war. Possibly the losses already sustained would have cooled the hot blood of the French and English, so that, as after the Napoleonic Wars, they would have eschewed arms for a generation. It is true, conditions are different. The modern world offers but a narrow margin for peace between war and revolution. The dichotomy between existing means of production, permitting an economy of abundance, and the control of production by private interests to maintain an economy of scarcity, according to communist doctrine, makes war inevitable in the policy of capitalistic nations as a means of absorbing production and averting unemployment. It is probable that peace in 1917 would have prevented the Bolshevik revolution in Russia. The Kerenski government would have been maintained by the Allies, and if Lenin had succeeded in overthrowing it Germany would have accepted the mandate of the Allies to bring Petrograd and Moscow within the *cordon sanitaire*.

3

An amusing aftermath of the Auditorium meeting occurred the next evening. I was out of the city during the day and returned to find Hyde Park sprinkled with circulars calling on citizens to meet in front of my apartment on Fifty-sixth Street, opposite Jackson Park, to demonstrate against my disloyalty. I was troubled by the fact that I had an important engagement, nothing less than a student's examination for the doctor's degree. I was hesitating between rival attractions when Bill Chenery arrived in his car and insisted on driving me to the university, arguing rightly that in my absence the demonstration would be a dud, while if I appeared even as a spectator, the newspapers would find it a *bonne bouche*. I was hanged in effigy. Next day someone brought me the collar of the effigy, in which was the laundry mark "Smith," explaining that the owner was an English alien.

Unfortunately Mr. Smith's interpretation of the Auditorium meeting was shared by most of my respectable fellow-citizens and my colleagues. I had opportunity to learn the truth of Samuel Butler's assertion that of three misfortunes, loss of money, loss of health, and loss of reputation, the last is by far the least. I was rather surprised myself at the ease with which I ceased to be a men-pleaser. I had, it is true, taken pains to mark the meeting as in no sense intended as an obstacle to the prosecution of the war, but the inveterate malice of the press demanded victims and would not be balked.

At a number of small neighborhood meetings we continued to insist on the distinction between anti-war and pro-peace. One day a reporter of Hearst's *Examiner* came to show me the report which he had written of one of these meetings. He had rewritten it a second time at the order of his superiors, who had finally themselves written the inflammatory account which was printed. Our proposal was, in fact, in accord with Mr. Hearst's personal editorials, but the popular appeal was to passion. The box office determined the policy of his papers.

A former student, in a flattering sketch of me written for La Follette's *Progressive*, stated that I attacked the war from auditorium platform and from the soap box, and even tried to spread disaffection among the armed forces. Nothing could be further from the truth. My son was in training at Plattsburg, and was sent to France in the following autumn. I shared his opinion that since the government had accepted total war, it remained only to carry through the dreadful task. In any case, I could not repudiate his sacrifice and that of his comrades. My only action during the war years was outlined by two letters in the *New Republic*. One warned the administration that by condoning acts of violence and suppression on the part of individuals it was in reality weakening the will of the nation to war. In this I was wrong. The actual weakening was of the will to peace, which was disclosed in the abandonment of Wilson at Paris. The other letter followed Professor Dewey in advising pacifists to avoid losing ground by opposing the war measures directly, particularly the draft, and to concentrate their efforts on protecting individuals who were the sufferers from such opposition, as in the case of conscientious objectors, or more particularly those who were the victims of false accusation and legal tyranny.

4

The sedition law, of which Senator Thomas Walsh was the author, was unnecessary in view of existing laws punishing anything leading to overt acts. Only after the war did Federal Judge Anderson in Massachusetts declare that ninety-five per cent of cases brought under it were without merit. Its mischievous effect was largely in its initiation of legislation by the states, under which hundreds of cases were brought to gratify public prejudice or private malice. These cases involved activity in strikes, distribution of literature, membership in peace organizations, but I believe in no single instance violence or incitation to violence. These laws gave color and countenance to the hysteria which was compensation to noncombatants for lack of military glory.

Many manifestations of synthetic patriotism were so extreme as to defeat their purpose. The outgivings of the apostles of hate among the clergy were so ludicrous as to recoil on their reverend heads. The atrocity-mongers, even behind the great name of Viscount James Bryce, could be ignored. The minute-men and other strategists of verbal warfare could be endured, though I felt for teachers and pupils of Chicago schools who were compelled to suspend education to listen to self-advertising patriots of the Council of Defense or the Chamber of Commerce. At the university a corps of the faculty drilled conscientiously. A German-born professor of chemistry proposed at a faculty meeting that all activities of the university not directly connected with winning the war should be suspended for the duration, whereat the professor of Latin, whose chief preoccupation was Catullus, asked plaintively where he came in. One great service the university rendered through Professor Manly, who became the most proficient decoder and reader of cipher messages in Military Intelligence. He gradually drew nearly all his colleagues from the English Department to Washington. As I directed the department in his absence I often thought of the picture in *Punch* of a curate who when challenged by the inquiry in regard to doing his bit replied that he was "carrying on with the young ladies."

The really dangerous and obscene phenomena of the war on the home front were the efforts on the part of civilians to profiteer in patriotism by bearing tales of the disaffection of their friends, neighbors, or merely accidental associates. This vile feature of Hitler's later conquest of Germany was anticipated in the United States during World War I and inexcusably continued for years afterwards.

During the Civil War there had been attacks on civil liberties, but these had usually been initiated by the executive and heads of military departments, while the courts in most cases had stood stanchly for the protection of individuals. During World War I the situation was reversed. Judges and district attorneys swung into action, often showing themselves avid of the public applause which fell to them as a result of the persecuting mania. President Wilson and at least some members of his cabinet tried to mitigate the popular fury. Secretary of War Newton D. Baker protested against the publication of lists of suspects by the Overman Committee of the Senate. Secretary of the Treasury William G. McAdoo went to Iowa to tell the farmers not to flog and hang their neighbors who were reluctant to buy so-called Liberty Bonds. In the end the administration too succumbed.

The uncompromising opposition to the war announced by the Socialist party at St. Louis led to a general proscription of Socialists. Eugene Debs was tried and sentenced for attacking the selective service law, which President Wilson described in honeyed phrases as "in no sense a conscription of the unwilling; it is rather selection from a nation which has volunteered in mass." Congressman Victor L. Berger was expelled from the House of Representatives. In the Chicago federal court there was a trial before Judge Kenesaw M. Landis of five members of the party, at which I was happy to appear as a witness for the Reverend St. John Tucker, who had done magnificent work for the Auditorium meeting.

Judge Landis was the judge before whom a hundred members of the I. W. W. were brought to trial on the charge of obstructing the war effort, on the evidence of various publications of the organization. I suggested to their attorney that there is a ritual of violence, as there is a ritual of pacifism in Christianity, to which the subscribers pay lip service without in the least intending to put the code into practice. This did not impress the jury, which after twenty minutes of deliberation brought in an indiscriminate verdict of guilty. On what basis Judge Landis apportioned the fund of some hundreds of years of punishment I could not imagine. Charles Ashley, an English journalist, whose association with the I. W. W. was that of a student of social phenomena, got his portion with the rest. They went to

Leavenworth, where they remained long after the armistice. In the failure of the Senate to ratify the Treaty of Versailles the United States remained technically at war with Germany, a fiction which Wilson maintained as a vehicle for his exasperation against all who had criticized him. The visit of wives and children of the condemned to the White House was a pathetic plea for clemency to which his successor listened. Whatever may be said of President Harding, he had the quality of compassion, which extended even to Eugene Debs.

The I. W. W. was the most bitterly hated of all labor organizations, not only by employers, but by the orthodox churches of labor led by Samuel Gompers. It was literally wiped out in blood by mobs with the connivance or assistance of the authorities and the approval of the public. Nor was the I. W. W. the only organization which vested interests made a casualty of the war. The Non-Partisan League had achieved a promising start among the farmers in North Dakota and was spreading into neighboring states. A former colleague on the *Harvard Monthly*, Horace Davis, who was engaged in marketing the bonds of the state to pay for erecting grain elevators and developing other means of making farmers independent of middlemen, told me of the rejection of the investment by bankers because of the opposition of boards of trade in Minneapolis and other marketing centers. Worse than this, the missionaries of the League in rich farming states such as Iowa were mobbed, beaten, tarred-and-feathered, left for dead. A device to discredit the organization, which became typical of tory propaganda in the United States, was the accusation that it advocated "free love."

A special cause of dissatisfaction with the conduct of the war was the treatment of conscientious objectors. At the outset, Secretary Baker and Assistant Secretary Frederick P. Keppel announced a generous policy, but it was not maintained. Some outstanding personalities, like Carl Hessler of the University of Illinois, carried off their protest with distinction. Hessler conducted a school at Leavenworth for political prisoners and won the respect of his jailors. On the other hand, we heard shocking stories of the treatment of men of obscure religious sects such as Doukhobors and Molokans, who in some cases were done to death in military prisons and then dressed in the uniforms which they had died for refusing to wear, and so sent back to their families. Later Judge Julian Mack was appointed to examine objectors and more reasonable treatment resulted.

The case of a former student of mine, Brent Dow Allinson, came home to me closely. Allinson transferred to Harvard before the war. There, as an editor of the *Monthly*, he wrote vigorous editorials against the participation of the United States. Brent was appointed to the Legation to Switzerland, but on the demand of his local draft board he was summoned to Washington, then returned to Chicago, and on his refusal to bear arms was sentenced to Leavenworth. His father and mother, who had long been devoted social workers at a settlement house in Chicago, were forced by the trustees to resign—an illustration of how easily the victory in war can be turned into the tragedy of useful lives lost to society.

The misuse of the war by the patriots who fought on the home front to eliminate competitors in business, to pay off grudges, to gain prestige, or merely to satisfy a desire for action, was painful to us whose sons were at the front. A case at the University of Chicago was that of the son of a professor of Romance languages. The boy's background was German and his grandparents were then living in Germany. In the privacy of his fraternity house his "brothers" badgered him into saying that he "would like to stick a knife into Wilson." They reported this seditious utterance to the district attorney, who had the boy arrested, jailed, brought to trial, and fined five hundred dollars. It is to the credit of the university that then, as always, it stood behind its members. The attorney for the university appeared in defense and a subscription among the faculty paid the fine.

It may seem that this recital of outrages on the home front is gratuitous and irrelevant. It is not. They were an essential part of my life during the years of war. My thoughts were divided between anxiety on account of boys at the front, especially my son, who I knew would give himself to danger rather than avoid it, and indignation against the perpetrators of deeds at home which make the minor horrors of war. On the one hand, I had new reason to hate war, and on the other, I carried in future years a resentment against the ruthless exercise of power by the strong against the weak, and a disgust at society which permits it and the government which condones it.

5

When on trial in 1935 before a committee of the Senate of Illinois, appointed to investigate communist teaching in institutions of higher learning, I was asked, perhaps irrelevantly, what advice I should give my son, or had given him, in regard to joining the armed forces in war. I replied truthfully that I should give, or had given, no advice whatever. This answer was unfavorably regarded as showing a lack of patriotism, but it was warmly defended by Mr. Evjue in the *Capital Times* of Madison, Wisconsin.

Robert had enlisted in the Harvard R.O.T.C., and on the declaration of war applied for training at Plattsburg. My friends James and Jane Wheeler invited Ida and me to visit them at Burlington, Vermont, across Lake Champlain, and their hospitality is one of my grateful memories of that time. After he was commissioned as second lieutenant Robert came to Chicago for a farewell visit. When he took his train for the East I rode with him as far as Englewood and, seeing him somewhat downcast, I encouraged him by reminding him that he had gone through the first hard initiation with credit, and now would have under him boys fresh from home, confused and homesick, whom he could help in many ways. He cheered up at once. "They'll be like my boys at South Boston," he said. "I must be a father to them."

The reality was rather different. He was assigned to Company E, 103rd regiment of the 26th (New England) Division, which was composed of militia regiments of Maine and New Hampshire. Company E was from Skowhegan, commanded by Captain James Healy—a hard-boiled bunch who must have resented the second lieutenant imported to bring the latest West Point technique by way of Plattsburg. Ida and I saw Robert in camp at Westfield, Massachusetts, doggedly putting his platoon through murderous bayonet exercises, a boy hardly twenty-one instructing veterans. His grandfather, a gentleman of the old school, asked the general in command of the division to have the boy transferred for further training on this side, and the general, also of the old school, was willing to oblige, but Robert refused any intervention on his behalf. The next we heard was of his voyage to France on the *Leviathan*, where he spent his time below watching the bulkheads.

Robert thoroughly enjoyed his military life. His letters were gay, amusing. He was always well, and never afraid. He became a favorite with the company, and his strong home-loving instinct found a place among men whom he loved. The top sergeant told me how he would carry the pack and rifle of an exhausted private at the end of a long march. Robert was especially concerned in his training with methods to save the lives of his men. The regiment was engaged at Cantagnies while he was away at officers' school, and men were killed. On his return, when he stood before his platoon he was in tears. Captain Healy said they used to tease him by threatening to report him for staff work because of his knowledge of German and French; and on being detailed for school he made a special request for his return to Company E.

On August 5, 1918, we received the dispatch from the War Department: "Killed in action." It had happened on July 18 in Belleau Wood, at the beginning of Foch's triumphant offensive. Later there came a letter from Maude Radford Warren, a former student, who was a correspondent at the front. She met by chance a week later a group of soldiers on the way to the rear, heard the familiar name, and stopped to inquire. Her letter stated that the 103rd Regiment was ordered forward early in the day to cross a wheat field and a narrow-guage railway track to occupy a wooded hill beyond. Robert's platoon suffered severely in the wheat, and he crawled back to report to Captain Healy, "Captain, they're sniping my men. Have I got to go on?"

The Captain replied that the woods had to be taken. ("I told Lovett he had to do it. I thought it was only a bit of brush. Anyway it had to be done.") So Robert said, "All right. I'll go on with what men I have left."

He started back and arrived safely to his men. They crawled on a bit further and then halted for a time; they had been losing men pretty heavily. Robert kept crawling up and down his line of men to give them instructions and see how things were going. At something like nine o'clock Robert was shot in the thigh. He said, "That's a funny place to get hit." That wound was evidently not serious. Some of the men I talked with say that at that moment the order came for the company to retreat and that Robert began to crawl back with the others. Some say that before the order came to retreat he was again shot . . . this time in the head. The two men beside him were also shot. It may have been machine-gun firing.

Mrs. Warren wrote of a corporal named Lancto, who was beside Robert at the end, but whom she could not find. I saw him some years later, a typical French-Canadian poilu. I gathered from him that the platoon had reached the embankment of the narrow-gauge railway and lay behind it while Robert watched for the expected counterattack.

"He kept talking to us," said Lancto, "and joking."

"What did he say," I asked. "Can't you remember?"

"Oh, he didn't say anything—he just knew we wanted to hear his voice. He was hit again, but he didn't seem to mind. After a while we didn't hear him. . . ."

The losses were very heavy. Captain Healy told me that his roll call, which in the morning showed a full complement of two hundred and fifty, at night was only twenty-nine. Nearly every family in Skowhegan was in mourning. Robert's body was recovered the next day and buried in the ruined village of Bouresches; later it was transferred to the American cemetery of Belleau Wood, where the white crosses mark the graves of so many of his comrades of Company E.

IX. *New York*, 1919

I

THE *Dial* was a fortnightly published in Chicago. It held a commanding position in the Middle West as a literary magazine by virtue of its editor, William Morton Payne, a critic of learning and authority. The principal of a Chicago school, he found time for immense reading in many languages. On his death, George Donlin became editor, and the paper was bought by Martyn Johnson. I had written for Donlin a number of reviews of biographies of Victorian statesmen, and on Donlin's retirement, in the autumn of 1918, Johnson asked me to take the editorship.

Johnson had large plans for the magazine. Like the London *Athenaeum*, the *Dial* had become a political as well as a literary journal, the organ of liberals who were concerned, under the term Reconstruction, with preserving the social values released by the war effort. There was a secondary group of editors, "in charge of the Reconstruction Program," consisting of John Dewey, Helen Marot, and Thorstein Veblen. The regular board included Harold Stearns, Clarence Britten, and Scofield Thayer, who helped to finance the paper. Florence Haxton put together and got out the fortnightly. In 1918 the new orientation necessitated removal of the paper to New York, where it occupied the building at 112 West Thirteenth Street.

The flexible quarter system of the University of Chicago made it possible for me to be absent in the winter and spring of 1919. I arrived in New York in December 1918 and found that my first assignment was to make it possible for both John Dewey and Randolph Bourne to remain with the magazine. Bourne had been bitterly opposed to the entrance of the United States into the war and scornfully hostile to the mediatorial position of Dewey, the *New Republic*, and other liberals. His article on "The Intellectuals and the War" in *The Seven Arts* had been the death of that brilliant journal in 1917.

Thayer was chiefly interested in the *Dial* as a vehicle for Bourne's writing, but Johnson refrained from placing his name among the editors because of Dewey's opposition. I always considered myself indebted to Dewey in philosophy, and I also admired Bourne. I hoped to bring about a reconciliation, but immediately on my arrival in New York I learned of the latter's death. I was disheartened at losing the most important contributor to the literary function of the *Dial.*

As it was, however, the little magazine was top-heavy, overstaffed, and underfinanced. Moreover, Johnson had contracted for articles to which our limited space was mortgaged. From George Moore in London came the manuscript of *Conversations in Ebury Street.* Communication with London was slow, and it seemed doubtful if corrected manuscript or proof would ever be returned. I made what I could of the wretched typescript. It remains on my editorial conscience that I had not the wit to change the name of an etcher typed as Frank Hall to Frans Hals.

Another manuscript from London was John Gould Fletcher's explanation of free verse. The examples he cited were so carefully marked that I could follow the text exactly. I did not intend to send him a proof, but according to office routine it was sent. Weeks later it was returned with the system of accents and caesuras so changed that I became skeptical of any theory underlying free verse.

A dereliction more seriously regarded by my colleagues occurred when in the absence of Miss Haxton I got out the paper. The compositors saw to it that nearly every page opened with a "widow"—i.e., an incomplete line closing a paragraph.

The problem of space continued to haunt me, especially after Veblen arrived from California to take up four or five pages in each issue. I tried to edit his articles until proof came back with cuts restored and a note of admonition to let them run. As Veblen's contributions were paid for outside the office by admirers, he was independent of editorial authority. It was with difficulty that we kept even with the book market, which I continued to think was the chief reason for our existence.

The new poetry pressed upon us until we made Conrad Aiken the arbiter. Nevertheless, the poets continued to flock to us in the afternoon, Maxwell Bodenheim always among the first, until in despair of getting my work done I would lead the party to the saloon opposite, on the corner of Seventh Avenue. I had prudently collected my half year's salary in advance and soon became the banker of the office. Thirst among editors and contributors was flagrant.

About this time the lost generation was coming back from Europe. One of the most engaging was Malcolm Cowley, who sometimes appeared early in the day to collect no fewer than three volumes for review. At noon the reviews were on hand, the pay check issued, the volumes exposed for sale at Frank Shay's bookshop—and Malcolm was lunching. One morning a tall handsome youth in khaki appeared—Lewis Mumford, in fact, just discharged from the Army. He qualified at once as a reviewer, as did Geroid Robinson, who arrived at about the same time. Martyn Johnson, with the aplomb of the captain of a sinking ship who thinks that one or two more victims will make no difference, engaged both as assistants. Mumford succeeded me as editor and married Sophie Wittenberg, our extremely competent and attractive stenographer. Robinson left us for Columbia.

2

The year 1919 was one of yeast-like fermentation. The makers of the new world were as busy in New York as in Paris. The great name of Reconstruction covered a multitude of movements and enterprises, to which the *Dial* was editorially committed. There was the Youth Movement, the Labor Movement, the "World for Christ" Movement, occupying a huge department store building on Sixth Avenue, where I could see many of my young radical friends solemnly pounding typewriters. The New School for Social Research was established for higher education independent of academic machinery, where the university outlaws, Professors James Harvey Robinson, Charles A. Beard, and Thorstein Veblen, could function with the support and blessing of Professor Dewey. There was the Forum Movement, for which the popular Reverend Percy Stickney Grant's Sunday evening forum at the Church of the Ascension furnished the model. Under his persuasion Martyn Johnson was ready to commit the future of the *Dial* by turning it into an organ of a national organization to establish clubs for the popular discussion of public questions. There was the Co-operative Movement, which assumed pretentious form in Charles Phillips' plan of organizing communities by blocks, to supply consumers' commodities. Mrs. Willard

Straight was its chief financial support. A lavish suite of rooms in the Metropolitan Tower housed the propaganda department, which was under the able direction of Dorothy Thompson, and to which we contributed the services of Harold Stearns. I believe that the plan was tried out in a selected area in Cincinnati but failed because the butcher, who was one of the consumers affected, could not go along with the purchase of meat wholesale from Chicago, nor could the fishmonger look with complacency on sending a truck weekly to Chesapeake Bay for community fish and oysters.

3

The political interest of the *Dial* naturally centered about the Conference at Paris, where President Wilson was honestly struggling to redeem his promises of the Fourteen Points, on which Germany had explicitly surrendered and which had been accepted no less explicitly by Great Britain and France as the basis of the armistice. We welcomed Wilson's first triumph in gaining the acceptance of the Covenant of the League of Nations, but after his return to Paris it was difficult to keep a note of skepticism out of our leading articles. I was in favor of maintaining faith in Wilson in spite of evidence that he was buckling. I demurred to a cautious editorial by Harold Stearns on "Reasons Why Wilson May Fail," but Johnson was for abandoning the leaking vessel of our hopes at Paris before it sank. The attitude of the administration in Washington, conducted by Wilson's surrogates, was puzzling to say the least. The only issue of the *Dial* which was held up in the mail was one containing an account of the Austrian proposals for peace in 1917, by our Paris correspondent, Robert Dell. Even two years after the event it was apparently seditious to write of the mistakes of the Allies.

For liberals in the United States, as for the Allies in Europe, the acid test was, as Wilson defined it, the treatment of Russia. Here, again, the ambiguous course of our government was disconcerting. On the one hand the President was inviting the Soviet leaders to a conference at Prinkipo, while on the other hand he was making war on them on two fronts. It might be argued that the expeditionary force under General Graves in Siberia served a useful purpose in restraining the Japanese, but the good was canceled by the aid given to Kolchak, Denikin, Wrangel, and other White Russians, and to the British in the Murmansk region. The excuse that our troops were sent to protect American supplies was too flimsy to bear repetition.

The *Dial* published the Constitution of the Union of Soviet Socialist Republics simultaneously with its publication by the *Nation.* Thayer disapproved our attitude and threatened a law suit "to protect his name." We published articles by Albert Rhys Williams and other firsthand observers of the Russian Revolution. We argued for the recognition of the Soviet ambassador, Peter Martens, and the dismissal of Bakhmetev, who represented the Kerenski government and was allowed the use of the two-hundred-and-eighty-million-dollar loan to that government for the purpose of supporting the White Russian counterrevolutionists.

From the outset I was in favor of the Russian Revolution, which Miss Addams called the greatest social experiment in history. I am inclined to accept the well-known opinions of Jefferson and Lincoln in regard to revolutions in general, though without committing myself necessarily to endorsement of the governments which they generate. The first speech I made in New York when I joined the staff of the *Dial* was in favor of toleration of the Bolsheviks. I quoted the cautious advice of Gamaliel to the Jews in regard to their treatment of the early Christians:

> Ye men of Israel, take heed to yourselves what ye intend to do as touching these men. . . . And now I say unto you, Refrain from these men, and let them alone: for if this counsel or this work be of men, it will come to nought: But if it be of God, ye cannot overthrow it; lest haply ye be found even to fight against God.

Later I came to know Mr. Martens, an engineer, a modest unassuming man, a very appropriate ambassador for a workers' republic. He was deported while Bakhmetev remained to spend the taxpayers' money, to carry on intrigues, and to balance the dinner tables of embarrassed hostesses.

4

The *Dial* was admittedly hanging on a shoestring, and finally the shoestring broke. Scofield Thayer was the only financial resource. I had once incautiously remarked to him on the anomaly of putting up money for a paper and letting others have the fun of running it. Whether he remembered this suggestion or not, he took up his option. The staff scattered. I returned to the University of Chicago. Martyn Johnson disappeared with the jocular remark, "I have got my sixpence and am off for the moon." Scofield Thayer and his cousin, Dr. J. S. Watson, with Gilbert Seldes, Kenneth Burke, and Marianne Moore successively as assistant editors, made the *Dial* for several years the most distinguished organ of arts and letters that America has produced.

5

My term on the *Dial* was important to me because of the contacts I made. The Civil Liberties Union took its new departure at that time under Harry F. Ward and Roger Baldwin, whose friendship I enjoyed. I had a special relation with Norman Thomas, under whom my brother Sidney had served his apprenticeship as assistant in the church for immigrants in Harlem. Thomas was much concerned with the situation of conscientious objectors imprisoned at Fort Leavenworth. Scott Nearing I had always regarded as an outstanding victim in the cause of academic freedom since his dismissal from Toledo University. His acquittal in his trial for impeding the war effort, next to that of Max Eastman and the editors of *The Masses*, was the most important victory of the people against the administration, which, in the Department of Justice, was becoming a fascist tyranny. The *Dial* gave me an opportunity to protest against the outrages perpetrated against civilians, with the countenance of the government, which seemed to become more flagrant after the armistice.

As editor of a literary journal I became responsible for the relief of one German writer. I received a letter from Fort Oglethorpe, written apparently under extreme nervous strain, signed by a well-known writer named Hanns Heinz Ewers. He described conditions under which he and other intellectuals, including Dr. Muck, the former conductor of the Boston Symphony Orchestra, were suffering concentration. Ewers asked me to write on his behalf to John Galsworthy, founder of P.E.N., the international association of authors, who was then in this country. Mr. Galsworthy replied sympathetically, pointing out that as a foreign guest he could not approach the government on such a matter, and adding that his brother-in-law was then in a concentration camp in England. I interested Norman Hapgood, who took up the case with Attorney General Palmer, and Ewers was released under parole to me. When he came to New York his publisher brought him to the Harvard Club to meet his benefactors. Norman and Hutchins Hapgood were waiting with me. As Ewers appeared they exclaimed, "Is that the man?" and incontinently departed. Hutchins recognized Ewers as a particularly loud and offensive member of pro-German circles in the first years of the war. Ewers had been on his way back to Germany from South America, via this country, when our declaration of war made him an enemy alien. Ewers was not a pleasant associate. He reported to me, often in the company of the charming German-American girl who had signed his bond, and whose verses he was always urging me to publish. His manner to her was that of a Prussian officer, which led me to think they were engaged, and I was glad for her sake when he sailed for Germany. He became an ornament of the Nazi school of literature.

6

One afternoon Rose Strunsky came to ask me to help the Indian revolutionists in this country, for whom the historic right of asylum had become a farce. Two years earlier, on the day after our declaration of war, a number of these refugees had been arrested and held for trial in San Francisco on the charge of conspiring to ship arms to India. Among them was Taraknath Das, formerly a fellow in Political Science at the University of Washington, and an American citizen. Das told me later how his apartment had been searched without a warrant, by Sir George Denham, head of the British police at Calcutta, with the complicity of local authorities.

The shipment had been arranged by German interests in 1915, and workers had been engaged as stokers through an Indian employment agent who represented the destination as India. The vessel had been captured in Honolulu and the stokers held for trial on the charge of conspiracy to violate the neutrality of the United States by engaging in an armed expedition against a friendly power. On trial with them for association in the conspiracy were a few Indian intellectuals. Six convicts were brought from Indian prisons by Sir George, who actively aided the prosecution throughout the trial. The official representative of American justice, a woman district attorney, was afterwards brilliantly feted by the British Empire Society.

The trial in 1917 had abounded in dramatic incidents, including the shooting in court of the employment agent by one of the prisoners, and the attempt of one of the imported witnesses to enlist the protection of the judge if he told the truth. The trial had ended with the conviction of Dr. Das and others, who became associates of my friends among the I. W. W.'s and conscientious objectors in Leavenworth.

All this was, of course, ancient history. Miss Strunsky was interested in protecting these prisoners from further persecution when they should be released on the expiration of their terms. We formed an association known as Friends of Freedom for India, of which Norman Thomas, Roger Baldwin, and Agnes Smedley were members. Miss Smedley was concerned about the persecution of Indians in New York and the complaisance of American military officers to British influences, of which she has given an account in her book *Daughter of Earth*. Among others, Sailendra Nath Ghose was held for months in the Tombs under an impossibly heavy bail, on the charge of writing to the Secretary of State without the authorization of a foreign power. Someone in the district attorney's office gave as the true reason for the imprisonment a suspicion that Ghose meant to marry Miss Smedley. When the case was brought before Judge Learned Hand, he pointed out to the district attorney that such honorable intention was no crime, and Ghose was soon released on reduced bail.

The chief danger was the Johnson immigration bill, pending in the Senate, which by amendment contained a clause having direct reference to the deportation of Indians to British India, where their fate would have been shooting or banishment to the Andaman Islands. In our leaflet for popular appeal we stated this obvious fact, whereupon Richard Gottheil, who as professor of Semitic languages at Columbia University was recognized as an authority on Indian affairs, wrote a letter to the *New York Times* in which he denied our allegation. From official records of the British we collected a number of cases of Indian refugees who, by kidnaping or other means, were brought back to India and suffered the fate indicated, but neither the *Times* nor Professor Gottheil took notice of our reply. Later I heard that the professor said that he had written his letter at the request of the British Ambassador, Lord Reading.

I went to Washington and interviewed many senators; they were, without exception, in favor of eliminating the objectionable clauses, which was done. Some of them declared that India had as much right to independence as the United States. I was surprised to find how easy it was to lobby in the Senate. I merely established myself in an alcove of the cloakroom and sent a page to the floor with a message to the senator selected. He always came. In the alcove next to mine was William Jennings Bryan, who was working to obtain a majority for the Treaty of Versailles. We chatted when we were both waiting like friendly spiders for our flies, and Mr. Bryan promised to put in a word for us when occasion offered.

My connection with the Friends of Freedom for India, especially with Agnes Smedley and Taraknath Das, who became my good friends, was rewarding except for one unfortunate result—it prevented visits to England. One of our members, who was in Great Britain, was deported. Another, James Maurer, chairman of the Pennsylvania Federation of Labor, was stopped at the gangplank as he prepared to cross the ocean to attend a meeting of British trade unions. Later Roger Baldwin was allowed to spend a week in England under parole to a member of Parliament. As the reason given in all cases was that of connection with the Friends of Freedom for India, I knew that, as president of the organization, I should be refused a visa.

I have always regretted that as a teacher, whose business was with English literature, I was not permitted to revisit England. I have always had nostalgia for the English countryside, of which I know so little. Contemporary authors are a compensation—W. H. Hudson for Hampshire, Sheila Kaye-Smith for Sussex, May Sinclair for the Midlands and Yorkshire, and Mary Webb for the Welsh border.

Apart from personal reasons, however, I have been more deeply irritated by the treatment of the Indians in the United States by British agents, acting through our authorities, than by any other instance of foreign interference in our affairs. I have spoken of this interference to Englishmen whom I have met in this country, to H. G. Wells, to H. N. Brailsford and Lord Robert Cecil and S. K. Ratcliffe. From all I received in effect the same answer—nothing doing. The British government was patient of American criticism in regard to its Irish policy and even of American support to Irish rebellion. It recognized that the subject had a political significance in this country. What legitimate interest did India have for the United States? The Indian vote numbered less than a score. It was little enough to ask that the citizenship be canceled of any who, like Dr. Das, resented the subjection of his mother country—and American judges were sometimes ready to oblige.

7

Among the happiest events of the year was the renewal of association with Norman Hapgood. Hapgood had made *Collier's* the most powerful magazine in the country. His smashing of Colonel Mann and his scandal sheet *Town Topics*, his exposure of the patent medicine frauds, were examples of militant journalism in the cause of public welfare. He had supported Wilson in 1912 although Robert Collier preferred to be with the young aristocrats behind Roosevelt. After that it had been easy for Hapgood's subordinates to undermine him and force his resignation. The Colliers felt no gratitude to the editor who had put them into the way of enormous profit and prestige from a great cultural enterprise—President Eliot's "Five-Foot Shelf of Books."

He was one of Wilson's advisers, particularly in regard to the Soviets. The President appointed him Ambassador to Denmark to watch the Russian experiment, but the Senate later showed no intention of confirming him and he resigned.

Before this catastrophe, however, Hapgood founded the League of Free Nations Association, in co-operation with Stephen A. Duggan and James G. McDonald, as a means of rallying support to Wilson's policies at the Peace Conference. On Hapgood's nomination I became a member of the executive committee. Our hope was that Wilson would triumph at Paris and that peace in Europe would be followed by a return to democracy at home. We tried to avoid discouraging criticism while the outcome was in the balance. The association was the chief meeting-ground of liberals on the subject of foreign affairs. At a general meeting in April, after Wilson's return to Paris, there was a considerable walk-out of members who thought that he was conceding too much to his opponents, but the executive committee stood by Hapgood.

When the committee met to consider the Treaty of Versailles I offered a brief resolution disapproving it. Dr. Duggan defended it in comparison with the Treaties of Vienna. As my resolution received only four votes, I walked out, followed by Mrs. Straight, Mrs. Henry Goddard Leach, and Mrs. Charlotte Sorchan. It was some consolation that within a few weeks the association reversed its position and invited us to return. As I was then in Chicago I did not accept.

X. *Chicago*, 1919–1920

I

I TOOK back to Chicago in the summer of 1919 many of the connections and interests which I had formed or strengthened in New York. Stuart Chase was then in Chicago, as an expert accountant for the government investigating the behavior of the packers during the war. Under his lead we formed a discussion group of Socialists and liberals of the Left, which borrowed the name of Fabian Club. When the Council on Foreign Affairs was formed I joined it as a malcontent. I recall the expressions of pain on the faces of the wise and kind whenever I rose to speak. On the occasion that General O'Reilly came from New York to recommend that arrangements for the peace of the world be committed to the general staffs, my remarks left a disconcerting pause, which Arthur Aldis ended by congratulating the speaker on his splendid address and moving that it be printed. Professor Irving Fisher came from Yale to discuss the economic consequences of the invasion of the Ruhr, and on his failure to touch the subject at all I exploded with a denunciation of the invasion as a monstrous violation of the treaty. This time it was my colleague Weber Linn who rose to save the situation by affirming the pleasure with which the audience had listened to Dr. Fisher. The complacency with which the treaty was accepted irritated me as much as the boasting of its artificers. In President Wilson's illness it was generous to try to forget that he had declared that the treaty was a literal fulfillment of his Fourteen Points.

The Foreign Policy Association under James G. McDonald used me occasionally as an *advocatus diaboli*. He invited me to speak at the Philadelphia chapter of the association along with David Hunter Miller. As he had been an active participant in drawing the treaty I tried to be courteous, and instead of calling it a lie I pointed out its futility. I closed by quoting the solemn words of Dean Inge in regard to our dead soldiers: "We may hope that in the paradise of brave men to which they have gone, the knowledge is mercifully concealed from them that they died in vain." David Hunter Miller waxed exceeding wroth at this statement and charged that I was dishonoring the dead.

One reason for mildness in discussing the Treaty of Versailles was the expectation that the United States would ultimately become a member of the League which it had forced on the world, and would insist on the application of Article XIX of the Covenant, which provided an escape from the strict application of the Treaty. The behavior of President Harding in repudiating the pledge of his platform, and of Secretary of State Hughes in ignoring for a year all communications from the League, seemed to me a monstrous betrayal. When the separate treaty between the United States and Germany, negotiated by Mr. Hughes, appeared, containing some of the worst features of the Treaty of Versailles including the clause imputing sole guilt for the war to Germany (the product of the American members of the Committee on Responsibilities, on which had been Robert Lansing, Secretary of State, and James Brown Scott, secretary of the Carnegie Endowment for International Peace), I felt that this country had fallen to the lowest point in our international relations.

I do not look back with satisfaction on my speeches of this period. I should have been more tactful or more forthright. On only one occasion did I find myself on the platform when, as General Booth used to describe it, "great freedom was given me." On February 23, 1923, a gathering of the German societies of Chicago crowded the Coliseum. The music, the faces, brought back the Germany that I had known and loved. My subject was the invasion of the Ruhr. The atrocious action of the French and Belgians in attacking a country which they had disarmed was, I foresaw, the prelude to World War II. It gave Germany a special reason to violate the disarmament clauses of the Treaty of Versailles, in addition to the standing one of non-fulfillment of the pledge by the victors to disarm. Today it is clear that the loss of its principal industry and the necessity of supporting the unemployed workers threw upon Germany the financial burden leading to inflation and to weakness in the financial structure which could not withstand the crisis of 1929–33.

2

My connection with the American Civil Liberties Union in New York made me a sort of corresponding member after I returned to Chicago. The chief defenders of the rights of man in Chicago were Clarence Darrow and his partner W. H. Holly, afterwards a federal judge. I had lived in the same apartment building with Darrow for three years before going to Germany. It is significant of my absorption in the university at that time that I had only a neighborly acquaintance with a most interesting and significant figure. Darrow was not an organization man. As a lawyer he declared himself ready to defend any person accused of crime, because crime originated with government. Holly, on the other hand, was the chief promoter of the organization for civil liberties in Chicago.

These were rudely challenged in December 1919 by the "Red raids" of Attorney General Palmer. In Chicago some five hundred men were arrested without warning, chiefly because they had avoided the draft or lacked enthusiasm for the war then actually if not officially ended. The city jails were not big enough to hold the prisoners; they were crowded into City Hall and held incommunicado. As most of the victims were of foreign birth, the fear of deportation was torture to them and their families. Great credit is due to one of our Chicago liberals, Louis F. Post, for his humane administration as Commissioner of Immigration and Naturalization. If Palmer intended this foray as a bid for the Democratic nomination for the presidency he was disappointed—audiences howled execration at the mention of his name. A committee of prominent lawyers issued an indictment based on his illegal actions in office.

But the witch hunt went on. In 1919 the Socialist party held its convention in Chicago from which the radicals, under the inspiration of John Reed and the Russian Revolution, seceded to form the Communist party. A "splinter" became the Communist Labor party, headed by William Bross Lloyd. Why this group attracted the special attention of the authorities I do not know, but what appeared to be the entire membership was arrested and accused under the state sedition law: they had signed a revolutionary document known as the Left Wing Manifesto.

Lloyd was the son of an outstanding liberal of the previous generation, Henry D. Lloyd of Winnetka, whose *Wealth against*

Commonwealth was, like Henry George's *Progress and Poverty*, a call to Americans to enter the field of higher politics, of which the fundamental concept is human welfare. The Bross family was part owner of the *Chicago Tribune* and Mr. Lloyd was thus able to provide for his own defense. His followers were anxious to have their own counsel, especially Darrow. I attended a meeting called by Jane Addams and was somewhat disconcerted at being elected treasurer of the defense fund. With an initial pledge of five thousand dollars from Long John Wentworth, descendant of a leading pioneer, we raised ten thousand.

There were about twenty defendants, some, like Ludwig Lore, John Engdahl, and Max Bedacht, who presumably knew what they were about, and others whose immature political consciousness left them open to suggestion. It appeared that the case was simple enough in fact and law to be decided at a single session. It lasted four weeks and involved a survey of the revolutionary situation of the entire world. The story of the first general strike in United States history, which had recently occurred in Seattle, was told by Mayor Ole Hansen, who was then passing as a savior of society, and by James Duncan, who had led the well-conducted strike. Raymond Robins, recently returned from Russia where he had served as head of the Red Cross, eloquently described the Bolshevik Revolution. When the current events class was finally dismissed the arguments to the jury came. I remember Darrow best in that scene, in his shirt sleeves, leaning forward in front of the jury box and, as it seemed, addressing each juryman personally as he pleaded for his clients: "They adopted a platform which they had as much right to adopt as the Epworth League had to adopt theirs. If their platform would accomplish what they hoped, then speed the day of its adoption. Unpractical dreamers! But we don't send men to the pen for trying to help their fellow men—we send them to the insane asylum."

His opponent, Frank Comerford, had been engaged as special assistant to the state's attorney. Comerford held the jury spellbound for hours under his emotional outbursts of loyalty. The jury gave its verdict to the United States flag. The defendants were found guilty.

While Lloyd appealed the case we kept most of the accused out on bail. The appeal was denied. Then on the day on which the convicted men were at the gates of Joliet, Governor Len Small issued a pardon for all.

3

Another cause in which I continued to be concerned was that of Ireland. It was through Arthur Upham Pope, the art expert, that I became identified with the movement in New York, but I cannot remember a time when I was not interested in Irish freedom. In the Boston of my boyhood the Irish exile John Boyle O'Reilly was a visible reminder of the patriots Wolfe Tone and Robert Emmet. Recent events had increased sympathy for the cause of Ireland. The crude incitements to violence of Sir Edward Carson and "Galloper" Smith—"Ulster will fight and Ulster will be right"—supported by the mutiny of English officers in Ireland in 1914; the outbreak on Dublin Green at Easter of 1916 and the savage reprisals of the government; the shooting of Sheehy Skeffington, a pacifist who had not borne arms, by a British officer who was merely pronounced insane; the execution of Sir Roger Casement; finally the outrages perpetrated by the "Black and Tans"—all these had stirred the Irish-Americans to indignation which was shared by press and public in the United States. I spoke at many Irish meetings and always made a hit by quoting Longfellow's lines:

> You know the rest. In the books you have read,
> How the British Regulars fired and fled,
> How the farmers gave them ball for ball,
> From behind each fence and barnyard wall,
> Chasing the red-coats down the lane . . .

Through Padraic and Mary Colum I gained personal impressions of the martyrs of Dublin Green, of their charm and their courage. Padraic appeared from beyond the sea like an elf, a perfect Cymric in appearance, in speech, in imagination. Mary had stood with the Countess Markovich on the coast to receive the guns to be taken to Dublin to arm the revolt. I knew Lawrence Ginnell, who represented the Irish Republic in Chicago, a gentle man, much broken by imprisonment. I approached him one day in the La Salle Hotel and tactlessly touched him on the shoulder; he whirled about with the look of a hunted man. Through him I met Miss McSweeney, sister of the Mayor of Cork, who had died in prison on a hunger strike. Mrs. Sheehy Skeffington was a guest at Hull House.

I met Eamon de Valera, tall, thin, austere, with a ravaged face and a consecrated earnestness which, as Jane Addams remarked in the case of Tolstoy, seemed actually a kind of moral violence. Oswald Villard of the *Nation* had a plan of sending a committee to Ireland to investigate and report on the outrages of Lloyd George's Black and Tans, and, I think at de Valera's suggestion, asked me to be chairman. Although I was already compromised with the British authorities by my chairmanship of the Friends of Freedom for India, and had noted the exclusion from the British Isles of two of my colleagues in that organization, I nevertheless applied for a leave of absence from the University of Chicago, which was refused. Meanwhile the whole group was denied passports. The committee, under the chairmanship of Jane Addams, met in Washington in 1920 with Senators David Walsh and George Norris as leading members. There was considerable skepticism as to whether such a proceeding would not result in hardening the hearts of the oppressors, but Villard and Miss Addams had correctly appraised the situation, and this evidence of feeling in America in regard to the Black-and-Tan outrages had its effect on public opinion in England, contributing to the final suppression of Lloyd George and his myrmidons.

My last meeting with de Valera was on the occasion of a great rally of the Irish in Chicago on January 30, 1921. I was invited to dine with him at the Edgewater Beach Hotel, whence we were to drive to the Auditorium. When I reached the hotel I found myself the only guest, though others had evidently been expected. De Valera made no comment. After dinner we found two limousines at the door. I was about to follow the leader when a priest intervened. Not to waste the second car he insisted that I should take it, "so that thim that doesn't get a look at the prisident will see the professor. They're alike as two pays." So we drove into the city, each alone in his glory, through a lane of green Bengal lights and cheering crowds. It seemed discourteous not to acknowledge such greetings. At the Auditorium we found Frank Walsh giving a history of Ireland. An hour passed. The speech that had been boiling up within me as we arrived subsided like a tired geyser. I felt it becoming tepid, then cold. Finally the crowd could be held no longer, and about midnight it surged onto the stage, shouting for de Valera, embracing him, trying to carry him aloft. I recognized my superfluity and said good-by, in spite of his courteous protests.

4

A third connection which I brought back to Chicago was with the leaders of the third party movement. The obvious failure of President Wilson to accomplish the aims of the war at Paris, his fallacious defense of the Treaty of Versailles, and the reactionary tendencies developing within his administration led to a great falling away from his following. At a meeting of the League of Free Nations Association, even before the treaty had emerged from the Paris Conference, a discussion was precipitated by those already critical of Wilson's compromises, and J. A. H. Hopkins, Amos Pinchot, Will Durant, and others walked out. At that time I favored standing by Wilson, but later I found myself in association with this group whose objective was to establish a political party to maintain the liberal traditions of Wilson's first administration and to oppose sanctioning a treaty which violated the promises which the United States had made to the world. The group assumed the name "Committee of Forty-eight"—claiming national standing by references to the full number of states represented. As the campaign of 1920 approached, it was decided to enter the field and to hold a nominating convention in Chicago.

At the Morrison Hotel we gathered in July, animated by the hope which grows perennially in the heart of America of salvation through politics. On the platform sat handsome Swinburne Hale, one of the twelve lawyers who had condemned Attorney General Palmer for actions which should have led to his impeachment; beside him, the expansively beautiful Mrs. Garland, whom he was going to marry, the mother of philanthropist Charles Garland, known to his intimates as Barley, and later to be the donor of a million dollars to found the American Fund for Public Service. There sat George L. Record, former congressman, the most statesmanlike figure of the company, "with Atlantean shoulders fit to bear," etc.; Amos Pinchot, long of face and limb, a liberal fanatic: Will Durant, keen and vivacious; and J. A. H. Hopkins, genial and rather nervous, the conductor of the show.

The best-known and most popular figure at the assembly was Dudley Field Malone. Like many others present, he was a disappointed man, seeking some way to rehabilitate his political fortunes. I had met Malone in Washington a few years before on the afternoon of the day when he escorted a parade of the Women's party, taking special care of Miss Doris Stevens. As she marched at the head of the line, bearing a banner aloft to which her eyes rose in Joan of Arc adoration, a mucker thrust out his foot to trip her up. Malone grappled with the hoodlum, and a few minutes later, when the paraders were arrested, rushed to the White House to protest hotly to President Wilson, and to throw up his job as Collector of the Port of New York.

It was obvious that to bring a third party into the field without the support of labor was futile, and our convention had been called to synchronize with one of trade unionists called, I believe, by the Chicago Federation of Labor. Our most impressive leaders, Pinchot and Record, were on the committee working by conference with the labor committee to bring forth a joint platform. Presiding over us was the gigantic figure of Parley Christensen of Salt Lake City, in immaculate white.

While we awaited the report of the platform committee we listened to Taraknath Das on India, to Eamon de Valera on Ireland, and to a number of other promoters of special causes. Working day and night, the two platform committees were within ten per cent of unity, but the rank and file, already jealous of the leaders, could not be restrained.

Swinburne Hale moved for immediate amalgamation of the two bodies. The measure was carried, and the Committee of the Whole marched out of the Morrison Hotel, across the city to the West Side where the labor men were meeting in a building sometimes known as Carmen's Hall. It was a bare auditorium with bad acoustics—a bleak change from the comfort of the Morrison Hotel.

There the fight over the slight differences in the two platforms was resumed. It was a full-dress debate. The hall was full of trade unionists, whether accredited or not, who greeted their champions with tumultuous applause and overwhelmed ours with the usual signs of disapproval. The vote was by voice and show of hands, and our defeat was foredoomed. As I wandered out Bob Buck, who edited the local organ of the Federation of Labor, embraced me cordially, crying, "We licked 'em. We licked 'em!" The demonstration throughout the hall could not have been more enthusiastic if the election itself had been won.

It had been hoped that the platform would be such that Senator Robert M. La Follette could stand on it as a candidate. However, his representative, Gilbert Roe, promptly notified us that the Senator would not accept if nominated and accordingly the evening session was devoted to naming candidates. The Committee of Forty-eight voted for Dudley Field Malone, but labor, in a placating gesture, gave the nomination to our chairman, Parley Christensen, who became the standard bearer of the Farmer-Labor party.

The next morning the rump of the Committee of Forty-eight was back in its comfortable quarters at the Morrison. The important question was whether we should begin the history of the third party with a split, but before we could answer it we had to listen to Mr. Roe explain at length Senator La Follette's position. I sat on the edge of my chair, my eye fixed on the new chairman. The moment Roe finished I was on the platform with the impassioned cry, "Men and bretheren, God in His infinite mercy has given us another chance," and I urged the delegates not to commit the last folly by bolting a party at its birth. As I was returning to my seat, feeling that I had saved our battered face, Amos Pinchot backed me against the wall with the solemn inquiry, "Lovett, have you lost your mind?" A moment later Parley Christensen, his white suit creased and soiled, stormed in with a group of his partisans to appeal for unity. He did not get it, and the convention of the Forty-eight melted like snow at the breath of the Lord. Fragmentation set in. All that day new parties were being born throughout the hotel. The word was passed —"Judge so-and-so of Nebraska has a new party in room 1445," or "The Oklahoma delegates are caucusing in room 1947 and invite other states to join them in forming an honest four-square party." The Committee of Forty-eight checked out.

Parley Christensen, thus raised to the status of a national figure, seemed to be the property of the journalist William Hard, who led him like a dancing bear to parlor meetings along the North Shore from Evanston to Lake Forest. The campaign might have been expected to get somewhere on a protest vote with the alternatives of Harding and Cox, but it ran to less than half a million votes. The chief result was the name Farmer-Labor, which remained a symbol of united action for future political adventures.

5

The "Red raids" of Attorney General Palmer furnished a model for the behavior of trustees and administrative officials in institutions of learning. At the University of Minnesota the dominant figure on the Board of Trustees was Pierce Butler, later Justice of the Supreme Court. He called suspected members of the faculty before him and gave them one, two, or three years, according to the degree of their offenses, to find positions elsewhere. At Illinois a local trustee was the patroness of the inquisition which had the cordial support of the university administration. An instructor in the Department of Architecture at the University of Michigan, an Austrian, who as a Tolstoyan had been recognized in his own country as a non-combatant, told me of his harsh questioning by a leader of the witch hunt in Ann Arbor.

One test of subversive opinion was the attitude toward the Treaty of Versailles. At the University of Chicago a dinner of the International Club was the occasion of criticism of the treaty by the president, Louis Wirth, now a distinguished member of the faculty. Two professors, present as guests, ran with the news to President Judson, and it was discussed whether to deprive Mr. Wirth of his degree at the next Convocation. The matter was settled by Professor Carl Buck, who remarked dryly that if the university intended to make approval of the Treaty of Versailles a prerequisite for a degree, it should be so stated in the entrance requirements.

The American Association of University Professors was formed under the leadership of Professor Arthur O. Lovejoy of Johns Hopkins to fight the battle of academic freedom. Members gave much time to hearing charges, sifting evidence, and deciding on conditions of tenure implied in the engagement of university teachers. Obviously, the results of these investigations by *ad hoc* committees varied with the character of their make-up, but on the whole the association marked a great advance in the professional status of university men and women. One of its chief concerns was the negotiation with the Carnegie Institute for the Advancement of Teaching in regard to the fulfillment of its pledge to provide retiring allowances for employees of institutions not provided for by state or church. The original endowment of ten million dollars proved inadequate for Columbia University alone. The settlement with the Carnegie Foundation ultimately called for a hundred and thirty-five million to make good claims only up to 1915.

XI. *The "New Republic,"* 1921–1929[1]

I

IN THE winter of 1921 Herbert Croly asked me to join the staff of the *New Republic*. The journal had been founded by Willard Straight of the Morgan firm in 1914 with a distinguished board of editors selected by Croly, whose *Promise of American Life* had marked him as one to be entrusted with the means for making good that promise. Walter Lippmann, Walter Weyl, Philip Littell, and Francis Hackett were his associates, later joined by George Soule and Alvin Johnson. At the outset the journal was confronted by the European war. Instead of contributing to the fulfillment of the promise of domestic progress in peace, the *New Republic* found its immediate function in dealing with the war in Europe, as it more and more nearly concerned the United States. The paper at first supported the policy of neutrality toward the belligerents so strongly as to be called pro-German. Later it argued that Germany should renounce the submarine in restriction of neutral commerce. It approved the declaration of war against Germany and rallied liberals to the support of the administration, while it stood for the preservation of civil liberties and the mitigation of the hysterical patriotism on the home front. It developed the policy of the "political offensive," which finally took form in the announcement of the Fourteen Points, with the view of driving a wedge between the German government and the German people.

[1] The next five chapters cover material of approximately the same years—1921 to 1939. I have thought best to divide this material according to the interests involved—i.e. journalism, literature, labor, relief, and peace.

In the summer of 1917 President Wilson's attention was called to the *New Republic*, and for a time the magazine carried in parallel columns excerpts from the speeches of the President and its own editorials. The suspicion grew that there was a connection between the two, and that the *New Republic* was in some sense an organ of the administration. Among candidates for the authorship of the Fourteen Points Walter Lippmann was frequently mentioned.

The *New Republic* remained true to itself. When the Treaty of Versailles was published it denounced that instrument as a violation of the terms on which Germany had surrendered, and thus forfeited the support of the Wilsonians. Willard Straight, who had guaranteed the budget of the paper, had died in Paris while in government service. Mrs. Dorothy Straight, however, continued her support and maintained the policy of complete non-interference with the editorial board.

As I have written, I had been in favor of using our declaration of war as the occasion of the immediate launching of the "political offensive" in the statement of terms of peace. The first contribution I offered to the *New Republic* was my address at the Auditorium meeting in May 1917. It was declined. During my editorship of the *Dial*, the *New Republic* was friendly. I dined with the editors on the evening of the day when they decided to oppose the ratification of the Treaty of Versailles. I remember Walter Lippmann's vigorous denunciation of the treaty as a breaking of faith with Germany and a violation of moral obligations to the world. In the winter after the collapse of the Committee of Forty-eight I found Croly sympathetic to the idea of a third party to the point of obtaining a contribution from Mrs. Straight toward the survival of the abortive Farmer-Labor party in Illinois. Nevertheless, it was a surprise to me when he asked me to join the staff.

In Croly's conception of the journal the editorial board was a soviet. Its decisions were reached in conference and were presumed to be unanimous. Contributions from outside were submitted to all the editors. Each number was issued with the *nil obstat* of the entire group and carried the unique authority of an elite board. How long this condition endured in its pristine vigor I do not know. When I joined the staff there were rifts in the fabric. Walter Weyl, whose intellectual authority and powerful political articles contributed to the unity of the board and the early influence of the journal, had died. On the declaration of war Walter Lippmann had entered government service, a desertion which Croly, to whom the journal was supreme in importance, resented. Francis Hackett insisted that the decision of the board to support the belligerency of this country had been taken without his consent. Between him and Lippmann there was inveterate opposition. Philip Littell was suffering from a long illness and rarely appeared at the office, confining his contribution to the admirable series of essays under the title "Books and Things." Alvin Johnson was the mediating influence and shed his beaming presence on the scene of controversy which Croly contemplated with anguish.

Herbert Croly was of an infinite seriousness and intensely romantic. His father had been a radical of the Chartist school who emigrated to the United States, where he edited the *Architectural Record.* His mother was a writer and speaker under the name of Jenny June. At her parlor lectures, to which Herbert was taken as a little boy, he suffered from shyness in the presence of affectionate ladies until he could reach the portieres within which to wrap himself. At Harvard, where, he told me, he partly supported himself by playing poker, his face was his fortune; and later his gravity was portentous. Whether it was shyness or courage, he was the only man I have known who could sit through a dinner without a response by word or smile. He was conscientious to a fault, high in standards, but tolerant and kind. And romantic; by temperament devoted to women and dependent on friends. His conception of the *New Republic* was romantic, a child to be brought forth from the functioning of creative purpose in the intimate intercourse of the editors. He spoke of "the paper" with reverence. He did not expect it to outlive him.

The basis of this religious regard for his work was the faith which the *New Republic* was founded to proclaim and defend, the faith of the nineteenth century—liberalism. To Croly liberalism was "an attitude of mind which seeks to bring understanding to bear upon action, which prevails in social life less through the functioning of liberal institutions than through the activity of an alert, aggressive, and disinterested public opinion." Liberalism was the means of progress, the child of humanism and science. "The essential task of the humanists was the discovery of some method of liberating human life, both in its individual and social aspects, by improved understanding of its processes."

2

The *New Republic* then occupied two old three-story houses at 421 West Twenty-first Street, opposite the grounds of the General Theological Seminary. It was a pleasant place of work. Croly's plan of unifying the board of editors involved setting up housekeeping. A French couple served luncheon and occasionally dinner, at both of which famous visiting Europeans appeared for the enlightenment and entertainment of the editorial board. Sometimes under feminine influence a luncheon went wrong. On one occasion an expert on the British coal situation was present, but one of the ladies turned the conversation to the Hall-Mills murder case, and there it remained.

From the first, the welcome of the editors of the *New Republic* was cordial. They called me Bob at once. My more intimate associations were with Francis Hackett and his wife Signe Toksvig. They lived in an apartment house, part of an architectural project known as Turtle Bay, in which two blocks of houses on East Forty-eighth and Forty-ninth Streets had been turned to face each other across a garden held in common. Frances Grimes, the sculptor, had a studio apartment on the first floor, which the Hacketts arranged for me to rent during the summer and autumn months when Miss Grimes was away. Across the garden lived Phil Littell, and I came to know him and his family well and enjoyed them immensely. With Robert Littell I shared the direction of the book pages of the *New Republic* after the withdrawal of Francis Hackett. The Littells and Francis contributed the humor sorely needed to keep the *New Republic*'s seriousness from turning sour, but all three were satirists. I recall Bob Littell's excruciatingly funny piece on a Shriners' convention in Washington, with its title drawn from the invitation displayed by taxicabs, "Hop in, Noble."

As a boy I had found my chief pleasure in reading, though I never expected to be paid for it. This pleasure, with the addition I mention, I carried into my work on the *New Republic*. I went to the book room of the paper every morning in a glow of anticipation to see what the night had brought forth. I wrote my articles in the office to maintain a decent appearance of industry. Luncheon was interesting whether with the staff and guests or alone with Croly. Afterwards I would gather up my plunder and retire to my studio, with the door open to that pleasant garden, to read, select, make notes. There were not so many books published in those simple days, and reviews in the serious journals were fairly contemporaneous. It was amusing to compare the reviewers—Margaret Marshall and Mary McCarthy in the *Nation*, Van Wyck Brooks in the *Freeman*, Henry Seidel Canby in the *Post*, and later Stuart Sherman and Irita Van Doren in the *Tribune*. Now and then there were skirmishes and reprisals. One week Mary Colum slew the academic critics, Canby and myself, for praising Booth Tarkington's *Alice Adams*. Once Margaret Marshall and Mary McCarthy performed the salutary exercise of reviewing the reviewers in a series of articles in the *Nation*. They generously gave me a B–.

I took reviewing seriously and conscientiously. I felt that the reviewer's first responsibility was to the public in the selection of works of value, and then to the author—last to himself as a member of the staff of his paper. I was especially anxious to bring to public notice works of my academic colleagues which might fail of a wider circulation than that afforded by the learned publications. In this connection I remember two reviews which did good. One was on Professor Emery Neff's *Carlyle and Mill*, which opened up the essential controversy of the nineteenth century between faith and reason, the unconscious and the conscious, which has had such fateful repercussions in our day. The other was Frederick L. Schuman's history of the diplomatic relations of the United States and the Soviet Union. My aim in criticism was recognized by Claude Moore Fuess in a letter which it gives me satisfaction to quote:

My Dear Dr. Lovett,

I cannot refrain from telling you how proud I am of your kind and appreciative review of my *Daniel Webster* in the *New Republic* for December 24, 1930. You have said, lucidly and tersely, just what I had dreamed,—but none too hopefully,—that some one of high repute in the critical world might discover in my book; and you have understood, and expressed perfectly, what I aimed to do. A writer is indeed fortunate when his work, over which he had labored for many long months, is placed in the hands of a critic so fair-minded, so discriminating, and so sympathetic. I am exceedingly grateful.

So far as I can remember, I have never before written to a reviewer of any of my books, but your review was so exceptional in its tone and style that I have yielded to an impulse. Please do not think it necessary to acknowledge my outburst.

The success of a literary department depends chiefly on the skill with which books and reviewers are selected. Since so many young writers begin by reviewing the work of others, my temptation was to be too generous in encouraging them. As I look back over the pages which I edited, however, I am happy to note the names of so many who have gone on to higher things.

3

I exulted in the opportunity offered by the *New Republic* to deal with issues in which I had already been interested. My first assignment in the office was fortunate. Bob Littell had obtained the loan of the four volumes of the report of the Lusk Committee of the New York Senate, dealing, in anticipation of the Dies Committee, with what it chose to consider unpatriotic or seditious. If any investigation of the type commonly known as a witch hunt ever condemned itself by its self-compiled record it was this one, conducted by a certain Archibald Stevenson. I never more enjoyed writing an article than "By Stevenson out of Lusk." I also wrote on freedom for India, and when Francis Hackett developed too much verbal heat over the Irish question, which had then become the long conflict between de Valera and Lloyd George, I took over that subject.

On another subject, connected with Soviet Russia, I caused considerable embarrassment to my chief. I had agreed with President Wilson that the treatment of Russia was the acid test of the sincerity of the Allied Nations. It was therefore with disappointment and chagrin that I saw the United States join the intervention of the Allies. To some extent as the result of the embargo on trade and of our support of the White Russian insurgents, there was famine in Russia, especially in the great grain region of the Volga. The conscience of the American people was aroused. The Friends Service Committee were already in the field, and other associations for relief were beginning to organize. Then stepped forth the Great Humanitarian, Herbert Hoover, with the American Relief Administration. His protracted negotiations with the Soviets, demanding for his organization substantially extraterritorial standing, seemed ill timed in the face of mass suffering and death on the Volga. Moreover, the Soviets were not to be blamed for looking on the A. R. A. as a wooden horse in view of the record of its director. Hoover had allowed his campaign biography of 1920 to claim credit for his use of the power of feeding the hungry for political purposes, in order to suppress revolution. His aide, Captain T. C. C. Gregory, had written an article in *World's Work*, boasting with insolent flippancy of his dealings with Hungary. Hoover was not a person to be accepted as a shining model of pure humanity. I wrote two leaders in the *New Republic* to that effect.

Croly, on vacation in Cornish, returned hurriedly to New York and almost with tears explained that Hoover was the only person who had ever been interested in buying stock in the *New Republic* —ten thousand dollars' worth. Croly's editorial conscience did not allow him even to suggest that we should withdraw or modify the articles, but would I write to Mr. Hoover, take responsibility, and give him an opportunity to reply? I gladly did so and offered to withdraw and apologize if the facts I alleged were not true. I expected a swift epistolary kick in the pants. What was I, a petty journalist, to put trivial obstacles in the way of a great human engineer who got things done in the only way in which they could be done? Hoover's answer was Christ-like in turning the other cheek, but his St. Peter, George Barr Baker, volunteered to come to the *New Republic* office to beat me up.

That Hoover intended to have Russian relief entirely in his own hands was soon apparent. I was then acting as chairman of a committee for the relief of Russian women and children. I gladly resigned in favor of Allan Wardwell, whose service for the Red Cross in Russia and whose prominent social position in New York made him a natural choice. We were going forward with the advice of a professional promoter, who, however, did not save us from a psychological blunder. We planned a banquet with tickets at ten dollars apiece, the food to be restricted to what the Russians were presumably eating, black bread and thin soup, to be followed, when the hearts of the guests were softened, by distinguished speakers in an appeal for funds. A large audience gathered in the banquet room of the Waldorf, looked with distaste at the menu, and adjourned to the regular dining-rooms. The hope that they would come back proved forlorn.

In spite of this setback we were carrying on with a strong advisory committee, which contained the names of President Eliot of Harvard and President Neilson of Smith (whose sympathy with Russia was always unflagging), when suddenly our enterprise folded up, with the understanding that Hoover had ordered its demise. At the same time an attempt by two journalists to obtain funds from the Mid-western states to buy surplus grain from the farmers for shipment to Russia was cut short by opposition from the same source. Undoubtedly Hoover, through appropriations by Congress, had access to, funds larger than all the other organizations together. Undoubtedly he feared that a general appeal for the relief of suffering might extend to sympathy with the revolution itself. At all events, only the Friends, whose work was already established, were allowed to continue, and then under hampering restrictions. I have always wondered whether Hoover also dictated the policy of the Red Cross. With Mr. and Mrs. Graham R. Taylor, Chicago social workers, I went to see its president, Dr. Livingston Farrand, to ask the Red Cross to take up famine relief in Russia. He assured us blandly that the Red Cross was already there—unable to work with the Bolsheviks, but right behind Wrangel's army. We left in stupefaction. For what did Dr. Farrand take us, thus frankly to claim credit for helping counterrevolution at a time, indeed, when one of the officers of the Red Cross was under the accusation of training Wrangel's troops!

The post-war years were those of disillusion and discouragement. The hopes for nations "safe for democracy," for countries "fit for heroes to live in," for "the world of Christ," all nourished for a time under the fallacy of Reconstruction, slowly faded; all the evils following in the train of war were nourished in an atmosphere of general malevolence. Ground was everywhere lost in futile experiments, political and social. Only from Russia was there light breaking on the world, and that light was stormy, serving rather to make darkness visible. The Bolshevik Revolution seemed at least one positive result of the war, and not a few liberals agreed with Sir Josiah Wedgewood's statement, in a letter to Norman Hapgood, that the "collapse of the Russian Empire was in itself enough to make the war worth while." President Wilson's reasoned policy of understanding, and "getting along with," Russia was defeated by his weakness in yielding to the Allies on the matter of military intervention and to the State Department, which adopted as a fixed principle that it would "continue to be animated by zeal against Bolshevism."

4

The *New Republic* had always been credited with assuming a haughty and superior air toward other liberal magazines. That it was a "kept" journal seemed rather shocking to Ellery Sedgwick, who was making a fortune out of the *Atlantic Monthly*, to Oswald Garrison Villard, who, I suspect, was keeping the *Nation* out of his own pocket, to Albert J. Nock, whose admirable *Freeman* was "kept" by Mr. and Mrs. Francis Neilson. Nock had no patience with Croly's high-church pretensions in journalism. I do not know whether he perpetrated the epigram "Crolier than thou." As editor of the *Dial* I had experienced the courtesy of Villard and Nock and was happy to find it renewed on my return to New York. Both had resented the wartime belligerence of the *New Republic* as a desertion of the fundamental principles of liberalism, but they apparently accepted me as evidence of the return of the paper to the fold.

Soon after my arrival in New York Villard invited me to meet editors of the *Nation*, the *Freeman*, and the *Survey* at a week-end party to discuss our common aims and interests. We projected a visit to Washington, to greet the new administration and estimate the prospects for a reversal of the trends that under Wilson and Palmer had become flagrantly reactionary. When we arrived in Washington we divided forces, Villard and others waiting on President Harding, while Professor Joseph P. Chamberlain of Columbia and I called on Secretary Hughes to discuss the threat of intervention of the United States in Mexico in consequence of the dispute between the Mexican government and the oil companies.

Chamberlain and I, by way of preparation, had already interviewed representative oil men in New York and had discovered that the Doherty group was in favor of an export tax by Mexico to limit competition with oil originating north of the Rio Grande. The Doheny interests were opposed. Chamberlain's easy mastery of the subject was in striking contrast to the Secretary's patriotic heat and vehemence. At last the latter sent for Henry P. Fletcher, who had been Ambassador to Mexico and could talk more quietly and intelligently about conditions. We parted cordially with a feeling that Hughes, for all his truculence, would not be made a tool of Doheny. The presidential party returned, satisfied as to the good intentions of President Harding with respect to amnesty for political prisoners, civil liberties, and European policy. We dined that evening with Senator Borah who, with Senators La Follette and Norris, headed the liberal Republicans, as Senators Walsh and Wheeler of Montana headed the liberal Democrats. Already plans for the Washington Conference were forming. Altogether the prospects for liberalism seemed bright in the spring of 1921. It is the pathos of the decade that they were frittered away by the frivolity and corruption of the administration which began with high hopes and bright prospects.

5

A subject in which I became interested through my connection with the *New Republic* came to me quite by accident. In the summer of 1921 Francis Hackett turned over to me an invitation to speak at a luncheon of the Cleveland City Club on disarmament. I have no recollection of contributing anything to the solution of that problem, but later in the afternoon I was introduced to a topic which I followed for years. A. R. Hatton, C. A. Dykstra, and Peter Witt asked for the support of the journal in their fight to maintain intact the city plan of Mayor Tom Johnson by adding to the imposing group of public buildings on the lake front a union railway station. The Van Sweringen brothers had made a countermove by selling to the New York Central their proposal to erect a station in the Public Square, in the center of the city, to accommodate not only the railways, but the interurban lines to their real estate subdivisions. The underground station would offer a large number of concessions, making it a shopping area. It would be surmounted by a huge office building, of which the air rights would belong to the Van Sweringens. Authorization of the plan rested with the Interstate Commerce Commission, where now the battle raged.

The chief advocate of the Van Sweringen interests was Newton D. Baker. Baker had gone to Cleveland in 1902 at the instance of Frederic C. Howe, and as city solicitor became a lieutenant of Tom Johnson in his plans for the building of the city. In 1912 he had succeeded Johnson as mayor, but even then, and certainly later, was the chief force in subverting those plans. After his term as Secretary of War Baker had returned to his law firm in Cleveland and was now counsel for the New York Central; why that railroad was subservient to the Van Sweringens was and remains a mystery. The chief opponent of the steal—for such it plainly was—of values that belonged to the public was Peter Witt, who had also been a lieutenant of Tom Johnson and who defended to the end his policies. I went over the ground with Witt and saw the disadvantages of the Public Square underground site, which would have to be reached by a long viaduct and tunnel. In spite of local opposition, my articles in the *New Republic*, and the refusal of the Pennsylvania and other roads, except the "Nickel Plate," to participate, the Interstate Commerce Commission, after repeated refusals, finally yielded, and the Van Sweringens had their prize. Their trolley lines were soon obsolete; options for space in the station were not taken up; the rents did not sustain the expense of the great office building; the shift of business to the Public Square proved a detriment to the city; and the New York Central was saddled with an annual obligation for interest on the bonds which it had guaranteed.

6

The third party movement fell naturally into the field of the *New Republic*. In 1923, Croly wrote: "No matter how difficult and hazardous it may be to start a progressive party . . . the ability to do so will prove to be the infallible test of the vitality of any progressive agitation." He added: "A farmer-labor coalition would unify the economic groups which are now suffering most severely from discrimination and have most reason to favor radical reforms."

The Liberals were moving in these years to develop issues on which a campaign could be fought in 1924, with Senator Robert M. La Follette as presidential candidate. A meeting at Cleveland, in December 1922, formed the Committee for Progressive Political Action. Public ownership of utilities was obviously a progressive doctrine, and a conference on the valuation of railroad property was held in Chicago on May 25, 1923. The scandals of the Harding administration, especially the transfer of government oil reserves to Doheny and Sinclair, which sent the Secretary of the Navy into retirement and the Secretary of the Interior to prison, furnished a significant background for a campaign for reform.

Senator La Follette was the obvious and necessary candidate of the Progressives in 1924. The cause of advanced liberalism was typified by the Senator from Wisconsin, the state which under his leadership had given a practical demonstration of government devoted to the interests of the people. La Follette had once before launched a national progressive movement, in 1912, but Theodore Roosevelt had edged him out. He had suffered temporary eclipse because of his opposition to the war, but by 1924 his steadfast isolation represented the mood of disillusionment prevalent throughout the country which had seen the fruits of victory turn into apples of Sodom.

The convention which formed the Progressive party met in Cleveland, July 3 and 4. It was united on the candidate but divided among a dozen groups and interests. It was most important to secure the adherence of the Socialists, who had a party organization and campaign experience. Morris Hillquit was their leader. I admired his renunciation of the party label and the place on the ballot, won in the previous election when Eugene Debs had polled nearly a million votes, in order to support the common cause. The nomination of Democratic Senator Wheeler for vice-president was fortunate since the next week the Democratic party, apparently bent on suicide, allowed Norman Davis and Frank Polk to pin the nomination on John W. Davis after exhausting itself in a convention divided for days between McAdoo and Smith. As I listened to the Democratic nominee's embarrassed speech before the convention in the evening, my hopes set strongly toward the Progressives, not to become at once the first, but at least the second party in the country.

My interest in the campaign was chiefly the foreign affairs plank in the platform. Mr. Hamilton Fish Armstrong projected a series of articles in *Foreign Affairs* on the three platforms and invited me to make the statement for the Progressives. I consulted Senator La Follette, but found him rather indifferent. He did not think the people would be interested and he felt that discussion of the subject would draw attention from the domestic issues which were vital. Accordingly he gave me practically a free hand. I interpreted the platform in the spirit of liberalism, as a repudiation of nationalism and especially of financial imperialism. I wrote:

> If Mr. La Follette is elected President we may expect to see his foreign policy directed to promote the pacification and prosperity of the world without subtraction or reservation in favor of the special interests of the United States—generously and whole-heartedly and patriotically, in the conviction that our own peace and welfare are bound up with those of other nations and that we are strong enough to act on that principle.

I believe today that if this policy could have been followed with respect to great powers as well as small nations, the world might have been spared a second world war.

One pleasant episode of the campaign was the relation between the candidate and Senator Norris. Together they had fought the battles for progressive causes in the Senate. The support of Norris was important to the solidarity of the movement. He was a candidate for re-election to the Senate as a Republican that year, but he offered to withdraw his name and give his full endorsement to the Progressive campaign. La Follette would not have it. He pointed out that Norris's presence in the Senate was indispensable and must not be sacrificed. In the end, Norris went to his summer home in Michigan and remained neutral in the campaign, certainly lending no support to Coolidge.

The failure of La Follette to carry more than his own state in 1924 was a blow to the hopes of the *New Republic* for a new political alignment. Croly had been dissatisfied with the conduct of the campaign, with the use of propaganda and the appeal to class interests. He accepted the defeat philosophically, finding comfort in the thought that liberals were now "in a position to attach less importance to politics and to devote themselves to the original task of liberalism—the search for a liberating knowledge of human nature and society."

Liberals apparently tended to accept this advice. In 1928 their vote was divided between Hoover and Smith, both of whom claimed the liberal designation, although the Socialist vote was significant with the candidacy of Norman Thomas. In the disappointment following Hoover's election a meeting was called in the autumn of 1929 by my university colleague Paul Douglas to form a Committee for Independent Political Action, which had as its textbook Professor Dewey's *The Public and Its Problems*. Professor Dewey's recipe for organizing the public in a democracy was the application of social science. "This inchoate public is capable of organization only when indirect consequences are perceived, and when it is possible to project agencies which order their occurrence." This doctrine was entirely in line with the social program laid down by Herbert Croly. Obviously, its practical application was a long-term proposition, and the rush of events proved too rapid for it. The depression and the New Deal immersed the public in problems of day-by-day existence.

7

One of the most passionate interests of the editors of the *New Republic* was the Sacco-Vanzetti case, not only because of the appealing personalities of the victims but because of the light cast on the processes of justice, both of nation and a state—"there she stands!" In the efforts of the Department of Justice under A. Mitchell Palmer to deport radicals a certain Salsedo was arrested in New York and held incommunicado on the fourteenth floor of a Park Row building. The next day his body was found on the street after his murder or suicide. Two of his comrades in an anarchist group in Massachusetts,

Nicola Sacco and Bartolomeo Vanzetti, were raising money for his defense, and also warning their associates to conceal any anarchistic literature which might result in their sharing his fate. Their efforts in this regard aroused the suspicion of government detectives, and the idea occurred of connecting the men with two hold-up crimes, one committed December 24, 1919, in Bridgewater and the other on April 15, 1920, in South Braintree, Massachusetts. When taken up on May 5, they assumed that their arrest was due to radical activities, and in trying to conceal these they exhibited what the trial judge finally stated was the basis of the whole case against them—"consciousness of guilt."

The trial judge was one Webster Thayer of Worcester, a favorite son of Dartmouth College. He presided at the trial of Vanzetti in Plymouth for the abortive hold-up in Bridgewater. Vanzetti was a fishmonger. His alibi rested on the testimony of customers, mainly Italian, who swore that they had made purchases from him on the day of the crime. Apparently Vanzetti's lawyer failed to warn the witnesses not to embroider their testimony with details which might seem false and discrediting. That nearly all specified that they had bought eels on the day in question was a damaging circumstance, the court being ignorant of the fact that eels are a usual part of the Italian feast at Christmas. Sacco's alibi for the Bridgewater crime was perfect because he had been at his work in a shoe factory at the time. Vanzetti was found guilty and sentenced to prison.

The second hold-up was a more serious affair. Two men in charge of payroll boxes containing some fifteen thousand dollars were shot dead in front of the factory by a gang who escaped in an automobile with their booty. Sacco and Vanzetti were accused of being in the gang and were brought to trial at Dedham a year later, on May 31, 1921, before Judge Thayer. The subsequent proceedings were admirably summarized by Professor (now Justice) Felix Frankfurter in his book *The Case of Sacco and Vanzetti*. Frankfurter was a director in the *New Republic* company, in close contact with the editors, and through him I followed the case.

The trial was conducted in circumstances calculated to appeal to the emotions of the jury, which was protected by keeping the prisoners in a cage. The two men had fled to Mexico to avoid the draft, and much of their cross-examination turned on their unpopular social views as anarchists, and their affection for this country, all calculated to appeal to patriotic passions of the time. The trial at first turned on the identification of the prisoners by witnesses of the crime. During the year this testimony had gained in assurance and definiteness, and when one witness was caught in discrepancies between her original and final statements the district attorney gave his endorsement by assuring the jury that during his long service he had never "laid eye on or given ear to so convincing a witness." The strongest witness, a Mr. Gould, who stood close to the murder car, who was himself shot in the getaway, and who reported to the police at once, was never called to the stand, and his existence long remained unknown to the defense. His statement was positive that neither Sacco nor Vanzetti was present. The worst feature of Judge Thayer's conduct of the case occurred in his charge to the jury when he distorted the doubtful testimony of the ballistics expert, Captain Proctor of the State Police, into an absolute assertion that the mortal bullet found in the body of the payroll guard was fired from Sacco's pistol.

My interest grew when Mr. William G. Thompson entered the case. As president of the Suffolk County Bar he had gone to Dedham to hear Judge Thayer's charge to the jury. He reported that while the judge's charge was correct in its text, his manner of addressing the jury, with facial innuendoes, was so prejudicial that he offered to associate himself with the defense. I had known Thompson at Harvard, where he suffered the reading of my junior year forensics. Now I renewed the acquaintance and saw much of him during the long-drawn-out proceedings. Thompson had built up a lucrative practice in Boston. His connection with the Sacco-Vanzetti case cost him nearly all his clients. He told me that but for the help of his associates he would not have been able to carry on his office.

The feeling that these Italians had not had a fair trial extended to others. Not since the days of the Abolitionists and the protest against the Fugitive Slave Law had Boston been so stirred with divided emotions. Mrs. Glendower Evans became a leader in this, as in so many other humane causes. Mary Donovan was secretary of a defense committee composed mainly of Italians, later expanded by Gardner Jackson. Herbert B. Ehrmann, as Thompson's assistant, devoted himself unsparingly to recovering hitherto hidden evidence for presentation to the court on the several occasions when motions for a new trial were argued. These motions were based upon the discovery of Gould as an eyewitness, upon the false interpretation of Captain Proctor's testimony in Judge Thayer's charge, upon the statement of a fellow prisoner of Sacco, a Portuguese boy named Madeiros, who confessed that he was one of the gang which had committed the Braintree murders and could testify that Sacco and Vanzetti were not among them. All motions for a new trial were rejected by Judge Thayer, who was in effect always passing upon the question of his own prejudice. Meanwhile, several witnesses testified to his behavior out of court, especially Professor Richardson of Dartmouth College, who told how the Judge came to him at a football game, eager-hearted as a boy, to exclaim, "Did you see what I did to those anarchist bastards?"

When at last the sentence of death was pronounced, efforts were redoubled by those who were determined that an unrighteous decision should not remain a black mark on the page of Massachusetts justice. The fate of the two men was now referred to Governor Alvin Fuller. He undertook a personal investigation of the case and at the same time appointed an advisory committee consisting of Judge Robert Grant of the Probate Court, retired, President A. Lawrence Lowell of Harvard, and President Samuel N. Stratton of the Massachusetts Institute of Technology. A worse selection could scarcely have been made. Judge Grant had already expressed an opinion on the case. He has told us in his autobiography that the Governor in naming him first naturally expected him to preside, as being familiar with judicial procedure, but that at the first meeting Lowell took the chair and thenceforth conducted proceedings. I had known Stratton as Professor Michelson's assistant in the Physics Department at Chicago, doing the routine work of his chief. Stratton was always a dependent.

Attention was now fixed on the proceedings before the commissioners. They reviewed the evidence *in extenso*, but it cannot be said that they exhibited high judicial competence. For example, an important point was the testimony of a clerk in the Italian consulate in Boston to the effect that Sacco had consulted him on the day of the murder in regard to taking his family to Italy. Sacco's alibi was further strengthened by the testimony of the editor of an Italian paper to the effect that Sacco had lunched with him and others on the same day. Asked how he identified the day, he remembered the discussion at table of a banquet to be tendered by Boston Italians to a Mr. Williams, a correspondent who had been in Italy during the war. Consulted in Washington, Williams placed the banquet at some time earlier, and Lowell enjoyed a triumph over the witnesses; but later Williams remembered that there were two banquets by different groups, of which one corresponded in date to that of the occasion cited. Lowell had to apologize to the Italians for calling them liars, but he continued to think of them as liars.

Hope was felt that when Judge Thayer came before the committee the essentially prejudiced nature of the man would appear, but Thayer proved to be a man after Lowell's own heart. Another hope was that Chief Justice Arthur P. Rugg of the Massachusetts Supreme Court would express his opinion as to Thayer's judicial competence. Thompson remarked that he hoped that Rugg would entertain the committee with his little imitation act which used to move the St. Botolph Club to laughter at the pompous silliness of Judge Thayer. Apparently he did not.

Rugg was on the defensive. The judicial system of Massachusetts was on the defensive. According to Massachusetts law no appeal to the Supreme Court was permissible after one year had elapsed since the passing of the sentence. What were two lives of obscure Italians in the balance?

As the date set for the execution drew near, efforts to save the doomed men became more desperate. Governor Fuller remarked in regard to Vanzetti's alibi that he had seen many people who alleged that they had bought eels of Vanzetti, but he had no evidence that Vanzetti ever had any eels to sell. Inquiry, therefore, was made of a merchant with whom Vanzetti had dealt and an inspection of his accounts was requested. The merchant had thrown out all accounts over seven years old. He permitted a search of the old papers in his attic by a group of Harvard Law School students under Ehrmann's direction. They found not only an entry of the sale on the date in question, but they obtained from the express company the record of the delivery of a barrel of eels with Vanzetti's receipt. Fuller remained impenetrable.

Other volunteers were on hand. Lawyers Arthur Garfield Hays, attorney for the Civil Liberties Union, Michael Musmanno from Pittsburgh, and John Finnerty from Washington came to Boston to reinforce the legal corps, as did Francis Fisher Kane, former Attorney General of Pennsylvania. The responsibility of the national government for the action of its agents in conspiring with local authorities had been brought out by the statement of two former detectives, who admitted that they did not believe Sacco and Vanzetti guilty but cynically declared that the Department of Justice wanted them deported and electrocution would serve as well. It was thought certain that the files of the Department contained reports of detectives who had followed Sacco and Vanzetti's movements that would certify their innocence. Hays and Musmanno went to Vermont to ask Attorney General John G. Sargent to open the files of the Department of Justice. They were refused. There remained an appeal to President Coolidge, then in South Dakota. At one of our conferences I heard the name of Charles Innes, the Republican leader in Boston, and remarked that "Chub" Innes and I had been classmates in the English High School. At once hopes soared. If Innes would call up the President long distance and request him to open the files the day would be saved. I saw Innes next day. He was sympathetic, though he did not give me a promise. He pointed out that the case concerned the state of Massachusetts and not the United States or the city of Boston. He thought the President would not go behind Fuller's opinion—and he added with distaste, "Fuller is a reformer." I remember that he either gave me a letter to Senator Butler, the Republican leader in Massachusetts, or telephoned an introduction. At any rate, Walter Frank and I drove to New Bedford that afternoon only to find that the Senator had sailed on his yacht, leaving no address.

Arthur Dehon Hill, a former district attorney of Boston, had joined Thompson for the defense. I think it was he who went to Beverly to ask Justice Holmes of the United States Supreme Court to grant a writ of certiorari. He also appeared before the Massachusetts Supreme Court with an eloquent plea that a legal technicality, such as the law that an appeal cannot be heard a year after sentence has been imposed, could not be invoked in a case which might become one of judicial murder. All in vain.

By this time public opinion in Boston had set strongly against the victims. Sacco and Vanzetti had become a bore, and, worse, an affront to the New England conscience. They must cease to disturb the peace of mind. Their cause with Boston was not helped by demonstrations of workers in cities all over the world. Ten years earlier such demonstrations had forced President Wilson to ask the Governor of California not to permit the execution of Tom Mooney. Now reaction was in the saddle. In Massachusetts what was a decent respect for the opinion of mankind compared with respect for the opinion of Mr. Lowell?

Young men and women who enjoyed some personal freedom as artists, writers, social workers, rallied in Boston. They picketed the State House; they held meetings on Boston Common. They were clubbed and jailed by the police, thirty-nine of them. On the night of August 21 they kept up their death march at the state prison while Thompson held a last interview with Vanzetti and took to Governor Fuller his firm conviction that his client was innocent. Not until the last moment was hope abandoned. But on August 23, 1927, Sacco and Vanzetti were electrocuted.

The aftermath of the famous case was important in the social history of the time. President Lowell was described to me as being privately on the defensive, but in public he hardened his heart. It might have seemed to an enlightened intelligence that the last person with whom he should associate was Judge Thayer, but with the opaque quality of mind which characterized him he attended a dinner of Dartmouth men in honor of their most distinguished alumnus and accepted the applause for what together they had done to the "anarchist bastards."

The believers in the innocence of Sacco and Vanzetti formed an association which undertook two tasks—the raising of a sum sufficient to pay for the publication of the voluminous records of the trial, and a volume of essays by eminent authorities dealing with different phases of the case. The first was taken out of our hands by William Flexner, who obtained the twenty-five thousand dollars necessary from a single source. The complete record in eight volumes (now in regular publication by Henry Holt and Co.) was circulated among libraries, law schools, and legal authorities throughout the world. I have yet to learn of an opinion adverse to the general view that Sacco and Vanzetti were denied a fair trial. The second objective was achieved so far as the collection of articles was concerned, which were entrusted to a highly competent professor of law for criticism and an introduction. Why the volume never appeared I do not know. Perhaps the editor did not approve the papers submitted, or possibly he thought that the number of books published meanwhile was sufficient, including among others Felix Frankfurter's, Herbert Ehrmann's, Norman Hapgood's, and especially Upton Sinclair's *Boston.* Our plan, however, looked not to a review of the case so much as to a discussion of it in its broad social aspects. It is unfortunate that this volume never appeared.

A third function devolved upon the Sacco-Vanzetti National League. After the confession of Madeiros, suspicion had been concentrated on the gang of which he was a member, headed by Jake Morelli, as the real criminals in the Braintree affair. Morris Ernst now established contact with Morelli and found him willing, for a sum of money, to give a full story of the hold-up, exonerating Sacco and Vanzetti and supplying corroborative evidence in the form of a bank account showing the disposition of the plunder, and especially indicating where the boxes containing the payroll money had been thrown into some lake or swamp. To pay Morelli and provide funds for an investigation of his statements it was thought would require some fifty thousand dollars. As chairman of the Sacco-Vanzetti National League I called a meeting of persons likely to be interested; Oswald Garrison Villard lent his house for the gathering. The assembled company and others subscribed some thirty-five thousand dollars, but before the remaining sum could be underwritten the financial collapse of October 1929 occurred. The largest subscriber could not meet his pledge, and others were embarrassed. Nevertheless, I think of my failure to carry this plan through as the most lamentable dereliction in my life. As I have realized more and more clearly and keenly what a complete and public demonstration of the innocence of the victims, and the fallibility, not to say guilt, of agencies of government and justice, would have meant in forwarding a revolution in political life and the discrediting of pursy, pompous pretenders to the confidence of the people, I have bitterly deplored my lack of a sufficient sense of responsibility and of initiative in failing to grasp the opportunity.

The Sacco-Vanzetti case was an emotional experience in my life. It forced me to accept a doctrine which I had always repudiated as partisan tactics—the class war. It is clear that the two Italians—the good shoemaker and the poor fish dealer—were in the end victims of class hatred. The legal questions were lost sight of in the hatred of the ruling class for two men who challenged it. The opinion so often heard that whether they were guilty or not, Sacco and Vanzetti must die, was the judgment of the rich and well-to-do against the poor.

8

It was probably on account of my connection with the Sacco-Vanzetti League that I became associated with a successful effort to prevent a similar miscarriage of justice. Early on the morning of Memorial Day, 1928, before the assembling of Italian-American fascists, the leaders of two wings of the party, orthodox and secession, were simultaneously murdered in the Bronx. Both were buried with military honors, wreaths from the Italian Ambassador duly in evidence. Certainly it was permitted to infer that both murders were inside jobs to remove obstacles to uniting the party, but clearly it was necessary to the dignity of fascism that guilt should be fixed outside and victims furnished. Suspicion fell upon two Italians in Brooklyn, Greco and Carillo, who had been concerned as anti-fascists in a disturbance a week earlier. All non-fascist Italian organizations in New York joined together to form a defense committee; I was asked to be the chairman. No refusal was possible, I was assured, since the union was in itself an incredible event and a fight over the chairmanship would shatter it at the start. We met regularly on Saturday afternoon, a rather stormy assembly but perfectly courteous to the drafted chairman, who, flanked by two interpreters, was enabled to preside with dignity and maintain a somewhat doubtful contact with the proceedings.

I believe the sum collected was more than twenty thousand dollars. It was needed because the Italian wing of the Police Department, largely fascist, was determined to provide a victim. Clarence Darrow and Arthur Garfield Hays were associated in the defense, which encountered obstacles similar to those in the Sacco-Vanzetti case. I asked Darrow how a district attorney could lend himself to such a proceeding. "Well," he replied, tolerantly as always, "he has his own career to consider. He can't let down the police. If he doesn't push the case to the limit he will be accused of collusion or indifference. If he obtains a conviction he may get to be governor; and then he can always save the men from the chair by admitting later that he isn't sure they are guilty and recommending commutation of sentence."

The defense was confronted by a special difficulty. As in the case of Vanzetti in Plymouth, the good will of witnesses frequently outran veracity. Greco worked as a tailor in the rear of his brother-in-law's shop, where musical instruments and records were sold. Many asserted that they had seen him at work there on the fatal morning, but on being asked whom else they saw in the music shop they assembled a substantial fraction of the people of Brooklyn, all buying piccolos, flutes, fiddles, and records. Darrow remarked that he feared his own witnesses more than those of the prosecution.

The first break in our favor was the announcement of the judge—Cohen, a Jew. A hope at least of justice! When the panel of the jury was complete and it appeared that four of the chosen were Jews, we considered the case won. I never saw Darrow in better form than when he cross-examined a hostile witness. He would lead the victim to the brink of the precipice, where one question more would topple him into the abyss of perjury, and then turn away as if discouraged. Four hands would shoot up in the jury box, and in spite of the judge's deprecation of such activity the fatal question would emerge and the shattered witness would retire in confusion. Greco and Carillo did not follow Sacco and Vanzetti.

9

Resignations from the editorial staff of the *New Republic* in the years after the debate over the Treaty of Versailles depressed Croly, who regarded continuity as the essential basis of his plan. Walter Lippmann went to the *World*, and later Bob Littell. Francis Hackett resigned to write a history of Ireland, and Alvin Johnson to direct the New School for Social Research. The great opportunity offered Johnson by this position did not impress Croly as compared with the claim of the *New Republic*. On the other hand, several recruits came in. Stark Young took over dramatic criticism; Edmund Wilson, whom I have always considered one of the leading critics of our time as treating literature with a background of philosophy, reviewed books; and Bruce Bliven became in effect the managing editor. His experience as managing editor of the *New York Globe* gave him a wide acquaintance among journalists, and "middle articles" on subjects of contemporary interest gradually outweighed in importance the editorials of the board. Croly withdrew more and more into the religion of liberalism—"Liberals have wished on themselves without knowing it the job of discovering some way of making themselves and other people experts in the art of leading the good life." One evening he explained to me the discipline, physical and mental, initiated by Gourdjef in France. The strenuous rule was too severe. In 1928 he suffered a stroke. He made a desperate fight for life, for he was convinced that the existence of the journal depended on his recovery. He had said indeed that he did not wish the *New Republic* to survive him. Mrs. Straight, now Mrs. Elmhirst, decided otherwise, and on his death the next year Bruce Bliven continued to carry on as managing editor. My active connection with the paper ceased at Croly's death, though I continued to write for it.

At Mrs. Croly's and Mrs. Elmhirst's request I planned a collection of Croly's articles. I made the selection for the book and Felix Frankfurter was to write the introduction. Meanwhile, however, Professor

Frankfurter had become a Justice of the Supreme Court. Without this introduction and without a financial guarantee the volume was declined by several publishers. They felt that the public had moved too far from the interests and temper of the nineteen-twenties to be recalled. I regret this, as the selections seem to me the record of a permanent aspect of liberal thought, and of an editorial conscience comparable to that of such great English editors as C. P. Scott of the *Manchester Guardian* and H. J. Massingham of the *Nation*, who was Herbert Croly's ideal.

XII. *New York and Elsewhere*, 1921–1939

I

MY SEMI-ANNUAL residence in New York brought me into relation with two causes having to do with life and death. Across the garden from my studio lived George and Juliet Rublee. George had been a notable figure at Harvard in my day, having the reputation of being the ablest student on the campus. He told me once that he had wished to be a teacher of Greek at Groton, but having entered the Law School to please his father he unexpectedly found himself at the end of his first year rated as the second man in his class. I had special sympathy with him as one whose career had been fortuitously determined by high marks. Though he rendered conspicuous public service in connection with the Ballinger case during Taft's administration, by temperament he was a most amiable Laodicean.

Not so Juliet Rublee, whom I had sometimes seen at a distance in my early years in Chicago. She was the second in a group of fascinating sisters, an ardent, I may say a flaming, spirit. She was a close friend of Margaret Sanger, and the driving force in the birth-control movement in New York. I saw this cause winning support among members of the middle class who were already convinced, but I felt that it would never advance among the masses until the Pope should be converted. I do not think this impossible, for His Holiness must eventually realize that the indefinite increase of population on the globe is the final and inescapable reason for some form of communism. At present, however, the attitude of the Church is uncompromising. We planned a public meeting for Mrs. Sanger one Sunday evening in a theater, and on arrival found a large audience outside. A cordon of police held the approaches. When asked who had ordered the theater closed, the captain in charge replied simply, "The Cardinal."

The second cause was capital punishment. Vivian Pierce, whom I had known as an organizer in the Women's party, asked me to become a director in the American League for the Abolition of Capital Punishment. I consented, and as long as I remained in New York I was a faithful attendant at meetings. Vivian Pierce was a personality to whom the overworked adjective "vivid" inevitably applies. With burning zeal she carried the campaign into other states, while maintaining the office in New York, where her salary was always in arrears (if it was ever paid) and her assistance was scanty. The important directors were Warden Lewis E. Lawes of Sing Sing, Professor George W. Kirchwey, then head of the Department of Criminology at the New York School of Social Work, and Clarence Darrow.

There are various arguments against capital punishment, such as factual uncertainty of conviction and psychological uncertainty in regard to fundamental guilt, as well as the question of the right of the state to take life in any circumstances; but the argument that most appealed to me was the vulgarizing of the public by providing sensational stuff for the press, forcing respectable papers to verge toward the yellow. One of Thackeray's *Roundabout Papers* had much to do with the abandonment of public executions. His argument applies to all executions. In view of the means of publicity available today the death house has lost its privacy, and the spectacle of execution has become a public function, adding a supreme sensation to those provided by crime. The writers of detective stories should be commended by Will Cuppy, the highest critical authority, for their good taste in usually permitting their villains to extinguish themselves.

On one occasion a number of us accepted Warden Lawes' invitation to visit Sing Sing. The "lifers" were his best prisoners, having made a tolerable and not useless existence for themselves within the humane and intelligent system inaugurated by Warden Thomas Mott Osborne and carried further by his successor Dr. Kirchwey. I remember meeting a radical who had tested prison life in many countries. The worst jail he found was at Oxford. Of Sing Sing he had only this to say: "It's a hotel."

The afternoon of our visit was enlivened by a baseball game between the teams of the New York Stock Exchange and the prison.

The latter won. I remarked innocently that they had the advantage of longer hours of practice.

"Oh, no," said Warden Lawes. "They all work in various departments. I have hard work to get the foremen to allow half an hour a day."

"What you need," remarked Bill Chenery, "is a strong alumni association."

"Well, we have one," replied Mr. Lawes. "They take a real interest in us, visit us occasionally, meet our graduates on leaving us and help them get started. Why, one of them is on the Stock Exchange team today."

2

In 1924 I had a very pleasant personal relation to Senator La Follette. He asked me to call on him one day in New York and told me that he wished that I should become president of the University of Wisconsin. He spoke of his great love of the university, of which both he and Mrs. La Follette were graduates. I was impressed, just as I had been when President Eliot asked me to do something at Harvard. Indeed, both men remain in my memory as superb gentlemen, genuinely kind and with extraordinary distinction of manner. I told Mr. La Follette that, flattered as I was, I could not consent to become a candidate unless I had assurance that the faculty was in favor of me. I had a firm conviction that a university faculty should have a voice in choosing its chief, and there the matter rested.

A little latter Herman L. Ekern, then the Attorney General of Wisconsin, called on me in Chicago with word that Governor Blaine would like to see me, and accordingly I spent an evening with him at Madison. I wrote for advice as to the situation to Professor John R. Commons, and received from him a fine honest reply. He told me frankly that I was not the man. While I had some friends in the Modern Language departments, these were not of first importance in an institution interested mainly in the natural and social sciences. The social science men wanted Dean Roscoe Pound of the Harvard Law School. Moreover, he added, a conservative reaction was due in the state; the new Board of Regents would promptly throw me out, and that would be a defeat for the liberals. I wrote him a letter of thanks and received a second letter saying that I had almost convinced him that he was wrong. He thought I might get away with it. "I like a man who doesn't take himself too seriously," he wrote.

Next Phil La Follette burst upon me one night to assure me that the Board of Regents proposed to elect me the next day. It seemed, however, that there was an unwritten agreement that the incumbent should be allowed to complete fifty years of service to the university, which he had entered as an office boy, and Phil had counted wrong. It was only forty-nine. The next year the Regents elected Dean Pound, who had promised his acceptance but finally decided to stay in Cambridge. That made it easy for me to withdraw as a candidate, having been rejected once for Pound; and Miss Zona Gale, who was a Regent, persuaded her colleagues in the general confusion to elect Glenn Frank.

I have always thought it unfortunate that Pound did not accept. He was a Midwesterner, a strong and genial man whose sense of humor was far more robust than mine. His stories would have delighted the legislators, and he could have swung a big fist on the faculty. He would have saved the state from the scandal of throwing out Glenn Frank, and he would have made for himself a brilliant and useful career, instead of lingering in Cambridge, out of tone with the faculty which had prevailed upon him to remain.

3

In those early days of the Volstead Act I had a rather special function in the *New Republic*—that of almoner. Herbert Croly, like many other liberals, held that it was the part of good citizenship to defy the law and thus force its repeal. I brought from Charles Wood of Lake Zurich a strong opinion that the Eighteenth Amendment was unconstitutional, having been recommended to the states by Congress without the necessary two-thirds of the membership of each House, but with only two-thirds of those present and voting. In the early days of the temperance regime, however, enforcement was seriously undertaken and defiance of the law was not the easy way out that it became later.

I had found a friend, through Hutchins Hapgood, in Luke O'Connor, the proprietor of the once famous saloon known as "The Working Girls' Home." Luke had been president of the Saloon Keepers' Association of New York, and had taken pride in the movement of the trade to reform itself. It was a surprise to him, in the face of these improvements, to find himself outside the law. He took up his cross, however, and bore it gallantly, opening an establishment at the corner of Fourth and Perry Streets, where he made it a point of honor, as he said, not to let his old clients down. As customers stood at the bar, occupying themselves with small beers, Luke would suddenly receive signs from his scouts from both directions, and quickly would shoot out his hands fan-like, his fingers separated by thin glasses like test tubes, holding what we came for.

When the chase became too hot Luke retired to the second story, where at little tea-house tables, behind lace curtains, his habitués looked a bit too refined to seem convincing. On the wall was a magnificent photograph of a banquet of the Saloon Keepers' Association with Luke presiding, looking like John L. Sullivan with his white curling mustache. It was one of Luke's principles not to mix wine and women, but in view of the feminine décor of the café I thought that he must have relaxed, and one day I had the bad sense to make an appointment to meet Hutch and Neith Hapgood there. On arriving I found Luke in a high state of indignation. I had put him in the position of turning an old friend from his door and "insulting the wife of him." I found my guests sipping chocolate in the delicatessen across the street.

I learned that it was in The Working Girls' Home that John Masefield had served an apprenticeship in the scullery. Luke was fond of the poet and liked to talk about him. I was unfortunately absent when Mrs. Lamont brought Masefield to lunch at the *New Republic;* but I was glad to know that he remembered Luke and found his way to Luke's present quarters.

4

One fortuitous connection with literature was my service on the jury granting the Pulitzer Prize for novels. My first appearance in 1920 was not auspicious. Hamlin Garland, the chairman, chose Stuart Pratt Sherman, then a professor at the University of Illinois, and me to act with him. Sherman and I agreed on Sinclair Lewis's *Main Street* as satisfying Mr. Pulitzer's condition—"the novel exemplifying the highest standard of American manners and manhood, and the wholesome atmosphere of American life." Our argument was that *Main Street,* by provoking discussion in regard to standards and atmosphere, advanced the tendency toward higher things in our way of life. We were surprised when the award went to Edith Wharton's

Age of Innocence, which, though a fine technical performance, seemed to fall outside of Mr. Pulitzer's frame of reference.

Some years later I was again invited to serve on the jury, with Professor Richard Burton of the University of Minnesota and Jefferson Fletcher of Columbia. I knew what Mr. Pulitzer meant by the conditions laid down and was insistent that we should try to meet them in spite of the raging of critics who naturally could always suggest better novels than the one we had chosen. My greatest disappointment was in my failure to persuade my colleagues to give the award to Elizabeth Madox Roberts' *Time of Man*, which was certainly the finest novel of the year and which fully satisfied the specifications. Another year I urged Upton Sinclair's *Boston*, but Burton and Fletcher voted for John R. Oliver's *Victim and Victor*, which certainly sets a high standard in an atmosphere Anglo-Catholic rather than American, whether wholesome or not. It was enjoined on us to leave the announcement of the decision to the trustees, along with the awards for poetry, plays, and journalism, but Burton revealed the secret as a *bonne bouche* in one of his popular lectures, and the trustees canceled the award. Later the trustees relieved our embarrassment by changing the conditions to the "whole atmosphere of American life," and finally abolished them altogether, leaving us free to choose whatever novel we thought best.

I do not remember whether it was under the conditions originally imposed or in the later period of free choice that we made the award to Sinclair Lewis's *Arrowsmith*. It would have been appropriate in any case. It was somewhat surprising to have the author publicly repudiate the award on the ground that the whole system of prizes was a detriment to literature as tempting authors to write with a view to satisfying the standards of the jury. We were flattered at the attribution of a power to alter the current of literature and realized more than ever our responsibility to exercise it wisely. We were happily surprised, however, when Mr. Lewis withdrew his objection a year or two later by accepting the Nobel prize.

5

My divided interests between Chicago and New York enabled me to be of some use to artists and writers seeking connections in one or the other city. One of my happiest relations was with Jo Davidson, who came to Chicago in the early days of his career with a letter from Hutchins Hapgood. From that time he has been a bright strand woven into the texture of my life, recurring in the pattern only too rarely. His enormous acquaintance with the great of this world, including the leaders of two wars, make him a source of footnotes to history. He told me of a charming episode with President Roosevelt. While doing a bust of the President at the White House he could not stop in time to dress for dinner and came to the table as he was. The next evening he appeared in a dinner jacket, but Mr. Roosevelt had not changed.

Another brilliant figure of occasional appearance in the pattern was Amy Lowell. Miss Lowell lived on Heath Street in Brookline. She sometimes called me by telephone at my father's house—once to borrow a pair of pants for Maxwell Bodenheim, whose careless dress had excited the suspicion of Miss Lowell's dogs. My aunt once remarked on Miss Lowell's democratic manner when calling, "She just says 'I'm Amy Lowell.' "

Dinner at the Heath Street house was exciting. On one occasion Miss Lowell and Professor John Livingston Lowes scolded me because of my favorable review of André Maurois' *Ariel: The Life of Shelley;* on another, Miss Lowell and Florence Ayscough (later the wife of a colleague, Professor H. F. MacNair, at Chicago) were immersed in translating or imitating Chinese poetry. After dinner Miss Lowell, smoking her long black cigar, commanded the company from her station in front of the fireplace, where she fed the flames from a pile of thin-cut hickory slats, six feet long. On her visit to Chicago I introduced Miss Lowell at a dinner at the Arts Club. As we looked down the long table after the waiters had withdrawn we saw heads thrust forward in our direction. "They're looking for me to light my cigar," remarked the poet. "I'm not going to do it."

My first summer in New York Vachel Lindsay and I seemed to be the only people in town. We took dinner nearly every evening on the roof of the old Majestic Hotel at Seventy-second Street, and watched the lights go on, following the long graceful curves of the park roads. The view inspired Lindsay to draw with a pen innumerable arabesque sketches of which he explained the rhythms. A more simple, candid, generous soul I never knew. I admired his chanting of the great flowing cadences of "The Congo" and "General Booth Enters into Heaven." The students at the university gave "The Chinese Nightingale" with my daughter Ruth as the princess. Vachel was infinitely pleased and wanted her to give up everything to follow him and accompany his poetry in dance, but "The Potatoes Dance" was not one of his happiest efforts. I remember the refrain, chanted in his Midwestern speech:

> Pertaters were the waiters,
> Pertaters were the waiters,
> Pertaters were the waiters,
> Pertaters were the band.

Ruth could not fit her carefully studied ballet steps to the homely rhythm.

Vachel was a bard in the old tradition, a free and spontaneous singer. He had a theory that every community, every neighborhood, should have its poet singing on the street corner. He began his career by wandering through the South, literally singing for his supper and night's lodging. He had his days of recognition in England and came back to Chicago in triumph. But though he could support himself by poetry he could not take care of a family. Worry and a morbid conscience toward his responsibilities were certainly the causes of his untimely death.

Renewed acquaintance with Carl Van Vechten brought me some of the richest experiences of my life. Van Vechten had found his vein in eccentric romances, *The Blind Bowboy* and *The Tattooed Countess*, which place him with Ronald Firbank and Norman Douglas. Through him I read and reviewed Elinor Wylie's lovely novel, *Jennifer Lorn*, and met the no less lovely author. In pure poetry I place her among the first.

Van Vechten also introduced me to a novel of exquisite artistry, *Love-Days*, by Henri Waste, who turned out to be Ettie Stettheimer, author of an earlier book, *Philosophy*, highly praised by Randolph Bourne. The Stettheimer family, mother and daughters, lived in a sumptuous apartment on the corner of Fifty-eighth and Seventh Avenue, where they made me welcome. Their circle was of a seventeenth-century distinction. I took Phil Littell there, and he was fascinated. The youngest sister, Florine, was a painter of scenes of eccentric beauty touched by irony, a world of romance flavored by the grotesque. One met at the Stettheimers Philip Moeller and members of the Theatre Guild, Archipenko the sculptor, Henry MacBride and Paul Rosenfeld, the critics, Rabbi Wise and Professor Seligman, Mr. and Mrs. Alfred Knopf, Virgil Thomson; it recalled a culture such as that pictured by Arthur Schnitzler in Vienna, before World War I.

A special interest of Van Vechten's was the Negro. At his apartment I met Langston Hughes, James Weldon Johnson, and other poets, as well as the singers Paul Robeson and Josephine Mills.

6

The author I knew best was Sherwood Anderson. I first met Sherwood at one of the studios on Fifty-seventh Street in Chicago which had been erected as shops at the time of the Columbian Exposition and since had served to house the flotsam and jetsam of Chicago culture. He came one evening to read part of a novel which he had begun much in the manner of Dreiser. He was in workman's clothes, which, I seem to remember, carried a seducing odor of paint. The reading did not impress his audience, except Floyd Dell, who a year later sent *Windy McPherson's Son* to John Lane in London. Then *Winesburg, Ohio* made a hit, with its individual biographies in the manner of the Spoon River epitaphs, which added up to an authentic character sketch of a town. Later I met Sherwood Anderson in New York, when I had written enthusiastic reviews of his successive volumes of short stories and rather severe criticisms of his novels. I thought that the former grew out of his intimate personal relation with his material, as so well explained in several passages in *A Story-Teller's Story* and in the preface to *Horses and Men*. His novels began with the same intimacy and mastery of material, but tended to lose their way and become merely badly imagined fiction, most pathetically true of *Poor White*. Only in *Dark Laughter* did he succeed in bringing through a work of the larger dimension. I wrote more about Sherwood Anderson than about any other contemporary, and though he protested my lack of sympathy with his novels we remained good friends, in testimony of which I quote a letter I received from him in 1923.

Your review of *Horses and Men* in the *Dial* has stirred up in me anew a desire I have long had to write you a note. It would be infinitely nicer if I could talk to you.

As for the review I have no quarrel with it, of course. You have always been whole-heartedly generous with me. However, you have written several reviews and articles after books of mine and in all of them I have thought there was—in minor but to me important directions—a misunderstanding of what I had aimed at and sometimes, it seemed to me, achieved.

You make a point which you have made before, of my having sacrificed intelligence to the emotional. Is that quite sound? Can emotional surrender to a theme get anywhere without guiding intelligence? Add to this your stricture about my taking people who are messed up. Perhaps the word messed up is too strong. I mean to imply that the [two illegible words] reacts on the lives of all sensible people. That I try to make the implication of my letter.

Dear friend, do you really know anyone who is not messed up?

Naturally I prefer, in life and in art, drawing close to rather sensitive people. Can a man be at all sensitive to life and be quite clear and unriled? It would seem to me a kind of stupidity to be so.

And does not the very point you make, that one person chooses a particular story as being my best, while another is untouched by that story and deeply by another, imply that the writer of these tales has used his head also?

You see that I am puzzled by you—frankly.

The wide divergence in the opinions you have heard is of course even more apparent to me. Ferdinand and Paul Rosenfeld (two widely different types of men I think) were both deeply moved by "An Ohio Pagan" in this book, a tale that apparently left you untouched.

You also take for granted the failure of my novels. That seems strange to me. Both *Poor White* and *Many Marriages* seemed to me to do what I wanted them to do. One does not go from the novel to the short tale for any reason but that some themes offer themselves for long, involved treatment, others for direct, simple treatment.

You see that I am not quarreling with you, dear man. I am interested to develop from you, some day, an amplification of what is your formula—if it can be written out and be expressed in a form that will answer for such men as myself.

Perhaps, after all, our difference is one of technical formula. Perhaps you have a formula on which you may depend. I wish I had. Your saying definitely that the novels are "failures" implies, doesn't it, that you know they are? And yet how deeply they have touched many people, how completely they have sometimes seemed to answer.

Not often I grant you.

I certainly do not wish to be impertinent, dear Lovett—perhaps I shall have to wait until some day when I can walk and talk with you.

7

As I came to a regular division of the year, giving summer and autumn to the East, I found refuge in several country places for week-ends and, after my engagement with the *New Republic* ceased to call for office work, for short visits. The most important was York

Village, Maine, where Herrick had reconstructed a farmhouse, and Jeff and Agnes Fletcher occupied an adjacent more pretentious residence known as the chateau. To their children I was endeared by the characters I had created for my own offspring—Ben Boon and Little Dog Fido. I followed young Jeff's career at St. Bernard's, St. Paul's, Harvard, and All Souls. When my own boy was killed he said solemnly to Agnes, "I must try to make it up to Uncle Robert." His death in an automobile accident was a sorrow in my life only less than my own boy's death.

With Robert Herrick, after the war which divided us, I spent many weeks in his cottage at York. The village was surrounded by woods growing about abandoned farms and grassy lanes which once had been roads, excellent country for walking. After Herrick's heart became a preoccupation he used to drive me to some vantage point for the start of a circuit, and several hours later would meet me at a terminal. He always gave me precise directions for the route. If on my return I reported any deviation he would remark with a sense of personal loss, "The walk was ruined."

For several years on these expeditions I had as my companion Micky, the Lupeta terrier which his master commemorated in his charming idyl, *Little Black Dog*. When I left the car Micky would bound joyfully beside me, then hearing the car start he would race back, but unable to forgo the walk he would return to me, and repeat the performance until the alternative became too great for his short legs. I sympathized with him as the type of a man making up his mind.

I never had better days than those which began in the early light of a brisk autumn morning, with Herrick impatiently sounding his horn. Then a drive to Kennebunkport, Cape Porpoise, or Old Orchard, by the sea, or inland to Liberty, Bethel, or the Limericks, and the return in the pleasant afternoon to chess, smoke, and drink by the fire. The autumn afternoon in Maine is unique in the brilliant color of flowers, the smell of ripe fruit and fallen leaves.

Always we took one long drive across New Hampshire to Cornish, Herrick to stay with Mabel and Winston Churchill, I with Louise and Ned Burling. After Herrick's appointment as Government Secretary of the Virgin Islands I was still welcomed there. The small circle of my friends was the most *simpatico* and the most concentrated in its gaiety, wit, and culture that I have known except at Florence. Up the road from the Burlings' was Judge Learned Hand

and his wife Frances, where one caught, now and then, glimpses of three lovely daughters. Then came George and Juliet Rublee. Up the hill by a wood path were Phil and Fanny Littell. Across hillside pastures we walked to the Churchills'. In later years came Margaret and Tiffany Blake from Chicago to rebuild Harlakenden, the original house where I had known Mabel and Winston Churchill years before. My classmate Jack Ames married Mary Goodyear of High Court, which I had frequented in Norman Hapgood's day. Working at the Saint-Gaudens' studio was Frances Grimes, whose tenant I was at Turtle Bay; and employed intermittently on *Fortune* was Katharine Hamill. Louis Dow was of the essence of the group.

These people formed a thoroughly self-sufficient community, meeting day after day, never bored with each other for long. Their kindly frankness or frank kindliness was illustrated by Ned Burling who, after dinner at his home, once asked Frances Hand, "Will you do something very special for me, Frances?"

"Why, of course, Ned. What is it?"

"Go home."

On my way south from Cornish I always stopped at Richmond, New Hampshire, where Neith and Hutch Hapgood had bought a farm. There and at Provincetown I continued my oldest friendship. Hutch had an extraordinary attraction for the greatest variety of associates, and, as I have noted, took pleasure in sharing them. At Provincetown he had Jig Cook, Susan Glaspell, and Mary Vorse. John Dos Passos and his wife lived next door. Hutch and Neith had founded the Provincetown Players, which first produced Eugene O'Neill's plays. Eugene and his wife Agnes lived across the narrow neck in the house which Robert Edmond Jones had designed for Mabel Dodge. Slender, dark, handsome, O'Neill would sit, courteous and silent, until late afternoon, when he would put to sea in his kayak to disappear on the horizon.

When Dorothy Woolsey was on the *New Republic* I used to visit her and Heathcote at Rye. One day we drove to Kent, where she found the farmhouse which under Heathcote's reconstruction became their year-round residence. I saw their children grow up in beauty and strength, and their homestead too.

Near by, at Ridgefield, Martha Dodd and Alfred Stern lived on an estate. It is in their large barn that I am supposed to be writing this book. Martha had been one of my pupils at Chicago; she had a subtle gift for stories that seemed to me as rare as Kay Boyle's. Her father was my liberal colleague on the faculty. I was in his study when President Roosevelt told him by telephone that he should go as Ambassador to Hitler's Germany. I took great interest in Martha's writing and enjoyed the success of her novel, *Sowing the Wind.*

The beauty of New England, though more exciting, is not more gratifying than that of New Jersey, where at Mendham I visited Agnes Cromwell. I used to see her and Seymour, who was my classmate, at the Crolys', and Agnes was often at luncheon at the *New Republic*, but only after Seymour's death did I come to know her well. Then it was Phil Littell who produced me as a novelty, for she had no recollection of my earlier appearances slightly above the horizon. Her veranda looked down to a lake over a rolling field, which, with the autumn-pale sun on the grass, seemed to invite to long afternoons of release. Mendham and its chatelaine were thoroughly in accord with my mood when we wore out.

> . . . packs and sects of great ones
> That ebb and flow by th' moon.

From 1922 on I enjoyed agreeable relations with Houghton Mifflin Company as consultant and editor of books on their English list, to which I contributed myself, first with *A History of the Novel in England*, in which I had the valuable co-operation of Helen Sard Hughes of Wellesley College; later with an anthology of *British Poetry and Prose* in collaboration with Robert Kilburn Root of Princeton and Paul Robert Lieder of Smith College. Among books in which I was concerned as editor I should mention *Eighteenth Century Prose and Poetry* by Odell Shepard and Paul S. Wood. My last service in this connection was with a really epoch-making book by Addison Hibbard of Northwestern University, *Writers of the Western World*. I also published in Chicago *A Preface to Fiction*, which Miss Elizabeth Greenebaum took down from my lectures and gave back enriched in style.

XIII. *The League for Industrial Democracy,* 1921–1939

I

THE INTERCOLLEGIATE SOCIALIST SOCIETY was founded in 1905 by Upton Sinclair, Jack London, J. G. Phelps-Stokes, and Harry Laidler for the purpose of encouraging the study of socialism in colleges. With a few exceptions—Simon N. Patten at the University of Pennsylvania, John R. Commons at Wisconsin, outstanding—the teaching of economics followed the lines laid down by Ricardo and Mill. Veblen gave a course in socialism at the University of Chicago, but I understood that his approach was cautious, as indeed was that of the Society. Its plan was to form groups of interested students, supply them with literature and if possible with speakers. A number of liberals and Socialists, including instructors in colleges, formed an advisory and supporting body. In spite of its laudable purpose and moderate attitude during the war, the Society came under the fire of the home-front guard, and persons of impeccable if tolerant conservatism were disgusted to find themselves pilloried in Senator Overman's list of subversives. It is true that the uncompromising stand of the Socialist party against the war made the Socialist label an impossible one for such an enterprise as the Society was undertaking with the middle class.

I attended meetings of the I. S. S. in the autumn of 1921, when a change of title was under discussion; and after the adoption of the name League for Industrial Democracy I was elected president, on the advice of Roger Baldwin, who as executive secretary of the American Civil Liberties Union was becoming the pope of the liberals. The new name indicated a change of purpose and attitude—a change from passive study to energetic opposition to the domination of the profit motive in industry. "Production for use rather than for profit" was its text. It continued its work by the same methods as before—addresses, publications, affiliated organizations—but it reached out beyond the colleges to the general public. The work among college students, however, remained a special interest of the League. Harry Laidler has continued as executive director. His *History of Socialistic Thought* was recognized as a standard textbook, and his presence in colleges, both on the campus and in the classroom, was welcome. Conferences were held every summer at such resorts as Camp Tamiment in Pennsylvania or Lake Mahopac. All these should be stated in the present tense, for the League continues to exist and prosper. These activities required elaborate organization. Laidler was an admirable chief, efficiently aided by an able staff of whom I remember in particular Mary Fox, Mary Hillyer, and Anna Caples. The Board of Directors, which met regularly with elaborate agendas, included Mrs. Walter Weyl, Elizabeth Gilman, Julien Schlossburg, and LeRoy Bowman. The original Socialist orientation was maintained by Helen Phelps-Stokes, Jessie Hughan, and Norman Thomas. A serious loss occurred when the college chapters voted to amalgamate with the Young Communist League and other youth organizations in the American Students' Union. Although I did not advocate this measure it was undoubtedly in accord with my general attitude of minimizing differences among liberals and radicals, and I raised no objection. For a time the Union worked harmoniously under the presidency of James Wechsler, but in the end the Young Communists, with superior organization and discipline, took control. The L. I. D. was obliged to re-establish its college work, which was the original cause of its existence.

The League bore a part in the movement to preserve the social gains won in the course of the war effort, especially as they were of benefit to labor. Other elements in the movement were the Brookwood Labor College, founded by A. J. Muste at Katonah, New York; a program of labor education financed by the American Fund for Public Service; the Labor Bureau founded by George Soule and Stuart Chase to give the assistance of trained economists to labor unions; and the Federated Press League to aid the labor press. A secondary school was founded at Pawling, New York, for the children of workers, of which Nellie Seeds Nearing became the principal. The plan was to charge a special tuition fee for the children of middle-class families who could afford to pay for the privilege of associating with the children of workers. At the meeting of trade unionists and liberals to draw up the curriculum Scott Nearing was insistent that the emphasis should be upon the economics of socialism, but the trade unionists were opposed. They wanted the conventional secondary school program that would fit their offspring for college.

2

One approach to the union of labor and middle class was through recognition of identity of interests. The real ownership of much of the industry of the country rests with the middle class, which, through shareholding, is just as subject to exploitation by the financial overlords and their appointees as is labor. A unique opportunity to demonstrate the possibility of this approach occurred in connection with the strike of textile workers in New Bedford in 1928, at the height of the great prosperity, which, however, had left out the cotton mills.

I had spent some of my happiest days in New Bedford and welcomed the opportunity, as reporter for the *New Republic*, to revisit the old town. It was an August morning and very pleasant. The city had grown from fifty thousand to one hundred and twenty thousand, and in place of four mills there were twenty-seven. The city was very quiet that day. Purchase Street was doing little business. Many men were working in little gardens on the outskirts of the city. There was a good deal of fishing from small boats in the bay. Toward noon, lines began to form outside of soup kitchens, conducted by the strike committee. There was little picketing and that ineffective. The *New Bedford Times*, favorable to the strikers, reported on August 3 that there were 267 pickets at all the mills, while 393 strikers "went in" to work.

New Bedford had taken its place in the manufacture of fine cotton goods with the establishment of the Wamsutta Mills in 1848. The whaling men put the revenues of their successful voyages into the mills in New Bedford as the merchants of Boston and Salem did in Lowell and Lawrence. New Bedford was fortunate in having ships to pick up cotton from Southern ports and labor from the Azores and Cape Verde Islands on their return voyages from the

Arctic. The industry suffered during the Civil War but prospered exceedingly during World War I. The older mills enlarged operations and declared stock dividends; new mills with improved machinery were opened. The capitalization of all the mills increased from nineteen million dollars in 1908 to seventy-one million in 1920. Then came the slump. The competition of Southern mills with their lower wage scales increased. Prices of goods fell. Petticoats were discarded. Dividends were passed. Corporations were liquidated, throwing real estate and workers on the market. The value of shares of all New Bedford mills on the stock market shrank nearly a hundred dollars per share. As much of the stock was held locally and represented the investment of the community over a century, the city was threatened by catastrophe. The population began to shrink. There was never a better example of "boom and bust."

The managements of the mills, except Dartmouth, belonged to the New Bedford Cotton Textile Manufacturers' Association, which in April declared a cut in wages of ten per cent. Among the workers were several hundred highly skilled British operatives who had been recruited in the boom period and who had brought with them seven small craft unions representing different stages in the process of manufacture. These refused to accept the cut, walked out, and were promptly joined by the great mass of workers, then unorganized. A Textile Council was elected, which was fortunate in having the services as adviser of Professor Norman Ware of Wesleyan University, who was recommended by the Labor Bureau of New York. The conduct of the strike was largely in the hands of the British skilled workers who had initiated it. Abraham Binns, who spoke with a broad Lancashire accent, had been in strikes in Manchester and knew that the first necessity was to feed the strikers and their families. He was very proud of the efficient and orderly working of his kitchens. He and his colleagues had the sympathy and good will of the mass of the citizens, especially the New Bedford Church Council and the press. A new paper, the *New Bedford Times,* under its able young editor P. E. Porter, was all out for the strike.

The occasion seemed made for a test of middle-class support of labor. The chief question was whether the wage cut was necessary to save the industry. Before the Massachusetts State Board of Conciliation and Arbitration the workers on three occasions very conclusively proved that it was not. Then, on August 3, three spokesmen for the Council issued a remarkable appeal to the actual owners, the stockholders. They argued that the failure of the mills to pay dividends and fair wages was due to inefficient management. They charged nepotism in the selection of officers of the mills in favor of the old families which had founded them:

> We saw sons and cousins of millmen promoted over the heads of men more competent than they, and able leaders who had fought their way up from the ranks leaving the city because they could go no further here because they were not socially acceptable.

Some of these men stayed, raised capital from investors who recognized their ability, and founded mills of their own, thus increasing the already more than sufficient number of spindles and looms.

Again, the management had allowed the manufacturing interest to be dominated by agents who both furnished raw material and disposed of the product. They were speculators in the cotton market. The workers protested:

> We saw fortunes lost through unwise buying of cotton, buying done through favored relatives and friends who waxed rich on sales which forced mills to pass their dividends.
>
> We saw cloth sold by New Bedford mills for 16 cents and finished for 3 cents more retailing for 76 cents and yet we were told that with all that 57 cents the retailers and middlemen were taking, the mills could not possibly get enough money to pay dividends except by taking away from the workers the 4 cents which was all they were getting for their share.

The statement closed with a pathetic appeal for what in a true sense is industrial democracy, a sharing of control with the workers:

> There are able millmen in New Bedford—millmen we would be glad to follow, but who are not allowed to lead us now. If there were more of them and they had fuller control there would be no question of lower wages for us or lower dividends for investors. . . .
>
> Dare we not hope that by co-operation stockholders and operatives may find some quicker, wiser way of ending the inadequacies which have made our joint lot seem so helpless, and may go forward together to rebuild a finer, wiser New Bedford?

I owned a few shares in the Wamsutta inherited from my uncle, who had taken great pride in the oldest and most famous of New Bedford mills. I went to see the president, Oliver Prescott, the bearer of an old New Bedford name. I had known Prescott at Harvard and remembered that when he had finished at the Law School he had given his furniture to our Prospect Progressive Union to enable us to carry out the settlement plan. I found him discouraged. I spoke of my plan of writing to some of the stockholders in favor of the workers' plea. "I wish you would stir them up," he said. I gathered that he would welcome a demonstration to strengthen his hand against John Sullivan, the czar of the Manufacturers' Association. Prescott was always spoken of with respect and liking by the strikers, who regretted his abdication of control.

I wrote to some of the stockholders, and the press presented the idea of co-operation. I wrote an article for the *New Republic* which Mr. Porter told me "sank home." An effort was made to persuade the unions and the management to introduce what is known as the Fiedler plan of lining up the work for greater efficiency, with the wage cut withdrawn, but Sullivan would not permit the workers to claim a victory. Then Wamsutta and Neild, oldest and youngest of the mills, threatened to leave the association, which thereupon reduced the wage cut to five per cent. The workers rejected this by sixty to forty per cent, but their unanimity was gone. The majority of the workers had joined the United Textile Workers of the American Federation of Labor, but there was a radical union under way which frightened the middle class. The community had borne the greater part of the two million dollars which was the estimated cost of the strike, and its sympathy was exhausted. Conciliation won the day.

I believe that in this strike was lost an admirable opportunity for putting in practice the principles of industrial democracy. The ownership was local and concentrated, with clearly defined interests bound up with those of the workers. The public, including shareholders, was sympathetic to the strike. The strikers included a group of highly intelligent operatives who had expert advice and the support of the press. Their statements before the Massachusetts State Board were a convincing presentation of conditions in refutation of the arguments of the Manufacturers' Association. Many of the managers of the mills agreed with them, but they had bound themselves to the association controlled by John Sullivan, and loyalty to class and business held them fast against their convictions.

3

After the death of Herbert Croly I ceased to be active on the board of the *New Republic* and the center of my activities shifted to Chicago, where my family was living at Hull House. The collapse of the stock market occurred on October 23, 1929, and after a few fallacious signs of recovery in 1930 it appeared that a far-reaching depression was under way. The L. I. D.'s interest in labor turned to the unemployed. The League received a grant from the American Fund for Public Service to pay the expense of a branch in Chicago, and on January 22, 1931, I find a record of its establishment by Mary Fox of the national headquarters, Clarence Senior, the executive secretary, and Karl Borders, who had recently returned from service with the Friends in the Soviet Union.

It seemed a natural proceeding to take advantage of the instinct for organization developed among the workers to promote a sense of unity among those who were left stranded by the shrinking of the unions. A Workers' Committee on Unemployment was formed. Centers were opened in various parts of the city, where workers shared experiences, discussed problems, and called for help. For two years the situation remained ghastly, with the horrid spectacle of thousands resorting for food to swill barrels and garbage dumps. We had occasion to thank the American habit of waste, to which Mr. Van Camp, the packer, referred in saying, "The swill barrel is my best customer." After the Works Progress Administration entered the field, the situation improved. Then at least the unemployed had a focus of application, and they made use of it.

The relief stations (W. P. A.) were directed by social workers whose assistants were often appointed by officials higher up. A bureaucracy naturally formed, with interests within itself to which the relief of the unemployed tended to become secondary. The latter pressed their claims, sometimes obstreperously. Meetings of protest were held outside of relief stations where the managers seemed indifferent. I had great sympathy with the social workers who in general did a good job in distributing food and clothing, and we tried to induce the workers to deal with them through committees rather than by mass demonstrations, which provoked the police to savagery. They seemed to have a peculiar hatred for the men of their own class who were the victims of social catastrophe.

The provisions of the National Recovery Act designed to protect workers in their union affiliations were sometimes turned against them by the local officials. On one occasion the members of a union of fur workers were laid off during a light season and on their return found that the proprietor had imported workers from New

York who belonged to the American Federation of Labor. He sought to take advantage of the regulations of N. R. A. to compel all his employees to join this organization. Naturally they refused. I took the case through successive local authorities, who invariably decided against the workers. Finally I put the case before Professor W. H. Spencer, Dean of the University of Chicago School of Commerce and Administration and then top man in the Chicago N. R. A. He overruled his subordinates and protected the workers in the union of their choice.

4

Through the Chicago branch of the League for Industrial Democracy and the American Civil Liberties Union I became interested in the strike of the coal miners in the southern counties of Illinois, and especially in Christian County, dominated by the Peabody Coal Company. I made my approach through Ed and Agnes Wieck in Belleville. Ed Wieck had been a pit committeeman and Agnes's father had been a charter member of the union. Both had grown up with the United Mine Workers of Illinois and were authorities on conditions. Economists like Professor Carter Goodrich and Powers Hapgood, son and nephew of my old friends, visited them. I had gone to see them in 1924 in connection with an article for the *New Republic*. It was natural to return to them eight years later when the complicated situation had developed of a strike of miners against their own organization.

The mining towns of Illinois have not the hideous, sordid aspect of those in Pennsylvania. Many miners own their own houses and gardens, and in the case of the smaller mines, practice subsistence farming during lay-offs. This tends to promote individualism and independence. The miners of Illinois were fully organized as early as 1898 and enjoyed district autonomy for thirty years thereafter, numbering at the peak about a hundred thousand members. They were steeped in the democratic traditions brought by British miners. They were the backbone of the United Mine Workers of America, setting the pace of that union in working conditions, living standards, and progressive outlook. Their paper, *The Illinois Miner*, under the editorship of Oscar Ameringer, was the leading journal of the U. M. W. A.

The Illinois miners were suffering from the competition of machines and cheap labor from the South when the depression of 1929 spread hunger and despair through the mining towns. It was at this crisis that John L. Lewis, who had tightened his control over national election machinery, made his attack on district autonomy in Illinois. Taking advantage of confusion in the ranks, he sent to the Washington office the president of the district, John Walker, and took control of the Illinois situation, negotiating a contract with the Peabody Coal Company. When the district rejected it, the contract was resubmitted, but the ballot boxes were stolen and Lewis, declaring a state of emergency, signed the contract without a referendum. Naturally this flouting of the constitution was met by a strike, which Lewis undertook to break by importing U. M. W. A. workers from Kentucky.

The mining counties were in an uproar with workers aligned against workers. An outdoor meeting and picnic was arranged by the strikers at Mulkeytown. On their way the cavalcade of cars carrying their wives and children was ambushed, shots were fired, and several participants were injured. Thereafter the strikers organized as the Progressive Mine Workers. The local merchants in most of the mining towns and villages, though anxious to have the strike settled, supported the Progressives, but local authorities of order and justice were generally with the U. M. W. A. Moreover the Governor ordered out the militia in Christian County, which reinforced the local authorities. In one case a Progressive was shot down by a corporal of the National Guard. The wounded man lay untended and bled to death. The corporal, who incidentally had a prison record, was summarily tried by court-martial the same day and exonerated, so that civil punishment was prevented. Altogether some ten Progressives were murdered with no action sustained by the courts.

Lewis exercised a complete dictatorship over three counties. No one was permitted to speak, except Norman Thomas who spoke in Franklin on one occasion. Even churches were under censorship, and the U. M. W. A. forbade meetings of certain of its locals lest they should revolt. Investigators from the Civil Liberties Committees of Chicago and St. Louis were barred from Lewis's territory, and a group of social science students from the University of Chicago was turned back at the border.

The election of Governor Henry Horner in the Roosevelt landslide of 1932 had seemed to promise the re-establishment of law and order. The Governor called a conference of both sides at which the Progressive miners offered to refer the question of union affiliation to a referendum vote, to which the officers of the United Mine Workers answered no. Then the conference was adjourned and the Governor set up a committee to investigate a situation which was clear to any reasonably naked eye.

The Progressives made an eloquent appeal to Governor Horner, charging that under an unholy conspiracy, law and order had been replaced by brute force:

> Human blood was flowing in Christian and Franklin Counties. . . . You saw ten thousand of our women march under the banner of their auxiliary to your office and petition you to re-establish their civil rights in this state. You also saw a group of these same women return to your office after they had been clubbed and beaten on the streets of West Frankfort. You saw them because they waited in your anteroom for hours, nursing their wounds until there was no way left for you to escape them. . . . Since your coal conference more human blood has been spilled. . . . We do not ask for special favors. We do not want the police force and the law of Illinois to compel miners to join our union. We do demand the right to attend our own meetings, to join or quit any organization we please, to conduct lawful picket lines, and to carry on the legitimate business of building up our organization. And that we are going to do and in spite of the oppression and terror.

Here was a case in which workers deprived of civil rights appealed to the middle class and the New Deal governor, but they remained as isolated as if entombed in one of their own mines. Occasionally Garry Allard, editor of the Progressive paper, came to the L. I. D. in Chicago to ask what we were going to do.

St. Louis was hundreds of miles nearer than Chicago to the mining counties of Illinois. Besides the Civil Liberties Union there was a strong middle-class organization in St. Louis, known as the Commission for Social Justice, which had already a number of successful interventions to its credit. The Commission, headed by Bishop Scarlett, called for a conference between Lewis and the leaders of the Progressives, and somewhat surprisingly the meeting actually took place in the parish house of Temple Israel synagogue. On the morning of the scheduled day I saw a number of Progressives loitering about the synagogue. Pearcy, the president of their group, said lightly, "They're here to see that we don't run out on them," but I suspected that he feared that some hothead might take a shot at Lewis.

At the conference Lewis treated the group of perhaps twenty leading citizens of St. Louis to an oration of over an hour, delivered with a sound and fury that befitted an audience of twenty thousand. Among other charges he asserted that the leaders of the Progressives were disappointed office seekers who left the U. M. W. A. in order to enjoy salaries and release from toil by holding office jobs. Someone inquired of Lewis what his salary was. He replied twelve thousand, with, of course, an expense account. When Pearcy was asked he answered twelve hundred, but added pleasantly, "Of course I don't get it." And expenses? "There aren't any." Then arose to her full five feet Agnes Wieck. She was head of the Women's Auxiliary of the Progressive Miners of Illinois, and she laid at Lewis's feet the recent outrage of her organization's mission to Governor Horner. Lewis, like Castlereagh in Shelley's "Masque of Anarchy," could boast:

> I am God, and king, and law.

For twenty minutes she excoriated him. Finally Lewis sprang up like a tiger and rushed at Mrs. Wieck, shouting, "I won't stand for that!" His two-hour oration was completely shot.

In the early days of the Roosevelt administration I called at the Department of Labor. I did not see Miss Perkins, but an assistant secretary, who seemed to belie his martial name of Battle. I urged the department to conduct a plebiscite, which Mr. Battle seemed to think should be restricted to the men actually at work. As this would have included U. M. W. A. workers imported from Kentucky and excluded most Progressives, I could not see that it would contribute to a settlement of the dispute. The atmosphere of the department as I sensed it was strongly impregnated with the odor of John L. Lewis.

The Progressive Mine Workers later affiliated with the A. F. of L. My last contact with them was at Benld, the center of the movement. It was a terribly hot Sunday afternoon in August. I spoke from the grandstand in an immense sun-stricken field, alone, the audience, if any, out of sight, having taken refuge under the bordering trees or porches of abutting houses. My host assured me that thanks to an exceptionally powerful loudspeaker my message went far. "Why, they must have heard you in Springfield," he said hopefully.

Benld had been on strike for years, and I suspect had been on short rations. It was just then rejoicing in a lucky fall of manna. A distillery at Peoria had burned, releasing thousands of gallons of whisky to enliven the waters of the Illinois. The fish had become so intoxicated that they could be caught by hand. In particular one great catfish, whose fame had become legendary, had fallen to the son of my host. The fish weighed seventy-five pounds and was delicious. I am told that my visit is still remembered as the day of the catfish.

As a final postscript, when Lewis left the C. I. O. and asked to rejoin the A. F. of L., William Green told the Progressive Miners to leave by the back door.

5

I have to thank the League for Industrial Democracy for the best part of my education in domestic policies. I was given a valuable travel course in the winter of 1933 when the depression was at its worst. I spoke at meetings arranged by local centers at Columbus, Dayton, Yellow Springs, Cleveland, Ann Arbor, Detroit, and Toledo. At Dayton interesting experiments were being conducted in distributing goods by barter in lieu of cash money. At Yellow Springs President Arthur E. Morgan of Antioch College had introduced a local currency to supplement legal tender. His faculty received half their salaries in this medium, which local merchants accepted on the same basis. We had paid much attention at the *New Republic* to the Antioch plan, under which students alternated terms of academic study with terms of practical work in industry or trade, thus gaining funds for self-support and meeting a condition on which I often spoke under the title "The Cleavage between College and Life." At Toledo, as indeed everywhere else, I found the middle-class groups in a chastened mood. Private enterprise was suffering an eclipse. Business was willing to discuss public ownership. Obviously, a depression furnished a favorable climate for social change:

> A Blessing, we should use it, should we not?
> And if a Curse—why, then, Who set it there?

How badly we did use it appeared in the years of partial recovery. The strikes of 1936 showed that the Bourbons of business management had learned nothing. With something of the impulse to set actual ownership against financial management which I had tried to invoke at New Bedford, I went to Flint, Michigan, in January 1937, where the workers striking against the General Motors Corporation had taken possession of the Fisher Body mills in what came to be called a sit-down strike. The occupation originated when the management planned to ship dies and special machinery to plants in other cities, by which device the strike in Flint could be broken in Atlanta. I had the chaperonage of Adolph Germer, who was on the board of strategy directing the strike.

I was introduced to the workers as their employer and was cordially received by the sitting-down strikers. My first anxiety was as to the condition of my property. The springs and cushions of partially completed cars had been appropriated as furniture but were uninjured. Some cars showed bullet holes, the result of sniping by the police from adjacent buildings. I gathered that the orderly administration of the plant was by committees. A court was held every morning to judge offenses, of which the worst were promoting physical or mental trouble by bringing in liquor or circulating rumors. Those found guilty were put out. Food was brought to the strikers by their wives and other sympathizers. On one occasion the police tried to close the street in front of the plant and force an entrance by means of tear gas, but they were repulsed by a shower of hinges and bolts, a battle referred to as Bulls' Run.

I found the safe, comfortable indoor strike an improvement on the usual procedure of picket lines dragging along in cold and storm, interrupting traffic, which made of them a source of legal disputes and contradictory court decisions, punctuated by encounters with the police. It raises, it is true, a question of *possession* as opposed to legal title. I wrote in an article on the sit-down strike:

Who has the better right to call the Fisher Body plant his—I, whose connection with General Motors is determined by the price of shares recorded on the New York Stock Exchange, or the worker, whose life and livelihood are bound up in the operation of making cars? I bought my shares at long odds and probably have collected the purchase price in dividends. When I place a winning bet on a horse race I do not claim part ownership of the horse. I know from political economy that my property is the result of labor and abstinence. Whose? Not mine. Obviously, the enormous mass of wealth represented by the capitalization of the General Motors Corporation is the surplus resulting from the toil of hundreds of thousands of workers over many years, who have not shared fairly in the wealth they have produced.

6

Some of the worst failures in the use of the depression were made by the statesmen of the New Deal, often with the best intentions. I was brought close to one of these in a second travel course given me by the L. I. D. In the winter of 1939 I was scheduled to speak at New Orleans, where I found a friendly liberal group. From there I drove with Professor Mary Allen of Sophie Newcomb College, daughter of my old friend Phil Allen, through Louisiana and Mississippi to Memphis. The great migration of expropriated tenant farmers had passed its crest, but still we passed families huddled over fires between the barbed-wire fences and the highway, father, mother, children, with nowhere to go. The amazing New Deal policy of paying farmers to shorten production; of distributing this largesse through the Farm Bureau among the owners to the exclusion of the sharecroppers; and of trying, futilely, to get the owning farmers to play fair, was bearing fruit. According to the Tolan report to Congress, four-fifths of the tenant farmers were deprived of status by the landlords, with the alternatives of becoming day laborers or scuttling across the country to California—the "Okies" and "Arkies" in Steinbeck's *Grapes of Wrath.*

On the way we stopped at Delta Farms where Sherwood Eddy was trying to colonize a dozen evicted families on a collective farm, which revealed a certain promise in comparison with the abandoned cabins and homeless families around it. At Memphis I stopped to see H. L. Mitchell, secretary of the Southern Tenant Farmers' Union, and heard terrible accounts of violence and murder practiced against its members by the rich farmers, with the acquiescence and connivance of the authorities, similar to stories I heard in the mining counties of southern Illinois, but here with the added incentive of race hatred because of the fact that five-sixths of the members of the union were Negroes. The Workers' Defense League published the letters of fifty sufferers in a pamphlet "The Disinherited Speak." The American Civil Liberties Union issued a summary of the exhaustive report of Professor Louis M. Hacker, "The Struggle for Civil Liberty on the Land," which dealt with conditions in the South and elsewhere, especially in California. The International Labor

Defense was active through its affiliate, the Share Croppers' Union, which preceded the Tenant Farmers' Union, having been founded in 1931. The Civil Liberties pamphlet cited the estimate of union officers that forty to fifty persons had been killed since the union started. A student, Howard Kester, set the example of a private citizen going into the field at the risk of his life to help the helpless. Members of the L. I. D. and others under the impulse of Miss Elizabeth Gilman furnished funds for his maintenance and work. Southern states had in effect seceded from the Union and abolished the authority of the federal government, while the government dared not attempt to revive that authority lest it reveal its impotence. After this experience in the South it seemed ironical to continue my tour giving lectures on "The Middle Class and Organized Labor."

7

I afterwards put my argument in a pamphlet for the L. I. D. I pointed out that the middle class is losing its independent status and economically and socially is coming nearer to organized labor; that the chief demand of both is for social security; that both are threatened by fascism, which is, according to President Roosevelt, "the growth of private power to a point where it becomes stronger than the democratic state itself." I showed that they could be of mutual assistance in the preservation of civil liberties and the maintenance of the legal right to strike, a right that has become important to white-collar as well as to manual workers. They could unite for political action, as in Great Britain. The middle class could use its economic power as investing and consuming public to support labor. To accomplish these ends I recommended as a necessary project the extension of organization throughout the middle class—already impressive in the case of teachers, journalists, lawyers, technicians, entertainers—and the education of such organizations to lead in breaking down social barriers and class distinctions and developing cultural solidarity with labor. Much of this now seems remote and academic. In any case, it applied only to the favored part of the working class that was organized and left out of account the vast mass of misery and helplessness which we call the proletariat. At the back of my mind I kept thinking of William Morris's answer:

How can we of the middle class, we the capitalists and hangers-on help? By renouncing our class and on all occasions when antagonism rises up between the classes casting our lot with the victims, those who are condemned to lack of education, refinement, leisure, pleasure and renown; and at the worst to a life lower than that of the most brutal of savages. There is no other way.

The possibility of middle-class intervention in the social struggle through its financial power is as old as Defoe's *Essay on Projects.* It was put forward in 1937, by Mrs. Dummer, a long-time liberal, in Chicago and her sister Mrs. Johnson in New York, in conferences on the duty of stockholders. Miss Zara Du Pont repeatedly went to stockholders' meetings to protest against such anomalies as in Bethlehem Steel, whose president, E. G. Grace, was taking in one way or another about a million dollars a year while no dividends were being paid and workers were on strike for a living wage. These efforts illustrate the difficulty of individuals, however high-minded, in making headway against organized management, a difficulty as great as that of members of a labor union attempting to free themselves from a leadership known to be corrupt and even criminal.

The abdication of control by both middle class and labor, in both corporations and unions, is a denial of democracy. It puts the economic future of the country at the mercy of managers and labor leaders whose self-interest is dominant, whether expressed in money or in power or in both. The basis of their authority is financial, and the primary appeal is to gain, whether dividends or wages. The motto of the L. I. D., "Production for use rather than for profit," may be scorned as unpractical idealism, but it marks an approach toward the good society, and inevitably will be accepted in the economic collapse of the future if the human race is to survive.

XIV. *Hull House,* 1921–1937

I

On September 14, 1889, Jane Addams and Ellen Gates Starr went to live at the old mansion of General Hull at the corner of Halsted and Polk Streets. Judged by its effects, this was perhaps as important an event as occurred in the United States between 1865 and 1914. It was the American initiation of the most characteristic social impulse of the last half of the nineteenth century, which sociologists call "compunction."

The nineteenth century found its chief problem in the separation of classes, as the twentieth finds its problem in the separation of races and nations. As early as 1845 Benjamin Disraeli defined it in his novel *Sybil, or The Two Nations:*

> Two nations between whom there is no intercourse and no sympathy, who are as ignorant of each other's habits and thoughts and feelings as if they were dwellers in different zones or inhabitants of different planets; who are formed by a different breeding, fed by a different food, ordered by different manners and *are not governed by the same laws*—the Rich and the Poor. [Italics mine.]

Separation of classes had always existed in the form of slavery or serfdom, but it became a bleeding wound in a democratic world. The first great effort to stanch it was the French Revolution, which united equality and fraternity with liberty in its slogan. Three years after Disraeli, Marx and Engels issued the Communist Manifesto to carry forward the revolution by means of the class war. Ten years later John Ruskin began his crusade in behalf of the disinherited with *Unto This Last;* and William Morris followed with what has been called "revolution by consent." Peter Kropotkin and Henry George offered solutions based on the proper distribution and use of land. Tolstoy pronounced the most eloquent denunciation of his class for making its chief preoccupation the ways of maintaining and increasing the separation of their lives from those of the poor. It was in this atmosphere of the end of the Victorian Era that Jane Addams grew up—an era in regard to which Lord Morley quoted the famous saying of Bacon: "The nobler the nature the more objects of compassion it hath."

Tolstoy's solution took the form of renouncing his class and becoming a peasant. Jane Addams and Ellen Starr remained gentlewomen, but they went to live among the poor. Readers of Miss Addams' *Twenty Years at Hull House* remember that as a little girl she wondered why she should live in a big house so far away from all the little houses, and determined that when she grew up she would still live in a big house, but that it should be among those little ones. The old Hull mansion was exactly suited to this purpose. Two years earlier Canon Barnet had founded the settlement in London named Toynbee Hall in memory of Arnold Toynbee, a pupil of Ruskin. Hull House soon was regarded as the American equivalent of the English settlement, but in its origin it was merely two cultivated middle-class ladies becoming neighbors to those whom it is polite to call the underprivileged.

Soon they were joined in residence by others, and the influence of Hull House as a pioneer in social experiment extended beyond its immediate purpose. From Hull House went Florence Kelley, as the first factory inspector in Illinois, and Julia Lathrop, as first head of the Children's Bureau in Washington. Among other early residents of Hull House was Dr. Alice Hamilton, who then stood almost alone as an expert in industrial diseases and the health of workers.

The settlement idea was simple, depending on individual initiative and leadership. It spread over the country. I have written of our imitation at Harvard of Hull House a year after its founding. At the University of Chicago a settlement was opened in rooms above a feed shop. Northwestern University soon established its settlement. In short, it was recognized that such an institution was part of the equipment of a modern college. In 1940 there were some thirty-five settlements in Chicago alone.

Hull House rendered two types of social service. It gave to the great submerged population of the poor a voice to demand necessities of which they were hardly conscious, and a hand to help obtain them—also a voice to protest against their wrongs. And it provided a way in which the fund of good will in the community could express itself.

2

In the spring of 1921 when I joined the staff of the *New Republic* for part of the year it became necessary to provide a home for my family in Chicago, where my older daughter was to study medicine at the Rush Medical School on the West Side. I consulted Miss Addams as to the possibility of finding an apartment. With her usual quiet modesty Miss Addams indicated that there were apartments at Hull House, and thus in a moment we were enrolled as social workers. Ida as a girl at Radcliffe had heard Jane Addams speak, and from then on had felt drawn to that gentle and lovable person. In our earlier years in Chicago we had often enjoyed the hospitality of the House, but we had not thought of ourselves as meeting the requirements of actual residents. Ida found at once a field for an executive ability which made her successful as a lieutenant. She became one of Miss Addams' close companions, sharing her company on journeys and giving her always the watchful care which became more necessary as the years passed.

My connection with the House was less constant, but I was well satisfied to exchange the stratified suburb of Hyde Park for the amorphous neighborhood of Halsted Street, even at the expense of a long daily journey to the university. I never changed cars at the corner of Halsted Street, on returning, without a sense that here was life, something incredibly vital though its stigmata were grim enough—poverty, squalor, crime.

The residents of Hull House were a group of strikingly original characters engaged in a common enterprise. The Hull House Players were directed by Mrs. Laura Dainty Pelham, supplemented by juvenile groups under Miss Edith de Nancrede. They staged the plays of Yeats and Lady Gregory, of Hauptmann, of Galsworthy and Phillpotts. Several of the players graduated to the professional stage. Miss Eleanor and Miss Gertrude Smith directed the Music School with the assistance of Miss Pillsbury and Miss Birmingham. Miss Benedict, the oldest resident, presided over the Art School. These activities stimulated cultural interests in the neighborhood and gave opportunities for young talent to develop. Two important organizations grew up at Hull House—the Juvenile Protective Association, directed by

Miss Jessie Binford, and the Immigrants' Protective League under Mrs. Kenneth Rich.

Dean of the House was George Hooker, who had been Secretary of the City Club. Victor Yarros, partner of Clarence Darrow and editorial writer for the *Chicago Daily News*, and his wife Dr. Rachel Yarros, chief exponent of birth-control and director of clinics, were among the most vivid personalities. Dr. and Mrs. Britton were among the most important, the doctor acting as house physician and supervising the boys' athletics and gymnasium directed by Messrs. Kirkland and Hicks, Mrs. Britton having the kindergarten.

Miss Ethel Dewey, Miss Mary Gleason, Miss Rose Gyles, and Mrs. Hicks were in charge of classes in English and citizenship. Mrs. Alfred Kohn and Miss Ella Waite were concerned with the general problems, especially financial, of running the establishment. Frank Keyser had been engineer from the beginning. There were many young people who took care of various clubs and classes. Altogether, when we went to Hull House, it comprised a family of about seventy people, residents of the block from Polk Street to Gilpin Place, which was occupied by a somewhat heterogeneous but well-adapted group of buildings designed by Allen and Irving Pond.

Hull House rendered a service to Chicago by offering philanthropic men and women an opportunity to take part in a practical solution of the social problem. First should be mentioned Mrs. Louise de Koven Bowen, who acted as treasurer of the Board of Trustees. Among many gifts she gave a beautiful estate at Waukegan for a country resort for mothers and children. Though differing in politics, especially in the matter of the war, from Miss Addams and most of the residents, she never wavered in her loyalty and faith. Mrs. Mary H. Wilmarth, Miss Mary Rozet Smith, Mr. Frederick Deknatel, Mr. Julius Rosenwald, gave not only money but time and thought to the House. Miss Helen Culver, the heir of General Hull, gave the original house and adjacent land, and started an endowment fund with a gift of one hundred thousand dollars.

3

The Hull House family and its non-resident relatives were held together by the personality of Jane Addams, who refused to be called head resident. She has written her experience and character in her books, especially *Twenty Years at Hull House* and *The Second*

Twenty Years at Hull House. She had inherited from her father, the friend of Lincoln, the finest tradition of the Middle West, as fine as, but so different from, that of New England. When she visited President Eliot at Mount Desert I would have given anything to be present at the meeting of two leaders, Miss Addams, gentle and persuasive, Eliot, vigorous and commanding, but both sincere, generous, courteous, of the best that human nature can show.

When I went to Hull House Miss Addams had already become a national and an international figure by virtue of her leadership in the cause of peace. She had presided at the International Congress of Women, which had met at the Hague in the spring of 1915 and formulated resolutions which anticipated the terms of peace finally offered by President Wilson in the Fourteen Points. After the adjournment of the Conference she had visited the chancelleries of both belligerent and neutral countries to promote the plan of a conference of neutrals to offer continuous mediation, pronounced by Walter Millis "one of the few really generous and rational impulses of those insane years." It was unfortunate that the first serious break in her health had come at this time, but she had recovered and visited Germany after the armistice with Dr. Alice Hamilton, to report on conditions of starvation resulting from the blockade by the Allies. Later she presided with dignity and skill over the committee, promoted by Oswald Garrison Villard, to investigate the atrocities perpetrated by the Black and Tans in Ireland.

All this was before our residence at Hull House. Dark days of reaction had set in. Attorney General Palmer had set afoot his raids for the deportation of the foreign-born. Miss Addams was denounced as a pacifist and an internationalist, and her name was first on the report of the witch-hunting Congressional committee. The Daughters of the American Revolution denounced her as disloyal, a factor in a movement to destroy civilization and Christianity and the United States government. She was wounded by the disapproval of many of her friends, and anxious for the future of Hull House. Her strength in those years was in her tolerance and understanding.

Jane Addams was a genuine pacifist whose idea of peace was not limited to matters of armament and war. She wrote after a visit to Tolstoy: "It seemed to me that he made a distinction between the use of physical force and that moral energy which can override another's differences and scruples with equal ruthlessness." She was an equalitarian, believing in equality as the solution of social evils. That was the spirit of Hull House. "I am not so sure," she wrote humbly, "that we succeeded in our endeavors to make social intercourse express the growing sense of the economic unity of society and to add the social function to democracy." The objective was there defined, and again: "Hull House was soberly opened on the theory that the dependence of classes on each other is reciprocal; and that as the social relation is essentially a reciprocal relation it gives a form of expression that has peculiar value."

With all the high seriousness of her efforts, Miss Addams retained an engaging modesty and a winning sense of humor. She once told with enjoyment of her discomfiture when, having induced a number of industrialists to witness the operation of a machine to record fatigue of the workers, something went wrong with the apparatus and the result showed less fatigue at the end than at the beginning of the trial. It was with rueful humor that she told of summoning a group of Italians of the neighborhood to inquire about the murder by one of that race of a Negro. A doctor who acted as spokesman said seriously, "You must remember, Miss Addams, that our people are becoming Americanized." But it was with a smile that she related an encounter with the dean of Bishop Paul Jones' cathedral in Salt Lake City. The dean was complaining of the addiction of the bishop to bad company such as I. W. W.'s and Communists.

"Perhaps," suggested Miss Addams, "he goes among them to do them good."

"No indeed," responded the dean, "he goes with them because he likes them."

When she was expelled from the D. A. R., of which she had been made an honorary member, she remarked, "I thought it was for life but it must have been only during good behavior."

4

The residents of Hull House were not necessarily exclusively social workers. Nearly all had vocations outside and gave as a minimum two evenings a week to the House. The humblest task of all was attending to the door and telephone in the evening, and this properly fell to my lot as initiation. It was interesting because it brought one close to the life of the neighborhood—everyone who was in trouble came in person, and news of fires, crimes, and arrests came by prompt report. Miss Addams thought that I was fitted for higher things. She had always believed in lectures as a contribution to the intellectual life of the neighborhood, and she looked back to earlier days when the lecture room was crowded with audiences to hear of science, art, and poetry from professors of the university or other gifted persons.

I pointed out that the community had changed. Instead of Germans, Irish, and Russians we had Italians, Greeks, and Mexicans, but I thought that a course on contemporary social and political topics might go over. I had excellent speakers, capturing as many as possible on their way to or from Washington or New York, and filling in with local talent, but the neighbors were not interested. Several times Ida raided the reading room, turned out the lights, and shepherded the "readers" into the lecture room, where they slept. Gradually the reading room lost custom on lecture nights.

My first real assignment was as a sort of scoutmaster to a hard gang of boys who had seceded from the regular administration of the gymnasium and clubs. I was cowardly enough to be glad when, after looking me over, they disappeared. I did, however, make an attempt at individual salvation. On a visit to the reformatory at Pontiac I met a boy whose ingenuous tale impressed me. He had been sentenced to a year, he explained, by an amiable judge who wanted to save him from bad company. I thought badly of his honor's judgment in choosing Pontiac for its uplifting influence and promised to have some job in sight for the boy as a condition of his release at the end of his term. Unemployment was then at its height and educational institutions were taking up the slack. I asked President Hutchins if he would favor admitting a student from the excellent preparatory school of Pontiac. "Certainly," he said, "if he can get by the examiner." I asked Miss Addams if she would object to a youthful delinquent becoming a resident of Hull House. Of course she welcomed the addition to our human curiosity shop. So all was well. The boy capitalized on his prison experience with the Department of Sociology. An interesting social experiment was being conducted known as the Area Project, by which a neighborhood notable for juvenile delinquency was delimited for intensive study of conditions and the introduction of remedial measures. After graduation my protégé was given a place at South Chicago. He was successful in his work. Again his prison experience was capitalized on to win the admiration of his young clients. He married a summer resident at Hull House and had a daughter. He betrayed them. I felt that if I had continued to watch him and hold him to his work and his family I might have saved him, but South Chicago is a long way from Hull House. I realized then that you can't launch a human being like a ship, and that you can do a lot of mischief by assuming a responsibility that you aren't willing to see through. I failed as badly as did the poor lad.

My chief activity at the House came to be meeting once a week with a group of young writers whose manuscripts I read for criticism in class, and corrected outside. Residents, neighbors, and even recruits from distant parts of the city made up a highly miscellaneous company whose writing, without benefit of academic influence, made up in spontaneity for what it lacked in conventional form. I remember especially a long narrative of exciting and dangerous experiences by Billy Ortiz, a waiter in the Coffee House, which might have been called "Up from Mexico." Wallace Kirkland, who directed boys' activities and spent his vacations exploring north of the Great Lakes, wrote articles on wild life which were published in various magazines. Our chief triumph was that of Oscar Ludmann, an Alsatian, who had been forced into service in the German Navy, had participated in the mutiny at Kronstadt, had marched with the sailors on Berlin, and later joined the abortive movement for the independence of his native province. His book, *A Stepchild of the Rhine,* remains in my mind as one of the most vital records of experience in the war. The account of the cruel fate of Alsace, torn by conflicting loyalties and crushed between opposing powers, deserves to be better known as another of the age-long tragedies of nationalism.

5

Hull House was emphatically the refuge of lost causes. The anarchist agitation had died out, but the fear of it was maintained by press and police to haunt the slumbers of the best people. Miss Addams was attacked for entertaining Peter Kropotkin at Hull House. The celebration of his birthday was an occasion for the visit to Chicago of the mild ghost of anarchism. I was always glad to speak in memory of that innocent and noble figure, a genuine humanitarian, whose doctrine Miss Addams revived in her book *Peace and Bread in Time of War*. I also enjoyed meeting the aged widows of the victims of Judge Gary's betrayal of justice, especially the Negro wife of Albert R. Parsons, a hero who voluntarily surrendered to join his comrades in court and on the scaffold.

Another dying cause was that of the I. W. W. More than a hundred I. W. W.'s had joined the conscientious objectors and Indian patriots in Leavenworth, and it became the function of the surviving members of the order to help their families and work for their pardon. This was refused long after the war was over. There seems to have been a streak of malignity in Wilson's character which showed itself in his refusal to release even Eugene Debs, whose original offense, of a technical nature in opposing the draft, had lost its meaning. Hull House was a center of the movement for clemency and pardon.

It was inevitable that the case of Tom Mooney should become a fixation of liberals. An aggressive labor leader in San Francisco, he was deliberately "framed" as having caused an explosion which resulted in the death of several participants in a "preparedness" parade. Felix Frankfurter, on a mission to examine and report to President Wilson on labor difficulties in the West, saw through the plot and warned the President of the danger in the execution of an innocent man whose fate was exciting workers all over the world. After commutation of the sentence to imprisonment for life, the long struggle began. One by one the folds of perjury were peeled away until the nucleus of the noxious growth was reached. The bluff cattle buyer "who had seen Mooney plant the bomb" was shown to have been miles away from the scene. He was also revealed as having written to a friend in Ohio to come to California to add another lie. Was he prosecuted for perjury? To ask the question is naïve. Year after year governors and the Supreme Court of California wriggled like snakes to avoid a formal admission of the criminality of the state. It was not until the Christmas of 1938 that Tom Mooney was pardoned.

The interest in the Mooney case waxed and waned until the Communists took it up. They arranged a conference with trade-union support in Chicago on April 30–May 1, 1933. I know it is usual for my friends to resent the efforts of Communists in such cases, and to argue that their advocacy serves to stiffen the opposition of the tories, yet it cannot be denied that Communist activity gave an impetus to a cause that had long challenged the impotence of liberals. If the Communists are charged with exploiting such cases for the prestige of their party, and with condemnation of the government and public which permits them, the answer is that government and public deserve all that the Communists can do to them.

6

Hull House at Polk and Halsted Streets stands almost at the exact center of the population of Chicago. It is near the eastern frontier of the vast hinterlands of Czech, Ukrainian, Italian, Greek, Hungarian, and Lithuanian settlements. Only the Poles on the far South Side are remote. Both the local and national interests of these groups were constantly before us. During the war there had been held in Chicago a congress of oppressed nationalities, in which the Poles played a leading part. It was somewhat disconcerting to have a sub-group, suffering oppression from the oppressed, appear in the case of the Ruthenians and Ukrainians, represented by Mr. Sichinsky, who had himself assassinated the Polish governor of Galicia where the Poles enjoyed the favor of the Austrian imperialism. One Sunday afternoon at Sichinsky's invitation I spoke to a gathering of Ukrainians called in protest against the atrocities of the Pilsudski government of Poland in 1934. I told the Ukrainians that they had the right to put the case of their fellow nationals before the State Department, since the inclusion of the minority of Ukrainians within the boundaries of Poland had been secured at the Peace Conference by the eminent Polophile, Professor A. M. Lord of Harvard, according to his own account. The other speakers did not speak in English, so that I do not know what they advised, but I judged from the applause that they proposed more radical action.

Among the residents at Hull House was Dr. Steiner, a Hungarian, the leader of the radical wing of his countrymen in Chicago. He invited me to speak at a mass meeting held in anticipation of the visit of Count Károlyi, whom the State Department after ten years of anxious deliberation finally decided to admit to our sacred shores. Mr. Hoover should have had a bad conscience in regard to Károlyi. As a liberal nobleman he had been made premier of Hungary, as had Prince Max von Baden of Germany, on the collapse of the Hapsburg and Hohenzollern regimes, in order to facilitate negotiations with the triumphant Allies. In Hungary the people starved while the American Relief Administration played politics. Although, as Count Károlyi told me, his government tendered a million dollars in gold, no food was forthcoming. The liberal government was forced to yield to the Communists; the Rumanians were permitted by the Allies to overrun the country and loot it, even carrying off the black earth of the Hungarian plain on flat cars; and Admiral Horthy took over as regent to the accompaniment of a White terror which lasted for years.

I saw much of Count Károlyi during his few days in Chicago. He seemed like an English peer, kindly, courteous, rather formal. He always apologized for an impediment in his speech, but when he was roused he spoke with eloquence. He was reasonable in talking of the future of his country, to which he had sacrificed his privileged position and estates, while his relatives and colleagues of the Magyar nobility continued to flourish in their feudalism under favor of the erstwhile Allies. Nowhere in Europe was the peace more decisively lost than in Hungary.

7

Toward labor Hull House was boldly sympathetic. It gave aid to strikers in industries whose owners were contributors to the support of the House. This was notably the case in strikes against the great packing firms, some of which, however, remained friendly. In the organization of the needle trades into the Amalgamated Clothing Workers by Sidney Hillman, Hull House played a significant part. When Ellen Gates Starr went on the picket line with the strikers and was arrested and jailed I am convinced that the public interest excited brought support to the strike, and that her action was a powerful stimulus to that change of policy which made Hart, Schaffner and Marx, the leading clothing firm in Chicago, formulate the agreement which, followed perforce by other firms, brought stability into one of the industries most subject to fluctuations by reason of season or caprice. I have heard Joseph Schaffner refer to Sidney Hillman as "my partner."

Having been so often a spectator and critic of the police, I could hardly claim immunity from their personal attention. A strike of Negro girls at an apron factory on Michigan Avenue was attracting attention because of alleged police cruelty to the strikers on the picket line. A number of social workers agreed to go to the scene as observers. Jessie Binford, executive secretary of the Juvenile Protective Association, was ill on the day fixed and asked me to go in her place. Accordingly I joined a party, chiefly of ladies, at six in the morning, June 26, 1933, and saw the attempt of the management to import strikebreakers against the persuasion and protest of the pickets. Everything was peaceful until the arrival of the police. They ordered the pickets off the block in one direction, and the spectators off in the other. As we paused on the opposite corner for consultation the police suddenly charged us across the intervening street, waving clubs and shouting war cries. I stepped up to the leader of the chase and asked to speak to his superior officer. "You'll speak to him in the wagon," he shouted, and in a moment I was sitting in the Black Maria along with Tom McKenna, secretary of the Chicago Civil Liberties Committee.

It was Monday morning, and in the cell into which we were hustled were forty or fifty Negroes who had been taken up for crap-shooting, bad language, or other offenses; they had spent a foodless Sunday, but were nonetheless cheerful and happy to see us. McKenna telephoned the press, and within half an hour cameras were directed at us through the bars, whereupon the captain of the station moved us into a private cell, not wishing, perhaps, to have the malign secrets of his prison house exposed. Dean Woodward telephoned to know if the university could do anything for me, but Miss Binford had already sent twenty-five dollars for my bail. The papers enjoyed the paradox of "the elderly professor" being rescued by the Juvenile Protective Association.

Judges who sit in police stations do not like to let the police down, and so on our first appearance we asked for a jury trial. My former colleague Henry P. Chandler took our case, and with the numerous witnesses available built up a formidable defense. When, however, he recognized Judge John Gutknecht on the bench, he promptly withdrew the request for a jury. Within a few minutes the Judge dismissed the case, convinced that it was groundless. When the representative of the state attorney's office threatened to alter the charge from unlawful assembly to disorderly conduct, Judge Gutknecht observed that in that case he should consider the young man himself in disorder.

I should have been willing to consider the incident closed, but learning that the captain of the district on leaving the court had assured the patrolman that he had done exactly right, I decided that I ought to teach the police a lesson and brought suit against the officer for false arrest. My attorney, John F. Cashen, took my case. When we went to court with our witnesses we were informed that the officer was ill. When this excuse turned up again we sent a bailiff to investigate—he found the officer on his beat as usual. I had heard of such a thing as contempt of court, but the court apparently had not. I could not continue to take the time of my witnesses and attorney and so dropped the case with an apology from the officer. The incident would not be worth mention had it not been made later a basis of the charge of un-Americanism by Congress.

The affair had other consequences. The plant owners were shocked that a professor should have suffered in connection with their strike. They invited me to inspect their factory and note the humane conditions under which their girls worked. The strike was soon after settled with a wage raise.

My presence as an observer began to be in demand in connection with other labor troubles. Early one morning I was urged to come to a clothing factory on Water Street where a strike was being broken. Captain John Stegey was in charge. I went fearing the worst. On my arrival, however, I was greeted by the first patrolman I met. "I saw your picture in the paper, Professor," he said cordially. "Come and see the Captain." Stegey also greeted me like an old friend and called my attention to the excellence of the police work. I congratulated myself on my presence, but I noticed that across the street a number of trucks were drawn up awaiting loading, the drivers of which, idle at the moment, were taking considerable interest in the proceedings. As Yellow Cabs drove up with strikebreakers they were deluged with rotten fruit from the trucks. The police would form a cordon from the cab to the door of the building—an arch through which the arriving girls ran crouching. The pickets insinuated themselves between the legs of the patrolmen and tried to reach their rivals. It was all a good-natured struggle which ended in more or less official embraces between officers and pickets after the strikebreakers had disappeared. Captain Stegey insisted on driving me to the jail where the only picket who had been arrested was being held. "She had a knife on her and we didn't want her to cut herself as she did one of my men. We'll let her out this afternoon," explained the genial officer.

8

How hard it is for a mere citizen to obtain a hearing when intrenched interests are involved was brought home clearly to me.

While my suit was pending, I went to Rockford to address a club at Rockford College and stayed with a leading Socialist, a Swede. He told me that he had run for mayor during the war and had been defeated by the accusation in the local papers that he was pro-German. He sued for heavy damages, but the chief paper was owned by a woman prominent in politics. For over ten years he had been unable to find a judge willing to hear his case.

An example of the injustice meted out to foreign-born workers involved a Yugoslav named Perkovitch. When conditions were at the worst in 1932–33 the unemployed on the West Side were in the habit of crossing the city to the South Side where food was sometimes obtainable from bakeries, disposing of yesterday's bake, and where, at least, the garbage was more lavish. One morning these itinerants were picked up by the police and held at the station house on the absurd pretext that a revolution was planned. Perkovitch told me that he and about one hundred others were kept in the basement all day without food. Once a lieutenant with a bodyguard of patrolmen raged through the room, striking and kicking the men in an ecstasy of sadism. At six the prisoners were released with no charges.

The whole story seemed past belief, but I told Perkovitch that if he could find four witnesses to support his account I would go with them to the police authorities and present the case. A day or two later he returned with his comrades, and I took them by appointment to see an assistant commissioner. He listened sympathetically, made careful notes, and assured me that he had the case in hand and something would be done. After waiting a week I asked a colleague, Leonard White, one of the civil service commissioners of Chicago, if he would arrange to let me bring Perkovitch to the chief of police. He readily agreed; an appointment was made, but Perkovitch, who was to join me at Hull House, did not appear. I had to go alone and apologize. It turned out that Perkovitch was ashamed of his ragged and dirty clothes and had tried to reach my apartment by a back door that was seldom used and where his knock was not heard.

In the spring I gave Perkovitch the job of making a garden on my small place at Lake Zurich. He had a room over the garage and fifteen dollars a week. He earned it. Early and late he could be seen bending over the acre of land that he loved. When I left for the summer I gave the cottage to my son-in-law, who did not need a man but offered Perkovitch board wages with permission to take any outside job that was offered—and there were plenty because his industry had excited the admiration of the whole community. Perkovitch refused. His pride of workmanship was insulted. He had done a good job; why should he be demoted? Later I used to hear from him from California, always asking when I wanted him back, always beginning "My friend," perhaps the only one he had in America.

9

In 1933 the Century of Progress exposition was held in Chicago in celebration of the hundredth anniversary of the incorporation of the city. Unfortunately medicine in the United States had not progressed so far as the general recognition of tropical diseases, which may be expected to accept the invitation of a world's fair. At all events, amoebic dysentery early appeared as a guest in the hotels on the lake front. The Commissioner of Health, Dr. Herman Bundesen, took steps at once to limit its ravages. Visitors at the Congress Hotel, where the disease first appeared, were followed to their homes by a questionnaire, inquiring among a number of innocent questions if the individual had experienced any illness during or after sojourn at Chicago, and if so requesting the name of his regular doctor. Then, if the answer was yes, a telephone call to the latter advised him of the probable nature of the disease and its treatment, and warned him on no account to operate for appendicitis, which would probably be fatal, as indeed it was in the case of Texas Guinan. Dr. Bundesen assembled a congress of medical authorities who highly commended his efficient procedure.

During the summer there was no disturbing publicity, but in October a physician in an Indiana town recognized the symptoms in several patients who had attended the fair in a party; he made his discovery the basis of a medical report. Chicago took the matter with its accustomed good humor. It was suggested cynically that as the toilets on the fairgrounds were provided by a concession held by a plumbing concern, the amoebae were introduced to swell their profits, a practice not out of line with devices known to the Federal Trade and Pure Food and Drug Commissions. The horrid irony of ornamenting the walls of the toilets with advertisements of Ex-Lax was also commented on.

I spent the summer in Chicago, and went east in the fall. When I was returning in January, I happened to sit on the train next to a distinguished colleague, Dr. Frank R. Lillie, professor of zoology. Having noted in a Chicago paper some remarks on the prevalence of the malady, I described certain symptoms which I had not thought serious. Lillie at once pronounced the verdict and ordered me to the hospital. I went to the Frank Billings Hospital at the university where his diagnosis was confirmed. I took a room and remained under treatment for three months, going out afternoons to meet my classes. It was an admirable arrangement and led me to suggest that instead of making aged professors "emeritus" they should be made "hospitalers" and kept on half pay. This made no hit with my younger colleagues.

I was rather irritated as a citizen of Chicago at being the victim of a pest obviously intended for strangers and at having no warning until the amoebae had resided with me for several months. I wrote an article for the *New Republic* on the subject and was sternly rebuked by Dr. Fishbein of the *Journal* of the American Medical Association, who wrote to Bruce Bliven that the *New Republic* did not have on its staff an editor entitled to express himself on the subject. I thought this rather hard in view of the quantities of emmetine and anyodin that I had absorbed.

I was back in the hospital after the spring vacation. This time the X-ray had discovered a growth in my colon described innocently as a polyp. I went to the operating table before a distinguished group of professional guests, among whom I saluted with pleasure my daughter Beatrice, who had come down from Minneapolis to see the distinguished surgeon Dr. Dallas B. Phemister do his stuff. For me it was a rather pleasant experience. The anaesthetic was introduced via the spinal column, so that I was conscious and enjoyed conversing with a pleasant girl in nurse's uniform who made the hour pass quickly. At the close I heard Beatrice saying admiringly, "Hasn't Papa a good heart!"

But I was a bad patient. I fought the stomach pump until I had blown out all the stitches and menaced Dr. Phemister's masterpiece. Back to the table, but this time without the éclat of my first appearance, and instead of compliments on my part in the performance I heard only the adjuration, "Don't do it again."

I had, however, another moment of triumph. It was about midnight. I woke up terribly cold, and was surprised to see my daughter in the room and even Dr. Phemister. I remarked, "Well, doctor, I see you have to work late nights like a professor," and went to sleep. It was only next morning that I reflected, "They were expecting me to pass out, and I treated them like casual visitors. What a *faux pas!*" And I was utterly unaware of an experience that Shelley would have enjoyed.

My convalescence lasted through the spring, during which time, and even in the autumn, the university gave me leave of absence with salary. One afternoon I read in the *Chicago Daily News* a statement from the Health Department to the effect that there were only some eighteen cases of amoebic dysentery in the city. I asked an intern how many there were in this hospital alone, and he replied about the same number. I showed him the item in the paper and suggested that he should ask a representative of the Health Department "how come." He did so and was rebuked by the reply, "Don't you know the world's fair is reopening next month?"

10

One of the responsibilities which I had was that of reporting on civil liberties in Chicago to the Union in New York. In March 1930 there was a police attack on Communist headquarters, in which the offices were wrecked, furniture and machines smashed as in a raid on a gambling house, and the officials beaten up. Roger Baldwin came on from New York, and W. H. Holly (later judge) arranged to have a hearing before the mayor, who was represented by the corporation counsel. The victims of the raid told their stories and showed their wounds. A treaty was made by which the Communists were allowed to hold a meeting in the Ashland Auditorium without interference, and also a parade along Halsted Street to a vacant lot for a picnic.

The auditorium meeting was held with some forty policemen on guard; they were obliged to listen to denunciations of their conduct a few days before. Roger Baldwin and I spoke. The next day I waited on the balcony of Hull House to see the procession, but it did not arrive. I learned later that the police guard of honor led the parade up quiet Jefferson Street instead of the main thoroughfare, Halsted. The chief result was the formation of the Chicago Civil Liberties Committee, of which Mr. Holly became chairman.

I continued as a sort of liaison officer with New York. One evening in 1934 Roger Baldwin called us by telephone to say that Colonel MacCormac, Commissioner of Immigration, had informed him that he was obliged to arrest for deportation John Strachey (later Minister of Food in the British Labour cabinet), who was lecturing that evening at a synagogue in Winnetka. Ida took the message and called Attorney Walter Fisher, Jr., who at once went to the rescue and obtained Strachey's release on his own recognizance to appear next morning before the immigration commissioner in Chicago. I put up a bond which allowed Strachey temporary freedom to continue his lecture tour. It was known that William Randolph Hearst had brought pressure on the immigration authorities to force Strachey's deportation, and it was obvious that Commissioner MacCormac was reluctant and thought that the American Civil Liberties Union should do something about the matter. There was a farewell meeting for Strachey in New York at which I presided and made some uncomplimentary remarks about Hearst. Thereafter I was the subject of attacks in the Hearst papers.

Early the next year a leading citizen of Chicago, Mr. Walgreen, a large advertiser in the Hearst papers, saw fit to withdraw his niece from the University of Chicago on the ground that she was being indoctrinated with communist ideas. He demanded a public hearing before the Board of Trustees. The Board was willing to hear Mr. Walgreen in private, but the latter insisted on his publicity. Next a bill was passed by the Illinois Senate, introduced by Charles Baker of Rockford, for the appointment of a committee to investigate charges of communistic teaching in institutions of higher learning. The committee was appointed and opened hearings on the University of Chicago.

As I was a teacher of literature I did not consider myself involved and did not attend the first session, but as I was told that my name was constantly mentioned by Legionnaires and others from the floor, I readily acceded to the request of President Hutchins and appeared before the committee. I was immediately confronted by a typewritten letter bearing my signature.

Some eight years earlier I had among the neighbors of Hull House seeking fame as writers a young man named Jacob Gordin who brought me a manuscript. He had gone to Russia after the Revolution and had not liked it; on his return he had described his experience in a book called *Utopia in Chains*. I corrected the manuscript and recommended it for publication. The book was not a best-seller. I inferred from a letter Gordin wrote me that he thought I had sabotaged his book because of my sympathy with the Soviet Union.

In reply to his somewhat heated protest I wrote him briefly that his criticism of administration in Russia was probably the reason why the publishers took his book and added: "I was anxious to have the book published as a human story, not caring in the least whether it reflects on the Russian government or the United States government or any other—all in my opinion being rotten." If I had been writing more carefully I should have quoted Lord Acton's classic remark: "All power tends to corrupt, and absolute power corrupts absolutely."

When I saw the letter, somewhat faded by time, it seemed incredible that responsible senators should take a private communication in connection with university teaching seriously. I merely identified it and left it at that. It was with surprise that I read in the papers a few days later that it was the basis of the recommendation of my dismissal from the university, the proponent of the committee noting that I had added to my offense by using the objectionable sentence during the administration of "the beloved Calvin Coolidge."

Two members of the committee of the Illinois Senate, Graham and Barbour, brought in a minority report which I recognized as a friendly gesture. They wrote:

> We cannot fail to express our feeling that the outside activities and some of the extra-campus affiliations of Robert Lovett are not conducive to effective or helpful service as a member of the faculty of the University of Chicago, and that in view of his long service and scholastic achievements in the field of English literature he is deserving of honorary [sic] retirement, with usual and suitable provisions for emeritus professors. It is in no unfriendly spirit that we express the belief that his long years of study and authorship and a family affliction incident to the World War may have weakened his judgment to the extent of causing him to a pen a letter in which he refers to all governments, specifically including the United States, as rotten.

Senator Barbour accompanied this gesture with a personal letter reasserting the friendly feeling of Senator Graham and himself, to which the obvious reply was "It is all very well to dissemble your love, but why do you kick me downstairs?"

The whole affair, which later was revived by a committee of the House of Representatives with more serious results, gave me a certain distaste for elected persons, a feeling confirmed when Congressman Samuel Dickstein declared to the Hearst papers: "If all the exhibits offered in evidence against Professor Lovett were disregarded except Exhibit 19 [the Gordin letter], proof of his disloyal conduct is conclusive."

The question of "outside activities and extra-campus affiliations" as affecting my effective or helpful service as a member of the faculty might properly have been raised as a matter for consideration by the president and trustees of a privately endowed and administered university rather than for interference by the state. It might fairly be said that I was giving too much time and energy to extramural activities. But from its beginning the University of Chicago was generously tolerant toward and even encouraged the extension of academic life beyond the cloister. President Harper was an extraordinary example of the wide range of such activities. President Judson was disposed to bring my position on the *New Republic* before the trustees with a view to forcing me to decide whether I should be a teacher or a journalist. This would have been fair enough if my arrangement with the head of my department for a leave of absence of two quarters had not been approved for the ensuing year. President Burton, who succeeded Mr. Judson, was sympathetic in accepting my dual role.

As to the right of an institution to control the expression of belief and opinion by a member of its staff outside of his professional engagements a question might be raised. Undoubtedly his position in the institution gives a certain influence and even authority to such expressions. The institution may even consider itself compromised by them. On the whole, however, it must be admitted that the gain arising from this form of academic freedom is greater than the loss. When I was at Harvard President Eliot was under ferocious criticism in Boston because he was a Unitarian and because of his advocacy of free trade. Harvard lived through it.

When the Illinois Senate committee recommended my dismissal to the Board of Trustees President Hutchins proposed to issue a scorching statement. He read it to Professor Linn, who advised a policy of silent contempt, which after all proved most irritating. "And," said Linn, "perhaps the trustees will not agree with you." Loyally, but perhaps mistakenly, he added, "If they fire Lovett you will receive twenty resignations from the faculty." "Oh, no," replied the President. "They will go to my successor. Mine will beat theirs to it."

The impinging upon the minds of students of beliefs and opinions expressed by a teacher outside his professional relation should be a matter of careful consideration by the individual concerned. For myself I can safely say, first, that I never used my university classroom or lecture hall as a place for expounding any doctrine whatever except the subject announced in the curriculum. Second, in spite of my belief that students are people, and should inform and express themselves on public questions at issue, I have never initiated the formation of groups or clubs for discussion (except the Poetry Club), though I have thought it part of my job to meet such organizations on their invitation.

II

Our years at Hull House were marked by personal and family events. In 1922 my mother died after long illness, in the true faith of a Christian. I sometimes think that those who really desire an afterlife, and deserve it, will receive it, on the terms of Matthew Arnold's sonnet:

> And who flagged not in the earthly strife, . . .
> His soul well-knit, and all his battles won,
> Mounts, and that hardly, to eternal life.

Five years later my father died at his Brookline home. He had become less rigid in his theology. It is recorded that when the deacons of the Harvard Church in Brookline discovered that their distinguished pastor was a Unitarian, and were discussing his retirement, my father impatiently rebuked a hot gospeler by demanding, "What do you or I know about the divinity of Christ?" He was eighty-six when he died, the oldest insurance man on State Street, still active, highly respected, and frequently called upon for addresses in reminiscence of the Boston Fire.

My sister Emily had married Dr. Horace A. Eaton, long professor of English at Syracuse University. Their home was a center of liberal thought and action. My brother Sidney had gone to Yale, and after enjoying two pastorates had returned thither as chaplain. He must be good, since they have made him a visiting preacher at Harvard.

My older daughter Beatrice had gone to Radcliffe College and then entered the University of Chicago. She took her medical course at the affiliated Rush Medical School. On her graduation she was at the Durand Hospital for Contagious Diseases. Later she was assistant to the resident physician for the McBride Sugar Plantation on the island of Kauai, whither her mother accompanied her to renew Hawaiian memories. After a year in the islands they went to Vienna, where Beatrice studied pediatrics. Unfortunately her promising career was deflected by tuberculosis, probably the effect of the unheated rooms and laboratories of Vienna, and she was exiled for a year to Trudeau. After her recovery she became a member of the staff of the Hennepin County hospital for tuberculosis near Minneapolis.

My younger daughter Ruth, having literally outgrown a career as a Russian dancer, consented to go to the University of Chicago and to Radcliffe. She married her classmate at Chicago, John Ashenhurst. They went to Paris to conduct the Drake Travel Bureau. John's sinus trouble threatened the loss of his eyesight, and they were advised to go to Baltimore, where our friend of early Chicago days, Dr. Llewellis F. Barker, took charge. He declared that there was no chance of saving John's eyesight, and that treatment must be directed to enabling him to live without seeing. It was remarkably successful. John has ethmoid blindness, with five per cent vision, yet so skillful is he in using this resource that his behavior is entirely normal. He is manager of the Edward Petry Company, radio advertising agency in Chicago.

To the Francis W. Parker School my family owes much. When the Ashenhursts were living briefly at Hull House, Ruth took her first-born, Nancy Jane, to see the principal, Miss Flora Cook, but was told regretfully that the enrollment was complete. When, however, residence at Hull House was mentioned, and my honored name was brought in, Miss Cook became enthusiastic and went over the limit. Nancy is now an assistant in the school, of which her mother is financial manager. The second child, my namesake, graduated last year, after passing the entrance examinations for Harvard (they are easier than in my day) and winning a national scholarship. The third infant, Ruth, is now in the high school. She displays remarkable acumen in connecting herself with the capitalistic system.

Nancy married a schoolmate, Haskell Wexler, and has given me two great-grandchildren, Katharine and Jeffrey, making me an ancestor.

12

A privilege of residence at Hull House was the connection with international affairs through the visits of representative men and women from Europe and Asia. I remember especially the visit of Mr. Oswald

Mosley, then of the British Labour party, and his lovely wife, Lady Cynthia Curzon. The latter, granddaughter of the old Chicago merchant, Levi Leiter, was in full sympathy with her husband's radical socialism of that time. After dinner the photographers gathered, and the Mosleys insisted on our posing with them in the rather magnificent dining-room of Hull House. The picture appeared next morning in a Chicago paper over the caption, "The Mosleys Abandon Their Lake Shore Drive Friends to Dine with the Poor" – which gave us much pleasure.

The chief privilege, however, was the association with Jane Addams. Her preoccupations increased constantly on account of the Women's International League, of which the triennial conclaves drew her abroad. In 1926 Ida went with her to Ireland. In 1929 the League met in Washington, where its reception caused much anxiety. The Daughters of the American Revolution considered it a patriotic duty to suppress Miss Addams. At the first meeting a D.A.R. representative strode to the front and began to speak. Miss Addams explained that the program was arranged, but she promised to allow the uninvited guest to speak later. After standing for a while in front of the rostrum the malcontent departed. The convention proceeded to Chicago, with visits to local chapters at several cities, and there were dire threats of what the local D. A. R.'s would do to the delegates. The newspapers joined the outcry, outraging the decency of this country in the presence of these distinguished women from other continents, who were naturally amazed. Miss Addams carried off the situation with dignity and good humor. She explained to the delegates:

> May I assure you that Americans are not by training and nature less tolerant than the people of those other countries who treated us with such fine and unvarying courtesy. May I beg you not to take the situation too seriously? The American delegation does not, for it knows only too well how easily newspaper attacks are manufactured, and how ephemeral they are.

And she illustrated the point by a reference to her visit to London in 1915, when the city was placarded with posters "To the Tower with Ramsay MacDonald," paid for by Horatio Bottomley, who in 1929 was himself in prison while MacDonald was Prime Minister.

As the aftermath of the war revealed more clearly the condition of the world it "reconstructed," the belligerence of patriotism abated somewhat. The depression of 1929 turned attention to the class struggle rendered acute by unemployment. A reversal of public opinion brought praise to Jane Addams. In 1931 she was awarded half of the Nobel Prize for Peace, the other half going to Nicholas Murray Butler, who had expelled members of his faculty for being opposed to the war, and who, as president of the Carnegie Endowment for International Peace, had placed the resources of that organization at the disposal of the government for war. Some thought the collocation unhappy, but Miss Addams was pleased at this evidence of reconciliation—a leading advocate of war and an absolute pacifist united in the prize for peace. Approaching her seventy-fifth birthday, she was given a banquet at Washington by the Women's International League, attended by the most distinguished of her countrymen, in recognition of her position as the leading woman of America. For once Miss Addams showed pleasure in praise, but with reserve. "Did you read what they said of me?" she asked on her return.

Two weeks later she had a recurrence of a severe illness that she had had the year before. It proved fatal. The funeral on May 23, 1935, in the courtyard of Hull House was simple and moving, but the real outpouring of the grief of her neighbors was at her bier. Hour after hour men, women, and children, thousands of them, passed up the stairs to look for the last time on the beautiful, worn face of their friend. All the noble tributes of her admirers at Washington were less eloquent than the spontaneous comments of these humble people among whom she had lived for nearly half a century. A Greek workman was heard to say, "She not Ortodox, not Catolic, not Presbytere—she all religions."

13

In the summer of 1937, as we were leaving Hull House, George Reynolds invited me to teach at the summer session of the University of Colorado. George had taken his doctorate at Chicago, and President George Norlin had been senior fellow in Greek at the time of my arrival at the university in 1893. Ida and Beatrice came out to stay at Columbine Lodge, and we drove to Livermore, where my cousin Ethel and her husband Gordon Johnson kept the old Poland ranch. Edward Davison, the poet, was directing a conference for several weeks, and among the attractions were Sherwood and Eleanor Anderson, John Peale Bishop, and John Crowe Ransom. I was happy to meet Evelyn Scott, whose books I had reviewed with appreciation, and Ford Madox Ford, the receiver of literary movements now liquidated.

Boulder is one of the most striking of university towns, sitting at the feet of two massive rock formations which turn perpendicular faces to the valley, each marked by a great naked scar. Several miles above the town the university has a camp which is a base for geological and botanical studies. The athletic department used it as a starting point for climbs up into the higher mountains. I remembered my ascent of Long's Peak seventeen years earlier, and learning that a party was forming for the next day I presented myself to the physical director as an adept. He accepted me with reluctance. It was too late for me even to get nails put on my boots. The route was by way of a chimney which cut off much of the distance, but the climb was difficult, up wet rocks with no sure footholds. I was shocked to find myself utterly fatigued, trailing the party to the summit and falling farther and farther behind on the descent—I who was upbraided by Jeff Fletcher and Robert for forcing the pace on our Alpine trips. I thought, however, that my exhaustion was the effect of breaking in after so many years, and that the next time I should be of the strength of other days. The next week the party went to Navajo Peak. I had the same weariness. As we rested and lunched on the saddle, perhaps five hundred feet from the summit, a black thundercloud rolled up. I caught at the excuse that I should be too slow for the climbers in their necessarily rapid ascent and would sacrifice myself and stay below. Professor Leisy declared that he would stand by me. We crowded together under a rock, the sleet beating down on our blanket, and watched the little black dots winding their way up the cone amid playful lightning and incessant thunder. I was never so comfortable in my life. The return, however, was as painful as before, and I drew a red line under my account with one phase of life.

The University of Colorado was the third institution at which I taught, and the contrast with Chicago and Harvard was suggestive. The high mountain atmosphere gave a peculiar quality to the students, unlike that of the prairie or the Eastern coast—a buoyancy in the present and a sense of self-determination toward the future. I found them magnificent. The university showed the way in which American universities naturally reflect and take advantage of the scene and social background of their situations. My visits to others in the years of my retirement gave further examples of this; California was characteristic of the "slope," Arizona of the desert; Iowa, Wisconsin, and Minnesota exemplified three types of Middlewestern scenery and strains of immigrational influence; Oklahoma revived the aboriginal culture of the American Indians. My experience at Colorado was important to me, and I was sorry to refuse a later invitation there because of my appointment to the Virgin Islands.

XV. *Peace*, 1919–1939

I

DURING the two decades in which I was successively editor of the *Dial* and associate editor of the *New Republic*, president of the League for Industrial Democracy and resident of Hull House, my constant interests were peace and civil liberties. The two are intimately connected. The freedom of choice between peace and war depends upon the exercise of civil liberty, and one of the worst of war crimes is the subversion of it.

The refusal of the Senate to ratify the Treaty of Versailles did not release the United States from responsibility for the peace of the world. This was recognized by both political parties in the election of 1920, by promises to join the League of Nations and the World Court–promises which were broken by both. It was as a sort of atonement that President Harding called the Washington Conference in 1921 for the reduction of naval armament. Charles Evans Hughes, as Secretary of State, was much praised for the token sacrifice of a few ships of our Navy, but during the first years of his incumbency he ignored persistently official communications from the League of Nations.

For two years after the armistice the United States remained technically at war with Germany, implying the continuance and exercise of powers by the government at variance with civil liberties. During the regime of Wilson and Baker undeclared war against Russia was fought on two fronts. Relations with Mexico remained uncertain, and in view of the pressure of the Hearst papers and the Doheny oil interests other adventures, like the Veracruz occupation or the stern chase after Villa, were to be feared. Only after President Coolidge sent Dwight W. Morrow as Ambassador to Mexico was the danger of a second predatory Mexican war eliminated. Meanwhile military intervention in the Caribbean continued as a legacy of the dollar diplomacy of President Taft and Secretary Knox, with the addition of the seizure of Haiti in 1915. The atrocities perpetrated in that island by our armed forces in putting down resistance repeated the ugly story of the Philippines. The people of the United States remained apathetic until a committee, including Professor Emily Balch of Wellesley and Professor Paul Douglas of Chicago, visited Haiti and reported on conditions there. Then General Smedley D. Butler, commander of the Marines, swung out in protest against the killing of Haitians, and our forces were withdrawn. In the Dominican Republic the Marines on withdrawing set up Sergeant Trujillo as commander of the native police, by means of which he established a complete dictatorship. It is difficult for the states of Eastern Europe to appreciate the concern of the United States in promoting their democratic procedure when they see the set-up in the Dominican Republic fostered by our government.

In Nicaragua the resistance to an American-controlled puppet government took the form of an active revolt under General Sandino, involving jungle warfare with the Marines. Except for Villard and the *Nation* the Communists were the most vigorous opponents of this undeclared war, and I did not hesitate to speak for the Communist-sponsored Anti-Imperialist League. I felt that the real un-American activity in this case was that of the United States government, a fact that would be generally recognized today.

During the twenties the European situation was ameliorating. The Dawes Plan followed by the Young Plan reduced the burden of reparations and contributed to financial recovery. The Locarno treaties in 1925 promised a return to political stability. In this year Count Coudenhove-Kalergi was speaking for the Foreign Policy Association on the idea of a United States of Europe which had the support of Aristide Briand in France. The general appeasement moved forward until in the last year of Coolidge's administration fifteen nations signed the Kellogg-Briand Pact to renounce war as an instrument of national policy.

The pact gave encouragement to those who made peace a primary object of thought and effort. It was the only notable contribution of this country to the cause of international security since the Nine-Power Treaty and other engagements of the Washington Conference in 1921. On the other hand, the weakness of the pact in providing no machinery for the judicial determination of violations, and no implementation for restraint or punishment of offenders, was a cause of derision to realists, who believe that war is inevitable in this human world or has roots too deep to be reached by hortatory legislation. The Kellogg Pact was signed by ambassadors because it was demanded by the public opinion of the world. No statesman, no government, dared to flout public opinion by refusing to sign. The treaty was among governments, but it was also between each government and its people, a promise that the world should be spared the horror and suffering of war. Although weakened in its authority by the skepticism of statesmen and the derision of publicists, it remained a proclamation of emancipation for the people from the worst form of slavery. Ignored and almost forgotten, the Kellogg-Briand Pact was made the basis of the argument of the United States prosecuting attorney, Mr. Justice Jackson, before the international court at Nuremberg in the trial of Nazi leaders for the crime of making war.

It was recognized by believers in the pact that to maintain its vitality it must be used. Walter Lippmann argued that because "the pact provides no machinery for judicial determination as to whether it has been violated or not," the United States had no ground for protest to Italy in regard to its attack on Ethiopia. Such reasoning implied that diplomacy works in a sealed tomb, in which statesmen exist, seeing nothing, hearing nothing, knowing nothing of the world outside. Obviously the pact gave to every signatory the right to protest when an act of war is committed or threatened by another signatory. This right became an obligation in the case of the United States as the initiator of the world agreement and the nation least likely to get into trouble, the one which could most easily suffer a diplomatic check if such should be the result. The protests of Secretary of State Henry L. Stimson on the invasion of Manchuria by Japan, and later of Secretary of State Cordell Hull in the attack on Ethiopia by Italy, are honorable episodes in the diplomacy of the United States. Although both were futile, the responsibility for failure in the first case lies with Great Britain, in the second, with weakness in the neutrality laws designed to uphold the pact.

It was also recognized by those who trusted the pact that no treaty is stronger than the will of the people concerned to uphold it. In view of the ease with which the volatile American public could be stirred to war almost overnight by the Venezuela boundary or "Remember the Maine," played as themes by the yellow press, it was an important aim of pacifists to strengthen the will to peace on the part of the public, against the time when other interests should find it profitable to arouse the will to war. The initiative was already being taken by American youth.

The so-called Oxford oath, not to fight for king and country, was adapted to an American form and was being taken by students en masse after the Kellogg-Briand Pact was signed. I realized that such an oath could not be kept, except in comparatively few cases, if the government departed from its original promise. I never administered the oath, but I heard it read and taken at meetings of students, and approved it as an individual affirmation of loyalty to the national pledge and an aid in keeping it.

Similarly the "strike against war," initiated by the League for Industrial Democracy, was a declaration of union in support of an announced national policy. With a sense of the incongruity of a strike in time of peace, I felt that it was justified as including opposition to those measures and policies of the government which could be recognized as leading to war. I spoke frequently at colleges, sometimes by invitation of the academic authorities, as at Michigan and Oberlin, sometimes at the request of the students and more or less with the disapproval of faculties. I defended the right of students to protest against war in their corporate capacity. I pointed out that the fact of their association exposed them to propaganda, and I reminded them of the shameless use of this weapon in the last war by college presidents, professors, headmasters, clergymen, and prominent alumni, who turned the young lives entrusted to them into cannon fodder, too often thinking of their prestige and that of their institutions more than of the justification of the war itself. At all events they had renounced he task of making good the promises made: they in their generation left fruitless the sacrifices for which they had called, a harvest of blood and tears.

2

One feature of the campaign against war was the Committee against Militarism in Education, of which the specific objective was to combat the indoctrination of boys in schools and colleges through the R. O. T. C. As an educator I had a profound distrust of the motives behind this military organization. I remembered my own experience in military drill in high school, a complete waste of pupils' time to give a sort of dignified employment to veteran officers of the Civil

War as drill masters. I suspected that the War Department, with the personnel of the expanded war machine on its hands, found this outlet convenient for their leftovers. It is usual in a college faculty to feel contempt for departments which profiteer in numbers by giving high marks and special favors. The R. O. T. C. demanded and received academic recognition of its courses, for which it offered inducements for registration in the way of uniforms and subsistence. A particular ground of objection was the handbook of citizenship issued by the War Department in which democracy was scouted as "government by the mob," and fascism was in effect advocated. This book was later withdrawn, as was another manual which was too realistic in its detailed instructions for killing. It is true, as Ruskin says, that we honor the soldier not for killing but for being killed. Nevertheless, killing in war is an obligation ancillary to being killed, and to minimize this fact in the interest of presenting only the pleasant side of war seemed to cast doubt on the sincerity of the War Department as an educator. Finally the exploitation of sex on the campus as a recruiting device was revolting. When an officer of the United States Army praised a student corps and predicted military success because it had "such a pretty honorary colonel," the degradation of the honor of the soldier, for us who had known soldiers, was complete.

The tendency of the government to conceal the terrible and ugly aspects of war called for corrective action. A speech of Congressman Ross A. Collins on March 14, 1932, called the attention of the House to the reply of Major General Irving J. Carr, chief of the Signal Corps, to George P. Putnam, the publisher, who wished to include photographs in possession of the Signal Corps in a book called *The Horror of It*. General Carr said that the Signal Corps would supply Army pictures which showed "the pleasant features of military operations," but declined to release others depicting "the repulsive side of war."

While the War Department declined to aid pictorially in the campaign against war it could no longer control literature. The suppression of books revealing "the repulsive side of war" necessarily ceased with the treaty with Germany. *Le Feu* by Henri Barbusse was translated as *Under Fire*. Miss Ellen La Motte's *Backwash of War*, written during the war and suppressed, entered circulation. Erich Maria Remarque's *All Quiet on the Western Front*, Arnold Zweig's *The Case of Sergeant Grischa*, Humphrey Cobb's *Paths of Glory*, and Thomas Boyd's *Through the Wheat* followed. Literature came back in power and significance to help develop and maintain a psychology of peace, especially in such revealing accounts as Walter Millis's *The Road to War* and Philip Gibbs' *Now It Can Be Told*. The English poets raised their voices. Siegfried Sassoon, Robert Graves, Wilfrid Gibson, Wilfred Owen, formed a school of anti-war poetry. A very simple poem that I often quoted, "Five Souls," by William Ewer, seems worthy of a place beside Southey's "Battle of Blenheim." I was regularly besieged for copies.

I was a peasant of the Polish plain.
  I left my plow because the message ran—
  Russia in danger needed every man,
To save her from the Teuton; and was slain.
I gave my life for freedom—this I know
For those who bade me fight had told me so.

I was a Tyrolese, a mountaineer.
  I gladly left my mountain home to fight
  Against the brutal treacherous Muscovite,
And died in Poland on a Cossack spear.
I gave my life for freedom—this I know
For those who bade me fight had told me so.

I worked in Lyons at my weaver's loom
  When suddenly the Prussian despot hurled
  His felon blow at France and at the world;
Then I went forth to Belgium, to my doom.
I gave my life for freedom—this I know
For those who bade me fight had told me so.

I owned a vineyard by the wooded Main
  Until the fatherland, begirt by foes
  Lusting her downfall, called me and I rose
Swift to the call, and died in fair Lorraine.
I gave my life for freedom—this I know
For those who bade me fight had told me so.

I worked in a great shipyard by the Clyde.
  There came a sudden word of wars declared;
  Of Belgium peaceful, helpless, unprepared,
Asking our aid. I joined the ranks and died.
I gave my life for freedom—this I know
For those who bade me fight had told me so.

A book which I thought of special value in this campaign was *It's a Great War* by a writer calling herself Mary Lee, who had served as nurse, Red Cross worker, and manager of a canteen. As nurse in a hospital behind the lines in France, she records the triumph of the military mind over professional ethics in the case of a distinguished surgeon, made a major, who insisted on the wounded men saluting him as he went his rounds, though some of them fainted at the effort. Miss Lee emphasized the sexual element in war, illustrated among others by the general who went about accompanied by two girls in uniform who were called secretaries.

3

An argument against war of which the public was largely ignorant was the shameless profiteering of business interests, exposed by a committee of the House of Representatives in 1922. The merchants in charge of operations in leather were a case in point. They cornered supplies to manufacture 41,100,152 pairs of shoes for the Army, 945,000 saddles for 86,418 cavalry horses, 2,850,853 halters and 2,033,204 nose bags for 500,000 horses, all of which superfluous stock they bought back after the war and presumably sold to their competitors at prices determined by the scarcity they had created. The scandals in connection with aviation had been exposed during the war in consequence of the protest of the sculptor Gutzon Borglum, but the inquiry was delayed so that the young men to whom the results were of special interest seldom heard of them. There was the fact that after the expenditure of over a billion dollars hardly a single American-built plane reached the front, and also the appalling fact that while 236 aviators, flying foreign planes, were killed in battle, 296 were killed in accidents caused by defective machines. The blame for this situation was placed squarely upon Colonel Edward A. Deeds, in charge of aircraft production, by Charles Evans Hughes, chairman of the committee of investigation appointed by President Wilson. He wrote:

> His former business associates were placed at once through government contracts in a position where they had assurance of very large profits upon a comparatively small investment of their own money, and in addition were able to secure generous salaries which they charged against the government as part of the cost of manufacture. The evidence with respect to Colonel Edward A. Deeds should be presented to the

Secretary of War to the end that Colonel Deeds may be tried by court-martial under Articles 95 and 96 of the Articles of War.

Secretary of War Baker, always lenient where "high-spirited businessmen" were concerned, arranged to have the charges dropped, and instead of a court-martial Colonel Deeds on leaving Washington was honored by a banquet. To Wilson's phrase "too proud to fight" might be added "and too ashamed."

In the light of such revelations, "To take the profits out of war" became one of the roads to peace adopted by the American Legion. Under this powerful sponsorship Congress set up in 1928 a Commission on War Policies, consisting of the Secretaries of War and Navy and a number of representatives and senators. Probably because of my articles in the *New Republic* on the work of the Graham Committee and the culpability of Secretary Baker, I was invited to appear before the commission. My argument boiled down to the conclusion that to take the profits out of war it would be necessary to take the profits out of peace. I received a very cordial response from the Secretary of War, Patrick J. Hurley of Oklahoma, who asked for literature on the subject. I referred him to Veblen's *The Nature of Peace*.

4

After the financial crisis of 1929, the collapse of the Weimar Republic and the rise of Hitler, the Mukden incident followed by the attack on Shanghai, and the invasion of Ethiopia, the world situation became more tense and was marked by increasing urgency on the part of peace forces in the United States. Many plans were drawn up and widely supported. Carrie Chapman Catt, president of the League of Women Voters, presented "The Cause and Cure of War." Salmon P. Levinson, with the distinguished patronage of Professor John Dewey, offered "The Outlawry of War." There were the "Emergency Peace Campaign" and the "Struggle Against War Committee." In the most comprehensive effort to implement the Kellogg Pact the Women's International League for Peace and Freedom initiated a People's Mandate to governments throughout the world, calling on them "to stop preparations for war, [to] use existing agencies to settle present conflicts and secure international action for disarmament and economic co-operation." Since a recent peace poll in Great Britain had already obtained twelve million signatures the League set its goal at fifty million.

In 1935 came the neutrality legislation designed primarily to keep the United States out of war and incidentally to supply a definite basis of neutral action in support of the Kellogg Pact by discouraging other nations from breaking it. It was hoped to obtain international support for the plan of smothering war at the beginning by cutting off supplies, of which the United States was the chief source. A fair statement on the neutrality legislation appeared in the "Foreign Policy Association Notes" of March 22, 1935, over the signature of the president, Raymond Leslie Buell:

> The United States can keep out of war in Europe or in the Orient if Congress at once adopts legislation making mandatory an embargo on the export of munitions and prohibiting American loans to all belligerents without discrimination as soon as war occurs; if it declares that the American Navy shall not be used to defend those of our citizens who attempt to make profits out of trade with "belligerents"; and if it reorganizes our military policy so as merely to maintain armed forces which, taking our geographic position and our control of potential bases into consideration, are adequate to defend the continental United States from invasion.

Mr. Buell added the question: "Are the American people willing to pay the price of a real anti-war policy?" As we continued to arm Japan against China the answer apparently was no.

The defect in all such plans was that they argued on the hypothesis that the question of peace and war rested with the United States. It was not recognized that another power might have a final voice in the decision. It was a fair statement that the neutrality legislation was directed to keeping us out of war in 1917 rather than in 1937.

In the autumn of 1936 on the invitation of Kirby Page I made a tour of the Southwest in support of the Emergency Peace Campaign. No special program was given me, but I tried to shape my arguments according to local circumstances in favor of strengthening of the neutrality laws. In particular, the Italian attack on Ethiopia might have been stopped by an embargo on oil. To argue before businessmen in Texas the importance of adding oil and cotton to the list of materials to be withdrawn from export to warmaking powers might seem a hopeless waste of time, but my hearers, if critical, were always courteous when I could get at them.

I remember that journey in fine October weather with reminiscent pleasure. Beginning at Little Rock, Arkansas, and going by Hot Springs to Dallas and Fort Worth, Texas, I had generous hospitality and appreciative audiences. I was joined by the Reverend James W. Workman, a veteran of the war and a genial fellow who was welcome everywhere. At Houston, however, my reputation—as delineated by the Hearst press—caught up with me. The papers carried screaming headlines, with the result that public buildings were closed to us. A protest luncheon was held by supporters of freedom of speech, and I spoke in the Negro high school, whose principal defied the order of the superintendent of schools.

The next day at San Antonio the situation was repeated. Here Congressman Maury Maverick swung out to our support. He was a bit disconcerted to find us at luncheon with the Rotary Club, of which Workman was a member. Here, again, although the white schoolhouses were closed to us, the principal of the Negro high school was unmoved by the storm. Maverick drove me to the schoolhouse, and I was amused to hear a conversation between him and the principal, who put him right on certain matters in regard to the Maverick pedigree.

5

The most vigorous demonstration of the will to peace was the American League against War and Fascism, afterwards the League for Peace and Democracy. When in 1932 the situation in Europe began to be appalling with the rising power of Hitler and the growing indications of the relation of fascist economy to war, an International Congress against War was held in Amsterdam. Delegates from the United States brought back a mandate to organize a supporting body in this country. As the Communists had taken a leading part at Amsterdam, they were active in the formation of the American branch, but the movement had a broader base and became the most typical of the so-called "united front" organizations. The League for Industrial Democracy sent delegates to the organizing committee, which was about equally divided between the Communists and the Socialist-Liberal group, but the former, it is to be observed, came to meetings regularly and promptly and were always ready to work. However, they were not allowed to control the meetings.

At the first convention, held at Mecca Temple in New York on September 29, 1933, local Communists made up most of the large audience. The guest of the occasion was the distinguished Communist Henri Barbusse. My first glimpse of him—a long, emaciated body, a haggard, tortured face under heavy black hair and brows—was as he sat alone on the deck of the steamer from which the other passengers had been landed, awaiting the decision of the Washington authorities as to whether our shores could receive so dangerous a personality.

The largest trade-union organization responding to the call was the Full-Fashioned Hosiery Workers of Newark. Sascha Zimmerman, its delegate, belonged to one of the Communist splinter parties, the Lovestoneites, and as such was more obnoxious to the Stalinists than even the Socialists. His admission furnished a test case between Communists and non-Communists in the steering committee. The latter held that refusal to admit Zimmerman was tantamount to destroying the united front and announced that they would withdraw if he were not seated and elected to the praesidium. After walking the quarter-deck for some hours Earl Browder finally gave way. How difficult his position was appeared when the name of Sascha Zimmerman was announced to the audience. There was an uproar which the chairman could not quell but which subsided as Browder stepped to the front and proclaimed, "Peace, be still." The same scene was repeated in the evening when it was thought proper to put the Lovestoneite on the list of speakers.

The next year the threatened split in the American League against War and Fascism became a reality. The great mass meeting in Madison Square Garden, called by the Socialists in honor of the workingmen of Vienna who died under the cannon of the fascist Dollfuss while defending their homes, ended in a disgraceful riot between Socialists and Communists. I was not present but I could envisage the situation—the Communists, who furnished a large part of the audience, getting out of hand at the mention of such speakers as Matthew Woll, their leaders attempting to control them, the Socialists unwilling to hold a meeting by the grace and favor of their opponents. At any rate, the League for Industrial Democracy, controlled by Socialists, withdrew from the League against War and Fascism. I sympathized with the feeling that led to this action, but I am always opposed to quitting. I saw in the A. L. W. F. a powerful weapon against war, and when it was reorganized in 1934 under the chairmanship of the Reverend Harry F. Ward, I became one of the vice-chairmen.

I was glad to work with Dr. Ward. He had been the first to arouse me to the desperate need of the underprivileged, in an address at my brother's church in Boston. I had followed his skillful direction of the American Civil Liberties Union as its chairman, and agreed with him, as did Roger Baldwin, that the League was an extension of the opportunity of defending freedom in respect to the most important subjects challenging its exercise—peace and democracy. Later I came to admire the statesmanship with which Dr. Ward guided the League, and to be amazed at the burden of work and anxiety which he carried. He was not strong and, I think, not entirely well, but he never spared himself.

His election as chairman was a recognition of the fact that the Communists alone could not carry the enterprise successfully. I presume that my selection was an invitation to the League for Industrial Democracy to return. I felt that in spite of the opposition between them, Socialists and Communists might be brought to combine on peace and opposition to fascism as objectives common to both, and that the common cause might act as a solvent for other differences. Co-operative action in elections was obviously desirable. I knew that in the election of 1932 in Chicago Norman Thomas and William Z. Foster, presidential candidates, lost in Chicago half the votes intended for them by frauds in counting, made possible by the lack of watchers at the polls. The L. I. D., however, proved immovable. Norman Thomas was not unapproachable on the matter, and Paul Porter, the student secretary, was favorable. I had at least the satisfaction of seeing Browder, Porter, and Zimmerman sitting together amicably in committee.

The League against War and Fascism held a second convention in Chicago in September 1934, when the prospects of peace offered by the neutrality legislation seemed hopeful, and a third in Cleveland in January 1936. By that time the rebellion against the Spanish Republic, led by General Franco and supported by Germany and Italy, was under way, and the failure of the neutrality laws was evident. In October 1935 President Roosevelt spoke brave words in regard to quarantining the aggressor, words which became part of the platform of the League. On Armistice Day a year later President Roosevelt declared: "We are acting to simplify definitions and facts by calling war war when armed invasion and a resulting killing of human beings takes place." His failure to find a state of war existing in China, in spite of an invasion by hundreds of thousands of armed men and the death of more than a million civilians, together with his policy toward Spain, showed the futility of relying on the government without the backing of a forceful public opinion.

6

All efforts to promote peace by treaties, disarmament, and neutrality legislation were thrown into confusion by the rebellion of General Franco and the resulting civil war in Spain. The immediate intervention on behalf of the rebels by the armed forces of Germany and Italy, followed by limited assistance to the Republic from Russia, posed a problem for the "peace-loving nations" that they met feebly. The English devised the Nonintervention Committee, apparently for the purpose of blinding their eyes to the obvious intervention of the fascist powers. The United States extended its neutrality laws to include civil war, in order to cut off supplies from the Republic, but took no steps to refuse such assistance to Franco by way of Germany and Italy. The situation was complicated by rivalry between Communists, Socialists, and other factions in the Spanish republican government and army, and by the support of Franco as a religious obligation by the Roman Catholic hierarchy, which had become the apologist of the rebellion. It was reported that the influence of Cardinal Mundelein, the "New Deal Cardinal," was responsible for President Roosevelt's reluctant decision to support Franco by accepting the farce of the Nonintervention Committee. The only redeeming feature of the behavior of the United States was the volunteering of recruits for the brigades bearing the names of George Washington and Abraham Lincoln for the service of republican Spain. Even this bright record was sullied by the action of the government in prosecuting the survivors as subversive persons on their return.

The Spanish Civil War was a concern of the League against War and Fascism. It was a clear indication of the rallying of fascist forces in Europe, of their preparations for war against the democracies, of the weakness of the latter in meeting them. When the atrocities of Franco became mass murders, as at Badajoz and Guernica, the people of the United States became somewhat moved, and the great increase in membership of the League, especially among the workers, was due to its unflinching stand for Spain. I spoke frequently in its support in 1937 and 1938.

In December 1937 a bill was introduced in the House by a member of the League, Jerry J. O'Connell of Montana, to stop up the manifest holes in the neutrality laws by making a clear distinction between an aggressor and a victim of aggression. The treatment of the Spanish Republic had now become the test of the sincerity of advocates of neutrality, and it was clear that the administration had decided to support the rebel General Franco. Every effort was made to smother any attempt to correct the neutrality laws and their misapplication. The chairman of the Foreign Affairs Committee of the House, Samuel D. McReynolds, canceled hearings on amendments to the Neutrality Act, scheduled to begin on March 29, 1938, with the assertion made to the *Washington Post* that "most of the demand for repeal or modification of the act stems from Communist or Communist-inspired organizations." He admitted receiving some forty-five thousand letters and telegrams asking for the repeal or modification of the Neutrality Act, but discounted ninety per cent because they came from New York City. A week before McReynolds released his statement the League had informed him that one hundred and seventy-four trade-union locals had passed resolutions in favor of the O'Connell peace bill, of which eighty-five per cent came from outside New York City; the number later increased to four hundred. Every effort was put forth to defeat O'Connell in his Montana district, which replaced him in the 1938 election with Jacob Thorkelsen, an outspoken reactionary.

7

While the question of peace was responsible for the more spectacular activities of the League, account was taken of developments in this country which resembled those preceding the rise of fascist parties and governments, especially in Italy. The year 1937 was a year of recovery in business. Although the United States Steel Corporation raised wages in conformity with the higher cost of living induced by prosperity, the companies of the second line, Bethlehem, Republic, National, refused to do so, thus precipitating the "Little Steel" strike. The worst event in connection with the strike, and one of the most horrible in the history of Chicago, was the so-called Memorial Day Massacre. The mills of the Republic Steel Works in South Chicago were kept in apparent activity by a skeleton force barricaded within. The strikers and their families planned a parade on the afternoon of May 30, 1937, in front of the mills, to induce the skeleton force within to join them. The route was over vacant land, with no interruption of traffic, and a permit had been granted. However, a force of some forty patrolmen was sent to the scene under command of a captain, who had been accused of using provocative tactics and brutal reprisals in connection with a meeting of W. P. A. workers a few months earlier. Among many regrets I count as one of the chief the fact that I ignored my feeling that there would be trouble. I spoke in the university chapel that morning on peace, and in the relaxation that followed I forgot to seek peace and pursue it. As the parade advanced, the police without provocation opened fire. Some ten persons were killed and fifty wounded. The Paramount moving picture taken showed policemen beating the fallen victims on the ground. Their friends were not allowed to give first aid. The wounded were put under arrest. Some died in the police cars in which they were being conveyed to hospitals many miles away. The Senate Committee on Civil Liberties, headed by Senator Robert M. La Follette, Jr., conducted an inquiry which revealed stupidity and cruelty which shameless perjury could not cover up, but the police who were summoned, including the Chief Commissioner, remained unmoved in the face of testimony by photograph and word. For months, however, the showing of the Paramount picture in Chicago was forbidden. The coroner's inquest was held in the Criminal Court Building, and took on the function of a regular court of justice, which found the wounded guilty of the riot. Later they were subjected to fine and imprisonment.

A meeting of protest was held in the Chicago Opera House. Paul Douglas and I spoke, but no influential citizens came to our support, as I am sure would have been the case with the generation I had known in earlier days. A former student, Meyer Levin, had just then published a successful book, *The Old Bunch*, and gave of his royalties and of his time and energy to rouse the city to a sense of shame. His book *Citizens*, based on the massacre, stands high in the record of the efforts of writers in behalf of justice. Mayor Edward J. Kelly was never repudiated for his failure in the primary duty of a chief magistrate of a city to care for the people entrusted to his charge. The division between the A. F. of L. and the C. I. O. showed its disastrous effect in the failure of labor to rally as a whole in political protest, and the middle class was indifferent.

Later that year I presided over a panel in Pittsburgh to take evidence from victims in regard to the strike of which the Memorial Day Massacre was the worst event. Some twenty men appeared. They told of the fight against unionization conducted by the National Steel Company at Weirton, West Virginia, by means of labor spies and thugs; they told of the provocative tactics of the police at

Massillon, Ohio, in consequence of which workers were fatally shot. The most significant report came from Bethlehem, Pennsylvania, where influential citizens were organized by a clergyman to aid the Bethlehem Steel Company in breaking the strike. The clergyman was indebted to the company and its officials for the support of his church, and in return he persuaded merchants, landlords, bankers, doctors, to refuse the strikers credit for food and rent, and to call in notes secured by mortgages on houses and cars. The alignment of the middle class against labor made us aware that we were in an early stage of fascism; it was a discouraging contrast to the attitude in New Bedford nine years before.

8

The League met in its Fourth Congress at Pittsburgh, November 26-28, 1937. It was attended by nearly fifteen hundred delegates, representing branches and labor unions claiming more than four million members. The League was now fully committed to the policy of collective security, "to keep the United States out of war by helping to keep war out of the world." I was still inclined to lay emphasis upon the first term of the syllogism by strengthening the neutrality laws, but I was converted by Reinhold Niebuhr's eloquent address against isolation and in favor of collective security. The program adopted for 1938 is to my mind a thoroughly statesmanlike document, but, like the proposals for the effective use of neutrality in World War I, it came too late to meet the menace of irresponsible power in the hands of Nazis and Fascists in Europe and Japanese imperialists in Asia.[1]

In 1938 the League changed its name from the negative "against War and Fascism" to the affirmative "for Peace and Democracy," its objectives remaining the same. As the most prominent of the united front organizations it early attracted the notice of the House Committee on Un-American Activities, headed by Representative Martin Dies, which came into being in this year. The first witness, who later became its chief investigator, was J. B. Matthews, who had been chairman of the first convention of the League in 1933 and

---

[1] PROGRAM FOR 1938

(1) Organize emergency citizens' committees for labor's rights wherever those rights are attacked either by employers or by public officials.

(2) Defeat legislative attempts to compel incorporation of unions and to

claimed to be an expert on its affairs. He candidly confessed at the first hearing that he had been a member of more "united front organizations than anyone except Professor Robert Morss Lovett." I was amused by this tribute, at being "by merit raised to that bad eminence," and wondered what was behind it.

I had been giving some attention to the activities of Nazis in Chicago, where the Bund was gathering great crowds in Riverview Park to listen to pro-Hitler propaganda. A Lutheran clergyman who had been invited to attend the assembly of the party at Nuremberg and to preach in Martin Luther's church boasted of converting his Young People's meeting into a military maneuver. I asked Secretary Ickes if he could refer me to any member of the Dies Committee who might be interested in my testimony, but he was unable to do so. Dr. Ward appeared before the committee at his own request and made a sworn statement disproving the allegation that the League was controlled by Communists. This document has disappeared from the files of the committee. Meanwhile the Washington headquarters of the League were raided illegally. The committee followed its usual tactics of condemning individuals, without trial, for membership in an organization which was assumed to be subversive.

As in the case of other so-called united front organizations, the League disbanded on the announcement of the nonaggression treaty between the Soviet Union and Nazi Germany in August 1939, and the declaration of war by Russia against Finland. The League could

---

PROGRAM FOR 1938 – *continued*

control or inspect union finances by governmental or other outside agencies.

(3) Press for an anti-lynching law; and measures to guarantee full rights for the Negro people and the foreign-born.

(4) Oppose vigorously the propaganda of race prejudice and discrimination.

(5) Defeat the War Department plan to conscript labor and industry and to regiment press and radio.

(6) Support the nationalization of the manufacture of arms, ammunition and implements of war, forbidding export except when ordered by Congress in cases of countries invaded by an aggressor.

(7) Promote the people's boycott of Japanese goods.

(8) Seek to remove and prevent restrictions on the access of the governments of China and Spain to our markets, applying regulations to purchases and shipments designed to remove the risk of our becoming involved in war.

(9) Demand a foreign policy based on:

The distinction between aggressors and their victims.

The necessity of denying our economic resources to the war-making, treaty-breaking aggressors and opening them up to their victims under conditions designed to remove the risk of our being drawn into war.

The necessity of concerted action to quarantine aggressors.

not approve these acts, and the Communists could not agree to denounce them. To that extent it may be said that the Communists controlled its existence.

A frank statement of the relations of Communists to the League by an employee of the latter appeared in the *New Republic* for March 18, 1940. A letter from Roger Baldwin in 1942 is authoritative:

> It is always difficult to say about any organization in which Communists actively participate whether it is really under their "control." I tried to make that clear in my article on "Liberalism and the United Front" for which you asked and which was sent you. Some organizations even with Communist minority participation are certainly under their control, since they hold the key positions. Others are not. I do not think it can be said of the League for Peace and Democracy that it was controlled by the Communist party or personnel, although many of its local branches were. But the policies made at the top, as you know, were arrived at by democratic consultation among people, a majority of whom were not Communists, neither party members nor fellow travelers. We were, of course, prevented from taking any position in opposition to Communist policy, for they would have withdrawn and thus wrecked the united front. But that area of conflict was comparatively slight. When it became acute, after the Nazi-Soviet Pact, it killed the League.
>
> I have tried to find in the Dies Committee reports what I thought was there, but apparently isn't—namely, an affidavit submitted after Dr. Ward's testimony in 1939 explaining exactly the degree and effect of Communist influence in the League. (I do not think any purpose would be served by making any such statement now.) I have reviewed Dr. Ward's testimony and he made the case against Communist domination perfectly clear—for anybody who believed him. The trouble with the Dies Committee and its supporters is that they just don't believe any ex parte testimony.

The League was an association of organizations of which the Communist party was one. It was the largest contributor by virtue of the size of its membership, and always had two representatives on the council of seventeen, one of whom was Earl Browder. He never dictated the policy of the League. In argument with Dr. Ward he invariably gave way and always expressed admiration for the leadership of the former in the cause which was of equal importance to Communists and to liberals and pacifists, the opposition to war and fascism. If the League followed the line of Moscow it was not because the policy emanated from Moscow but because it was our own line, especially in the matter of collective security and the punishment of aggressors, to which the Soviet Union had given the lead through Maxim Litvinov in the Council of the League of Nations. Russia needed peace even more urgently than did the United States, and the error at Munich in leaving Russia out has long been obvious. It is discouraging to find that the League was condemned by Congress for its intelligent foresight.

XVI. *The Virgin Islands,* 1939–1944

I

SOMETIME in the autumn of 1934 Dr. Ernest Gruening, then Director of the Division of Territories and Island Possessions in the Department of the Interior, sent me a telegram asking me to come to Washington. I knew that Gruening wanted Robert Herrick to be Government Secretary of the Virgin Islands, and also that Secretary Ickes, remembering Herrick's somewhat aloof manner in the early days of the University of Chicago, was suspicious of his "social attitude." In those days tourism was much in mind as the chief economic resource of the Virgin Islands. "What we need is a greeter," said the Secretary. I assured him that Herrick had two styles in social behavior, one deriving from George Washington and one from Warren Gamaliel Harding. The reserve of the first would maintain a gracious dignity in official relations with the residents of the islands, and the glad spontaneity of the second would gratify tourists. Herrick was appointed. Having so much on my conscience, I felt bound to visit the Virgins to observe the Government Secretary in action. In November 1935 I took the Furness Line steamer *Nerissa* for St. Thomas.

To enter the harbor of St. Thomas at sunrise is an experience that one is not likely to forget. The channel leads between land masses projecting like two long arms to enclose the basin of blue water. Along the shore clings the little cluster of white and red roofs, rising in terraces to the hills, as at Amalfi or Sorrento. The hills catch the sunlight, one by one, beginning at the west, bringing out the white faces of houses amid the green. When a drought prevails, the landscape is subdued to a tawny brown, golden at sunrise. Today the contours are defaced by gray catchment areas of concrete for the water supply of the town, but ten years ago there were too few to do more than excite the curiosity of visitors. The little steamer crawls up to the long dock of the West Indian Company and the Government Secretary comes aboard.

2

The Virgin Islands are fortunate in their history. To begin with, they were linked with the discovery of America by the supreme discoverer. I have always been sorry for the Elizabeth Islands because they were introduced to the world by such an obscure character as Bartholomew Gosnold. It is true that the Virgins were found by Columbus only on his second voyage, but a second in a great tradition is preferred to a first in some parochial order.

The Virgins are fortunate in the name that the great discoverer bestowed upon them, a name so rich in association, and so seldom deserved, as to constitute a distinction in itself. Some six hundred and fifty of the islands, large and small, they reminded the pious Christopher of the eleven thousand virgins martyred at Cologne with Saint Ursula. Happily Columbus was not aware of the latest scholarship which reduces XIM from eleven thousand to eleven martyrs.

The Virgin Islands of the United States enjoyed a happier fate than their West Indian companions in falling to Denmark in the scramble of the seventeenth century among the powers for overseas possessions. They escaped the brutalities of the Spanish and the revolutionary violence of the French islands. Denmark was neutral in the European struggles after the Thirty Years' War, and this neutrality extended to St. Thomas, which became a convenient post for exchange of communications and goods, incidentally acquiring a pleasant odor of piracy. Of the three large islands, St. Croix shared in the great prosperity based on sugar and the slave trade in the eighteenth and nineteenth centuries. St. Thomas continued to profit by its magnificent harbor, where the Danish West Indian Company built what is said to be the longest dock in the world. Today on the water side of Dronningens Gade, or Main Street, the old merchant buildings lead back through the increasing darkness, like tunnels, until they emerge on decaying wharfs where once their goods were landed and shipped.

Above all, the Virgin Islands were, and remain, fortunate in their transfer to the United States. They owe this happy fate to their strategic situation, at the eastern end of the line of the Greater Antilles and at the northern end of the arc of the Leeward and Windward Islands which curves southward to South America. Negotiations for the purchase of the islands during the nineteenth century were twice defeated, but the opening of the Panama Canal and the penetration of St. Thomas by German commercial interests made their acquisition inevitable. In the earlier proposals the figures under discussion had varied from five to seven and a half millions. In 1917 Mr. Lansing handed over twenty-five millions. I used to flatter the Virgin Islanders by pointing to the fact that for their one hundred and thirty-three square miles the United States paid two hundred and ninety-five dollars per acre, while for Alaska it gave two cents; for California, three; for the Louisiana Purchase, four; for the Philippines, fourteen; and for the invaluable Canal Zone, thirty-five dollars. There is historical precedent for payment to Denmark in the interest of national defense. A thousand years ago Saxon England was paying what was known as Danegelt to the Danes in pursuance of a policy of appeasement. Today the Virgin Islands can quote Pinckney's epigram: "Twenty-five millions for defense; not one cent for tribute."

Immediately on assumption of control by the United States the Virgin Islands were turned over to the Navy. The names of ten admirals and captains supplement the long list of Danish governors on the tablets in Government House. The naval administration was efficient within the limits of its mentality, but its attitude was expressed by an admiral who remarked, "The islands cost as much to run as a battleship, and we'd rather have the battleship." The islanders were in an ambiguous position as regards citizenship, and there were frequent delegations to Washington, inquiring pathetically about the constitutional rights and civil liberties of which they had heard so much. Economically a staggering blow was dealt by the application of the Volstead Act, which deprived the remaining sugar plantations of St. Croix of the only market which made sugar growing profitable.

In these circumstances President Hoover transferred the administration to the Department of the Interior in 1931 and appointed Paul M. Pearson as Governor. He brought to the islands the men who have played the chief parts in their development: Lawrence W. Cramer, Lieutenant Governor, later Governor; Boyd J. Brown, Government Secretary, later president of the Virgin Islands Company; and Harry E. Taylor, Commissioner of Industry, later administrator of St. Croix.

On his visit to the islands President Hoover described them, in words which rankle today in the minds of the inhabitants, as "an effective poorhouse." The conditions were indeed deplorable. Governor Pearson's first report is full of evidence of preceding maladministration and neglect.

> Conditions in the islands have been desperate.
>
> Most of the laborers were out of work, and during the preceding months the Red Cross had been feeding as many as twenty-five per cent of the population.
>
> Renters are required to pay cash to their landlords, a rental running from ten to twelve dollars an acre for land that would sell for from thirty-five to fifty an acre.
>
> The pressure is always to reduce the standards of labor to the cheapest possible.
>
> The standards of life are so low that in St. Croix sixty-five per cent of the burials are pauper burials.
>
> The death rate is abnormally high, being about three times that of the United States.

Against these conditions Governor Pearson and his successors fought vigorously, with the support of the Roosevelt administration. Public Works replaced Red Cross relief. The Virgin Islands Company was formed with federal funds to continue the growing of sugar on St. Croix and to revive the manufacture of rum, so imprudently sacrificed to the prohibition mania. Roads were built and improvements initiated. The Bluebeard's Castle Hotel was constructed on St. Thomas as a resort for tourists. Homestead and low-cost housing projects were set up on St. Croix and on St. Thomas. The Virgin Islands Co-operative was established to provide work at home, and under the management of a public-spirited merchant of St. Thomas it had in eight years done a business of over two hundred and twenty thousand dollars. The Civilian Conservation Corps camps and the National Youth Administration made a notable contribution. A decline in population which had been going on for nearly a century, marked by a fall from twenty-six thousand in 1917 to twenty-two thousand in 1930, was arrested, and an increase of thirteen per cent to nearly twenty-five thousand was recorded in 1940.

Of this number approximately eleven thousand live on St. Thomas, about thirteen thousand on St. Croix, and something more than seven hundred on St. John, which is connected with St. Thomas in municipal government. The two larger islands differ in physiography. St. Thomas is mountainous, with comparatively little good land for farming. Its chief resource is the excellent harbor, and its people are "harbor-minded." All but some eleven hundred live in the town of Charlotte Amalie. The population is counted as ninety per cent Negro, but many of these by virtue of interrelations of the races are light in color, and economically hold the status of an aristocracy. About a century ago Breton and Norman immigrants began to arrive from the French islands, St. Barthélemy and St. Martin. They settled as farmers on the north side of the island, which receives more rain than the south and contains some excellent springs. Others became fishermen at the west end of the town. Both groups have maintained their individuality by marriage among themselves.

St. Croix, topographically considered, is not one of the Virgin Islands, but belongs with Puerto Rico and Vieques. A range of hills along the north side guards a central plain, the sugar bowl which made the planters rich in earlier centuries. The round towers which dot the landscape, truncated cones in shape, are reminiscent of this prosperity. Two towns, Christiansted with three thousand inhabitants and Frederiksted with two thousand, are some twelve miles apart and maintain a rivalry as acute as any twin cities. The natives of St. Croix are rural in type, living close to the soil, but like the St. Thomians they carry as an inheritance from slavery a sense of the degradation of manual labor. Unlike St. Thomas, St. Croix has a white aristocracy. In the former, the leading citizens were Danes and a considerable number left the island on its change of nationality. In St. Croix the chief families were Scottish or American in origin, and remained closely allied by birth and marriage, dominating the social and business interests of the island. They have turned from sugar to cattle raising.

The island of St. John was ruined by a revolt of the slaves in 1828. It is almost entirely overgrown with bush, and the roads have become rough bridle paths. Most of the land is owned by the capitalists of St. Thomas.

3

This then was the little world in which I visited Robert Herrick some forty-two years after we had made our first venture together

into the megalopolis of Chicago. I found him in high spirits. He had indeed fallen into a hot spot on his arrival, owing to personal conflict between Governor Pearson and Judge T. Webber Wilson. President Roosevelt had summoned both officials with witnesses to Washington for a hearing, which became such a mess of recrimination that Roosevelt put an end to it by promoting both antagonists to higher-paid positions on the continent. The islands reflected the controversy in some disturbances, trivial but enough to establish Herrick in the opinion of Washington as the man for an emergency. He successfully urged the promotion of Lieutenant Governor Cramer to the governorship. When I arrived for my first visit Governor Cramer was in Washington and Herrick was living in Government House and enjoying his command. He used to say that of his three careers, teaching, writing, and administration, he was happiest in the last. He had warm friends among the continentals who had settled on the islands and among the original inhabitants, and they became my friends also and remembered me cordially when I returned year by year.

It was just before Christmas in 1938, shortly after my third visit to the islands, that I received in New York word from Ernest Gruening of Herrick's severe illness, and this was followed by news of his death. He was buried in York Village, where I had passed so many happy weeks with him in the house that he loved.

I never expected to see the Virgin Islands again, but early in January Gruening asked me if I would care to become Herrick's successor. I was pleased that he thought of me, but I did not take the proposal too seriously. I was planning my life very differently. I had finished my career at the University of Chicago, three years beyond the age for retirement. I was giving lectures for the League for Industrial Democracy on the middle class and the labor movement. I had engaged to teach at the Garrett Biblical Institute of Northwestern University during the early summer and later at the University of Colorado. Above all, Ida had found at Tucson the best climate for the arthritis from which she suffered. I joined her in January.

Tucson lies in a broken square of mountain ranges, surrounded by desert. We were both impressed by the beauty of the landscape. It was here that my all-time chief, John Manly, was making his last fight to live to complete his great variorum edition of *The Canterbury Tales*, and even then projecting future undertakings. "If I can't work, of course I don't want to live," he said one day, and added, "At least six or eight times a day I don't know whether I shall be alive minutes hence." We had many friends, especially Paddy and Mrs. Walsh, who had found a house for our permanent residence that was precisely what we wanted. I saw myself sitting under the remada doing what President Ernest Wilkins of Oberlin College once told me was his idea of retirement—reading the books that we referred to so confidently in our lectures.

While negotiations for the house were in progress, which I was glad to leave in the capable hands of Paddy Walsh, we made a rapid descent on the coast. We stayed with Herrick's wife and son at Los Angeles and had a lively visit with Upton Sinclair. At Berkeley I renewed an unforgotten friendship with George Noyes, who, first known as an obstreperous freshman at Harvard, a somewhat inconvenient hanger-on, had become a great scholar of Russian and Polish. His first lieutenant was Alexander Kaun, who had been my pupil at Chicago. Rudolph Schevill was head of the Spanish Department. A colleague for many years at Chicago, James Westfall Thompson of the History Department, and his wife were our devoted hosts. Altogether matters seemed to be drifting toward a quiet, happy sunset of life among books, pictures, music, friends. I was ready to cry with Antony:

> Unarm me, Eros. The long day's task is done,
> And we must sleep.

It was with some surprise that I received early in April an invitation to dine at the White House, but I was not unduly disturbed. The dinner was in honor of Rachel Crothers, the dramatist, and Miss Crothers was the cousin of my dentist. Besides I had written a play myself twenty years before. I was an obvious choice for the occasion.

The next day I was told that Secretary Ickes wanted to see me. I called on Gruening, who told me that the government secretaryship might come up at the interview, but I was not disappointed when the Secretary led me to understand at once that he was not going to appoint me to that office. He was interested, however, in the report of my last visit to the islands and the death of Herrick, for whom he had achieved a warm admiration. I was therefore startled when he turned to the telephone, called the Solicitor of the Department, and inquired, "Does Lovett have to go to the Senate for confirmation?" A day or two later I received President Roosevelt's appointment, dated April 25, 1939.

The University of Colorado courteously released me from my contract, but the Garrett Biblical Institute was less complacent. As soon as I finished giving young clergymen something of the literary background of the great faiths that are gone, I went to Washington to take my oath of office and meet Governor Cramer, who was there with a delegation from the Councils of St. Thomas and St. Croix trying to persuade Congress to return to the island treasuries the excise taxes on goods exported to the continent.

The islands are not a territory but a possession, an entity unknown to the Constitution. The laws passed by Congress do not apply unless the Virgin Islands are specifically mentioned. I have seen a document from Washington in regard to them marked "foreign." In fact, with respect to the tariff they are foreign: St. Thomas is a free port at which imports pay only a small *ad valorem* duty, the added imposition being collected at a continental port in case of reshipment of goods.

In administration, the islands are under the Secretary of the Interior through the Division of Territories and Island Possessions, which maintains a complete service in Washington, but they have business with every one of the several departments represented in the cabinet, and with the large semi-independent administrations, such as the Maritime Commission, the Bureau of Animal Husbandry, the Rural Electrification Administration, the Treasury Procurement Service. Finally there is the Bureau of the Budget, which exercises a final decision, too often a veto, upon expenditures.

4

I sailed from New York on July 20 and three days later arrived at San Juan, Puerto Rico. The next morning I was awakened in my stateroom on the inter-island steamer *Catherine* by the friendly voice of Dr. Knud-Hansen, the Commissioner of Health. That greeting was the first note of the major theme of my experience in the islands, a constant and cordial association with the people. On going ashore I met Morris de Castro, the Commissioner of Finance, and Jacob A. Robles, the efficient head of the Government Secretary's office. They had arranged a brief ceremony of induction, with the members of the administrative force and the municipal government present—all those with whom I worked most happily for nearly five years. Mrs. Cramer gave a reception at Government House in the afternoon.

The next day de Castro had arranged to have me call on the captain of the Coast Guard vessel *Unalga*, which on our departure fired the governor's salute of seventeen guns. "It will please the people and let them know that you're here," remarked my sponsor. It pleased me and made me sure that I was there.

The day after we flew to St. Croix, where the administrator, Harry E. Taylor, gave a reception for me. Taylor did a remarkable job in handling the finances and social problems of that community. He was one of the leading figures in the group which Governor Pearson had brought with him to establish the first civil government. He and his wife and our daughter became intimate friends. Their hospitality and friendly associations with the old families on St. Croix, which they shared with us, made our visits to Government House in Christiansted always happy.

Another day we flew to St. John to meet its administrator, Dr. George M. Hughes. In St. Thomas there was a series of cocktail parties, dinners, picnic suppers on the ridge which looks toward the Atlantic and where the summer temperature is ten degrees cooler than on the water front. I joined the Brewer's Bay Swimming Club for sea bathing, which when Governor Cramer returned became a daily event. The two families would go to the beach together after the day's work. The Cramer baby, known as Oskie, began to call me Bobus without any prompting. Herrick had built up an interest in chess, and in Lee Francis, Fred Dixon, the Superintendent of Education, and Canon Swinson of the Anglican Church I found worthy antagonists.

My notebook for summer and autumn is full of records of these pleasures, as well as of meetings of the Municipal Council, the Harbor Board, the Tourist Board, the Board of Control of Alcoholic Beverages, the Police Commission, the Lottery Board, and others. I enjoyed these as I did the dinners, cocktails, chess, and swimming, all of which made a charming and variegated pattern of life. Altogether, the atmosphere, personal and official, was cloudless.

In these early days I owed a debt beyond accounting to de Castro and Robles. I did not know then that Governor Cramer had quite properly proposed de Castro for the post of Government Secretary and that I had unwittingly stood in the way of his promotion. It would have been easy for him and his brother-in-law Robles to leave me to find my way through the intricacies of official protocol and island politics, but, on the contrary, they went far beyond any conceivable obligation to make my course smooth, to foresee mistakes I might make and warn me of pitfalls, to give me public recognition and credit for their own fine work. The basis of my enduringly happy relations with the Virgin Islanders was laid in those first weeks of my residence.

The house appointed for the Government Secretary was known from Navy days as Quarters B. It was a stone's throw from Government House on Kongens Gade, the first terrace above the water front. The upper floor on the level of the street was a superficial affair of recent construction, but the lower story, built into the side of the hill, was of solid Danish masonry with a charming grass plot and flowerbeds on one side and a row of outbuildings on the other from which descended what might have been a kitchen garden. The center of the house was occupied by a magnificent mahogany staircase, the replica of one of the *Kronprinzessin Cecelie*, for the builder of the house had been German consul and agent for the Hamburg-American line. Quarters B belonged to the Navy. Apparently it had been forgotten when the Interior Department took over the administration of the island, and for a time the Navy manifested a disposition to take possession, very disconcerting since no other residence was available. Finally President Roosevelt wrote a letter assigning it permanently as the residence of the Government Secretary. I suppose that someone else wrote it and slipped it across his desk, but I have always liked to think that his signature represented a conscious act of kindness toward an obscure official, whose pleasure and comfort as well as efficiency were dependent on his consideration.

After Ida's arrival in September life in Quarters B took on a pleasant routine. People dropped in for cocktails on Sunday afternoon, sometimes one or two, once thirty-four. When the Governor was away, as Acting Governor I had the pleasure of entertaining the official guests. We especially enjoyed the visits of our British neighbors.

The greatest potentate who visited St. Thomas during my stay was undoubtedly Generalissimo Trujillo. He came from witnessing the maneuvers of the Atlantic Squadron off Culebra, for he was a factor in the defense of the Caribbean. We gathered that Admiral

Leahy, then Governor of Puerto Rico, had objected to his coming to that island because there were too many Dominican refugees there to make it entirely safe for the "benefactor" of his country.

The Generalissimo's daughter, Madame de Brea, arrived in advance, a very beautiful and attractive girl, for whom the only entertainment we could provide was the routine affair of bathing at Brewer's Bay. The great man arrived on his yacht, a gorgeous affair acquired from the estate of an American millionaire. I was in doubt whether as Acting Governor I should call or wait for him to call on me, but as de Castro was of the opinion that he should be regarded as head of a state, though not then actually in office, I took the initiative. His interpreter and chief of staff, a former United States Marine, met us at the dock and explained that the Generalissimo was a poor sailor and had had a bad night. "He's hanging his hardware on," he added. We spent an hour over champagne and cigars. Finally the great man appeared, his breast gleaming with orders and decorations of which the papal collar was supreme. A review of the Marines was held, the consuls of the Dominican Republic gave receptions, and finally we had a banquet at the Bluebeard's Castle Hotel. I got thoroughly tired of making speeches of felicitation. Fortunately his plan of allowing a hundred thousand refugees from Europe to enter Santo Domingo, a contrast, on paper at least, to the niggardly policy of the United States, offered one subject for congratulation. My oratory was perhaps not sufficiently Corinthian for Trujillo's Latin taste. Just before his departure he showed me the effusive address made by the Papal Nuncio on the presentation of the collar.

In those days St. Thomas was a port of call for ships of the Atlantic Squadron. My notebooks are full of entries of the names of ships and commanders. There was a regular procedure. On the arrival of a man-of-war, the commander notified the Governor and asked when it would be convenient for him to call. Then the ship's boat would convey the Governor and his aide for the return call. When the Governor left the vessel, the boat stood off while a salute of seventeen guns was fired. If Governor Cramer was in residence I went with him as his aide; otherwise, as Acting Governor, I had the guidance of de Castro in that capacity. I attribute something of my decline in hearing to standing at salute in a rocking gig while the guns roared over my head.

Our relations with the Navy were entirely pleasant. The commander at Bourne Field on my arrival was Colonel Mulcahey, with whom I enjoyed our joint authority. I remember that one Sunday about six in the morning a councilman appeared from St. Croix. He had come over in a motorboat to obtain a coffin from the Marine stores for the funeral of one of the matriarchs of the island. In considerable doubt I called up Colonel Mulcahey and invited him and the doctor of the post to breakfast. They both were reluctant to release a coffin except in case of an emergency. To the Crucians it seemed an emergency—the death of a great lady in the back seat of her automobile, on her way to the christening of a grandchild, so suddenly that her daughter who was driving did not know what had happened until she opened the door to help her mother out. To the Marines it was sad, but death could hardly be called an emergency—it was routine. Finally Colonel Mulcahey agreed that if the Secretary of the Navy would authorize the release of a coffin he would have it broken out of stores and ready before noon, the latest hour for the return trip in time for the funeral. I hesitated to cable Secretary Edison at his home on Sunday morning, but I did, and received his affirmative reply about fifteen minutes before the deadline.

5

Governor Cramer was concerned heart and soul with every plan for the progress of the islands. As all plans were finally developed in the Interior Department and supported before the Bureau of the Budget, it was necessary for one of us to be in Washington much of the time. I have some sixty letters written in Governor Cramer's own hand, covering every aspect of affairs between July 1939 and December 1940. His long experience in the islands had given him an intimate knowledge of conditions. In Washington he had built up connections with the administrations of many of the official agencies. He knew what needed to be done and how to set about it.

As the Governor had to be away so much, his attitude toward my position was important. It should be explained that the office of Government Secretary was retained from the Danish regime. He was in no sense the secretary of the governor, but rather a check upon him. He reported directly to the Crown, or, in the United States administration, to the Secretary of the Interior. In the absence of the Governor he became Acting Governor. Following historical precedent, it is natural for the politics of the islands to turn on the friction between the two officials, in an effort to build up the heir-apparent at the expense of the incumbent. Such a situation had come between Governor Cramer and Robert Herrick, and a warm friendship had turned into bitter hostility.

Cramer and I were always the closest friends and co-workers. He gave me a free hand in matters directly pertaining to my office and allowed me full scope for the exercise of such ability as I had to serve the people of the islands. He did not question my action when as Acting Governor I reversed one of his most important decisions. The occasion is significant as a comment on colonial administration.

The supreme legislative authority of the Virgin Islands is the Legislative Assembly, composed of the Municipal Councils of St. Thomas and St. Croix, meeting in a joint session at the call of the Governor at least once a year. Hitherto the meetings had not been productive of great results. The islands were too different in their economy and social conditions to make feasible general legislation. However, a new school law was imperatively needed. The existing law, passed in 1921, was no longer operative. It provided for a single school system, under a general superintendent for the Virgin Islands. By force of circumstances St. Thomas and St. Croix had come to have separate authorities. The draft of a new law passed by the Assembly in 1939 provided for membership in the respective school boards of representatives of the Councils; Governor Cramer promptly vetoed it as violating the doctrine of the separation of powers by allowing legislators to sit on executive boards. I remember that in the discussion between the Governor and the Assembly a member from St. Thomas read a transcript from the decision of the Supreme Court in a similar case which arose in the Philippines, without noticing that it was the dissenting opinion offered by Mr. Justice Holmes.

Governor Cramer was absent when I called the Assembly together the next year to revise its work. I tried to persuade the members to bring their legislation into conformity with the Constitution of the United States, but it was argued that the preservation of certain customs and prerogatives of the Danish system was envisaged by the Organic Act of the islands. We were then seeking an opinion from the Solicitor of the Department of the Interior in regard to the moot point in the educational bill, and pending its arrival I agreed to sign the bill as passed, against the advice of District Attorney James Bough. I thought it not unlikely that Governor Cramer would resent this departure from his announced policy, and perhaps he should have done so. I gave notice, before signing, that I should propose certain amendments to the law at the next meeting of the Assembly. I expected that there would be general agreement in accepting the opinion of the Department Solicitor on the crucial point of separation of powers. I was, as it appeared, the only one so thinking. The opinion duly arrived, but the Assembly refused to be bound by it. It was objected that it was not from the Attorney General. I was vigorously denounced for trying to coerce the legislature and was turned down by unanimous vote. I am bound to say, however, that at heart I believe that Mr. Justice Holmes' dissenting opinion is sound in application to colonial administration. The presence of members of the Municipal Councils on the school boards of the Virgin Islands has been useful in facilitating action for the benefit of the schools. Laws determining standards of training for teachers, a scale of salaries, promotions, and so on, might not have been passed by the respective Councils without the efforts of their representatives on the school boards. There has been some attempted political interference on behalf of individuals, but the general effect has been good.

6

I was better equipped for my work as Government Secretary of the Virgin Islands than for any other position that I have held. My experience in teaching was an advantage, for the progress of the little community was largely a matter of education. I knew from former visits the Superintendent of Education in St. Thomas, Fred Dixon, and Thurston Child, who had the same position in St. Croix. During my stay in the islands I worked closely with them, following their plans and giving such help as fell within the functions of the executive. I visited the schools and came to know many of the teachers.

My incursion into social work at Hull House was also of value to me. I found in Roy Bornn, the Commissioner of Public Welfare in St. Thomas, a personal friend, and one ready to accept me as an ally. Probably the government secretary's work is more closely connected with welfare than with any other department. From my arrival I made it a practice, as at Hull House, to see everyone who came to me, either at my home or at the office, where the door was always open.

One group of cases properly belonged to the Government Secretary's department. The United States, in taking over the islands, had allowed the inhabitants to choose whether to remain Danish citizens or not. Those who chose at this time to become Americans were made second-class citizens of the United States only on a certain date in 1929, although an additional date was assigned a few years later on which a choice might be made. These arrangements, of course, left out of account the natives who were not at either time in the islands. They became men and women without a country. Obstacles were put in the way of their return, especially during the war, and if they succeeded they could secure citizenship only by the procedure of naturalization. Through the effort of the Virgin Islands Civic Association, composed of natives of the islands living on the continent, a bill dealing with this injustice was introduced into the Senate by Senator Mead, but Congress was too busy to pass it.

Another set of problems arose in consequence of the informal sexual relations prevalent among the islanders. Illegitimacy ran about fifty per cent. Governor Pearson in his first report commented severely on this situation as affecting adversely the economy and social life of the islands by "producing an abnormal increase of population without the proper assumption of responsibility for that increase or provision for its employment." The support of the children born outside the family fell chiefly upon the women. When the father could be identified he was obliged to pay from two to six dollars a month to the mother, a sum fixed by the District Court and collected through the office of the District Attorney. Even so the burden was heavy upon the women. I felt it infinitely pathetic when a girl came with her baby and replied to my question, "Fatherless." The women showed a certain loyalty to one another in a tragedy which they all shared. One afternoon three young women were in my office, two with children and one, a mere girl, whose child had not yet been born. They represented still a fourth woman in a unanimous petition for the pardon of the common father who had recently been sentenced to the penitentiary at St. Croix for rape. The older women urged that if he could not be pardoned, at least would I not arrange for his sentence to be served in the fort at St. Thomas instead of in faraway St. Croix, so that he could be near by to comfort their young colleague, in whose favor they were prepared to renounce their prior claims to the person of the great lover.

I found other cases in which the women were good to one another. A girl came in one day with her baby to say that it was dying in consequence of the sheer overcrowding of the tenement in which they lived. I went with her to see. It was a room on the ground floor, dark, with a single window. It was occupied by a great-grandmother with daughters, granddaughters, and babies. At night they were nine, sleeping on two or three beds in that hovel. The girl who had come to me was not a relative, hardly a friend, but since she had nowhere to go they had taken her in. The family of her lover was well-to-do, and we arranged for a dwelling and a job.

The most serious aspect of the situation was the children. When a woman kept her own, her work usually prevented her from doing much about her family. Often she farmed the children out with grandmothers, godmothers, aunts, or neighbors. With no responsible guardianship they fell into delinquency of various types. Petty thieving was common. Little boys, as well as adolescent girls, became the willing victims of sailors and Marines. A vigorous effort was made by the judicial authorities to curb this evil. A month or two after my arrival Herman E. Moore was appointed Federal District Judge. He and Mrs. Moore brought strong reinforcements to all the powers for good in the islands. Under his inspiration a meeting of citizens was held which in time resulted in the establishment of a juvenile school for boys at Calabash Boom, on St. John, later transferred to St. Thomas.

7

My long association with the League for Industrial Democracy had given me an introduction to various forms of social and economic planning which were useful to me in my job. The economy of the Virgin Islands was being determined by the experiments of the New Deal. Low-cost housing projects had been established on St. Croix and St. Thomas. The Civilian Conservation Corps was doing good work on both islands. On a visit to Washington I persuaded Mr. Frith, of the C. C. C. high command, to send a group of experts with a well-drilling outfit to St. Croix to open subterranean water resources. The project was to be carried out simultaneously with a program of soil conservation to dam the beds of watercourses and check the run-off by contour plowing. Always I followed with the greatest interest the work of the Soil Conservation and Farm Security workers in St. Croix. The Agricultural Experiment Stations both on St. Croix and St. Thomas had been taken over from the Department of Agriculture by the Department of the Interior in accordance with Governor Pearson's policy of extending practical advice and help to the farmers. Both stations did valuable extension work on limited funds, and promising experiments were going forward at St. Croix, especially after Norman Skeoch became director.

One project which occupied much of the attention of the administration had to do with the promotion of animal industry in the islands through the eradication of the fever tick. Dr. J. R. Mohler, then head of the Bureau of Animal Industry in Washington, was a firm believer in the program of eradication, and under the direction of Dr. Still the councils in St. Thomas–St. John and St. Croix were persuaded to appropriate funds for the erection of vats for dipping animals in an arsenic solution. As farmers were obliged to drive their herds of cattle, flocks of goats, horses and donkeys to the nearest vat once every fortnight, the process became very irksome and some losses occurred. The case of a family of women on Levango Cay off St. John particularly excited my sympathy. Their herd, originally of some thirty animals, was transported by sloops to Cruz Bay for dipping, at a cost of two dollars per head. Of necessity, this expense rapidly ate up the value of the herd. It was an immense relief when St. Thomas–St. John was declared "tick free" and the dipping ceased.

In St. Croix the execution of the program was complicated by the presence of wild deer in the hills, whose destruction was necessary to preserve the results of dipping the cattle. In an effort to deal with the herd at the east end of the island the C. C. C. boys built a high wire fence across the island and attempted to capture the deer by driving them against it, but the deer leaped it, struggled through its meshes, or back-tracked through the cordon of beaters. The Wild Life Division of the Department of the Interior financed a project for camouflaging the destruction as preservation, by trapping some of the deer, freeing them of ticks, and keeping them for export to other islands. Unfortunately the official appointed to carry out this delicate operation, through overzealous interpretation of his duties, shot an old man who was suspected of having killed deer for meat, and though his plea of self-defense was accepted, public opinion reacted so strongly against him that his removal was necessary and the project lapsed.

8

As Government Secretary it fell to my lot to spend more than half of the four years of my official life in the Governor's chair. An executive function in which I took great interest was the pardoning power. One case that came to my attention concerned two young Puerto Ricans who had been involved in a shocking murder in St. Croix to which the wife of the murdered man was accessory. All had been sentenced to prison for life by Judge Wilson. The woman, dying of cancer, was later released on probation by Governor Cramer. The two young men had already served several years in the penitentiary when their case was brought to me by one of the clergy, whose intelligent social interest gave weight to his plea. After correspondence with Judge Wilson, and on his advice, I released the older of the two, who had been an accessory to the crime. We had a conscientious parole board, which after much consideration recommended the release of the second on probation, on the ground that there was no likelihood of a repetition of the crime. I was glad to use the executive power to act accordingly.

Another case attracted much attention because of a curious coincidence. An old man named Knight had committed murder in St. Croix, where this crime by law is punishable by death, although the penalty had not been exacted for nearly a century. The evidence against him was conclusive, and the jury, taking note of the atrocious circumstances, recommended the death penalty. The court sentenced him to be hanged on June 17. In such cases the condemned has an automatic appeal to the District Court in Philadelphia, which is in effect a court of appeals for the islands. I visited him in the penitentiary with the St. Croix Chief of Police, thinking it might be well to learn something of his state of mind and attitude toward the crime in case the court should confirm his sentence. I was disgusted to find him contumacious, repudiating the account which had been established at the trial, and throwing the guilt on his son, who was serving a five-year sentence as accessory. I assured him, however, that his execution would be postponed, probably because the hearing on appeal would be delayed and certainly because June 17 was Bunker Hill Day in Boston, when an execution was no more to be thought of than on Christmas Day or the Fourth of July. As we left I asked the police chief if he thought Knight was at all anxious about his fate. "Oh, no," he replied. "He figures that he's an old man and will die anyway before we get around to hanging him."

On the morning of the 17th Knight was found dead in his cell. He had not committed suicide. The story went out that he died of fright, and much sympathy was expressed in newspaper editorials and by letters. We sent the vital portions of the body to San Juan for examination and received information that there were six natural causes from which he might have died. I took some satisfaction in communicating these findings to sentimentalists who thought death by fear was more cruel than death by strangulation. At any rate, as a member of the Association for the Abolition of Capital Punishment I was relieved of a serious responsibility.

9

Almost as urgent as the problem of the criminal classes was that of the mentally ill. The psychopathic wards both in St. Thomas and in St. Croix were horrible. Governor Cramer had interested Dr. Winfred Overholser, director of St. Elizabeth's Hospital in Washington, in these conditions, and he agreed to accept such of our inmates as were American citizens. We had to persuade the relatives of the patients that they would be better cared for at St. Elizabeth's than in the islands and would have a chance of recovery. The description of the hospital with its modern equipment, including a beauty parlor where hair could be straightened as well as curled, was an effective argument. Then it was necessary to obtain appropriations from the councils for transportation. St. Croix had to borrow the money.

The Alcoa Company made excellent arrangements for conveying the patients to New York. Two corridors of staterooms on C deck were appropriated to our use, cut off from intercourse with other parts of the vessel. Dr. Nathan Rifkinson of the St. Thomas municipal staff was placed in charge. I was instructed to go along as supercargo.

The voyage was of the pleasantest. We had a bit of a scare the first night when one of the patients was noticed walking in the corridor, apparently returning to his stateroom. A big-shouldered fellow, he had worked his way out through his porthole, and catching the "cat's walk" with his feet had crawled along until he could climb over the rail to the deck. Why? "You left my toilet locked." We feared at first that the patients might develop a destructive interest in the plumbing and instructed them to knock for an attendant when necessary. Later we gave them all the comforts of first-class travel. The only peculiarity was the sudden interest in laundry. Some of the women resumed a former profession and spent their days in washing every available article—sheets, towels, their own clothes.

Another accident threatened when one of the men tore the paper plaster off the full-length mirror and, seeing his image as an enemy, hurled his soup bowl at it, shivering the glass. Dr. Rifkinson tied him to his berth, but he succeeded in stretching his rope until he could reach the mirror and pick out pieces of glass with his toes. He was put in shackles, *l'homme enchainé*.

At the dock in New York the Baltimore and Ohio omnibus picked us up and took us to a special car in Jersey City; outside of Washington, it was switched to a side track running to the hospital grounds. There Dr. Overholser took over. Since then I have made several visits to our patients, who seem to form a little enclave of Virgin Islanders in the midst of the cosmopolitan mass, and who generally remember their home.

10

Soon after my arrival the federal government began to put the islands in a state of defense. The work of enlarging the air base at Bourne Field, of establishing a submarine base at Krum Bay, and eventually of building cantonments for the Army, was assigned to a continental company. In the face of the demands of the contractors for defense workers, the problem of administering the restrictive laws of the United States against alien labor became perplexing. Although the immigration service was under the Department of Labor, the Government Secretary acted as the local immigration officer, and it was a great relief when the Department of Justice took over.

Learning that jobs could be had in St. Thomas, men came in sloops from Anguilla, St. Kitts, St. Martin, and St. Barthélemy. They landed on remote parts of St. Thomas and made their way to the bases under construction, where they were received without too many questions. We soon had nearly two thousand aliens added to the normal population of Charlotte Amalie. There was a shortage of houses and they slept in abandoned sheds, sometimes twelve in a small room, cooking their food outside, with no sanitary conveniences. There was danger of pestilence, of fire, of violence arising from too close contact in congested quarters, and perhaps from friction between alien and native workers. Happily none of these dangers became serious. When I went to inspect the living conditions of alien workers I was amazed at the good-natured response of the British West Indians to our concern. They promised to notify the medical authorities in cases of illness and to keep fires at a distance.

The continued flouting of United States immigration and labor laws and the acute need for labor led the Department of Justice to issue an order to the effect that the illegal entry of five hundred alien workers already in the islands should be ignored, and that five hundred more should be enlisted in the British islands and registered at the point of departure for temporary stay on American soil. In May 1941 I flew to Antigua to meet the British authorities and put the plan into operation. I knew Governor Lethem of the Leeward Islands from his occasional visits to St. Thomas, a fine type of British colonial governor. I suspect his sense of humor was in play when he received me as Acting Governor at the water front, turning out his entire military establishment for my inspection. I expressed surprise at the concourse of citizens gathered, to which Sir Gordon replied, "Oh, they think you have come to take us over." I had a telephone conversation with the labor officer at St. Kitts, and he agreed to the plan sent down from Washington. He properly insisted on formal contracts for the workers whom he provided, with stipulations as to housing in St. Thomas and return passage home, and here the plan broke down. It was obviously simpler for the Army and the Navy to hire men illegally on the island, with no responsibility for them, than to enter into contracts, especially since it was never certain how far the defense work would be carried. The immigration service was helpless. *Silent enim leges inter arma.*

During this period there were frequent individual disputes between native workers and foremen, bosses and pay clerks. These regularly came to my office. The Arundel Company was represented by Commander H. S. Johnson, an engineer of the Naval Reserve from Wisconsin, who had both the civilian and the military points of view, and adjustment was easy. Later, after the Navy and the United States Engineers took over the direction of the works of defense, any intervention by local authorities in labor disputes was resented. The later commandant assumed a typically hard-boiled attitude toward native labor, and apparently as a kind of reprisal for my well-meant efforts to adjust disputes he suggested that I appear before an investigating board of officers for examination as to my social views reported in the press. It is unnecessary to say that this proposal met with severe reprobation from Secretary Ickes, who reported the matter to Acting Secretary of the Navy Forrestal.

II

In the early summer of 1940 I received a letter from Jack McMichael, chairman of the American Youth Congress, asking me to join a committee then being formed "to Defend America by Keeping Out of War" and to sponsor and arrange an Emergency Peace Mobilization to be held in Chicago August 3 and 4 (1940), the twenty-sixth anniversary of the outbreak of the First World War. The object of the plan and what was then the policy of the Youth Congress was thus stated in the letter:

In the Mobilization the American people will insist that the best defense of America is not aid to either side but a policy of strict neutrality. They will express their determination to protect labor standards, the rights of religious and racial minorities, social welfare, and civil liberties. This is the test whether our present defense policy is really one of defense or one of preparation for participation in the war.

I felt at that time that the immediate danger was that the United States, under powerful political leadership, would be drawn into a declaration of war as in 1917, and for that reason I signed the call for the Mobilization. Later I wrote McMichael a letter which I quote in full as expressing my attitude.

I am obliged to dissociate myself from one of the announced objectives of the proposed Emergency Peace Mobilization. Recent events have convinced me that the policy of absolute neutrality is not only impracticable but against the interests of the United States.

I believe that we should use our present relative immunity from war to anticipate and if possible prevent conditions in the future which we shall not be able to control. We owe this immunity in part to the resistance of China and Great Britain to aggression. It appears that neither can win without our economic support. It is therefore a wise policy to aid them by economic measures. It further appears that in the long run the plans of Japan and Germany so far as they concern the United States will not be changed by our aid to their opponents except in so far as this aid is effective. At present the choice of war or peace is in our hands. If Japan and Germany win, the choice will not remain ours. On the other hand, it is obvious that if they are defeated the immense preparations which we are making for future war with them, including conscription, will not be necessary.

There is, undoubtedly, danger in aiding China and Great Britain. There will be reprisals and provocation. If our aid becomes a decisive factor it is conceivable that Germany will seek to tempt us into war, as in 1917. The choice, however, will remain ours. To strengthen the will to peace in spite of provocation is a major function of the Mobilization. Above all, its effort should be to hold government responsible for suppressing the incipient civil war of persecution and violence against unpopular minority groups, which under the guise of preparedness is directed to sinister ends by false patriots. With these objects of the Conference I am in cordial sympathy. I hope that the question of neutrality, in regard to which there is an honest difference of opinion among those seeking the same ends, will not be a major issue of the meeting.

A year later I was asked to sign the call of the League of American Writers for its annual conference. My attitude was similar to that in regard to the Emergency Peace Mobilization. I signed the call but added a statement disagreeing with one sentence:

Today, we must ask whether the present policy of the administration and the program of big business are not leading us toward war and fascism in the name of resistance toward war and fascism.

I wrote in answer to the question:

In response to your request for a statement in regard to the meeting of the Congress of the League of American Writers June 6 [1941], I wish to make my position clear in regard to one subject of debate. I have constantly held that the possibility of freedom and peace in the present world is bound up with the victory of Great Britain. With Hitler in power the United States will never be free from the fear of war and the burden of preparedness with all the suppressions and persecutions that characterize such a situation. It follows that I believe in all aid to England. I believe this as the most likely way of avoiding war for the United States. Germany is less likely to declare war on the United States while England is fighting, than afterwards. Undoubtedly, if our aid to England becomes decisive, as it must, Hitler will seek to provoke us to declare war as in 1917. It is for the American people then to refuse to be stampeded by attacks on property or insults to national pride, and to give full support to the administration in keeping its pledge to give full aid to democracies without submerging our own democracy in war. I believe that this is the line which intelligent Americans should follow, and for which I should speak if I were able to be present at the conference.

My signature to the call was badly received in Washington. Secretary Ickes wrote me personally, April 25, pointing out the impropriety of my action:

In view of the international situation and the announced and deliberate policy of the administration, of which you are a part, to give all possible aid to the nations that are resisting Hitler and Nazism, your signature to this call represents an indiscretion of a high order and is embarrassing to this Department.

In reply I apologized for my "indiscretion," but pointed out that I was in sympathy with the policy of the administration of aiding the victims of aggression, especially Great Britain, and hoped to use my influence with those with whom I had always worked for peace but who now seemed to me to be inviting war rather than avoiding it. I enclosed a copy of my letter to the secretary of the League, but I doubt if my explanation appealed to Mr. Ickes as anything more than casuistry. It is all to his honor that when my associations with Communists became grounds for my dismissal from office, he went "all out" in defense of my loyalty.

I believe that the conference of the League justified the comment of the State Department as cited by Secretary Ickes: "This League of American Writers is generally regarded as a Communist subsidiary. Its policies, of course, always parallel those of the Communist party." The action taken denounced as imperialistic the war against Hitler, with whom the Soviet Union had concluded a pact of friendly relations. Almost within a matter of days Hitler's armies were invading Russia, and the League was obliged to reverse itself. Its political subserviency destroyed its function in American letters and it died.

I still believe that liberals and Communists can work together for good in local causes, and both are deeply concerned with civil liberties in the United States, but after the League for Peace and Democracy and the League of American Writers, I am suspicious of organizations which enjoy their existence on sufferance and depend on the variable policies of a foreign power.

Since so much of my record has to do with my attitude toward war and peace, I have put down in full the documents which illustrate my position in the years 1939 and 1940. Undoubtedly I was affected by a sense of the responsibility of the United States for its possessions in the Caribbean, already threatened by Hitler's submarines. If I argued for delay in entering a war that was inevitable while assisting the nations which were already involved and thus acting in our defense, I can offer a pragmatic apology. It is fortunate that the immediate cause of our entrance into World War II was the action by the enemy at Pearl Harbor.

Ida and I were in St. Croix when, on Sunday afternoon, December 7, 1941, Harry Taylor called us up at Government House to tell us what had happened in the Pacific. From that day I find a distinct change in the character of my notes. There were no more visits of warships. Before Pearl Harbor, we had set up a Council of Defense under de Castro. The Red Cross was active in promoting first-aid education. There were blackouts and rehearsals of anticipated bombings, to which the people reacted loyally. Later there was rationing of fuel and tires, and the Office of Price Administration was set up under the direction of Robles, whose good sense and good temper contributed much to the spirit with which restrictions on food were accepted. There were rumors of submarines seen in waters near the islands, but the incidents which brought the war most nearly home to us were the arrival of the crews of torpedoed ships, after many days in lifeboats, some men suffering from burns or wounds which proved fatal. Another poignant reminder of the war was furnished by a company of some thirty refugees from Europe, who had come by way of Africa only to be torpedoed in the Caribbean.

XVII. *Washington,* 1941–1947

I

GOVERNOR CRAMER was devoted to the interests of the Virgin Islands, always thinking and working to those ends. He was aided by a group of loyal supporters in the local administration, but he had a hostile Municipal Council in St. Thomas. At the first meeting which Ida attended as a spectator she was appalled at the violence of denunciation and amazed at the perfect calmness with which the Governor met it. "He reminds me of Jane Addams," was her comment, "or perhaps of Jesus Christ." This proved to be a superficial judgment, but at least it could be said of him that "when he was reviled he reviled not again."

When in 1939 Ernest Gruening was appointed Governor of Alaska, Dr. Rupert Emerson succeeded him as Director of the Division of Territories and Island Possessions. His visits to the islands brought him rapidly into intelligent mastery of our problems and his presence was most welcome. He felt as I did about Governor Cramer's value to the islands, and it was a shock to him when during a reception in his honor at Government House in December 1940, a telegram from the Department of Interior was handed to Governor Cramer calling for the latter's resignation.

The case was a chapter of accidents. A member of the Municipal Council of St. Thomas had become especially unpopular owing to his opposition to the attempt to introduce public service for light and power through the Rural Electrification Administration. When in Washington he had called on Secretary Ickes and informed him that the islands were on the verge of a race war, that the whites were arming, that he had (quite unnecessarily) engaged a bodyguard for himself. I arrived in Washington a few days later and disabused Mr. Ickes. Fortunately I had the report of Professor Angus Campbell of Northwestern University on the "St. Thomas Negro," which put at rest any apprehension of race trouble on that island. Unfortunately, however, the Secretary had believed that the situation called for investigation and had sent a man from his secret service, who behaved maladroitly, ignoring the responsible authorities and collecting personal gossip from hostile sources. Of course, Governor Cramer was furious. On his next visit to Washington he had demanded to see the investigator's report. Secretary Ickes, who had already shown his attitude by dismissing his agent, did not refuse. On the day of my departure from Washington I lunched with the Secretary and found him willing to forget the whole affair. On the same day I dined with Governor Cramer and so informed him. Nevertheless, after reading the file he wrote the Secretary a vigorous letter which the latter could not pass over, nor, in spite of a genuine liking for Cramer, could the President.

We had a melancholy Christmas season that year, for Governor Cramer was in bed after a bad fall on the precipitous north side of the island, where we used to go for evening picnics. As soon as he could be moved Sir Gordon Lethem offered him a residence at Antigua until his recovery enabled him to return to Washington for public service in another department.

2

Governor Cramer was succeeded by Charles Harwood, who arrived in St. Thomas with Mrs. Harwood in February 1941 for inaugural ceremonies, which were extended to St. Croix and St. John under the able showmanship of de Castro.

My only thought in connection with the change of Governors was to continue in the position in which I enjoyed the confidence of my superiors in Washington and of the people of the islands. I assured the new Governor, on behalf of the staff, that we would be loyal to him and never let him down.

A few personal questions arose which I did not think of as seriously disturbing our relations. Governor Cramer had been living in temporary quarters while Government House was being rehabilitated. As entirely new furnishings had been ordered he sent some articles when he left his temporary home to Quarters B, of which the furniture was riddled by termites and generally disreputable. Governor Harwood objected to the makeshift arrangements which he found at Government House—eating off a ping-pong table, sleeping in a bed such as he had not known since boyhood. Of course, we turned over the dining-room set and the comfortable bed, which Mrs. Cramer had specially designated in view of Ida's arthritis. When the new furniture arrived Government House rejoiced in a dining-room with two large tables and twenty-four chairs, and the Governor's naval aide slept in the four poster. Months later when I noted in my list of government property in Quarters B a sideboard, originally in Government House, Governor Harwood asked for the article in view of the approaching visit of King Carol of Rumania and Madame Lupescu. As Acting Governor I had properly the use of the Governor's car, but Harwood instructed the chauffeur not to let me have it.

All these things seemed too trivial to worry about. I did not suspect the Governor of any intention to make us uncomfortable, merely of a strong sense of possession as applied to government property. However, an episode revealing his attitude toward me occurred when his private secretary, inherited from Governor Cramer, resigned. As he was then in Washington I wrote advising him to find a satisfactory substitute there. I was surprised to read in the St. Thomas papers a communication from him to the public quoting my letter with the implication that I did not think a native fitted for the post. The editors saw through the maneuver and were amused at the effort to discredit me with the people. Emerson wrote me a scathing comment on the Governor's letter, and offered the information that from the time of his appointment Governor Harwood had sought my dismissal from Secretary Ickes, who, however, assured him "that you had his backing and could stay as long as you liked."

I realized then that Governor Harwood would succeed in the end, but I did not propose to gratify him by anticipating his triumph. Meanwhile our relations continued normal. I wrote his speeches for him on public occasions, and they were good ones, though I was always amused at his deprecating reference to my carefully prepared manuscript as a few little notes he had hastily thrown together in the interstices of a busy life. It is part of the political game in the Virgins to drive a wedge between the Governor and the Government Secretary, but when the *Daily News* referred to differences between us I always took occasion to scout them. I explained and defended the Governor's long absences from the islands. I was determined that the public service should not suffer from a break in the administration. In this I was helped by de Castro who, when the Governor tried to set me aside, insisted that I should be duly called into conference and my proper functions recognized.

It was Harwood's conduct toward others that I most resented. He seemed to prefer to disoblige. Especially was this the case when the relations of St. Thomas to our British neighbors were in question. He would never realize that St. Thomas is in effect the capital of the Virgin Islands, both British and American. The boundary line had been almost forgotten under the Danes, and families divided between St. Thomas and Tortola passed freely back and forth. Indeed, Tortolans had no easy way of reaching the outside world except through St. Thomas. Immediately after Governor Harwood's arrival he took up the case of the daughter of a leading merchant of Tortola who passed regularly through St. Thomas on her way to and from school on the continent. My assistant, Jacob Robles, had always handled such cases, and was disposed to let the girl proceed again this time, but the Governor spent most of a day fussing about the matter, and having elicited the information that the girl intended to study law and also might get married, decided that her education was a subterfuge and did not let her proceed.

During the war the State Department, apparently not realizing that the American Virgins are practically as close to the British islands as the continental United States is to Canada or Mexico, exacted passports for American citizens leaving St. Thomas for the British possessions. The Governor insisted that every application for a passport should be sent to the Federal Bureau of Investigation at Washington to make sure that the fingerprints were not those of someone in its rogues' gallery. With a decrepit mail service this proceeding resulted in a delay of weeks, and obviously the possibility of the identification of a lifelong resident of the Virgin Islands with a subject of investigation on the continent was infinitesimal. A woman who had been a schoolteacher for thirty years in St. Thomas, wishing to return to her old home in Antigua, was kept waiting for weeks until she died.

It was a mistake on the part of the Secretary to try to keep the Governor on his job in the islands. He did better service in Washington. He took over the plan drawn up by John Carmody and Frederick H. Walton for the expenditure of a large sum in public improvements. Advocacy of this plan before committees of Congress gave him a reason for being on the continent, and whenever the Secretary tried to "punish him"—his own expression—by keeping him in the islands, he could arrange for a summons to Washington from his political friends in Congress. These put through the authorization of the expenditure of more than ten million dollars for the building of roads, schoolhouses, hospitals, and sewers. The island legislatures have made February 7, the day on which Governor Harwood was inaugurated, a permanent public holiday. I trust that I shall live to see the translation of the program from paper into material, and be privileged to join full-heartedly in the celebration of Governor Harwood Day.

3

Governor Harwood in Washington met the sub-committee of the House of Representatives on Appropriations for Islands in a session at which no member of the Interior Department was present. Subsequently Congress took action for my removal from office.

Various circumstances favored this step. The report of the Illinois Senate committee on communistic teaching was available. Moreover, the Dies Committee, instead of investigating the notorious and dangerous attempts of the German Bund to promote the formation of a fifth column in the United States, had become a receptacle for vague and malicious accusations against liberals, progressives, and pacifists. It had found more than eleven hundred federal officials guilty of un-American activities and recommended their dismissal. A special sub-committee of the House Committee on Appropriations was appointed to sift the charges and in 1943 reported adversely in the cases of Goodwin B. Watson and William E. Dodd, Jr., of the Federal Communications Commission. I understood the animus of Congress against this Commission, which had charged Congressman Eugene Coxe of Georgia, but had not brought him to trial, with taking money illegally for services rendered in obtaining a license for a radio station—an animus which took effect in the appointment of a committee to investigate the F. C. C. under the chairmanship of Cox himself. It was with surprise, however, that on April 12, 1943, I received through Governor Harwood orders to proceed to Washington for hearings before several committees.

I arrived at Washington at four-thirty on the morning of April 14, in a sleet storm, and unable to find a room after an hour's search I made an elaborate toilet in a hotel washroom. At eleven I went to my first appointment with the sub-committee of the House Committee on Appropriations in charge of the Interior Department appropriations.[1] I was supported by Warner W. Gardner, Solicitor of the Department, Abe Fortas, Undersecretary, and William A. Brophy, of the Department staff.

I was confronted by a list of the organizations, compiled by the industrious Mr. Matthews, the Dies Committee investigator, with which my name had been connected in the past twenty-five years. Most of these had been temporary in character, addressed to immediate situations, and included Communists and others. No attempt was made to examine them in detail in regard to objectives or membership, but the menacing question of Chairman Jed Johnson gave weight to the proceedings: "You do know, however, that the Attorney General has found several of these organizations subversive?" Of course I did not know it, and I subsequently learned that he had not stated accurately the Attorney General's finding.

Then appeared Secretary Ickes' letter in regard to my signature of the call for the convention of the League of American Writers. As this was the only matter which I had reason to think would be an occasion for calling me to Washington, I had taken my letters with me, but in Miami, in spite of my protest, they were held by the military censorship until my return. For the rest, the committee indulged in an expedition which brought a variety of fishes to their net—my speech in support of Norman Thomas for president in 1936; an article in the *New Masses* protesting against the favorable attitude of the State Department toward Franco; a contribution to the League for Mutual Aid; a letter to Mother Bloor of Iowa on her seventy-fifth birthday; a letter from someone addressing me as "Dear Comrade"; a clipping from the *Daily Worker* stating that I had tried to get into Madison Square Garden on the occasion of the Communist convention in 1936; a contribution to the defense fund of the managers of the Oklahoma City bookstore illegally arrested. But the focus of the investigation turned on the private letter to Jacob Gordin that referred to all governments as rotten. As in the case of the Illinois Senate committee, this indiscretion was pursued with pertinacity.[2]

My hearing before the special sub-committee[3] of the House Com-

[1] On the committee were Congressmen Jed Johnson, James M. Fitzpatrick, Michael J. Kirwan, W. F. Norrell, Alfred E. Carter, Robert F. Jones, and Ben Jensen.

[2] See Appendix A.

[3] Its members were John H. Kerr, chairman, Albert Gore, Clinton P. Anderson, D. Lane Powers, and Frank B. Keefe.

mittee on Appropriations was scheduled for the next afternoon. I had been informed that I might obtain a copy of the charges against me from the attorney for the committee, whom after some false starts I discovered about noon. He showed me a mass of material, probably that published in the appendix to the report of the committee as an indictment; it included fifty-four exhibits, filling fifty-seven pages. I was not given a copy and had opportunity only for a rapid glance over the contents. I had no attorney at this hearing.

I appeared before the committee in executive session. The conversation followed the lines of the hearing of the day before. My connection with the American Peace Mobilization was brought up, to which I admitted my signature of the original call with the explanation that I believed in aid to the Allies, who were fighting for the principle of collective security, and indicated my separation from the organization on that issue. In spite of this statement my connection with the Mobilization was included in the report of the committee. I had a pleasant but somewhat irrelevant debate with Congressman Gore on production for use and production for profit, the profit motive and the profit system. The only new subject was my arrest by the Chicago police in 1933.

Anticipating that a fishing excursion could hardly miss this item, I had asked Henry P. Chandler, who had defended me on that occasion, to write a letter to Chairman Kerr explaining the case. Chandler, now head of the Courts Department of the Supreme Court, remarked that he knew Kerr and would speak to him personally. It was perhaps unfortunate that he did so, for when Congressman Powers alluded to the matter Kerr came to life and made his only contribution to the proceedings.

The Chairman: I think you said a while ago while Mr. Gore of Tennessee was asking you some questions that you advocated law and order?

Mr. Lovett: Absolutely, sir. Yes.

The Chairman: Why could you not have allowed the policemen to go down there rather than take the law into your own hands and go there also? The police are an arm of the law and are under the direction of the law, and they went down there to look after those strikers.

Mr. Lovett: I did not take the law into my own hands. I merely exercised the right of every citizen to investigate, to see if the law-enforcing agency was exceeding its proper powers.

The Chairman: You went down there to judge the action of the bona fide officers of the city to see whether or not they were doing their duty. Is that what you were doing down there?

Mr. Lovett: I have known policemen to beat up—

The Chairman (interposing): Wait a minute. Would you say that that was what you were doing? Answer that question, and then you can make any explanation of it that you wish.

Mr. Lovett: I went down to see if the workers were being deprived of their legal rights to picket and if they were being beaten up by police in the course of their effort to exercise those rights. I went as an observer.

The Chairman: You were not willing to leave everything to the process of the law to take care of a situation of that kind in this country?

Mr. Lovett: I am certainly willing to leave everything to the process of the law. I was merely invoking the process of the law.

The Chairman: Why didn't you leave it to the legal officers to take care of a situation of that kind rather than to go down and get into a riot yourself about it?

Mr. Lovett: I might explain that the group of people with whom I went were interested in seeing justice done to a group of exploited girls, workers, and I went with them at their invitation to see if their charges of such treatment as they made were true.

The Chairman: And got into trouble yourself?

Mr. Lovett: Yes. I am sorry. I seem to have been a scandal to the community by being arrested; but I am perfectly willing to have the case examined in detail. The record is there. The statement of my attorney is there. . . . He would be glad to testify in my favor.

After the conclusions of the hearings, at the request of Warner Gardner I wrote a final statement of my position to Chairman Kerr for submission to the committee. Whether it was ever submitted I do not know. As it did not find a place in their report, I print it here.

The Committee of Congress on un-American activities has collected published evidence of my membership over a period of twenty-five years in various associations and committees which included Communists. I submit that in fairness the occasions and objects of such associations should be taken into consideration, as well as the entire make-up of such published lists. A hearing at which only the names of Communists were specified might give the impression that I associated only with members of that party. The time at which these organizations functioned should also be considered. An attitude toward peace in the years in which the Kellogg Pact was hopefully regarded as a statement of national policy should not be a basis of a charge of un-Americanism today. A protest against military intervention in Latin-American countries twenty years ago should be regarded favorably in the light of the good neighbor policy of today.

I have been concerned for many years with certain causes which may be summarized as education for a better social order, the maintenance of civil liberties, and world peace. While my constant connections have been with the League for Industrial Democracy, the general orientation of which is socialistic, and the American Civil Liberties Union and its Chicago branch, the orientation of which is liberal, I have not hesitated to join committees and organizations directed toward specific objectives, namely the support of groups or individuals subject to discrimination, such as the Committee for the Protection of the Foreign-Born, the National Association for the Advancement of Colored People, a committee for relief of political prisoners. I have joined with others for the defense of Tom Mooney, Sacco and Vanzetti, and the two anti-fascist Italians in New York, Greco and Carillo.

In respect to world peace, I have passed through a number of phases since 1918. Like most of my fellow countrymen, I welcomed the Kellogg-Briand Pact of 1928. In the spirit of this treaty, I was in favor of the neutrality legislation of 1935, not as a means of isolating the United States from war, but as a measure to enlist other nations in the policy of suppressing war at its source by cutting off the trade in munitions and supplies. When the cases of China and Spain left the application of the neutrality laws in doubt, I retained my hope in peace through united action of peaceful nations. This was the attitude of the American League against War and Fascism (afterwards the American League for Peace and Democracy), of which I became a vice-president in 1934 and resigned in 1939. The League was a strong supporter of President Roosevelt's policy of "quarantining" the aggressor nations. The Communist party was represented on the Board of Directors, but Communists were never a controlling factor. A fair and accurate account of the League is given in an article in the *New Republic* for March 18, 1941. When the World War broke out in 1939, and after the signing of the treaty between the Soviet Union and Germany, many persons with whom I had been connected in efforts for peace went over to the "America First" policy of isolation. In signing the preliminary call for the American Mobilization for Peace, I stated my settled opinion that peace could be secured only by the combined action of peaceful nations. Since these nations had been attacked it was incumbent upon the United States to give all possible aid to them, even if it involved war with the aggressors. I maintained that the issue of peace or war in the United States would be decided by Hitler, and that the only safety for this country was in anticipating his action and supporting the nations which already were fighting our battle. As my views did not prevail I took no part in the Mobilization.

Organizations for such purposes as indicated are a natural phenomenon of democratic action in the United States. In those cited by the Dies Committee, Communists were frequently members, in some cases in a majority. I state emphatically, however, that my motive in joining such organizations was always the purpose sought and not the enhancement of the Communist party. In the course of twenty-five years I have been associated for worthy ends with men and women of many schools of thought. I did not regard any such association as subversive of our institutions. So far as Communists are concerned, I have viewed them as human beings capable, like the rest of us, of giving aid to humane and generous causes. I have stated at hearings before committees of Congress that I do not regard it as proper for an official of the federal government to be a member of any organization listed as subversive by the Attorney General even though I disagree with his opinion. Nearly all the organizations listed were formed for temporary purposes, and have ceased to exist, and in none have I been active since becoming Government Secretary of the Virgin Islands.

4

While the report of the committee was pending a number of my friends wrote to Congressman Kerr in my favor, among them Thomas W. Lamont, Judge Learned Hand, and Edward B. Burling. To them all I am grateful. The sheaf of letters collected by Burling from many sources I leave as a bequest to my descendants unto the fourth generation. The Municipal Councils of St. Thomas and St. Croix promptly took action in a statement to Kerr of which I am proud.[1] Secretary Ickes wrote Kerr a letter which moves me to tears.[2] The Virgin Islands Civic Association of New York joined in the protest. Nonetheless, on May 14 the committee recommended my dismissal from federal service.

Pursuant to the sub-committee's report the Committee on Appropriations offered an amendment (Section 304) to the urgent deficiency appropriation bill (H.R. 2714) to deny the use of federal funds for the payment of salary or other compensation for the personal services of Goodwin B. Watson, William E. Dodd, Jr., and Robert Morss Lovett after November 15, 1943.

When the report was brought before the House of Representatives on May 18, the debate was chiefly devoted to personal attacks on the

[1] See Appendix B.
[2] See Appendix C.

three men named. Kerr, it is true, "could not refrain from mentioning" a picture in his grandfather's library of George Washington giving the command, "Put none but Americans on guard tonight," and Congressman Hobbs of Alabama, while professing honor and respect for "our great Committee on Appropriations," regretted his inability to support its amendment because it was in effect a bill of attainder. The amendment was carried three hundred and eighteen to sixty-two.

The amendment was then sent to the Senate. On May 20 Secretary Ickes appeared before its Committee on Appropriations to make a statement which, in addition to being a generous defense of me, was important in influencing the decision of the Senate.[1]

The Senate struck out of the appropriation bill the amendment eliminating the salaries of Watson, Dodd, and Lovett. On June 8 Senator McKellar, on behalf of the Senate conference, moved that the Senate insist on its disagreement, and Senators Lucas, Mead, Overton, and others supported the motion on the basis of Congressman Hobbs' argument that the House had in effect passed a bill of attainder. The Senate was unanimous in disapproving the House amendment, but the House refused to recede; finally, at the close of the month when the fiscal year was nearly at an end, in order to save the appropriation bill as a whole, the Senate agreed with Senator McKellar's reversal of his former position. The President, also to save the financial structure of the government, reluctantly signed the bill, with a protest which he repeated on September 14 when Congress reassembled after the summer recess.[2]

In addition to this action, Congress eliminated the position of Government Secretary of the Virgin Islands, an office established by the Organic Act for the government of the islands in 1936. As Secretary Ickes considered that the people of the islands were entitled to the services of such an official, he appointed me to the office of Executive Assistant to the Governor, defining my duties as those hitherto pertaining to the Government Secretary. After November 15 I received no salary, but I continued to perform my regular duties. On March 13 the Secretary wrote me that in view of the threat to the entire appropriation for his Department he was obliged to ask for my resignation, which I promptly tendered.

[1] See Appendix D.
[2] See Appendix E.

5

Our departure from the Virgin Islands I remember as an occasion of which any government official might be proud. Both Councils passed resolutions recognizing my services and protesting against my recall. Departments with which I had been especially concerned passed similar resolutions. A testimonial meeting was held by the Business Men's Association of St. Thomas, attended by over one hundred and fifty citizens. A happy feature of this meeting was the presence of my old friend Oswald Garrison Villard, who was visiting the islands, and who spoke warmly of our long association in causes for which I was now being dismissed. Some forty organizations of all types under the lead of the Chamber of Commerce united in a testimonial statement which was in itself a sufficient answer to the charge that I was unfit to hold office.[1]

On the night before our departure from the islands a general reception was given us in Emancipation Park in Charlotte Amalie, at which addresses were made, resolutions read, and nearly three thousand dollars presented to establish a foundation in my name for the granting of aid to the people of the Virgin Islands. Such foundations have been established in the past by Danish governors and other benefactors, and I am gratified to know that my name will remain permanently among them. At the close of the meeting the people crowded about us, shaking and kissing my hands, some kneeling and weeping. We both felt how little we deserved such gratitude, but were regretfully happy in such affection.[2]

6

The question of the right of Congress to terminate an executive appointment to office by cutting off the salary attached thereto had been debated in House and Senate and had been answered emphatically in the negative by Secretary Ickes and the President himself. It was obviously a matter to be passed upon by the Supreme Court, which had already many decisions to its credit affirming the separation of powers under the Constitution. The way to the Supreme Court lay through the Court of Claims. Burling, who had already la-

[1] See Appendix F.
[2] See Appendix G.

bored valiantly in my behalf, now offered the services of his firm, and on my acceptance Charles A. Horsky undertook to handle my case along with those of Watson and Dodd. When the Attorney General declined to accept the case for Congress, the latter appropriated thirty-five thousand dollars and engaged John C. Gall as attorney. The Department of Justice intervened with a brief in behalf of the executive, drawn by Assistant Attorney General Francis M. Shea. The case was argued before the Court of Claims in May 1945. The decision handed down November 5 was a victory for the plaintiffs. All five judges wrote opinions concurring, two, however, holding that while the salaries earned should be paid, no constitutional question of a bill of attainder was involved. The opinion of Judge Madden, emphasizing the fact that the action of Congress was directed against individuals for the express purpose of doing them injury beyond the mere withholding of money and that it was, in effect, a bill of attainder, went to the root of the matter.[1]

The attorney for Congress appealed to the Supreme Court for a writ of certiorari, to which the plaintiffs agreed. Briefs were filed on behalf of Congress, the plaintiffs, and the Department of Justice, the last supporting the position that Section 304 is unconstitutional. The case was ably presented by Horsky. As in the Court of Claims, two members of the Court, Justice Frankfurter and Justice Reed, held that Section 304 was not a bill of attainder on the ground that it "lacks the characteristics of the enactments in the Statutes of the Realm and the Colonial Laws that bear the hallmarks of bills of attainder," and that "this Court reaches constitutional invalidation only through inescapable necessity." On the other hand, the majority of the Court, in an opinion written by Justice Black, declared:

> We hold that Section 304 falls precisely within the category of congressional actions which the Constitution barred by providing that "No Bill of Attainder or Ex Post Facto Law shall be passed."

The decision was handed down on June 3, 1946. There was still valid in the appropriation for the Virgin Islands for 1944 (which did not expire until June 30, 1946) sufficient money to pay my claim for wages, but for some reason the Interior Department refused to release the funds and preferred to include the claim in a deficit appropriation

[1] See Appendix H.

bill submitted to Congress in the spring of 1947, together with the sums due Watson and Dodd. Chairman Taber of the Appropriation Committee reported that the amount had been cut out of the bill on the ground that "these people did not owe their first loyalty to the United States." Mr. Hobbs of Alabama argued strongly for an amendment restoring the amount to the bill on grounds of obligation to support the Constitution:

The question is: Shall we repudiate these debts of our government? . . . Each member's answer to those questions depends not so much on how fiercely he hates the victims as upon how much he loves our government. . . . If you don't like the decision rendered by the Court of Claims which Congress created you have more legal right to vote to abolish that court than to repudiate a judgment Congress empowered it to render.

As the debate proceeded on lines indicated by Mr. Hobbs, it appeared that hatred of the victims was more in evidence than love of the government. When the question was called the vote was announced as ayes eighty-six, noes ninety-seven, but when tellers were appointed the House reversed itself, ayes ninety-nine, noes ninety-eight. The Senate concurred, and the bill including Hobbs' amendment became law.

It is clear that both investigations to which I was haled had certain similarities. The committee of the Illinois Senate, so far as I remember, made little reference to my teaching, which it was appointed to investigate. Its attention was concentrated on my offhand opinion that "all governments are rotten." By committees in Washington little understanding was shown of the organizations with which I had been connected. The members remained ignorant of their composition and purposes. The inclusion of a single Communist on a letterhead was sufficient. Here again the chief animus was directed to my remark in the Gordin letter.

The extreme sensitiveness of congressmen to this remark would appear to suggest a consciousness of guilt. Apart from its vulgar wording I make no apology for it. As Secretary Ickes pointed out in his address to the Senate committee: "There are not enough jails in the United States to contain all of the men and women who on one occasion or another have condemned their government as 'rotten.' . . . If this be conclusive evidence of a desire or an interest to overthrow the government of the United States or of subversive tendencies, then we are indeed in a bad case." Even as I read the news of the day I note that Senator Lee O'Daniel of Texas is quoted as saying: "More and more people are beginning to understand how rotten the New Deal dynasty has been."

How should it be otherwise with any government less than that of Plato's Republic, since, as Harold J. Laski says, "Society is the result of our virtues; government is the result of our vices." Naturally we find in it vicious men who appeal to our vices. We need not go to Hitler and Mussolini for examples. We have only to look at the representatives of the people in our own government who use the power granted them for public service to advance their own interests. And the appalling evil is that their colleagues uphold them in their corruption.

I take it for granted that representatives of the people are for the most part quite unconscious of the injury to public interest involved in their pursuit of private ends. They do not think in those terms. Recently we have had the example of Senator McKellar's vendetta against David Lilienthal with the knowledge and support of a great number of his colleagues. And Mr. Ickes called attention to the behavior of Congressman Jed Johnson of Oklahoma in bringing pressure upon the Commissioner of Indian Affairs to appoint to office his favorites under pain of meeting his opposition in Congress. An Army officer, charged with functions connected with the defense of the country at war, admitted to the committee investigating Senator Bilbo that he had given contracts on the latter's solicitation, as otherwise "we should have had Bilbo on our necks," meaning that he feared the Senator would have used his power to impede the Army officer in the performance of his duties. It is noteworthy that a member of the committee stated that he saw nothing wrong in Bilbo's effort to obtain lucrative contracts from the Army for his constituents, but only in his taking bribes for his services.

At the risk of substantiating the charge of communistic teaching, I "cannot refrain," as Congressman Kerr would say, from quoting John Milton's warning to his countrymen in his "Second Defense of the English People."

Milton's account of the weakness of representative democracy should arouse us today. The first duty of an elected person is to secure re-election; and in an economy of private enterprise concrete private interests, including those of the representative and his supporters, tend to outweigh public concern. This is a platitude, but it demands repetition as the chief danger to our country both in peace and war.

For who would vindicate your right of unrestrained suffrage, or of choosing what representatives you liked best, merely that you might elect the creatures of your own faction, whoever they might be, or him, however small his worth, who, would give you the most lavish feasts, and enable you to drink to the greatest excess? . . .

For should the management of the republic be entrusted to persons to whom no one would willingly entrust the management of his private concerns? . . .

Are they fit to be the legislators of a whole people who themselves know not what law, what reason, what right and wrong, what crooked and straight, what licit and illicit means? . . . who neglect every other consideration for the corrupt gratification of their friendships or the prosecution of their resentments? who disperse their own relations and creatures through the provinces for the sake of levying taxes and confiscating goods; men for the greater part, the most profligate and vile, who lay up for themselves what they pretend to expose to sale, who thence collect an exorbitant mass of wealth which they fraudulently divert from the public service; who thus spread their pillage through the country and in a moment emerge from penury and rags to a state of splendour and of wealth?

7

The case just summarized has gone into the textbooks and has given to Watson, Dodd, and me a place in history in spite of ourselves. I believe that we have nothing to regret; on the contrary, there is reason to congratulate ourselves on an opportunity, though unsought, to render service to our country. For myself, I may say that the evidence of confidence and friendliness on the part of so many people, especially those of the Interior Department and of the Virgin Islands, was ample compensation for the disapproval (had I been capable of suffering from it) of Congress. The firm which defended us, and especially Mr. Charles A. Horsky, profited in prestige and public estimation by their generosity in giving their efforts gratuitously to a cause of justice to individuals. The Department of the Interior, especially the Secretary and the Solicitor, profited in public opinion by standing loyally and eloquently behind a subordinate. The people of the Virgin Islands profited by an opportunity to show themselves united in a course in which they expressed their feelings in a style of restraint and dignity which bears honorable comparison with the crudity, vulgarity, and malignity which mark the pages of the *Congressional Record*. Finally, the case was of benefit to Congress. It is true the two Houses wasted many hours which they might have better employed in passing legislation acutely needed by the Virgin Islands, especially a law defining citizenship. On the other hand, many members who are incapable of sustained thought consider that the violence with which they attack private citizens who cannot reply appeals to their constituents as statesmanship. Congress challenged both the concurrent powers of constitutional government, the executive and the judicial. It claimed power to dismiss any executive appointee (including, presumably, members of the cabinet) by withholding salary. It barely defeated the attempt, put forward by Congressmen Taber and Dirksen, to defy the order of the Supreme Court. Congress should be grateful to Congressman Hobbs and others whose love of their government triumphed over hate of certain fellow-citizens.

XVIII. *Puerto Rico,* 1944–1946

I

ON MY departure from the Virgin Islands Governor Tugwell of Puerto Rico and Mr. Jaime Benítez, chancellor of the university, invited me to join the faculty of that institution. The morning after my arrival in San Juan, April 1, 1944, to take up my duties I was startled by headlines in the papers *El Mundo* and the *World Journal* announcing that Congressman McGehee had introduced a resolution in the House of Representatives calling for the removal of Governor Rexford Guy Tugwell on a number of charges, the first of which was his approval of my appointment to the staff of the university. The same day, I believe, a resolution was carried through the lower House of the insular legislature inquiring into the circumstances of my appointment. I was naturally disturbed by the prospect of involving my friends in Puerto Rico in my difficulties, but I found them merely amused. Governor Tugwell was already bearing affably so heavy a load of congressional displeasure that the addition of my weight was merely a straw. Señor Muñoz Marin, leader of the Popular party and President of the Senate, brushed aside the action of the legislature as "only the lower House." Chancellor Jaime Benítez replied to the House of Representatives with an affirmation of his belief in my integrity. Villard, who was then visiting the island, issued a warm defense of my character, including an appraisal of my service in the Virgin Islands. The association of teachers passed a handsome resolution in my favor. Altogether, my introduction was a fitting prelude to an experience which made the next two years among the best of my life.

It is true that I had known Puerto Rico already under happy auspices. On my way to the Virgin Islands to take up my duties there I necessarily had disembarked at San Juan and had been hospitably received by Secretary Walter Cope, who enabled me to see the low-cost housing projects and other improvements under way through the Puerto Rico Reconstruction Administration, and to meet a group of Puerto Ricans who were a prelude to agreeable personal relations of a later date. Frederick Bissell, the head of the English Department at the university, recognized me as a colleague. The next year he invited me to give a lecture on the occasion of Shakespeare's birthday, and a year later he asked me to be chairman of a conference of Inter-American writers, four from Latin-American countries, of whom Don Jorge Mañach of Cuba was chairman, and four from the United States. The ceremonies of the conference occupied ten days, and were conducted with great dignity and, I may add, enthusiasm. Señora Muñoz Marin, whom I had met in Chicago as Muna Lee, on the occasion of the award to her of the poetry prize, was an important factor as liaison officer in the success of the conference.

Again, I must note that when I went to San Juan to meet Ida on her way to the Virgins I quite fortuitously became an official representative of the islands on the occasion of the inauguration of Admiral Leahy as Governor of Puerto Rico. As we lunched with the Admiral and Mrs. Leahy, I recognized the old school tie in that Mrs. Leahy and Ida had attended the same dancing school in San Francisco—although in different generations. Governor Leahy visited the Virgin Islands occasionally as a release from an administration which he did not pretend to enjoy but in which he was very successful. He used to offer Governor Cramer an exchange of positions in the interest of efficiency and personal satisfaction. After Tugwell became Governor we exchanged official visits frequently in consequence of our involvement in common problems of insular administration, rendered acute by the war. My respect for his ability and my feeling for him and Mrs. Tugwell grew as I knew them, and I appreciated their devoted service to the island.

2

When I consider my affection for Puerto Rico I have to put first the voluptuous beauty of the island: its northern coastline varied by gracefully curving bays; the wide coastal plane of living green leading to the first range of mountains, cut by high steep valleys;

the second range, bolder and more austere, opening to highways which lead down to the tropical southern coast. This is the aspect of the island as seen from San Juan. Toward the west the higher mountains approach the northern coast. The whole scene is enlivened by picturesque towns—Cayey, Coamo, San German, Aibonito in the mountains; Humacao, Guayama, Ponce, Mayagüez, on the coast. I particularly remember Barranquitas for the gracious aspect of its houses, Comero for its precarious perch on the steep bank of its river. I found my favorite drive on the road from Rio Piedras to Cayey, the ascent to Jajome, where the Governor has his summer home, and the winding descent into tropical brightness and gaiety of the road to Guayama. At Coamo Springs there is an old-fashioned resort, suggesting New York's Saratoga Springs in the middle of the nineteenth century. One of the pleasant incidents of the Writers' Conference was a visit to the Springs, with a reception on the way at Coamo. As our cars approached the town the inhabitants lined the road to greet us; they escorted us to the house of the president of the local literary circle, where a program of music, poetry in Spanish and English, and polite conversation in both languages held us, hungry but grateful, for three or four hours.

In many of these towns there is an exclusive group of Spanish blood with a culture certainly equal to that of provincial towns in the United States. The Puerto Ricans of all classes are musical. I never enjoyed an evening of classical music more than in Ponce, at the home of Señor Feré, the president of the Ponce Iron Works. The host, a graduate of both the Massachusetts Institute of Technology and the New England Conservatory of Music, was the cultural inspiration of the city, the second in importance in the island. In San Juan the admirable Ateneo is a center for music and art.

Literary production is rife in Puerto Rico. Volumes of poems, short stories, novels, and plays, of beautiful typography with covers of attractive design, make gay the windows of the booksellers. At a luncheon given to the Writers' Conference by the publisher of *El Mundo* and *Ilustrado*, the chief newspaper and magazine of the island, I spoke of the desirability of Puerto Rican writers seeking an audience in the United States, but I could not be unaware that my remarks did not strike fire.

This stratum of culture rests upon the great mass of Puerto Rican peasantry, the *jíbaros*, a mixture of Spanish, Negro, and Indian strains, who constitute three-fourths of the inhabitants. The Borinqueños, who met the conquistadors on their arrival, were mild and peaceful and lent themselves to assimilation. Later, Negro slaves were imported to add to the mixture. I did not see much of the *jíbaros*, but the unanimous opinion was that they are the true Puerto Ricans, both in their virtues and defects; they are hard-working, loyal, affectionate, hot-blooded, passionate in love and hate. They furnish the mass of labor for the sugar plantations and new industries, but many live in the hills, squatters for the most part, working small holdings. According to the W.P.A. guidebook, the displacement of many of them owing to the destruction of the coffee plantations by the hurricane of 1916 gave rise to the horrible slums surrounding San Juan and other cities in which human life seems actually to fester. It is to the degraded peasantry of the slums that the Puerto Rican immigration to New York is largely due.

Even in the most distressing conditions the people show a persistence in living and holding fast to the narrow margin of existence left them. Along the estuary which divides San Juan from Bayamon lies the worst slum, well named *El Fanguito*, the mud. Here pitiful little shacks of tin or wood crowd each other at the edge of tidewater; every heavy rain submerges them. I have seen the raised highway lined by women and children, hovering under umbrellas, actual or improvised out of boxes and cartons, waiting hours for the waters to subside so that they could return to their dwellings. Many times I passed a man who lived by the roadside in a dismounted automobile top, his feet protruding to the weather. No one seemed to be moved to either pity or amusement until I wrote to a newspaper calling attention to the phenomenon, whereupon the man became such an object of public interest that the police removed him. After the election of 1944 a rumor spread that the triumphant Popular party was going to allow an extension of El Fanguito by draining the marsh adjacent, whereupon little houses began to rise above the water; men worked on them submerged to the waist or standing on boxes or barrels, eager to obtain a little foothold for existence. There was disappointment when the authorities forced the squatters to take down their constructions and crowd back to shore.

The Puerto Ricans are gregarious. Among the lonely hills they raise a multitude of offspring. In the slums they enjoy the human contacts. They love their *Fanguito*. When the authorities tried to remove the entire settlement to a better site there was bitter resistance by the people, who clung to their holdings, claiming titles and values based on long occupation.

3

My personal contacts with the Puerto Ricans were chiefly through the university. The Chancellor and several of the faculty, including Professor Maurice Segall, the acting head of the English Department, had been at the University of Chicago, so that I found agreeable associates at once. The Chancellor and Mrs. Benítez were indefatigably hospitable. Dr. Bissell had joined the Navy, but Mr. Segall accepted me cordially as a colleague and friend. My first employment was as adviser to the Chancellor on English studies. The university maintained extensions in several cities, Arecibo, Mayagüez, Ponce, Guayama, Humacao, and these were inspected from time to time by committees of the central faculty. Professor José Rosario, director of this extension program, added me to his staff, and thus I had the opportunity to survey the entire island. I tried to visit high schools as well as the university extensions, with special reference to the teaching of English, and found in those I saw, notably at Cayey, Ponce, and of course at the Central High School in Santurce, excellent teachers and instruction not inferior to that in similar schools in the United States. Most of the English teachers in these selected high schools had been from one to four years on the continent and spoke English easily and well. The chief defect on the part of pupils was in speech, owing to their subjection to bad models furnished by teachers in elementary schools, who were compelled for years by the United States government to give all instruction in English although their command was imperfect. My chief recommendation to the Chancellor was that the best service to the English language in Puerto Rico was to eliminate the bad English—to forbid its use in the classroom by teachers who conscientiously could only mutilate it.

In the English Department of the university I had nothing but respect and admiration for the group of able teachers selected to conduct the basic course, in which with infinite patience they enforced the principles of English grammar and usage and tried to correct the speech habits acquired in lower schools. My own teaching began in the summer of 1944 with a course in English poetry, and the impressions I had of that class were confirmed by every subsequent group. In Puerto Rico, as elsewhere, the attendance in advanced courses in literature is largely feminine, and Puerto Rican college girls are a delight to the eye. I find in a letter of the time a summary of their perfections: ". . . beautiful hair and so abundant, tender eyes, fine regular features tinted to a dark pink prettiness, exquisite hands, and the best legs ever." Later on, when I gave a second-year course in introduction to literature and had a fair division of the sexes, I found Puerto Rican students in general a joy to a teacher. They are exceedingly attentive and courteous, eager and responsive. I was a stranger, knowing little Spanish, not enough for communication, but my students were most considerate, always ready to help me out. For years my teaching had been by lectures, but now that I resumed work in the classroom and had to get down into the arena I found the experience stimulating. I began to flatter myself that I was a good teacher. At any rate, I looked forward to a class as to a cocktail, and felt the usual enlivening effects afterwards.

Next to the university in importance is the Polytechnic Institute at San German, a few miles from the western end of the island. Established by a Presbyterian missionary, Jabez Harris, some forty years ago, it was under Dr. Morris during my years on the island. Early in my residence the head of the English Department, Mrs. Belle Palmer, invited me to speak to their assembly, and later Thurston Child gave up his position as Superintendent of Schools in St. Croix to become a teacher in the Institute, another reason for our visits. The buildings are scattered among hills and woods with the guest house commanding the magnificent landscape bounded by the group of higher mountains at the center of the island.

4

After a summer on the continent I returned to Puerto Rico for the academic year which began in August, leaving Ida to follow after the hot weather was over. Unfortunately she broke her hip and was unable to move from Chicago. I found a pleasant residence in the family of Señora Ramona Anca in Santurce, the suburb between San Juan and Rio Piedras. Dr. Nathan Rifkinson, after his summary dismissal by Governor Harwood, had quickly made his place in Puerto Rico on the staff of the School of Tropical Medicine and the staff of the municipal hospital at Bayamón, across the bay from San Juan. He and Mrs. Rifkinson came for me every Sunday morning to drive to the lovely beach at Vega Baja for bathing, followed by dinner and an afternoon of chess. I pursued the elusive Spanish language with an excellent teacher, Señorita Harriet Wagner. Ferd Schevill came that winter to give lectures at the university. He and I spent the Christmas recess in the Virgin Islands with a week at Caneel Bay, St. John. I was also fortunate in persuading a former colleague, Percy H. Boynton, to come as visiting professor. I wrote him that he must learn Spanish, and he and Mrs. Boynton promptly began their study, which they continued to such purpose that Percy could address audiences acceptably in that language. He became much interested in the Institute, especially in the choir, which he inspired to make a tour in the States. The Boyntons were concerned in the revival of Renaissance music played on the instruments for which it was written, and gave concerts which were much appreciated.

During this year I had classes at the university only on the first three days of the week; hence when the Chancellor suggested that on the other days I give a course on the eighteenth century at the Convent of the Sacred Heart I accepted with enthusiasm. The Sagrado Corazon occupies a handsome pile of buildings in a park on the outskirts of Santurce. There some four hundred girls, from five or six to eighteen, are well taught by Redemptorist sisters. Dressed in white blouses and navy blue skirts, they were a distinctive group, though most secondary girls' schools have a similar uniform, green, brown, red, or blue. Whether I saw them in procession or in informal groups, they had a certain precision of movement and manners that seemed the result of careful training.

My class went along pleasantly through Swift, Defoe, Addison. When I introduced the novel with *Pamela*, Dean Guevara came to me with the remonstrance, "We are not allowed to read that." I was nonplused, but seeing a set of Fielding in the library I inquired whether he was permitted. He was. I had forgotten how shamelessly vulgar *Tom Jones* could be, but I led my seven virgins bravely through the hero's adventures. They said of him, "He was bad." Of my pupils I remember especially two, Señorita Ferrer, dark and serious, who intended to become a dentist, and Marguerita Esteves, bright and fair as an angel, whose intelligence and industry carried her the next year to Bryn Mawr where she took her bachelor's degree and was given an appointment in the Spanish Department.

5

While I was in Puerto Rico a book by Wenzel Brown appeared, bearing the alarming title *Dynamite on Our Doorstep*. It was hard to imagine that the dynamite was Puerto Rico. Mr. Brown was one of the American teachers who had gone to the island a dozen or more years ago when one of the recurrent spells of interest on the part of the Interior Department took the form of adopting Machiavelli's advice to force a conquered people to adopt the language of the conqueror. Mr. Brown recounted a number of incidents of discourtesy and even insult and threat on the part of Puerto Rican pupils, in school and out—incidents for which other American teachers could furnish no parallels. There have been times when special causes of discontent with foreign rule aroused something like exasperation on the island, but the almost universal testimony of North Americans is to the courtesy and kindness—even the affection—of the people.

The record of the United States in colonial administration is not a happy one. The conquest was an accident in consequence of another accident—the Spanish-American war. The Chief of Staff of the Army of the United States, Major General Nelson A. Miles, envious of the military glory won by Shafter and Roosevelt in Cuba and Dewey at Manila, looking about for other worlds to conquer, espied Puerto Rico. He landed his column at a point on the southwest coast and marched practically without opposition upon San Juan, which the Navy, eager to participate in the conquest, helpfully bombarded. At this time, Puerto Rico had, after years of effort, finally succeeded in obtaining autonomy from Spain. The defeat of this ambition, and the imposition of military government without the consent of the people, was an inauspicious beginning of relations between a democracy and its colony.

The independence movement which had gained such momentum under Spain refused to die. It gathered strength from governors who, according to the American custom, were too often appointed to serve special interests (including their own) and who believed firmly in the doctrine of racial superiority and discrimination. It found a leader of eloquence in Pedro Albizu Campos, who brought it to a formidable height. To the Governor, General Blanton Winship, the cry of independence was treason. The Chief of Police of San Juan, for reasons not entirely clear, was assassinated. The two assassins were arrested, and simply disappeared. Whether their crime was political or not, the Independentistas were held responsible; Albizu Campos and seven followers were tried and sentenced to six to eight years in Atlanta Federal Penitentiary. A campaign for funds for their defense spread through the island, but was met by suppression. Public meetings for the cause were forbidden. Teachers were forbidden to express themselves politically and were compelled to take an oath of allegiance to the Federal Constitution. Officials sympathetic to independence were dismissed.

A meeting and parade were scheduled in Ponce for Palm Sunday, March 21, 1937, but the permit was withdrawn an hour before the demonstration was to take place. Evidently in preparation for what was to occur, squads of police, including machine-gunners, were posted about the square where the paraders gathered. As the march began, they opened fire. As at Amritsar, the exits from the square were blocked, and for fifteen minutes the police fired upon the helpless crowd, killing and wounding upwards of two hundred. A hundred and fifty were arrested. Governor Winship's excuse was like that of the British General Dyer, the hero of Amritsar. "They would have laughed at us."

In October Governor Winship staged at Ponce a celebration of the American landing, a provocative gesture which resulted in the death of two of his aides and the arrest of several Independentistas accused of the shooting. It is characteristic of the Puerto Rican spirit of independence that these young men, sentenced to prison for life, refused to recognize the alien government even to ask for pardon. They were finally freed by Governor Tugwell, who dispensed with this formality. Governor Winship was dismissed by President Roosevelt through the summary process of appointing his successor. Later Albizu Campos was released on account of illness. I visited him in Columbus Hospital, New York, and found him cheerfully recalcitrant, firm in his belief that Puerto Rico by reason of natural resources and the capacity of its people could become an industrial nation—the England of Latin America.

6

The violent stage of the independence movement came to an end with the triumph of Luis Muñoz Marin and the Popular party in 1940. Don Luis is the son of Luis Muñoz Rivera, the leader who won a qualified independence from Spain. After the annexation, Muñoz Rivera had represented the island in Washington; his son had acted as his secretary and become thoroughly acquainted with the United States political scene. He inherited the independence cause, but he realized the importance of winning the campaign by a display of strength. He organized the Popular party for the election of 1940 by appealing directly to the people on the platform "Land and Bread." Although Congress, with singular foresight, had early passed a law limiting the holdings of a corporation to five hundred acres, the act had never been implemented, and the sugar plantations had expanded over most of the arable land of the island. The program of the Populares looked toward the recovery of this land and its division into small holdings. In support of this measure Don Luis warned the *jíbaros* against selling their votes. He went over the island, speaking to them in groups and individually, giving them one simple bit of political education—"The mark under the hat," the broad-brimmed straw hat of the *jíbaro* being the party symbol on the ballot. The other three parties, Republican, Socialist, and Liberal, formed a coalition, but they could not quite break even with the Populares, who controlled the Senate by one vote, and, by alliance with the Liberal member, controlled the House as well.

This was the situation when Rexford Guy Tugwell was appointed Governor. He found himself in accord with Muñoz Marin on the general policy of developing industry and agriculture to make the island more self-supporting. "Authorities" were set up for the extension of the control of water resources for power, for transport, for housing, for industry, for agriculture, as well as an over-all planning board. These measures were bitterly opposed by business interests in the island and on the continent. The ideal situation for both is for Puerto Rico to give itself entirely to growing sugar to pay for imports of every description from the United States. The disturbance of this *status quo* led to charges that Governor Tugwell was setting up a communist regime. So bitter was the opposition that a social boycott was drawn against the Governor's residence, the

Fortaleza, and when the Governor appeared to open a session of the legislature the opposition members rose and walked out.

The disgruntled businessmen of the island found sympathetic hearers in Washington. As Tugwell has noted, the ultimate government of Puerto Rico is in the hands of committees of the Senate and House of Representatives in Washington, which number together some forty-one members. When we read of the mischief wrought during the war by predatory attacks on the War and Navy Departments by congressmen, of whom Andrew J. May is an example, we may estimate the evil potential in these forty-one statesmen. The outpost of the New Deal in Puerto Rico offered them an opportunity to attack the Roosevelt administration, and committees of both the Senate and the House visited the island in 1943 to investigate Governor Tugwell. The latter was, however, in a strong position as a war governor. He handled the problems of feeding the island and its dependencies when the Caribbean was at the mercy of the German submarines. In particular, he enjoyed the confidence of the military and naval autorities of occupation so that there was no witch-hunt of the Falangistas, no suppression of Independentistas, no martial law as in Hawaii. Fortunately, too, all the officers successively in command of both military and naval forces were intelligent and reasonable men.

The Senate committee under Senator Chavez saw the importance of maintaining in our own colony the democracy for which we were fighting elsewhere. The House committee was more factious. It was natural for statesmen in Washington to look at the great importing market of Puerto Rico from the point of view of their own constituents who had things to sell. Accordingly, when it was proposed to import wheat, instead of perishable flour, and set up mills for grinding it in Puerto Rico, there was an outraged cry from Chairman Bell of the House Committee, who spoke for the flour mills of Kansas City.

The election of 1944 was a triumph for Muñoz Marin and an endorsement of Governor Tugwell. The election laws are so precise in Puerto Rico that fraud is impossible. Indeed, so rigid are conditions that some eighty thousand would-be voters (including the Governor) were disqualified for errors in their registration papers. During the hot campaign there were some disturbances, in the course of which several men were killed. Thereupon all parties agreed to hold no more mass meetings before the election—a self-denying measure that would have little chance of adoption in a campaign in the United States.

For the election Governor Tugwell appointed some seventy-five personal representatives to cover the entire island; I was sent to Cayey. When I presented myself to the election commissioners on the evening before election I found them starting on a tour of inspection of the eighty-three polling places, to see that all was in order for voting. Early on election morning *jíbaros* from the hills began to fill the town, and long lines formed in front of the *colegios*. I went with the entire board, representing the four parties, to each one of the eighty-three stations, and to some of them a second time on call. At one a ballot box was apparently full. The key was handed to me, and under close surveillance I stuffed the box to make more room. There seemed to be an unusual number of blind and crippled voters exercising the suffrage. The Republican committeeman protested against the police being allowed to assist old women to the polls. I listened to the argument between him and the Popular party chairman, which I decided by asserting that it was the duty of the police to help women under all circumstances.

It began to rain, as usual in Cayey, about noon, but there was no flinching. The lines held until the last voter had deposited his ballot. I quit with him. I considered that the climbs to many of the eighty-three *colegios* amounted to the ascent of a mountain, and I realized that mountain climbing was no longer a sport for me.

7

Even before the election of 1944 the status of Puerto Rico and its relations to its stepmother country had been increasingly under discussion both in the island and in Congress. A commission sent to Washington had worked out a plan for an extension of home rule, including an elected governor, but this fell short of the demands of the Independentistas, who had found an ally in Senator Tydings, chairman of the Committee on Insular Affairs; he sponsored a bill for complete independence. Although Muñoz Marin declared that status was not an issue in the campaign of 1944, the result of that election, concentrating power in a single party, gave an impetus to the discussion. If that party through its leader could be committed to independence, and so defined by a plebiscite, the battle was won. As in the case of the Philippines, the continental sugar growers might be expected to unite with Cuban interests to put Puerto Rican sugar outside the tariff wall. Shortly after the election an all-day meeting was called at the race track outside of San Juan by the Independentistas, who confidently expected that Muñoz Marin would announce his policy by radio before the meeting. His speech was not forthcoming, and the speakers at the meeting were left to wander in the desert of hortatory eloquence.

Both Governor Tugwell and Muñoz Marin realized that a plebiscite was futile without authorization by Congress and a promise that its result would be binding upon that body. Three proposals had to be considered: statehood, which had been set as the goal by President McKinley on the annexation of the island; an extension of the present relation into dominion status; and independence. Businessmen generally favored the first; the mass of *jíbaros* were satisfied with the second; the intellectuals, students and some professors, and ambitious young people of the middle class, including the Communists, were for the third. It was doubtful whether Congress would grant statehood, because of the language difference (although New Mexico furnished a precedent) and its inveterate race prejudice, but to leave out statehood would be an insult to the island and a repudiation of the historical development of the American commonwealth. The plebiscite proposal accordingly languished in Congress. In the island it was generally believed that the authority of Muñoz Marin would be decisive with the *jíbaros*, and this accounted for the urgency of the Independentistas in seeking his announcement. For his part he spoke sadly of "a one-man plebiscite."

He was indeed in a dilemma—in a spot, to use the vernacular. The economy of Puerto Rico had become almost completely meshed with that of the United States. When the island was taken over it was on a coffee economy; its trade was largely with Europe. Under the influence of American capitalism it was given over to sugar and became a one-crop economic unit. The production of sugar is profitable only by reason of government support—the so-called sugar benefits paid from the United States Treasury either for growing or refraining from growing sugar cane. At first these adventitious profits were returned almost entirely in the form of dividends to stockholders on the continent, but at present the ownership of the plantations is said to be about equally divided between Puerto Ricans and Americans. Puerto Rico has other financial benefits from its present situation. It enjoys free trade with the United States, which is of no value to the coffee grower, since coffee is outside the tariff wall. It has the unprecedented largesse of the return to the insular treasury of internal revenue taxes collected in the United States on island products. In 1944, when the manufacture of whisky was restricted and the great American drinking public turned to rum, this gift of taxes paid by United States consumers to Puerto Rico amounted to some sixty-four million dollars. It receives outright gifts for relief, amounting in the case of the Puerto Rico Reconstruction Administration (the P. R. A.) to a quarter of a billion dollars for housing, schools, hospitals, highways, and other public works. During the war Puerto Rican youth enlisted in large numbers, nearly seventy thousand of them. By a curious oversight on the part of Congress a "differential" of twenty-five per cent on salary payments to persons serving off the continent was made available to Puerto Rican soldiers who, though technically offshore, were in fact largely serving at home. Some of these financial advantages would be lost under statehood; all of them under independence. The situation was summed up by Governor Tugwell in saying, "As an American I am for independence; as a Puerto Rican I am against it." In the negotiations with Senator Tydings and the Committees of Congress on Insular Affairs, Muñoz Marin has always insisted on the retention of these financial benefits, at least in part, a policy which Villard described as "divorce with alimony."

Muñoz Marin has stated that Puerto Rico was in fact self-supporting up to 1935. It must have been on a lower standard of living than the present, which is the highest in the Caribbean. He is of the opinion that by extension of industry, increase of production, and limitation of population, the island may achieve independence in a real sense by ceasing to be dependent. Undoubtedly the appeal of independence to the patriotic ambition of self-conscious Puerto Rican youth may be expected to raise the spiritual temper of the island, whether sufficiently to meet the sacrifices which must be borne by rich and poor may be questioned. The Puerto Ricans are a mercurial people. It would be a misfortune if after starting on an experiment of self-government they should relapse into the condition of another of the foreign countries which the United States is trying to tempt away from communism and save from starvation by relief. It would be to the advantage as well as the honor of the American government to give disinterested advice and aid to Puerto Rico in solving the problems which had their origin in a criminal war and their development in flagrant imperialism on the part of a democracy.

8

The problems of Puerto Rico have been detailed at length by Tugwell in the record of his administration[1] and by Senator Muñoz Marin in many articles and speeches. To some extent they all depend for solution on the decision in regard to status, but pending this the collection of statistics and the making of surveys go on and reports and economic and social studies are issued. The activity of the university under Chancellor Benítez is notable.

The immediate pressing duty is the education of teachers for the elementary schools, which are unable to give instruction to one-third of the children of school age. The School of Education is the largest department of the university. Of course, the attempt of the Interior Department to make the English language the exclusive vehicle of education has proved a great handicap. The enforcement of this requirement varies with the attitude of superintendents, principals, and teachers, giving an uncertainty to its operation. In a questionnaire addressed to students of the basic course in English at the university, only twenty-six stated that they had had all their work after the seventh grade in English. Of the others, to the number of several hundred, less than half had had the greater part of their work in that language. I should say that the English spoken in business houses, banks, and shops in San Juan, where employees are in contact with continentals, is on the whole better than that spoken on the university campus. A bill has twice passed the legislature making the use of Spanish obligatory in all schools, including the university, except in specifically English courses, or by teachers unable to use Spanish. In other words, English would be treated as a foreign language, required in high schools and college, and taught by qualified teachers with the precision and discipline regularly applied to foreign language study. Governor Tugwell vetoed this on the ground that it would be too rigidly applied, especially to the university. As provided by the Organic Act of the island, the Gover-

[1] See his *The Stricken Land,* which is a textbook on colonial government as administered by a democracy. It becomes more valuable as the United States extends its empire.

nor's veto may be appealed to the President, who may or may not uphold it. In this case President Truman upheld it, but two days later than the time specified—a perfect instance of the carelessness with which matters of deep moment to Puerto Rico are treated in Washington. The Supreme Court of the island has decided that the President's action was too late and that the new law stands.

Undoubtedly the policy of the Interior Department was adopted in good faith in order to forward the preparation of the island for statehood. I found the advocates of statehood in the islands in general in favor of enforcing English speech in the schools. My friends in Ponce, Señor Feré and Señor Rosalie, president of the Bank of Ponce, assured me that they had learned their perfect English in the Ponce High School from continental teachers. But in their school days the number of pupils had been small and the government had then made a determined effort to induce American teachers to go to the island. I doubted whether these gentlemen appreciated the sheer weight and mass of the burden of maintaining a standard of literacy throughout the island where a third of the children receive no school education at all.

Apart from educational considerations, the attempt of an alien administration to supplant the vernacular seems like an attempt to subvert the native culture of which Puerto Rico is properly proud. It could not work toward harmonious relations between a suzerain and a colony. It is one of the ironical principles of Machiavelli but is opposed to the practice of colonial empires, British, Dutch, French.

Another duty assumed by the university is the training of public officials. With the extension of the functions of government into industry as well as into human welfare the need of men and women trained in administration is obvious. One of the bitterest outcries against Governor Tugwell was his employment of experts from the continent, necessarily at higher salaries than those generally in vogue throughout the island. The outcry was never louder than in connection with the establishment of a School of Public Administration to enable Puerto Rico to provide its own experts. It was regarded by *El Mundo* as a reflection on the ability of Puerto Ricans to direct complicated enterprises by virtue of *élan vital.*

One of the needs of Puerto Ricans is to vary their diet from the staple rice and beans. The Department of Home Economics of the university, directed on a part-time arrangement by Professor Lydia Roberts of the University of Chicago, is the center of missionary efforts in this direction. The School of Social Service is next to the School of Education in number of students. The island needs doctors, and the establishment of a medical school has been discussed, but the expense of its foundation on a basis comparable to that of the schools of the United States would seem to be prohibitory. The immediate cause of delay, however, is rivalry between Ponce and San Juan for its site. Reminiscent of former battles in many Western states is the claim that as San Juan has the university, Ponce should have the medical school. Meanwhile the Health Service shows generosity in providing fellowships for study on the continent.

All attempts of Puerto Rico to solve its problems, to raise itself by its bootstraps, as Grace and Rexford Tugwell express it, are overshadowed by the fact of overpopulation. The insular government cannot provide schools, hospitals, houses, industrial employment, or farm holdings rapidly enough to keep pace with an increase of fifty thousand a year, which by 1960 will raise the number of Puerto Ricans on the island to three million. There seems literally to be no solution. Even the directed emigration of a million would apparently be only a temporary alleviation. Dr. Fernos Isern, lately Commissioner of Health, and Muñoz Marin seem to believe that improvement in living conditions would result, in Puerto Rico as in other countries, in the establishment of an equilibrium, but the question remains whether such improvement can under any foreseeable circumstances occur rapidly enough to overtake and head off the annual birthrate. The Puerto Ricans are not religious with the same fervent faith as the Mexicans, but in the secular conduct of life they respect the authority of the Catholic hierarchy and priesthood, and the attitude of the Church on birth control is not determined by social considerations. Possibly such a campaign as Muñoz Marin conducted to free politics from subservience to the rich might free the population from control by the Church. Possibly!

9

During my last half year at the university Profesor Segall took advantage of my presence to leave me in charge of the department while he went to the continent for a needed rest. The Chancellor was doubtful as to the propriety of giving a visiting professor this distinction, but I was glad of the chance to round out my experience by some contact with university administration. I was already familiar with the excellent teaching of my colleagues. I found my chief problem in arranging for their leaves of absence for further study on the continent. Both teachers and students at the university are extremely ambitious and it is hard to balk them in their quest. I was very dependent on Mrs. Besosa, who directed the overgrown basic course, but overwork compelled her temporary retirement. Everyone in the department took on additional work without a murmur; the *esprit de corps* was perfect. Mr. Segall left me a youthful but competent secretary whom we all called Olga. As continentals we were much above the Puerto Rican average in size, and as I saw Olga moving gracefully and efficiently among us I thought of the Bible verse, "A little child shall lead them."

As chairman of the English Department I was invited to take an active part in faculty discussions by Dr. Gonzales García, Dean of the College of Humanities, and Dr. Morales Carrión, head of the Department of History. The subject of chief importance was the old moving-picture conflict, familiar to me from Harvard and Chicago, in which the beautiful heroine, *Litterae Humaniores*, seeks to defend herself from a foul ravisher who has already torn off her beautiful garments, Latin and Greek. In Chicago the assailant was Science; in Puerto Rico it was Education.

In view of the crying need for teachers, and the fact that teaching afforded the most immediate economic resource for women, the School of Education had become the largest division of the university both in faculty and students. Its active head, Dean Pedro Cebollero, was naturally eager to take advantage of his power to mold the curriculum in favor of an extension of the requirements in his division, with the consequence that registration of students in history, literature, and other humanistic studies tended to diminish. As the ground was familiar, I was able to follow discussions in faculty which were of a high order of intelligence and expression. Necessarily I spoke in English, urging that the School of Education should not push its advantage to the point of changing the essential structure of the university as a school of liberal studies, thereby sacrificing the culture of its students. On one point I was thoroughly in accord with Dr. Cebollero—the handicap placed on education by the requirement of English as its vehicle. That this superstition is maintained in Washington was shown when the university recommended one of its ablest young professors, Mario Villaronga, for the position of Insular Superintendent of Education, and his examination by committees of Congrees turned largely on his attitude on this question of language in school.

10

My memories of Puerto Rico are entirely happy. After Ida recovered from her accident and joined me, we were fortunate in obtaining the house of a colleague, Professor Warrek, who took his family to New York for his leave of absence. Opposite lived Professor Lewis Richardson, who conducted the English Workshop for the study of methods; next door lived Rafael Cordero, the auditor of the island; they both had neighborly families. Professor Segall was an active promoter of extracurricular activities, the organizer of a men's club (*Varónes*) and promoter of holiday excursions to neighboring resorts on which he made me welcome. He had been a follower of Ferd Schevill at the University of Chicago, and had come to Puerto Rico some twenty years earlier to be principal of the high schools in several cities. Later he had joined the university faculty. He had friends everywhere, especially in Ponce and Mayagüez. Of other American colleagues, Tom Hayes, the librarian, and Bill O'Reilly, of the English Department, I regarded as special friends. I had met Harry and Margaret Besosa through Fred Bissell on my first visit to the island, and now enjoyed their hospitality. Mr. and Mrs. Tugwell were close friends. They came to live at the Governor's House near the university, where, as earlier at the Fortaleza, we found much hospitality, crowned by a long visit before our departure in July 1946. Just before this we went with the Tugwells' party to St. Thomas on the happy occasion of the inauguration of W. H. Hastie as Governor of the Virgin Islands.[1]

I am aware that I have written of Puerto Rico more in terms of the island itself than of my personal experience there. This is obviously a matter of proportion, but I may add that my chief interest during my stay was in the history of the American occupation and its effect upon the people. In my last summer quarter I had as pupils in a course in writing several ladies; through family connections and childhood memories they could re-create the Puerto Rico of the previous cen-

[1] When Secretary Ickes reported to President Truman that Governor Harwood had spent in the preceding year only ninety days in his satrapy, the President called on him to resign, and on his failure to do so removed him by the summary process of appointing Hastie as his successor.

tury, when the coffee economy lent itself to something like the plantation system of dependence of workers and protection by masters. Traces of this civilization survive, but in general the separation of classes, the rich and the poor, is painfully apparent. One effect of Tugwell's administration was an awakening of interest in voluntary efforts of social charity. Mrs. Tugwell was chairman of an organization of ladies to supply milk for babies at stations throughout the island.

Through younger students I gained glimpses of the present discontent. These students were frequently Independentistas, from a sense of pride so often needlessly affronted by representatives of the United States, and from a belief that they would themselves then have a better chance for a career. On the other hand, the young administrators of the native agencies which had been set up to direct island activities were against adding another small nation but favored greater autonomy. I did not discuss politics with Muñoz Marin from a sense of tact, although I was particularly anxious to ask about his relations with the Governor; as his bearing was always frank and cordial I fancy that he would have responded, but I never did ask. It was obvious, however, that co-operation between Governor Tugwell and the leader of the dominant party in the legislature was necessary to the orderly development of the island, and furthermore that together they have accomplished more for the island and people of Puerto Rico than any previous administration. At the same time I sensed growing differences between them, as between a ruler responsible to God and a minister responsible to a party, which is his instrument for making the will of God prevail. Probably Governor Tugwell thought that Muñoz Marin should have had greater trust in God: Muñoz, that Tugwell should have been more of an instrumentalist.

XIX. *Lake Zurich*, 1946—

I

On our return from Puerto Rico in the summer of 1946 we encountered the housing shortage, and after a visit to Beatrice in Minnesota we settled in the cottage which we built nearly fifty years ago at Lake Zurich. This is a perfect place of retirement, which is now definitely my career. Forty miles from Chicago, the rural village has been promoted to a suburb, an hour's journey by automobile. It has prospered. The inhabitants are well clothed, well fed, well housed. The function of hired domestic service, at least so far as we are concerned, has been abolished. An excellent high school which serves the township of Ela sends half its graduates to various colleges. The golf club, which was the original cause of our settlement, flourishes with new members, among whom I am a veteran. The links behind us are our private park except on Saturday, when there occurs what Milton called a "gaudy night." The lake in front, whether fluent in sunshine or bound fast in ice, is the redeeming feature of the humble prairie landscape. In the morning when I walk to the village for mail I chant Milton's "L'Allegro"; in the evening, when I stroll in the moonlight, it is "Il Penseroso"—without the nightingale.

I am in an elegiac period of life, all for the quiet ending. With Landor I say:

> Mild is the parting year, and sweet
> The odor of the falling spray;
> Life hastens on more rudely fleet,
> And balmless is its closing day.

My favorite poems are the "Elegy in a Country Churchyard," the *Rubáiyát*, "The Waste Land." A sentence in one of Chekhov's letters comes to my mind: "Everything is crumbling and decrepit, but poetical, sad, and beautiful in the extreme." If I were God I should feel that the beauty of the world in decay is full justification for its creation, and the last obligation of humanity is to die gracefully.

With ample leisure for the contemplation of the world in its present state I do not find myself unhappy. I have as the first line of defense a satisfaction in the mere movement of time. Even in enjoyable experiences, a concert or play, a gay dinner party or a happy visit, a term of professional service or a vacation of travel, I am acutely conscious of its passing. I have my watch in hand at least once an hour, and the calendar is registered in my mind. In beginning a book I always note the number of pages and mark with satisfaction my progress toward the end. The division of the academic year at the University of Chicago by quarters certainly stimulates this temporal obsession. I remember even in childhood my mother's admonition: "Don't wish the time away"—but a line of a song by Charles Kingsley which she used to sing to me always consoled me: "The sooner 'tis over the sooner to sleep." Once, at a banquet of the L. I. D., the quotation occurred to me as I was about to introduce our guest, Mr. Sol Lewisohn. He urbanely turned it off with the hope that sleep would not occur before he finished his speech.

The obvious triumph of time is decay, in the phenomena of which I have always been interested. I like to see material things in process of wearing out. My friends have thought that my addiction to old clothes was a sign of thrift. Not at all: I enjoy them in their well-worn shabbiness. My only embarrassment is deciding when the process is so nearly complete as to justify resort to the rag bag, a matter on which my family and I often fail to agree. When I was in the Virgin Islands the house assigned to me as quarters was being eaten by termites. Officially I reported their ravages from year to year to Washington, but privately I cheered them on.

2

One of my chief interests in literary study has been the decline of faith in the nineteenth century—faith in the importance of man through his relation to the cosmos. One of the most powerful elements in that belief, and one which gave inspiration to its expression, was Nature. Through the century the sense of nature as the symbol of a friendly universe declined, leaving a spiritual vacuum. The process has been traced by Professor Joseph Warren Beach in his fine book, *The Concept of Nature in Nineteenth Century English Poetry*. He concludes: "One of the hardest things for man to bear is spiritual isolation. The sense that he stands alone in the universe goes terribly against his gregarious sentiments." I do not suffer personally from loneliness or homelessness because I accept Professor Beach's suggestion that social solidarity will increasingly supply incentives to action and give values to living and animate an art of the future from which God and Nature have disappeared.

My own work with institutions, so far as it is worth recalling, has been in the direction of social solidarity: peace through unity among nations; peace through unity among classes; peace especially within the movement for social progress. In the first category I shared in the international spirit which characterized Hull House; I tried to have faith in the promise of nations to renounce war, and encouraged young men and women to believe it; and I supported the neutrality legislation as an example for an international pattern in the Emergency Peace Campaign, and concerted action against aggressors in the League against War and Fascism. Among the institutions of the second category, peace among classes, I place Hull House again, the *Dial*, the *New Republic*, and the League for Industrial Democracy in its persistent attempt to educate the influential middle class into an understanding of and sympathy with labor. Among the third I count new political parties, beginning in my case with the Committee of Forty-Eight and the Farmer-Labor party, extending through subsequent conferences and committees which led to the Progressive party campaign of 1924, the League for Independent Political Action, and the Progressive Citizens of America behind Henry Wallace.

In all these movements for peace, for labor, and for political action I have consistently stood for admission of Communists. It is almost an axiom that the world cannot be unified under the United Nations, and a lasting peace assured, without the participation of the Soviet Union. I believe it equally axiomatic that the effective unity of social forces in this country depends upon participation of both Communists and liberals, although I am aware of the difficulty of getting along with Communists in view of their absolute social philosophy, their tendency to use their disciplined strength to assume control of any organization, their subjection to the policy of a foreign nation.

I recognize that the chief objection liberals must feel to joining united front organizations with Communists is the dependence of the latter upon the foreign policy of the Soviet Union now that its policy has become the extension of communism by force. I have already indicated my attitude toward that great social experiment. All revolutions tend to lose something of the splendor of their birth. What has become of the American Revolution, announced by Jefferson in a Declaration that has recently been called a seditious document, is evident in the Eightieth Congress. The French Revolution, welcomed by Wordsworth as "a pleasant exercise of hope and joy," brought forth Napoleon and universal war. The Russian Revolution proclaimed by Lenin has led to the subjection as satellites of a dozen peoples who won fame in history through their fight for freedom.

A short while before his death, John G. Winant was quoted in the newspapers as inquiring whether we can afford the liberty without which life is not worth living. That liberty in our democracy includes private enterprise, individual possession of social goods, and suppression of minority races. It fosters the chief enemies of social solidarity—greed, ambition for what William James called "the bitch goddess Success," and intolerance. Obviously, the question in Winant's mind, and in many another, is whether liberty must be purchased at such cost. I should not like to live in a communist state. Of Russia I hear various accounts, from those of Anna Louise Strong to André Gide, but the net result seems grim. I should find myself addressing Swinburne's line to Karl Marx instead of Jesus:

> Thou hast conquered, O pale Galilean; the world has grown grey from Thy breath.

And yet the managed economy and the social leveling of communism may be the only way of achieving the unity and social solidarity without which the world will destroy itself. For American communism is a challenge to the right of free speech. It appears as a contender in what Justice Holmes called the competition of the market place. It offers a test of the classic doctrine of liberty, as stated by John Stuart Mill, and recently affirmed by the President's Committee on Civil Rights, presided over by Mr. Charles E. Wilson. A résumé of Mill's argument is timely when hysteria has reached the point where sympathetic echoes can be heard in Congress of such a statement as, "If I had my way I would take them out in the yard tomorrow morning and shoot them, and the next day would have a trial to see whether or not they were guilty." Mill argues for the toleration of an unpopular opinion on three hypotheses: First, the opinion may be right.

Communism may become a categorical imperative for survival. As Harold Laski points out, communism is the only living faith held today by great masses of mankind, inspiring individuals to fight and die for it. For parts of the world it seems to be without a foreseeable alternative if freedom is won—for the peoples of India and China, the nations of Africa, and the peons of Latin America.

Mill's second hypothesis is that the new belief may be wrong. In that case, he holds that it should be tolerated for the sake of the challenge it offers to the existing faith. He points out the tendency of any accepted system to lose vitality, to grow cold and stiff for lack of exercise, and to yield easily to corruption. That this is the case with our economy of private enterprise is seen especially in the records of two wars. Already the effect of the Communist challenge is seen in the frequent utterance of the view that the way to avoid communism is to prove the greater value of democracy in promoting the health, welfare, and happiness of mankind. It may be proper in this connection to recall the warning that, in 1852, four years after the appearance of the Communist Manifesto, Mill wrote in his *Principles of Political Economy* (a textbook which, used largely in colleges, seems to have escaped the notice of the Dies Committee and the National Association of Manufacturers):

"If . . . the choice were to be made between communism with all its chances, and the present state of society with all its sufferings and injustices; if the institution of private property necessarily carried with it as a consequence, that the produce of labour should be apportioned as we now see it, almost in an inverse ratio to the labour—the largest portions to those who have never worked at all, the next largest to those whose work is almost nominal, and so in a descending scale, the remuneration diminishing as the work grows harder and more disagreeable, until the most fatiguing and exhausting bodily labour cannot count with certainty on being able to earn even the necessaries of life: if this or communism were the alternative, all the difficulties, great or small, of communism would be as dust in the balance.

As a third choice Mill suggests that the practical truth may, and usually does, lie between the two hostile theses and may be reached by a Hegelian synthesis—a revolution by consent. This is the conclusion devoutly to be wished. Such experiments, undertaken in a good faith enforced by bitter need, may be betrayed by the purchase by the United States of a democracy of free enterprise, or by the imposition by the Soviet Union of communism by military power. In either case the historical judgment passed by such writers as Oswald Spengler and Arnold Toynbee will be sustained, and another great civilization will go the way of Nineveh and Tyre.

For the only salvation worth asserting and working for is clearly that of the unity of humanity—not to reduce to uniformity all differences of belief and practice but to induce toleration among them—peace among nations, peace among classes. This is the meaning which the old maxim of Bishop Wilson, so often repeated by Matthew Arnold, bears today: "To make reason and the will of God prevail." Both reason and God, if we think in theological terms, command the suppression of greed, of ambition in the vulgar terms given it by success stories, of intolerance. Especially among those professedly working for social change is such sacrifice of intolerance called for. So far as I have been permitted to work with them this has been my doctrine. Whether or not we are making progress, a hope exists by virtue of the very exigency of the crisis, the widespread realization of its nature and of its cure. Two functions of humanity are involved, intelligence and will. Present conditions in the United States show an enormous advance in knowledge as the basis of intelligence through the gathering of information by literally hundreds of fact-finding bodies, governmental and private, with direct and immediate application to evils and dangers from which we suffer, within and without. Yet the good will necessary to give validity to reason remains feeble and vacillating. We still profess faith in the people, in their fundamental rightness, honesty, and generosity, and then we remember sectionalism based on color, the enclaves of prejudice based on race, the blind apathy which makes for inertia in politics and subjects good men and good causes to defeat.

3

During the last year I have had several occasions to recall certain aspects of my experience which served to put it in perspective. On recent visits to Boston I stayed with my cousin Joe Poland at his home in Boxboro, Massachusetts. Our reminiscences brought back the most interesting part of my boyhood.

Last June I attended the fifty-fifth reunion of my class of 1892. It was a moment of pride when Greely Curtis, who was marshaling the members for the day at Cameron Forbes' farm in Norwood, greeted me as Robert Morss Lovett, *summa cum laude*. In the evening at dinner I sat beside Neal Rantoul and recalled the old Beverly, whence our families had sprung, and Dr. Frank Newell, whom I first saw in the third grade of the Lewis Grammar School and in the Walnut Avenue Sunday School. We missed Thomas Lamont, the benefactor of the class and of Harvard, absent because of illness, and Allen Benner, now one of the *Stelligeri*, and many others of whom we spoke. All the romantic feeling for Harvard and Eliot which I had at twenty-one came back in gratitude and affection.

I spent an evening with Dr. Harry F. Ward, who, as I have written, was the first to lead me into a path of social service, which I have tried feebly but honestly to follow. I value the days when I was his colleague in the American Civil Liberties Union, and the American League against War and Fascism, now, eight years after its passing, pronounced disloyal by the Attorney General.

I was invited to Hull House, to speak on the anniversary of Jane Addams' birthday to the Women's International League for Peace and Freedom, and was glad to remember some of the "acts of kindness and of love" which illustrated the most perfect type of humanity I have known, and also her wise and brave leadership in the cause of peace. In conclusion I quoted the last lines of Arnold's "Rugby Chapel," which apply so exactly to Jane Addams and all true leaders:

> Then, in such hour of need
> Of your fainting, dispirited race,
> Ye, like angels, appear,
> Radiant with ardour divine.
> Beacons of hope, ye appear!
> Languor is not in your heart,
> Weakness is not in your word,
> Weariness not on your brow.
> Ye alight in our van; at your voice,
> Panic, despair, flee away.
> Ye move through the ranks, recall
> The stragglers, refresh the outworn,
> Praise, re-inspire the brave.
> Order, courage, return.
> Eyes rekindling, and prayers,
> Follow your steps as ye go.
> Ye fill up the gaps in our files,
> Strengthen the wavering line,
> Stablish, continue our march,
> On, to the bound of the waste,
> On, to the City of God.

Recently I spoke to a joint meeting of the Graduate English Clubs of the University of Chicago and Northwestern University. Some of my former younger colleagues were present, and perhaps a hundred students and their wives. What I said was trivial. A student consulted me afterwards as to whether I approved of a strike to close the university for three hours in protest against racial discrimination. I who had spoken often in favor of student strikes against war could only advise cautiously that it should be considered how such a strike would affect the trustees who had the power. But what the audience brought back to me most strongly was the reflection that my happiest hours had been spent in the classroom and lecture hall. Perhaps my most useful hours have been given to consultation. Above all else, I have been a teacher. I count myself fortunate to have had the privilege of sharing my years with thousands of young Americans who are the hope of the Republic and of the World.

Appendix

A.

EXTRACT FROM EXAMINATION BEFORE THE SUB-COMMITTEE OF THE HOUSE COMMITTEE ON APPROPRIATIONS IN CHARGE OF DEPARTMENT OF INTERIOR APPROPRIATIONS, APRIL 14, 1943.

Mr. Norrell: I believe you were interrogated by the Chairman with reference to a letter that you wrote in which you said that the United States Government was rotten. You made that statement in connection with a statement regarding Russia.

Mr. Lovett: I said that all governments are rotten in the sense that all are in a sense corrupt, and I wish to further explain that if I had been writing carefully I should have used the historical statement of Lord Acton that all power leads to corruption.

Mr. Norrell: You are a very smart man and I assume you knew what you were doing when you wrote this letter.

Mr. Lovett: I was writing to an individual. I don't believe that that letter ought ever to have been brought into—brought before—a committee which was investigating communist teaching in universities.

Mr. Norrell: Well, you do say, though, in this letter that the United States Government, in your opinion, was rotten.

Mr. Lovett: I said all governments.

Mr. Norrell: And you included the United States Government.

Mr. Lovett: Yes, sir; in the sense in which the writer of the letter, which I was answering, understood it; that is to say, corruption.

Mr. Norrell: We cannot go into the realm of what somebody else understood.

Mr. Lovett: Well, I admit it was a careless statement and if I had been writing more carefully for a publication, I should have chosen my words more carefully, but the man to whom the letter was written understood it in the sense in which I meant, that there were rotten spots in every government.

Mr. Norrell: Would you make a statement to a most confidential friend that the United States Government was rotten?

Mr. Lovett: I would say that all governments contain elements of rottenness.

Mr. Norrell: That is not what you say here. You made the statement that the United States Government is rotten.

Mr. Lovett: That was an unguarded and extreme statement, which, as I say, appeared in a private letter and would be understood by the man to whom it was written.

Mr. Norrell: Now, for the record, we would like you to state what part of the United States Government you consider rotten today.

Mr. Lovett: At that time I was—

Mr. Norrell (interposing): Now, wait just a moment, I want a statement for the record, as brief as you can make it, being fair to you today, now, as to what part of the United States Government presently you consider rotten.

Mr. Lovett: The officials of the United States Government who use their political power for private advantage or persecution of their enemies so that use of power, that misuse of power, is what I should characterize as rotten.

Mr. Norrell: Now, Doctor, you are too smart—

Mr. Lovett (interposing): I beg your pardon? I am not in the least smart; no, sir. I should not think, having written that letter, that I had been smart.

Mr. Norvell: Well, assume that you are, for the sake of the record.

Mr. Lovett: No, sir. It is an assumption contrary to the fact.

. . . . .

Mr. Norrell: All right, Doctor. To be as brief as I can myself, and I would like for you to be as brief and to the point as possible, I want to ask this question again: Will you state for the record if any part of the United States Government, as a government—not as officials but as a government—is rotten? Now I want to know what part of the government you consider rotten, if any part?

Mr. Lovett: I said only officials of the Government, who are part of the Government, and who use their power for corrupt ends. There are such individuals. There are such officials.

B.

LETTER FROM MUNICIPAL COUNCILS OF ST. THOMAS—ST. JOHN AND ST. CROIX.

April 28, 1943

Honorable John H. Kerr,
Chairman, Sub-Committee on Un-American Activities,
House Appropriations Committee,
Washington, D. C.

Sir:

It has come to our knowledge that the Honorable Robert M. Lovett has been examined before your Committee on Un-American Activities, and that a move is under way to have him removed as Government Secretary of the Virgin Islands.

This action has come as a surprise to the people of the Virgin Islands, since Mr. Lovett is known by all to be a man of very high humane qualities, in whom the people have implicit confidence.

Mr. Lovett has worked with us in the capacity as Government Secretary for the past four years and has gained the confidence of our people. We feel that any attempt to have him removed at this time, when our nation is at war to preserve the principles of democracy as assured us by the Constitution of the United States and the Atlantic Charter, for reasons which are not clear and definite, would give an indication that that action would be a direct reversal of the principles for which millions of human beings are today sacrificing their lives in anticipation of a better world in which to live after the United Nations have won the war.

We, the people of the Virgin Islands, through the duly elected representatives of the two Municipal Councils in joint conference at Christiansted, St. Croix, do hereby in all seriousness and sincerity protest against any action which might be taken, or which might be presented as of notoriety to be taken, in the case of what we suppose to be the United States *versus* Robert M. Lovett, on charges based on subversive and un-American activities. We humbly submit that we have known Mr. Lovett for the past four years and that during that time he has been Government Secretary and Acting Governor of the Virgin Islands, we have never found him or have had cause to find him other than an American gentleman, a patriotic citizen, and a humane administrator under the laws of the United States Government and the Virgin Islands.

Dr. Robert M. Lovett has evinced in all his policies, decisions, and actions in the Virgin Islands, the principles of democracy, which have been fully appreciated, admired, and followed by the people of the Virgin Islands. We find in him a wonderful spirit of co-operation and interest in the economic, social, and educational welfare of the natives of the Virgin Islands, who are patriotic, law-abiding American citizens.

While, unfortunately, the Virgin Islands are not included in the Selective Service Act of the United States, there are thousands of Virgin Islanders dying in the Armed Forces of the United States to show their patriotism to the Flag for which Robert M. Lovett stands as a symbol, in full support of the President of the United States, the illustrious Franklin D. Roosevelt.

In view of the above-mentioned facts, we, as American citizens, most respectfully request that the Honorable Robert M. Lovett be not removed from his present position as Government Secretary of the Virgin Islands.

This document is presented to your Committee with the unanimous approval of the members of the Municipal Councils of St. Thomas-St. John and St. Croix, the legislative bodies of the Virgin Islands.

Respectfully,

THE MUNICIPAL COUNCIL OF
ST. THOMAS AND ST. JOHN
By: /s/ Omar Brown,
Chairman.

THE MUNICIPAL COUNCIL OF
ST. CROIX
By: /s/ Joseph Alexander,
Chairman.

C.

LETTER FROM SECRETARY OF THE INTERIOR ICKES.

THE SECRETARY OF THE INTERIOR
Washington

May 7, 1943

My dear Mr. Kerr:

In my letter of April 15 with respect to three employees of this Department I stated that I would not comment on the case of Robert Morss Lovett because I had not yet received a report from the Federal Bureau of Investigation as to him. I have recently received this report and am now in a position to comment on the charges against Mr. Lovett. Since this report is very elaborate I find it unnecessary to take advantage of your kind offer of May 5, in response to my request of April 22, to allow me to examine the basic evidence accumulated by Congressman Dies against Mr. Lovett.

Mr. Lovett has had a distinguished career as an author, educator, and social worker. He was professor of English Literature at the University of Chicago for forty-five years. The current "Who's Who" lists eleven books which he has written in his field, and he was an associate editor of "The New Republic" for twenty years. His only son was killed in action in Belleau Wood in the last war. He has quite literally thousands of friends and admirers, ranging from bank presidents to paupers, and including judges and professors, Republicans and Communists, manufacturers and social workers. He is now a vigorous young man of seventy-three who has for four years been Government Secretary of the Virgin Islands and has won the respect and affection of the entire population.

I have known Mr. Lovett for more than forty-five years. I have been personally acquainted with him for many years. I feel, therefore, that my judgment of him has been tried by long experience and found correct.

Throughout his long life Mr. Lovett has been profoundly interested in civil liberties, the maintenance of peace, the rights of labor, and an orderly and constitutional improvement of our economic and governmental procedures. He believes in the right of men to say and write what they please without fear of punishment. He believed in the twenties that this country should not undertake armed intervention in the affairs of the Caribbean nations. He believed that the nations of the world should outlaw war by banding together against aggressor nations. He has lent his efforts to see that workers were free to join their chosen unions. He has sought to improve the status of the colored people. He has opposed the fascist revolution in Spain and the then policy of this Government which seemed to him to aid our present enemies and to cripple the cause of the democracies. He has been active in adult education and in promoting economic studies by college students. He has sought to lend aid to immigrants not yet able themselves to take full opportunity of the privileges of American residence. He has opposed the Japanese aggression in China.

In these many interests and activities I find none which can even remotely be considered to be subversive. Mr. Lovett has simply typified one of the best traditions in American life, that in every generation there should be a group of disinterested and active liberals who should labor prodigiously to remove the imperfections of the contemporary society. Thomas Jefferson, Thomas Paine, William Lloyd Garrison, Carl Schurz, and George Norris are examples which come to mind. I do not say that Mr. Lovett has achieved the public stature of these men, but I do say that he is made out of the same stuff.

I do not believe that any member of the Congress would think that this makes Mr. Lovett unfit for governmental service. His only offense in the eyes of Congressman Dies seems to be that he has far too readily joined and lent his name to almost any organization that was directed to one or the other of the ends which he has cherished. He has, for example, worked with a number of organizations which he knew to contain a number of communists. But this does not mean that he was a communist sympathizer. It means only that he would work alongside of anyone who sought to obtain a worth-while objective—whether relief of the needy, the preservation of civil liberties, or the maintenance of peace—without any concern as to their other activities or beliefs.

Most of us would be more critical and discriminating in our associates. I, for example, would refuse to join any organization if I knew that it contained a large number of communists, whatever its professed objective might be. But I am a far more suspicious man than is Mr. Lovett. He has, for the seventy-three years of his life, found it difficult to think ill of any man, and so far as I know has never questioned the motives of anyone who sought a good objective. If the sub-committee will appreciate this essential goodness of Mr. Lovett it will find the answer to why this man, who obviously is not a communist, has frequently associated himself with them in one non-political enterprise or another.

I am anxious that the sub-committee should understand that although some of the organizations which Mr. Lovett has joined included communists, a few of which were probably controlled by communists, the organizations also included many non-communists. Among the persons associated with Mr. Lovett in connection with one or more of these organizations which Congressman Dies has so loosely called subversive are: Wendell Willkie, Thomas E. Dewey, Henry Wallace, Frank Murphy, Robert H. Jackson, James Farley, and Cordell Hull; Senators Pepper, Logan, Thomas, Wagner, Green, Murray, Frazier, and Murdock; Congressmen Thomas F. Ford, Kent E. Keller, Ed. V. Izac, Lee E. Geyer, John M. Coffee, John Lesinski, Caroline O'Day, Emanuel Celler, Matthew Dunn, Michael J. Bradley, and Adolph Sabath; Federal Judges William Holly, Julian Mack, and Lewis Schwellenbach; William Green, Philip Murray, and A. F. Whitney; Newbold Morris, Bernard Shaw, Edward Corsi, and Clarence Darrow; State Governors Dickinson, Jones, Moses, and Olson; and, innocently associating with Mr. Lovett and some of these sinister figures, Harold L. Ickes.

There is, as the sub-committee doubtless realizes, much unequivocal evidence that Mr. Lovett is not himself a communist or a communist sympathizer. For twenty years he was president of the League for Industrial Democracy, a socialist organization bitterly attacked by the communists except for the brief honeymoon of the so-called "popular front" period. After the Stalin-Hitler Pact of 1939, no communist or communist sympathizer advocated preparedness or aid to the Allies before June 1941. Mr. Lovett was a vigorous and outspoken advocate of both; so much so, indeed, that on one or two occasions I felt it necessary as his superior officer to restrain him from his lifelong habit of public speech. He has been active in an organization which investigated political persecution in Soviet Russia. While friendly to that experiment in government, and appreciative of it as a Russian solution to the Russian problems, he was willing to aid in the publication of a book exposing and attacking graft in the Soviet government.

The issue is not, then, whether Mr. Lovett is himself a communist, or himself believes in the overthrow of our form of government, but simply whether a man is to be branded as "subversive" because he is willing to work with communists toward non-communist, non-political ends which none of us would criticize as unworthy. Frequent association with communists, in the absence of any evidence to the contrary, may raise an inference of communist beliefs. But in the case of Mr. Lovett, there is abundant and unmistakable evidence that he is not a communist, and his periodic association with communists in non-communist enterprises cannot possible raise any such inference. There is in his case, accordingly, no ground for the Congress to accept and act upon any "contagion" theory of subversion.

I know that Mr. Lovett is a close and cherished friend of many persons who could not possibly mingle with one who had subversive sympathies: for example, a partner of Morgan, Stanley & Co., the president of the First National Bank of Chicago, a Republican judge of the United States Circuit Court of Appeals for the Second Circuit, the president of a large industrial concern, and the senior partners of some of the largest law firms in Chicago and Washington. If a man is to be judged by his friends and associates, it would seem at least as likely that I should be condemned for hiring a conservative Republican as that Mr. Lovett should be condemned as subversive.

Mr. Lovett has been a reformer, and an enthusiastic and possibly undiscriminating adherent of every cause that seemed worthy to him. He is also a completely selfless and generous man interested only in the good of his fellows, and a man of real nobility of character and spirit. Thousands of people throughout our nation owe a personal debt to Mr. Lovett's generosity, and I think that the entire country has to an appreciable degree been benefited by his untiring efforts to see that the American form of government and the American habit of life should be of benefit to all Americans, whatever their race, creed, or station in life.

Mr. Lovett mentioned to me that the sub-committee seemed troubled by the fact that in 1933 he was arrested because he protested to policemen interfering with peaceful picketing. It seems to me highly important in this respect that Judge John Gutknecht of the Chicago Municipal Court, before whom the case was tried, wrote to President Hutchins of the University of Chicago when the Illinois Senate committee recommended the retirement of Mr. Lovett and, although he did not otherwise know him, urged that he be retained. His letter of July 5, 1935, states that "I presided at the trial when he was accused of disorderly conduct, etc., and I want to say that not one word of evidence was given that in any way even remotely could be construed as a violation of law on his part. I cannot say as much for the arresting officers."

I should, finally, like to discuss Mr. Lovett's work in the Virgin Islands, where he has been Government Secretary for four years. I recommended his appointment because I could think of no man who, through his warm-hearted sympathies and his concern for the common man, would more graciously represent our Government in a poverty-stricken island. My confidence has been justified. I have been sent a copy of the letter from the chairmen of the two legislative bodies of the Virgin Islands, unanimously approved by both councils, which expressed to you the high regard which the people of those islands have for Mr. Lovett. They have found him, throughout his four years of service, "an American gentleman, a patriotic citizen, and a humane administrator," and see in him the symbol of the American flag for which their sons are fighting.

I also find it significant that, of the many contributors to the Federal Bureau of Investigation report, the one investigator who talked to people who knew Mr. Lovett presented a quite different report from those who did no more than studiously to accumulate the very large number of organizations with which he has been connected. Special Agent Willis took the trouble to talk to the people in the Virgin Islands who were acquainted with Mr. Lovett. Not one said that he was a communist or harbored subversive sympathies. Typical comments are: "Well-liked by most of the residents," "a loyal citizen," "a wonderful person, thoroughly loyal to the United States," "a kind-hearted old man," "a grand person who was inclined to help the poor and unfortunate," "a fine person who . . . wanted to do everything possible for the poor people," "a fine old man and a loyal American citizen," "a kind and gentlemanly old man," "always ready to come to the assistance of the underdog."

Both the *Daily News* and the *Progressive Guide*, on learning the occasion of Mr. Lovett's last trip to Washington, published splendid tributes to him. He was, the *Progressive Guide* said, "one of the most genuine and broad-minded Americans sent to the Virgin Islands." The *Daily News*, after pointing out that it is often critical of the administration and its officials, says that "Mr. Lovett is doing a good job here and no one realizes it better than the people for whom he has worked so selflessly. It is from such characters as Dr. Lovett that this nation, the United States of America, can draw its full strength and endless resources to inspire a sick world and remain an assurance of worthy ideals for the future." The editorial concludes by saying, "No continental official sent here has been more loyal and honest in practice than this venerable man. . . . In Dr. Lovett is embodied what we love to call the very essence of Americanism." For the benefit of the sub-committee, I enclose copies of both editorials.

In short, I am convinced that the sub-committee has before it a man whose only offense is that he is a genuinely good man, and whose service for the Government in the Virgin Islands is a credit not only to my Department but to the United States. If it were to recommend his discharge because he knows and has, in non-political enterprises, worked with communists, as well as Republicans, Democrats and Socialists, it would in my opinion injure the Government's repute, not only without our own borders but also in the hearts of thousands of Virgin Islanders who through him have come to respect and to admire our Government.

I enclose a statement prepared by Mr. Lovett which he has asked me to transmit to the sub-committee.

I have also taken the liberty of sending a copy of this letter to Congressman Jed Johnson, Chairman of the Interior Department Sub-Committee of the Appropriations Committee.

Sincerely yours,
/s/ Harold L. Ickes
Secretary of the Interior

Hon. John H. Kerr,
Chairman, Sub-Committee on Appropriations,
House of Representatives.
Enclosure 2927709

D.

STATEMENT OF SECRETARY OF THE INTERIOR ICKES BEFORE THE SENATE COMMITTEE ON APPROPRIATIONS, MAY 20, 1943.

I appear before you to ask that you do not permit a man against whom nothing disloyal or subversive has been shown to be branded for life by a reckless piece of legislation nailed on to an urgent war appropriation bill.

That item is Section 304 of H.R. 2714, now before this Senate committee as a rider placed on an urgent deficiency bill in the House. It attempts to convict Robert Morss Lovett, Government Secretary of the Virgin Islands, of being "unfit for Government service" and to kick him out with a stigma attached to his name without his having had a decent opportunity for defense anywhere. This proposed punitive legislation by the Congress of the United States is a performance which this democracy cannot tolerate.

Mr. Lovett is not accused of breaking any law and he is not guilty of breaking any law. He is accused, at the most, of just one thing—holding opinions which some members of the House of Representatives do not agree with, and the holding of which is no crime in this country. In large part he is convicted by the House, not even for his own opinions, but for those held by others with whom he has had some fugitive connection.

I

The proposed rider is unconstitutional because it invades the executive powers of the President.

This is not by any means a new issue. It was discussed in the First Congress, which included many men who had participated in drafting the Constitution. The Congress was entirely clear that it had no power whatever to remove any executive officer (1 Ann. of Cong. 576-591).

The Supreme Court, from as early as 1839 to the present day, has always followed the same rule. It has said that it is "the settled and well-understood construction of the Constitution that the power of removal was vested in the President alone." (*Ex parte Hennen*, 13 Pet. 230, 259). Chief Justice Taft, in *Myers* v. *United States* (272 U.S. 52, 161), said that if Congress sought to remove an executive officer, or even to participate in his removal, it would "infringe the constitutional principle of the separation of governmental powers."

The framers of the Constitution took pains to specify the offenses for which and the procedures by which the Congress could remove an executive officer. There is no suggestion that Mr. Lovett has been guilty of treason, bribery, or other high crimes and misdemeanors, for which he could be impeached. The Constitution provides an elaborate procedure for the removal of officers, including impeachment by the House, trial by the Senate on oath or affirmation, and conviction by a two-thirds vote. It is inconceivable that the framers of the Constitution would have supposed the Congress could avoid this carefully designed procedure by the simple expedient of attaching a rider to an appropriation bill.

Even apart from the constitutional requirement that the Congress shall not invade the executive power of removal, the proposed rider is invalid as a bill of attainder. The Supreme Court in *Cummings* v. *Missouri* (4

Wall. 277), held a law to be an unconstitutional bill of attainder because it forbade holding public office, or teaching, unless one swore that he had never been hostile to the United States. Its decision applies with even greater force here, for the Court said (p. 323) the statute was unconstitutional because "the legislative body . . . exercises the powers and office of judge; it assumes, in the language of the textbooks, judicial magistracy; it pronounces upon the guilt of the party, without any of the forms or safeguards of trial; it determines the sufficiency of the proofs produced, whether conformable to the rules of evidence or otherwise." This language is more elegant than I would use with respect to the House "trials" of these accused men, but fits the case exactly.

II

The Kerr sub-committee assumed a very delicate and responsible task when it undertook to pass judgment upon a man's life. The job was particularly difficult in the case of Mr. Lovett, who already has seventy-three active years to his credit. I know and have a great respect for a number of the members of the Kerr sub-committee, and I am sure that they were trying to do a fair and honest job. But the procedures which the sub-committee unfortunately adopted made a sound result impossible and served to deny to Mr. Lovett rights which have always been basic under our form of government.

On April 14, Mr. Lovett received a note asking him to appear before the Kerr sub-committee on the next day. There he was examined by the sub-committee in a secret session of about two hours' length. He had no detailed specification of the charges against him. He had no counsel. Indeed, the sub-committee denied the request of the Solicitor of this Department that he be allowed to attend merely as a departmental observer.

I do not know what happened in that secret session but I gather that it consisted only of answering questions and making explanations of the particular charges. There was no opportunity to bring witnesses on behalf of Mr. Lovett. There was no chance for him to undertake the extended work necessary to verify or qualify some of the things attributed to him by Congressmen Dies. Most important of all, in the case of Mr. Lovett, there was no adequate opportunity to develop the great variety of facts and circumstances which demonstrated that he has been a loyal, patriotic American, and one who is rendering a real service to the people of the Virgin Islands and to the United States. The transcript of the hearing was not shown to Mr. Lovett, to the Department of the Interior, or even to the House of Representatives which voted his conviction.

A man under our Constitution is entitled to counsel when tried even for minor criminal offenses, where the only issue is whether or not a simple act was done. Here the charge, subversive activity against our Government in time of war, is far more serious. The penalty, a reflection upon the man's good name and the loss of his livelihood, is far greater. The issues, involving the balance of the whole of his past life, are far more complicated. Yet the Kerr sub-committee not only denied the right of counsel but conducted its interrogation in a secret session, the transcript of which is still unavailable. This, I submit, is not the American way to do things. This indeed is an "un-American" activity.

III

The lack of constitutional power to attach such a rider as this, and the unfair procedures used, may be more basic than the actual guilt or innocence of Mr. Lovett of subversive activities. But the Senate, after all, is asked to participate in the judgment of condemnation and, in fairness to Mr. Lovett and to the Senate, I should like to show what a serious mistake the House has made as to the man.

I have known Mr. Lovett for all of forty-five years. I feel, therefore, that my judgment of him has been tried by long experience, and I believe it to be correct.

Mr. Lovett has had a distinguished career as an author and educator. He was professor of English Literature at the University of Chicago for forty-five years. He has written eleven books in his field, and he was an associate editor of the *New Republic* for twenty years. His only son was killed in action in Belleau Wood in the last war.

Throughout his life Mr. Lovett has been profoundly interested in civil liberties, the maintenance of peace, the rights of labor, and an orderly and constitutional improvement of our economic and governmental procedures. This record obviously does not make Mr. Lovett unfit for governmental service. His only offense in the eyes of Congressman Dies and the Kerr sub-committee seems to be that he has far too readily joined and lent his name to almost any organization that was directed to one or the other of the ends which he has cherished. Some of these organizations have included communists among their members. But this does not mean that Mr. Lovett was a communist sympathizer. It means only that he would work alongside of anyone who sought to obtain a worthwhile objective without any concern as to his other activities or beliefs.

The evidence shows quite plainly that Mr. Lovett was himself neither a communist nor sympathetic with the political objectives of the communists. For twenty years he was president of the League for Industrial Democracy, a socialist organization bitterly attacked by the communists except for the brief honeymoon of the so-called "popular front" period.

After the Stalin-Hitler Pact of 1939, and before June 1941, no communist or communist sympathizer advocated preparedness or aid to the Allies. On the contrary, Mr. Lovett was a vigorous and outspoken advocate of both. He has been active in an organization which investigated political persecution in Soviet Russia. While friendly to that experiment in government, and appreciative of it as a Russian solution to the Russian problems, he was willing to aid in the publication of a book exposing and attacking graft in the Soviet government.

The test of the fitness of an officer of the Government cannot fairly be the political views of persons with whom he has in the past been associated for non-political objectives. The very organizations used by Congressman Dies and the Kerr sub-committee to brand Mr. Lovett as "subversive" could be used to pin the same label on Wendell Willkie, Thomas E. Dewey, Frank Murphy, Robert H. Jackson, Cordell Hull, James Farley, and Harold L. Ickes; Senators Pepper, Elbert D. Thomas, Wagner, Green, Murray, and Murdock; Congressmen Thomas F. Ford, Ed. V. Izac, John M. Coffee, John Lesinski, Emanuel Celler, Michael J. Bradley, and Adolph Sabath; and Federal Judges William Holly and Lewis Schwellenbach.

The only satisfactory or fair test is how the man is doing his job, what the people whom he serves think of him, and what is his standing among his neighbors. The people of the Virgin Islands have known Mr. Lovett continuously and intimately for the past four years. The strength and the unanimity of their tribute to him is really remarkable.

The two municipal councils of the Islands, meeting in joint session, unanimously approved a letter from their two chairmen to Congressman Kerr which declared that the people of the islands have found Mr. Lovett throughout his four years of service, "an American gentleman, a patriotic citizen, and a humane administrator," and see in him the symbol of the American flag for which their sons are fighting.

Both the *Daily News* and the *Progressive Guide*, the newspapers of the Virgin Islands, on learning of the Dies charges, published splendid tributes to Mr. Lovett. The *Daily News*, after pointing out that it is often critical of the administration and its officials, says that "Mr. Lovett is doing a good job here and no one realizes it better than the people for whom he has worked so selflessly. . . . No continental official sent here has been more loyal and honest." The St. Thomas Business Men's Association recently cabled the President and me in emphatic terms to urge the retention of Mr. Lovett. The agent of the Federal Bureau of Investigation who talked to many people in the Virgin Islands found not one who had seen any indication that Mr. Lovett was a communist or harbored subversive sympathies. Typical comments are: "A wonderful person," "thoroughly loyal to the United States," "a kind-hearted old man," "a fine person who . . . wanted to do everything possible for the poor people," "a fine old man and a loyal American citizen," "always ready to come to the assistance of the underdog."

These are the people who have been in daily contact with Mr. Lovett. These are the people of the none-too-prosperous islands which we govern. These are the people whose interests are at stake. There is not a man in Washington, and I venture to say not a man in our state capitols, who could draw such an impressive tribute from the people whom he serves and the legislature with which he works.

This committee, I hope, will not believe that it is some peculiarity of the Virgin Islanders that they see a kindly and lovable man where Congressman Dies and the Kerr sub-committee see a subversive and dangerous character. I may say, without any exception known to me, that everyone who has known Mr. Lovett as a man, and not merely as one who joined too many organizations, is of the same opinion.

I have just learned that a number of his lifelong friends have written to the Kerr sub-committee on his behalf. So far as I have been able to obtain copies of these letters they entirely confirm the conclusions of the Virgin Islanders. They come from men who would have no sympathy whatever with any communist or subversive character, including Thomas W. Lamont, chairman of J. P. Morgan & Co., who has also telegraphed me on behalf of Mr. Lovett; Edward Burling and George Rublee, the senior partners of Washington's largest law firm; Judge Learned Hand, of the United States Court of Appeals for the Second Circuit; Christopher Chenery, president of the Federal Water Service Corporation; and Laird Bell, senior partner of one of Chicago's outstanding law firms.

The Senate, through the regrettably hasty procedure involved in attaching a rider to an urgent deficiencies bill, must decide in a short space of a day or two whether it will accept the judgment of the Kerr sub-committee, which met with Mr. Lovett for about two hours, or that of these men some of whom have known him for half a century. The choice should be clear.

IV

In making the choice, the Senate should, I think, carefully examine the report of the Kerr sub-committee. I believe that the members of that sub-committee have been imposed on by Congressman Dies, and that more adequate staff work might have led them to a different conclusion.

The Kerr report, to show what Mr. Lovett himself has done or said, quotes only one letter and one election speech of Mr. Lovett. The letter was written in 1926, while the Teapot Dome scandals were fresh. It encourages an author of a book attacking graft in Soviet Russia and says that the Russian Government, the United States Government, and all others, are "rotten." This is permissible comment, not subversion. In 1936 Lovett said that the workers should vote for Norman Thomas, since neither of the two older parties offered hope, and since the Communist party did not have the right approach. If none of us has ever said worse in election campaigns, he is fortunate indeed. There are not enough jails in the United States to contain all of the men and women who on one occasion or another have condemned their Government as "rotten." This expression or some picturesque synonym has been in common use during these latter days. If this be conclusive evidence of a desire or an intent to overthrow the Government of the United States, or of subversive tendencies, then we are indeed in a bad case.

The six organizations on the basis of which the Kerr sub-committee condemns Lovett are stated to be found "within the scope of Public Law 135 and Public Law 644" by the Department of Justice. This sounds very sinister. Just what does it mean? The Attorney General in his report to the Congress on September 1, 1942, said that it meant merely that, since *some* of the members were communists, membership in these organizations should be investigated (H. Doc. No. 833, 77th Cong.). He was careful to explain that membership did *not* prove the man was a communist or subversive, since the programs appeared innocent and most members were not communists. The Attorney General, in a subsequent letter to me, says of these organizations that "needless to say, the 'fronts' were not regarded as 'subversive,' " because their programs "were legitimate and frequently commendable on their face. They had attracted the membership or participation of large numbers of persons who were animated by liberal and patriotic purposes."

One may ask, then, what else the Kerr sub-committee has discovered about these organizations. Two are said to have paralleled the communist election program of 1940 in twenty-one respects, and a third in sixteen respects. So did the Republican and the Democratic platforms of 1940 "parallel" the communist platform in many respects, it being the custom of all political platforms to promise prosperity, civil rights, international peace, and universal happiness. What else? One organization was said by Browder to have had assistance from a communist organization. Another was said to have followed the communist party line, although the Kerr sub-committee had before it evidence that Lovett himself was on record as *opposing* this line followed by the organization. Another was "alleged" to have been financed by Amtorg. Another opposed the Dies Committee, and more praise to it. I have not only opposed the Dies Committee, I have denounced it on more than one occasion. I do so today. I will continue to do so so long as I believe in the constitutional rights guaranteed to us by the Constitution. The sixth included, as the report itself says, "many non-communists unaware of its communist control."

This is a pretty weak pail of garbage with which to find a man guilty of being disloyal to his government, particularly a man as to whom evidence to the contrary is overpowering. There is in the report only one shred of so-called evidence suggesting that Mr. Lovett had any reason to think any of the organizations were subversive. This is a quotation from Dies' own chief snooper and smearer, Prof. J. B. Matthews (ex-preacher, save the mark!), the first chairman of the American League against War and Fascism. He said, as part consideration for his seventy-two hundred dollar a year job with the Dies Committee, that the organization was designed to involve the United States in any war on the side of the Soviet Union, and to cripple it if it fought against Russia.

I do not know whether the professor received a communistic accolade for that one. Certainly, any such purpose must have been very well hidden for the American League to have been supported by so many reputable people. For example, at the 1939 convention of the successor organization, the American League for Peace and Democracy, more than two hundred groups were represented. A very small sample includes: the Fourteenth District Democratic Club of Los Angeles, the Building Trades Council of New Haven, the various locals of the Brotherhood of Railroad Trainmen and of the carpenters, paperhangers, and painters unions of the A.F. of L., the Epworth League of the Asbury Methodist Episcopal Church, and the Y. M. C. A. of Washington, D.C. No one in his senses would suggest that these organizations are communist in nature.

I need spend very little time on the other organizations mentioned in the Kerr report. More important are the sources of this part of the report. I am shocked, gentlemen, that a committee of this Congress should undertake to discharge from Government employment a loyal American citizen on the basis of two statements, one by a woman under Federal indictment for sedition and the other by a fascist sympathizer.

At page 11 of the Kerr report is a list of cabalistic initials which I suppose are intended to list Lovett's organizations. I do not know what the initials mean and I doubt if the Kerr sub-committee does. But the interesting thing is that the same list, word for word, is found, at page 302 of the unsavory *Red Network*, by Elizabeth Dilling, who is now under indictment for sedition.

Again, at page 10 of the Kerr report is found another list of organizations. This bit is advanced as a part of the text of the committee's own report. But in fact it is taken from one Walter S. Steele, who on August 17, 1938, made the same statement, word for word and comma for comma, to the Dies Committee. His statement is found at page 681 of volume I of the 1939 Dies hearings. Steele, for the committee's information, is the editor of a sheet called the "National Republic." He represents fascist or semi-fascist groups such as the Christian American Crusade, the Paul Reveres of Chicago, and the Vigilant Intelligence Federation. These organizations peddle anti-Jewish propaganda and whip up Red scares. They have been on the regular mailing lists of the German propaganda machine, and are officered or endorsed by men such as Aryan and Sanctuary, now under indictment for sedition.

These are the people used by the Kerr sub-committee to brand as disloyal a patriotic American citizen. What are the sinister organizations which this fascist pair have served up for the Kerr sub-committee? They include the American Civil Liberties Union, the American Birth Control League, the *New Republic*, and organizations to aid China and Spain. The fact is also mentioned that Mr. Lovett also once signed a petition for the recognition of the Soviet Union. The only fitting comment seems to be "Mercy me!" I hope that Mr. Steele, as well as the man who jockeyed his statement on the Kerr sub-committee, each looks under his bed for communist burglars every night. They might ask the ineffable Professor Matthews, who was brought up on the communistic practice of confusing political opponents by the clever spreading of lies, to hold a torch for them.

This, then, is the report on which the Senate is asked to condemn a man as disloyal to his Government in time of war, and a man, moreover, who is proved by the Virgin Islanders whom he serves, as well as by his conservative Republican friends, to be one of great nobility of character and of complete loyalty and integrity.

I therefore ask the Senate to strike Section 304 from the bill, and thus avoid an unconstitutional usurpation of legislative power and a lasting plot on the name of an American who has never had any thought except to help other people and to serve his country.

E.

STATEMENT BY THE PRESIDENT OF THE UNITED STATES, SEPTEMBER 14, 1943.

TO THE CONGRESS OF THE UNITED STATES:

On July 12 I reluctantly signed H. R. 2714, the Urgent Deficiency Appropriation Act, 1943. I felt obliged to approve it because it appropriates funds which were essential to carry on the activities of almost every agency of government during the recess of the Congress.

If it had been possible to veto the objectionable rider, which has been attached to this Urgent Deficiency Appropriation Act, but which has no relevancy to it, without delaying essential war appropriations, I should unhesitatingly have done so.

This rider prohibited any government department or agency from employing at any time in the future, after November 15, three named individuals who are now employed by different government agencies, unless they are appointed to office by the President and confirmed by the Senate prior to that date.

There is no suggestion that the three named individuals have not loyally and competently performed the duties for which they have been employed. They are sought to be disqualified for federal employment because of political opinions attributed to them.

The provision aimed at these men does not define the offices they hold and does not seek to make appointment to those offices subject to Senate approval. As a matter of fact, the clause permitting them to remain in government employment after November 15 subject to Presidential appointment and Senate approval was inserted only after the Senate had refused to accept a provision requiring their immediate removal from government employment and their permanent disqualification for the federal service. The Senate rejected the compromise as incorporated in this bill once, and agreed to it only after the House conferees had refused to agree to any bill without a provision aimed at the removal of these three named individuals. The Senate yielded, as I have been forced to yield, to avoid delaying our conduct of the war.

But I cannot so yield without placing on record my view that this provision is not only unwise and discriminatory, but unconstitutional.

The Supreme Court has defined a bill of attainder as "a legislative act which inflicts punishment without judicial trial." The rider in this bill operates perpetually to disqualify three named individuals from holding office in their government unless they are nominated by the President and confirmed by the Senate before November 15. It is dircted at named individuals and not at specified statutory offices. No judicial trials have been held. No impeachment proceedings have been instituted. This rider is an unwarranted encroachment upon the authority of both the Executive and the Judicial branches under our Constitution. It is not, in my judgment, binding upon them.

FRANKLIN D. ROOSEVELT

The White House,
September 14, 1943.

F.

DECLARATION BY CITIZENS' ORGANIZATIONS OF THE VIRGIN ISLANDS.

TO

Mr. and Mrs. Robert M. Lovett

It having been our great pleasure and blessing to have you in our midst for nearly five years, it is with a deep sense of gratitude that on the eve of your departure from our shores, we, the People of the Virgin Islands, tender to you this expression of our esteem.

Our island home, our community, and, in no small measure, our own lives have been enriched by your faithful and devoted service and by your shining example of citizenship. Your zealous concern for the well-being of even the poorest citizen, your firm and unrelenting demands for justice to the humblest; your vigorous fight for the blessings of the Four Freedoms for us, the people whom you chose to serve, will ever remain amongst our treasured memories.

We are proud to have known you, to have worked with you, to have shared your dreams of a better Virgin Islands; proud to have had your friendship; proud to have had the rare privilege of association with a lady and a gentleman.

It is our earnest hope that you will find happiness wherever you may go, and we know, sad though the loss of your presence may be, that you will still be with us in the many good and noble causes you championed and in those deeds of kindness which neither man nor time can efface.

On behalf of a grateful People reluctant to let you go, we subscribe ourselves.

UNITED CITIZENS' ORGANIZATIONS

Civic & Fraternal

1. St. Thomas Business Men's Association, D. Victor Bornn, President.
2. Virgin Islands Progressive Guide, Oswald E. Harris, Supervisor.
3. St. Thomas Community Chest, Roy W. Bornn, Chairman, Exe. Com.
4. American Red Cross, C. Frederick Dixon, Chairman.
5. Parent-Teachers' Association (C.A.H.S.), David Monsanto, President.
6. American Federation of Labor, Joseph Francis, Vice-Chairman.
7. St. Thomas Women's Club, Mrs. Lambert George, Pres.
8. Goodwill Lodge No. 11316, Willfred Bell, Past Noble Father.
9. Beloved Strs. of Mary & Joseph Society, Alfredo Thomas, President.

10. United Brethren of St. Joseph Society, Barthold Testamark, President.
11. United Laboring Association, Maximillian Wallace, President.
12. Harmonic Lodge, #356, Dr. John S. Morehead, W.M.
13. Old Unity Lodge, Gustave Norman, Noble Grand.
14. Democratic Club, Ralph Paiewonsky, N.C.M.
15. Civic League, José Gomez, President.
16. St. Thomas Community Band, Alphonse Donastorg, Asst. Leader
17. Municipal Employees' Association, Bertha C. Boschulte, Pres.
18. The Lion's Club.
19. Charlotte Amalie High School Alumni Association, Aubrey C. Ottley, President.
20. St. Thomas Teachers' Association, Antonio Jarvis.
21. Household of Ruth, Luther Robles, Pres.
22. Taxicab Association, Louis Lindqvist, President.
23. Civil Service Employees' Organization, L. W. McIntosh, President.
24. The American Legion, L. Venegas, Post Commander.
25. The Ministers' Association, Rev. Edward Lewis.
26. St. Thomas Police Association, Sgt. H. Simmonds, Pres.
27. St. Thomas Distillers' Association, Harry Rosenblum, Pres.
28. Boy Scouts of America, Scoutmasters Jackson & Essanason.

G.

EDITORIAL IN THE *Daily News*, ST. THOMAS, V.I., U.S.A. TUESDAY, MARCH, 28, 1944.

FAREWELL TO MR. LOVETT

The United Citizens' Organization, comprising almost every single civic and fraternal organization in the community, which last night held a farewell program in Emancipation Garden in honor of Dr. and Mrs. Robert Morss Lovett, is about as good a cross-section of island opinion as can be found, since its membership is drawn from all social and economic strata. Its wholehearted endorsement of Mr. Lovett's record of service as Government Secretary and Executive Assistant to the Governor of the Virgin Islands is further evidence of the unanimous admiration and respect he has won during his four and a half years of exemplary service.

Dr. Lovett leaves tomorrow for Puerto Rico. His passing from the local scene will bring a lump to the throat of many. He is a truly great public figure, who served the people with notable fidelity and singular rectitude, and who will be sadly missed by the community. He is the liberal, outspoken, honest type of American which made this nation so great and powerful. In times like these when the nation is in its greatest peril we need men like Lovett in high office. We need his guidance, leadership, his ideals more than ever. His successor will have a tough job trying to fill the place of so eminent a public servant.

Mr. Lovett brought us no million-dollar appropriations to satisfy our great wants, no legislation to solve existing social and economic problems. His contributions were deeper and of more far-reaching importance. Back of every move for the advancement of the islands has been his guiding hand, his helpful suggestions, his sincere co-operation, his great wisdom and experience. He has been a constant source of inspiration to the islands, and has spurred the people on to the realization of greater things. He was another Abe Lincoln in the qualities of his character, and his broad interest in humanity. He was a man of the masses of the people, to whose level he brought the government.

As you depart, Mr. Lovett, you do so with the love of the Virgin Islands. Even though repudiated by Congress, you should not feel that this is the end of the road. There is a place for you in this great democracy of ours. You cannot spend your remaining days better than by spreading the liberal and refreshing principles that guided you in your useful life. All the people thank you, Mr. Lovett, for what you have done for us. You go with our fullest blessings. May God bless your remaining days on earth. May they be happy ones.

H.

EXTRACT FROM DECISION BY THE COURT OF CLAIMS OF THE UNITED STATES, NOVEMBER 5, 1945. CONCURRING OPINION BY JUDGE MADDEN.

Has Congress the power to remove, by statute, named individuals from Government service, and make them perpetually ineligible to hold positions in Government service because they have engaged in conduct which was entirely lawful? Section 304 purports to do this. If it in fact accomplishes it, it has accomplished, under the guise of law, a shocking and outrageous injustice, unique in our history, and discouraging because it follows one hundred and fifty years of experience under the best Government men have devised. The court's problem is not, of course, whether Section 304 is unjust, but whether it is unconstitutional. But when the injustice of the particular law is so shocking, and the threat of its repetition and extension is so menacing to our institutions, as in the case of Section 304, one can hardly be blamed for saying to himself, even before he consults the text of the Constitution, "If the Constitution is the charter of liberty and free government which I have always supposed that it is, it does not permit this."

If Section 304 is valid, Congress can disqualify for public office or service racial minorities, political minorities, and probably, religious minorities. To do so would, indeed, be less unjust than what is done by Section 304. If a racial minority were excommunicated, the statute would at least have one quality of what we have been accustomed to regard as law, the quality of generality of application to all persons of an ascertainable class. No individual would have the finger of the state pointed at him, as these three plaintiffs have, saying, "You are degraded, not because of the kind of person you are, for there may be thousands of persons just like you in all essential respects, who are still full citizens; not because of what you have done, for there may be thousands of persons who have done the same things, so far as those things are relevant to a rational state, as you have done. You are degraded because the state has selected you for degradation." And a racial or other minority could, under the constitutional protections which would apply even to second-class citizens, pool their resources and agitate for the repeal of the statute with some slight hope that in the turn of political events a powerful party might need the votes of this minority to insure its success, and hence would espouse its cause. But three individuals, such as these plaintiffs, are helpless. If they speak, who will listen? If they should happen to have the money to publish, who will read? Their appeal would appear to be completely selfish. The reaction would be: "Who are these persons, of the dominant race, of many generations of honorable American ancestry, to be complaining of discrimination? I don't know just what has happened to them, but if they can't take care of themselves, nobody can." And nobody can, if Section 304 is valid.

Nothing is claimed to have been done or said or written by any of the plaintiffs which was unlawful. . . .

What they did was completely innocent and of no interest or consequence to the law of the land as it then was, or, as to all persons except the three plaintiffs, as the law still is. . . .

But as a consequence of their having done what they did, the three plaintiffs find themselves excommunicated, reduced to the status of three second-class citizens among all of the millions of their fellows. They find themselves subject to the same obligations as their fellow first-class citizens to obey the laws, pay taxes, and serve in the Armed Forces and on juries; but completely and perpetually disqualified from serving their Government in any of the thousands of positions in which any of the rest of us, if technically capable, may serve. It is not claimed that the three plaintiffs were not competent to perform, or did not faithfully perform, the duties of the positions they held.

Section 304 is asserted by the plaintiffs to be unconstitutional because (1) it purports to remove the plaintiffs from executive offices, and no power of removal resides in the legislative branch of the Government, except by impeachment; (2) it is a bill of attainder, or its equivalent, a bill of pains and penalties, which the Constitution forbids; and (3) it deprives the plaintiffs of liberty and property without due process of law, in violation of the Fifth Amendment.

I have no doubt that Section 304 is a bill of pains and penalties and is therefore unconstitutional. It has the ancient flavor of the bills of attainder which were so odious to the makers of our Constitution that they forbade such laws in the main body of the Constitution, and before the bill of rights later embodied in the first ten amendments was thought necessary, in that it, like the bills of attainder that the fathers were familiar with, selects its victims as named individuals, and not as persons belonging to any describable class. It punishes them by removal from office and income and disqualification from ever again serving their Government for compensation except in military or jury service. It thus imposes the same penalty which the Senate is authorized to impose, on conviction by a two-thirds vote after impeachment by the House, upon officers guilty of 'treason, bribery, or other high crimes and misdemenanors.' "[1]

[1] Pp. 32, 33, 34 of decisions of Court of Claims of the United States, Nos. 46026, 46027, 46028 (decided November 5, 1945), *Robert Morss Lovett* v. *The United States, Goodwin B. Watson* v. *The United States, William E. Dodd, Jr.* v. *The United States.*

Index